...And with a Light Touch

Learning about Reading,

Writing, and Teaching with

First Graders

CAROL AVERY

Foreword by Donald Graves

HEINEMANN
PORTSMOUTH, NH

HEINEMANN

A division of Reed Elsevier Inc.

361 Hanover Street   Portsmouth, NH 03801–3912

Offices and agents throughout the world

Library of Congress Cataloging-in-Publication Data

Avery, Carol
    And with a light touch : learning about reading, writing, and
teaching with first graders / Carol Avery.
        p.   cm.
    Includes bibliographical references (p.).
    ISBN 0-435-08787-8
    1. Language arts (Primary)   2. English language—Composition and
exercises—Study and teaching (Primary)   3. Reading (Primary)
4. First grade (Education)   I. Title.
LB1528.F67   1993
372.4'044—dc20   92–42680
                                                          CIP

Cover design by Jenny Jensen Greenleaf
Cover illustration by Tiffany Hostetter
Design by Debra Kam
Photographs by Nathan Avery
Printed in the United States of America on acid-free paper
97 96 95   EB   4 5 6 7

For
Kinsey Rochelle Avery
and
Adessa Denise Avery
my "trailguides to the future"

Table of Contents

Acknowledgments

. . . And with a Light Touch could not have come to publication without the support, encouragement, and plain hard work of many people. I am grateful to all who helped along the way.

Where does the story of a book begin? Where does the story of a teacher begin? While it's impossible to trace all of the influences on a writer or a teacher, I know that I was fortunate to have had many excellent teachers. My parents opened the world of books to me and encouraged exploration, risk-taking and problem-solving. I had many fine teachers in my public education in Waterville, Maine and later in Pennsylvania, but the most memorable for me were those whose teaching style paralleled my parents' approach to children. I learned much about being a teacher by *how* my best teachers taught.

The undergraduate education in library science and English I received at Millersville University in Pennsylvania planted many seeds for the teaching that would emerge in my classroom in the late 1970s. The library education department under the leadership of Dr. Joseph Blake was one the finest around. Extensive reading and responding to literature was the focus of many classes. We studied the work of Jeannette Veatch and addressed the importance of children's books for reading instruction and the role of the librarian in all of children's schooling. The grounding for writing and reading workshops and a responsive teaching style were laid for me in Veatch's work. In an English course, "Contemporary Poetry," taught by Dr. John Huzzard, we wrote no papers and took no tests but rather read and discussed poetry in class and in a final hour-long individual conference with our teacher. Dr. Huzzard taught me about reader-response theory long before I read Louise Rosenblatt. That class became a community that I still enjoy today when I run into former classmates or read their published articles.

During the early years of working with writing and reading workshops, several people played a significant role in helping me structure these approaches and in providing encouragement. In the summer of 1982 I studied with Mary Ellen Giacobbe, a former first grade teacher in whose classroom Don Graves conducted research on the writing of young children. In a course based on the writing research in her classroom, she demonstrated ways to establish classroom writing workshops by sharing what had worked for her and by encouraging us teachers to create writing workshops in response to the needs of our students. Without the model Mary Ellen provided I doubt that I would have been able to establish successful writing and reading process environments in my classroom.

Another early teacher was Glenda Bissex under whose guidance I conducted a year-long teacher-researcher case study in my classroom. Glenda validated the importance of teacher observations and insights and enabled me to refine the process of teacher as researcher. In 1983 Glenda urged me to send three case studies I had written from my first year with writing and reading workshops to Tom Newkirk at the University of New Hampshire. One of these case studies was eventually published in *Breaking Ground.* I would not have considered wriiting professionally had it not been for Glenda's encouragement of that first manuscript and most likely this book would never have been written.

Through Mary Ellen I met Don Graves. For several years they came to Pennsylvania to conduct workshops for a group of teachers from across our state and together provided not only new perspectives but the necessary "shot in the arm" so needed by classroom teachers bogged down in the daily hassles of classroom life. Don's work and words have enabled change in classrooms throughout the country and I know I am not alone in the debt of gratitude I owe to him. I am especially honored by the words he wrote to open this book.

Mary Ellen, Glenda, and Don were my early teachers as I moved into process approaches to teaching. They not only shared new ideas and approaches to teaching but also, just as important, constantly demonstrated *how* to teach. The trust and encouragement each one offered buoyed my confidence as I tried new practices. The gentle and genuine support from Mary Ellen, Glenda and Don sustained me through the tensions of those early years as well as validated my classroom practice and stimulated me to consider new directions for growth.

In the Summer of 1985 I took a course entitled "Reading, Writing, Teaching and Learning" from Mary Ellen and Nancie Atwell. Nancie's passion for teaching and her high expectations for her students provided another demonstration of what the teaching/learning process can be in classrooms. In addition, Nancie's model of reading workshop with her eighth graders validated my daily use with first graders of the literature response time and the reading time which I had been developing in my own classroom parallel to writing workshop. I thank Nancie and all of these teachers who have inspired me, who have contributed so much of our educational theories and practices, and who continue to learn collaboratively as colleagues in our profession.

I owe much to the first graders in my classes at Neff, Nitrauer, and Schaeffer Elementary Schools in the Manheim Township School District in Lancaster, Pennsylvania. They have been my teachers who have shown me what learning is and what teaching can be.

Two administrators from that district, Rose Stetler and Jim Bowman, supported me years ago as I ventured into new territory as a classroom teacher; without their trust the stories that are the foundation of this book could not have occurred. The first draft of much of this book was written while I was a teacher in the Manheim Township School District. I no longer teach there but the various supportive relationships within the district, along with the encouragement of children and their parents, inspire me to want to return soon to the classroom.

In my recent role as consultant and workshop leader, I have met hundreds of teachers who have been striving to improve the teaching-learning processes in their classrooms. Talking with and listening to these teachers guided me through the revision process as I worked on this book and influenced the content of several sections. The teachers are the front-line experts and, for the most part, are committed to the ideals of learner-centered education.

John Meehan, now retired from the Pennsylvania Department of Education, brought Donald Graves, Mary Ellen Giacobbe, and Nancie Atwell to Pennsylvania long before writing process became well known in education. John's creative vision pioneered new directions for our state, and I was fortunate to be part of the workshops he planned.

As a classroom teacher I might never have considered writing about my classroom had it not been for several college educators. Ironically, each one told me that they considered the classroom teacher—not the university theorist—to be the expert on teaching and learning. Those individuals include: Glenda Bissex, Janet Emig, Donald Graves, Ken and Yetta Goodman, Jane Hansen, Donald Murray, and Tom Newkirk. I thank each of them for their continuing support of classroom teachers.

Louise Rosenblatt graciously opened her home to me and, for the large part of an afternoon, shared her ideas about readers, reader response theory, and young children. I believe her work provides a solid foundation for elementary teachers as we formulate our theories of teaching reading. I thank her for that work and also for the time she spent discussing it with me.

I am also grateful to my fifty-nine colleagues from the English Coalition Conference in 1987. It was with them that I began to articulate what I know about children and learning. We represented elementary, secondary, and university faculty and the three weeks we spent together bonded us as professionals all concerned about the future of the teaching of English.

I thank the Research Foundation of the National Council of Teachers of English for a teacher-researcher grant, which supported my classroom research on strategies first graders use when learning to read without a basal reader.

No one writes alone. Many individuals contributed to the process of writing and rewriting *And with a Light Touch*. Thank you to those who read and responded to portions of the manuscript: Mary Ellen Giacobbe, Linda

Hansee, Kathy Kerlin, Tom Romano, Barbara Rynerson, Susan Stires, Rosemary Winkeljohann, Carol Zartman. I'm especially grateful for the encouraging response of Michael Ginsberg that came midway through the writing. Had I not had his words to read over and over I might have abandoned the entire project. And I owe much to the support of a special group of writers and teachers. The Sugar Hill Writers' Group (also known as "The Eagles") gave me a much needed nudge—more than any of them probably know. That group includes: Nancy Blampied, Sara Casassa, Judy Douds, Ray Harrison, Joe Heinen, Christina Nicolson, Christine Picariello, and Norine Reichert.

Jennifer Avery salvaged pages "lost" in the computer and her typing saved me countless hours. No one put forth more effort or provided more encouragement than Carole Beech who read every word of this book several times, set me to revising again and again, and provided invaluable expertise in the final revision and editing of the manuscript. I am also indebeted to Carole for the development of my own writing skills. Carole has spent over thirty years as a writer and editor and has been my primary writing teacher for the last decade—responding, suggesting, encouraging, and always showing me specifics to improve my writing, thus enabling me to grow as a writer and a teacher of writing.

I am grateful to the editors at Heinemann who shared their expertise and talent. Philippa Stratton nodded her head and gave a thoughtful "yes" at just the right moments. She knows how to nudge and nurture writers. Toby Gordon gave compassionate and sensitive guidance. Joanne Tranchemontagne guided this manuscript through the production process.

And finally, a special loving thanks to the family members who gave so much throughout all of the writing.

Foreword

I didn't realize how much I needed this book until I'd read it. Over the last two decades we've seen an explosion in research concerning young children learning to read and write. Researchers have invaded classrooms, observed children, formulated theories, completed dissertations, and written books and articles. Most of the writing about young children and their literacy has been written by researchers from the outside. Finally, we have a book written from the inside by a practicing teacher who may understand our researchers' theories better than we, as researchers, understand them ourselves.

"There is nothing more practical than a good theory," someone once said. Well, this is the most practical inside-the-classroom book about the primary years that I've read to date. This book is for first-grade and primary teachers what Nancie Atwell's *In the Middle* (1987) and Linda Rief's *Seeking Diversity* (1992) are for middle-school teachers.

A practical book in this case doesn't mean cookbook recipes with first-grade activities. Rather, "practical" refers to the author's approach to teaching us how to observe children. Her premise is simple: Children are meaning makers; listen to them; observe the world through their eyes, and then help them express what they wish to say. We see the author in myriads of learning situations with all kinds of children ranging from the learning disabled to the gifted.

Carol Avery sheds prescriptive teaching for listening to children. Many of us have written about the importance of listening but we haven't applied sound theory to the classroom. The soundness of Carol's interpretations of first-grade children is no accident. She's taught first grade for twelve years, been a high school English teacher, school librarian, and mother.

She connects the child's fundamental urge to make meaning with the long-term view of what reading and writing are for—a lifetime of enjoying and learning to live in the world. This is no filmy-eyed work that ignores child problems. You will meet angry children; troublemakers crying, moaning, and swearing; and children of divorce. There are children with severe learning problems who at first don't want to read and write. We follow their progress from troubling moments through first scribbles and stuttering decodings to fluency.

There aren't too many texts that follow children from day to day over an entire year as they learn to read and write. Most texts, including my own, aren't always helpful to teachers who wonder what to do after introducing certain skills, or new learning procedures. This text documents children's learning right in the midst of a conference, then follows their gradual upward spiral to confidence and achievement.

With all of these individual cases, Carol doesn't neglect the overall class-room picture. "Books become the common ground that hold a class together," she says. There are numerous transcripts of children talking and learning together. We have that rare look at the understructure of her classroom—one usually lost to the casual observer or visitor—which shows the rock-ribbed tacit understanding children have about how a room works. In the author's room children learn to listen and help each other. Carol Avery shows us the details of developing a partnership with children, which, in time, becomes part of the understructure. Thus, new and experienced teachers, as well as academics who spend too little time in classrooms, can see how a classroom learns to take responsibility and enjoy reading and writing.

Carol Avery invites us to learn with her. This means that we will witness what doesn't work as much as what does. Most texts ignore how the author learned. We simply say it is a good idea to do this or that approach without showing the process of dealing with the problems or bugs that go with new practices. Carol goes one better and shows real children in the process of learning to learn. As readers, we learn from Carol because of her own appetite for learning. It is the quality of her own reading, writing, and learning that cannot be underestimated as the basis for successful teaching. It is her partnership with children and the questions they ask that move her to read still more literature, peruse journals, and consult with other professionals.

This book is filled with a wide range of literature for children. The author knows children and books and demonstrates the ways in which she helps children to begin to meet authors and choose books appropriate to their ability.

And with a Light Touch is a liberating book. Carol Avery listens to children, their wantings and intentions, and helps them to become lifetime readers and writers. As Carol frees the children to enjoy their world, we learn with her how to become professionally free ourselves.

Donald H. Graves

Prologue:
The Butterflies Are Being Born

The little boy yawned. His name was John and he sat at my feet in a circle of five or six of his first-grade peers for his daily reading lesson. Carefully, precisely, he printed a word on a line in his workbook, then looked up and yawned again. And then I yawned too. I opened my eyes to find John watching me. We exchanged quiet smiles and then waited for the others to finish writing the same word in their workbooks so we could continue the fill-in-the-blank exercises. I glanced around the classroom where the other three reading groups spent their seatwork time writing. And it hit me. The energy in this classroom was there: with the children *writing* at their seats.

I looked back to John and his group, now patiently waiting to continue their reading lesson. These six—my "top group"—listened, followed directions, behaved themselves, and read well. They produced neat, perfect work day in and day out. They'd begun reading almost immediately in September and my job had been rather easy—to teach them the essential "skills" of a good reader. How many times through the years had I gone through lessons such as this on digraphs, short vowels, main idea, or whatever? Thank goodness this group caught on with the first presentation. They were spared most of the agony of the "skill 'em, drill 'em, kill 'em" approach to reading.

I glanced at the involved expressions on the faces of the children around the room, then back to the passive, compliant group seated at my feet (who would soon return to their seats and the writing they loved as much as their classmates). I suddenly knew: "It will work!" The *it*, a gentle suggestion by Rose Stetler, the reading coordinator in our school district, was to abandon the basal reader and "to teach reading through writing." When I'd first heard this notion the previous fall I'd thought, "That's crazy!" Now, on a morning in early March, I saw clearly that children did not need worksheets or prescriptive lessons or a scope and sequenced program to learn to read. I realized that my first graders learned more about reading from the writing they were doing at their seats than they did from the carefully orchestrated lessons I presented to achievement-ranked reading groups. In that brief moment I knew that Rose's suggestion was anything but crazy. Writing was a powerful, efficient, and natural way to learn language.

Rose was one of several language arts specialists in local school districts involved in writing a grant in the late 1970s to develop the teaching of writing in the schools. Write-to-Write, as the proposal was known, became the current educational buzzword in our area. In fact, the phrase was so well known that many teachers thought Write-to-Write was a national program and were surprised to learn that this term was familiar only in the educational circles of Lancaster and Lebanon counties in Pennsylvania. Rose had learned about the research Donald Graves was doing in Atkinson, New Hampshire, with writing in elementary classrooms. Because children in those research classrooms spent time writing every day, their teachers devoted less time to teaching reading. Despite this shift in time distribution, the reading scores went up. "Writing made the difference," was the answer coming from this research. Hence the phrase, "learning to read through writing."

I had been following the research myself as it appeared in *Language Arts*, a journal from the National Council of Teachers of English geared for elementary education. The research on writing intrigued me and already I'd begun experimenting with writing in my classroom. The research seemed so real, so different from other research reports, that I found myself thinking, "I bet my kids can do that." Following the New Hampshire model I started my first graders writing, allowing them to use invented spelling and to choose their own topics.

In order to find time for writing every day, I asked the children to write during the seatwork time while I worked with reading groups. I enlisted the help of an aide and two mothers so that every day during the reading instructional period, an adult sat in the back of the room and listened to the children read their writing. Sometimes the adult lightly penciled in words or phrases that were undecipherable because of the invented spelling, but basically she listened and talked with the child about the ideas in the writing. Now, in early spring, I'd cut back to only the barest essential worksheets. The children quickly completed that work (regarded as a chore) in order to get to their writing.

The results astounded me. I discovered that not only could first graders select topics, but also they could present coherent and detailed information about those topics on paper. I chose the best of their pieces, corrected spelling and punctuation, typed them, and bound them into little books. We had a whole shelf of these books, and they were the favorite reading material in the classroom. Though I felt comfortable developing writing among my first graders, I dismissed any hint of "abandoning the basal and teaching reading through the children's writing" as foolish and irresponsible.

Eileen Sabaka, who taught in the classroom next to mine, kept the idea alive all year. "You ought to think about this writing program," she'd say as we stood in the hall greeting the children in the morning. "I bet you'd really like to do this reading through writing," she'd add when I'd show her some of my students' pieces. "Not me," I'd answer. It was too scary to consider teaching without a prescriptive program that had a sequential presentation of skills to lead kids in an orderly and uniform manner into reading. I had no idea how children learned to read; the program provided security. My vision was limited by well-entrenched, traditional reading instruction and the culturally endorsed basal reader.

Now, on this morning in March, I saw a brief vision of a different way in the faces of the children. After school I told Eileen, "I've been thinking about this reading through writing business, that maybe it might just work."

"Go talk to Rose," Eileen urged, and the next day I approached our reading coordinator about the prospect.

"We will need to do some planning and maybe get you some training," Rose responded, and then she went to work. She contacted Jean Robbins, the principal in Atkinson, New Hampshire, and arranged a visit. On a Monday morning in April I found myself trudging through fresh snow to visit the classrooms at Atkinson. That day I helped children out of boots and listened to them read books they had authored. In writing workshops I talked with first graders writing about going to see *Annie* on stage and I watched fourth graders working on reports about New Hampshire. I returned home enthused about children's writing and eager to encourage my students to write even more. I'd also learned of a graduate course, "Teaching Writing in the Elementary School, which Mary Ellen Giacobbe and Lucy Calkins planned to teach that summer for Northeastern University. Mary Ellen was the first-grade teacher in Don Graves's study and Lucy was a research assistant. Within a few days I'd sent my registration for the course.

I spent the remainder of the school year reading articles funneled to me by Rose and thinking about the following year. Sometimes I fought off misgivings: What kind of imprudent undertaking had I gotten myself into? But reading the stories from the New Hampshire research buoyed my optimism. I sensed that I had touched on something authentic for the children and for myself. I couldn't turn back. And I had administrative support from Rose Stetler and Jim Bowman, the district curriculum coordinator, who also had been involved in the initial Write-to-Write project.

On the last day of school, as the children hurried out the door, a quiet boy named George stopped to hug me. "Good-bye, Mrs. Avery," he said and he was gone. I felt a tinge of sadness. The reading program hadn't served George very well. He was in the low reading group and probably would stay there throughout his school career. I watched him leave and remembered the butterflies. In the fall George had brought a caterpillar to school in a jar. A few days later he brought a plastic box especially designed to hold caterpillars. His parents had gotten it for him, he explained, and he'd caught more caterpillars. Several caterpillars crawled around inside the box and from the lid hung a dozen or more green chrysalises, each with a fine strand of gold beads along one side. They were exquisite. We kept the box on the corner of my desk. In a couple of days the remaining caterpillars hung in tiny green and gold sacks. After a time the chrysalises turned black. Thinking them dead, I came close to discarding them or sending them home with George. Then one day in the middle of my teacher-directed reading lesson, monarch butterflies began unfolding from those seemingly dead chrysalises. George spied them first and cried out, "Look, the butterflies are being born!"

The principal, who had stopped in for an observation, sat with his pad and pencil. I glanced at him and struggled a moment, for I was well aware of administrative judgments concerning "time on task" behavior, account-ability, and following the preplanned lesson—all the agendas of school. Then I looked at George and decided. "Let's watch the butterflies for a few minutes." The principal left in a short while (I later learned that he appreci-ated my decision). We watched those butterflies unfold and dry their wings throughout the day. By the following noon a delicate sea of orange and black fluttered under the box lid. A couple days later we quietly, carefully carried the box outside. George lifted the lid and held it while, one by one, the butterflies took their leave and headed on their migratory journeys. George watched them until the last one was out of sight. He had known all along that inside those black chrysalises lived the developing butterflies. George knew lots of things that I didn't. I realized that there was much about George I didn't understand. I'd been too busy to see really, too busy "teaching," implementing programs. In that empty classroom I felt a stab of guilt. Those programs had barely touched George's capacity as a learner.

This school year was over. Though the children had been different as they were every year, in many ways—except for the writing—the year had been like all the others before it: We'd read the same books, followed the same sequence of lessons, completed the same drill and practice exercises. Worst of all, the spread in reading achievement—the basic measurement of success in first grade—had widened. Every year brought children like John to the classroom, who ended as they began—on the top. And every year there were others like George, who for one reason or another moved through the system but never really became competent readers. This year, writing had brought life to an otherwise boring landscape by providing a forum where every child participated successfully.

A couple of weeks after school ended I headed for New England to learn more about this new phenomena of teaching writing and, through writing, reading. The challenge of a new program kindled a renewal for teaching within me and put at bay an encroaching sense of burnout. I had no clue that I was embarking on a course that would change me as a teacher and turn me into a learner in my own classroom.

Awakening

CHAPTER 1

An Invitation
to Teach

Why are we doing all this writing? I came here to learn how to teach reading through writing, not to write myself. When is this course going to get down to business? When are they going to tell us how?

The course was split into two sections and except for our concluding read aloud and a session Lucy Calkins presented on writing across the curriculum, my class time was spent with Mary Ellen Giacobbe. I was eager to learn from another first grade teacher. Gradually I came to understand that Mary Ellen Giacobbe's and Lucy Calkins's course would be unlike any teaching methods course I had ever taken. We spent half of the four-hour meeting time each day in a writing workshop, drafting and struggling to refine our own pieces of writing. We reflected on our processes of writing and considered their implications for our teaching. The only graded project was one of our own choosing, which we were to produce during the month after the course ended. Giacobbe made it clear that she did not expect us to write a paper that fed back her theories, but rather to create a project that would be helpful for us in our own teaching.

The most startling aspect (and somewhat frustrating at the time) was that no one provided a precise formula for teaching writing, let alone a curriculum for "teaching reading through writing." No prescriptions. No activities to replicate. No recipes. I soon learned that my expectation—discovering how to teach reading in a new way—was shared by the other primary teachers in the course. Although we valued writing, the truth was that reading was the basic skill to be reckoned with in our classrooms each day; writing was a secondary skill. The course transformed my thinking.

At first I felt terribly anxious about writing each day. I had always written alone—never in a community of writers. But I soon found myself immersed in composing a personal narrative, sharing that writing with other teachers, and receiving responses. My fears subsided. As I wrote I experienced what professional writers come to anticipate: tension as thoughts emerged, exhilaration as writing flowed from my pen to the page, stagnation when the words would not come, surprise when a sentence worked beautifully, and the commitment and hustle of editing and polishing a piece for a deadline. The writing workshop gave me an important tool for thinking and learning—my own writing. In addition, working in a supportive community of fellow writers provided powerful evidence of the importance of establishing a writing community in my classroom and for setting the tone and procedures essential to the development of that community. We read and discussed articles reporting these new theories and practices and were challenged to begin articulating our own theories. Mary Ellen shared the structure of writing workshop in her classroom as well as numerous procedures, examples and tips that enabled that structure to run smoothly. She showed us examples of children's writing development and led us through role play of writing conferences. She accompanied all her examples with the reasons *why* she made the decisions she did in the classroom. I came home energized and with a new vision of what teaching and learning could be, as well as many ideas for implementing workshops, but establishing the precise model that would work for *my* classroom and *my* students was the task that lay ahead of me.

Planning

So much of what I heard and experienced in the Giacobbe workshop just *made sense*. Yet I viewed the work with children's writing as breakthroughs in education. Compared to the traditional theories and practices entrenched in the schools, this work was certainly avant-garde. When I returned from New England, as my course project, I wrote an action plan for establishing a classroom with daily writing and reading workshops. In the first part of this paper I traced the development of two children from the previous school year when I had begun playing with the new ideas about children and writing. Even today, when I read these pages, I feel the energy I experienced then, the first time I *really* began to think about children's learning. Here are excerpts from that report:

> Graves says writing is "an important means of developing thinking and reading power." I saw this evident in my students. In the beginning, many worked at connecting letters to the sounds in words. Later, they struggled for clarity and wrestled with sentence structure, punctuation,

and organization. In September, Lori drew a picture and labeled it: W (on the wagon), B (beside the ball), H (beside the house), T (on the tree). Lori could recognize beginning sounds and match them to objects in her picture. She verbalized a lot more than she was able to commit to paper. She told in elaborate detail her summer play in the scene she had drawn. Lori's classmate, Jenny, who was already reading, wrote: "I have two goldfish that my Mommy wane at the Ephrata fare. Golldy and Sunny." Jenny had written a complete sentence of twelve words, only three of which were misspelled. She also punctuated. But most important, both girls wrote from their own experiences. They communicated to their readers. What is more, both were vitally interested in reading what the other had to say. There was absolutely no idea that one was better than the other.

Lori gained confidence from the encouraging class atmosphere. She learned from reading the writing of her peers that words can be written together to communicate complete thoughts. Only two weeks after her initial writing she, too, was able to write a sentence: I LRto GOTSO to SVATONIS (I like to go to the zoo to see the animals).

Classmates praised her success and inquired about her trip to the zoo. They also received compassionately Jenny's piece concerning the fate of her fish.

> My goldfish did (died)
> goldey did (died) and suny did. (died)

By March Lori published her seventh book, "My Last Birthday."

> dedicated to Paige
> I whant to the stikyard [Stockyard] and
> beside it there was a restaurant.
> The rastarint was croutdid. There where difert rasterris rooms.
> I wnt in the six [sixth] room.
> I went in the room and every butty jumped out at me.
> My hart jumped up
> We are super there   we had shirbirt with froot under it.
> We had cake and ice cream after super
> Then last we opened my prests.
> The end of my birthday bok.

Jenny produced a 575-word story about the Easter bunny that began, "One day as easter bunny was hopping along mindding his onw binssis when sundlen he saw an egg." Her entire text is too long to reproduce here. However, her development was evident in the complicated story line, the use of quotation marks and punctuation, including a correct colon, and many correct spellings. The growth in both girls was amazing. It was also typical of the growth patterns in the entire class.

Not only could Jenny and Lori read each other's pieces, but so could most of their classmates. . . . Before my eyes a writing program was developing in my classroom that was also a total language arts program. As children read and reread their own and their classmates' writing, reading skills improved. Word recognition strengthened and comprehension skills became keen. Oral expression and listening skills developed as students presented, explained, clarified, and questioned their own and others' pieces of writing. It had become important to communicate effectively; all of the elements that contribute to effective communication were being sharpened. . . .

The writing became integrated across all areas of the curriculum. Science, health, and social studies lessons became part of the children's experiences that they chose to write about. When the class studied a weather unit, the published works included "Tornados" and "Thermometers." . . . The study of China produced "China" and "Pandas."

From the first day of school, the teacher must carefully and deliberately establish the norms and procedures of the classroom. . . . Children write every day. They choose their own topics. The teacher conferences [Yes, I really used a noun as a verb in that paper!] frequently with individuals and small groups. The conference approach is extremely effective because it responds to the children at the points of their strength and knowledge. When Lori began writing by picture labeling, the class and I responded to the content of the picture she had drawn and praised her efforts at using correct sounds. Lori's confidence grew and she was soon able to expand and write a complete thought. The conference system provides support for individual achievement. . . . When well established, the predictable environment of the classroom fosters responsible learning. Children know what to expect and what is expected of them. When they know they are going to write daily, they begin to think about writing when they are not writing. "I was thinking last night in the bathtub about what I'm going to write about today," said one child when he came in the door. The remark is not unusual. . . . The predictable environment is highly conducive to the high-risk activity of learning. It allows the unpredictable to occur. One day in a class discussion, Michael said, "The hard part about writing is that when you write you're sorta telling secrets about yourself and somebody might laugh."

. . . In this atmosphere, teacher and students become partners in the search for understanding and knowledge. Trust of each other, the environment, and of the self, support and encourage solid learning. The teacher must at all times be sensitive to the atmosphere of the classroom. It is important to be flexible. It is crucial to be responsive to the attitudes and idiosyncrasies of the children. Pacing becomes a significant factor. A rigid time schedule for instruction will handicap progress. Above all, it is important for the teacher to be truly interested in what the child has to say, to want to know what the child knows, and to help children to know what they know. . . .

The day after Jon presented his book "Clowns" to the class for the first time, he came to me and said with delight, "When I read my book about clowns everybody laughed (because it was funny). I didn't know I could write something everybody would laugh."(sic) Jon's learning is exciting. His classmates responded not only to his product, but to Jon himself. He learned skills in the process. He also learned something about himself. Jon has taken ownership of his learning. . . .

Ownership, a goal of process teaching, develops when students have a high degree of involvement with their learning. It produces strong learners who are honest writers and aggressive readers. . . .

I wrote this part of the paper to help administrators and parents understand this new approach, but the writing helped me clarify my thinking as to *why* I had seen amazing results from my first-grade writers. In the second part of the paper I mapped out my plan for next year's writing workshop, slowly building the structure with mini-lessons, writing folders, group sharing, etc. I included plans for establishing procedures for reading workshop, for creating awareness of authors and authorship, ways of publishing, establishing a parent library, and (in three paragraphs!) the role of children's literature in the classroom. (That's ironic to me now because children's literature eventually became the central component for both reading and writing development.) I even mapped out the physical layout of the classroom.

Procedures for recording the progress of each child composed a large section of this plan and were, of course, of keen interest to administrators. I also compiled a list of first-grade skills from the scope and sequence chart in the reading program and from other skill checklists provided by Rose Stetler. Later I realized that this list dealt almost entirely with reading skills, giving no attention to the skills of writing. From time to time throughout the school year I would refer to this list to be sure I addressed all the skills considered essential for a successful first-grade experience. The children, I indicated, would take the tests from the reading program as one means of documenting their progress.

I now recognize that in writing an action plan I did far more than prepare for a school year. The writing required me to think beyond the mandates of the curriculum and to delve into the complex, elusive processes of teaching and learning. My audience—administrators and, to a degree, parents—needed reassurance that these children would learn to read and that they would be ready for second grade. The plan was not as important to me as the *process of writing* it, though I didn't recognize this at the time. I was still looking for the recipe but I saw myself as writing my *own* recipe—one I'd eventually nail down. Planning boosted my confidence to start the school year, but I ended up abandoning or modifying much of the plan when school started.

Writing did help me synthesize the new ideas emerging from Graves's research. Two ideas were of particular importance to me. First, the behaviors of writers are idiosyncratic and highly variable. I could have substituted "learners" for "writers" in this statement. What classroom teacher couldn't? Here was a statement from researchers that validated what teachers *knew* to be true. Although Graves noted similarities among children as they wrote, he and his colleagues found they could not make generalized statements about the writing process and apply these statements to all children. Every classroom teacher I knew viewed research findings with skepticism and occasionally voiced those doubts with comments such as, "That may be true in *that* case, but it wouldn't apply to *my* classroom." Graves noted that many factors (self-concept, topic choice, organic factors, etc.) influence a writer's process on a given day. In capital letters, in his book *Writing: Teachers and Children at Work*, Graves (1983) wrote, "WRITING IS A HIGHLY IDIOSYNCRATIC PROCESS THAT VARIES FROM DAY TO DAY. Variance is the norm, not the exception" (p. 270).

Throughout the next school year, when doubts crept in, I took comfort in the knowledge that children wrote in "highs" and "lows," that I could not expect a steady upward spiral of growth, and that I must allow children the luxury of failure and the gift of time. I would remember a line in my summer notes: "In a class of twenty-five on a given day, only five or six children may be working on 'hot' topics with the writing going well."

The second important idea was that good teaching encourages individual differences rather than promotes uniformity. I'd seen differences in children's writing and in every aspect of their participation in classroom life. I hated attempting to blot out their differences and make them conform, but success with the curriculum and programmed teaching seemed grounded in uniformity. I much preferred the responsive style of teaching that this research suggested. Remembering to listen for the differences and gently to encourage and coax the individual voices of the young writers in my classroom became a guiding principle.

In addition, Mary Ellen added some specific suggestions for teaching that I included in my written plan:

- Respond to the writer not the writing.
- Be careful with general praise and with praising too much.
- Build on what a writer has accomplished rather than on what they haven't done.
- Look for growth over time.

These are all common sense, yet radical thinking when compared to educational practice at the time. I found it helpful to remember these refreshing attitudes about children and learning whenever I was tempted to revert to archaic teaching formulas or whenever I needed reassurance that it was all going to work.

Mary Ellen spoke of three essentials for writers of any age—even young children: time, ownership, and response. Today these terms have become synonymous with the teaching of writing. Mary Ellen Giacobbe was the first to use these terms and Nancie Atwell would later articulate them in *In the Middle*. When I looked back over my notes and reflected on the structure of that summer workshop, I recognized that time, response, and ownership were embedded components of the entire course and that they contributed to my learning. I discovered experientially how those elements of the environment enable learning to occur. In writing my action plan I connected experiences from the summer workshop and the new research findings to my own knowledge and my own teaching history. This writing thrust me out of the doldrums of programmed teaching and launched me on a personal and professional journey.

The action plan had another value; I believe it established confidence with administrators. As I went into the new school year, I needed their trust. Rose Stetler and Jim Bowman continued their support and, thankfully, nobody looked over my shoulder. I had enough anxieties of my own without the complication of hovering administrators.

My action plan for implementing a process-approach classroom contained no schedule. Previously, I had segmented the school day into time slots for all the curricular areas after receiving the assigned times for special subjects such as music, art, library, and physical education. My schedule was driven by the requirement to cover all of the district-adopted curricular programs for first grade: math, handwriting, health, language, reading, and science and social studies units. One of the first things I learned when I became a first-grade teacher is that being an elementary classroom teacher requires incredible time management skills but not necessarily a lot of thoughtful planning for instruction. The *schedule* took us through the day and *programs* established the classroom structure. Marking out little slots for individual subjects gave me a sense of security, as well as a guide to get through the increasingly complex school day and the bulging curriculum, most of which revolved around the reading program. Now, without the reading program, I was suddenly confronted with a vacuum. There was all that *time!*

When Rose Stetler read through my action plan she inquired, "And what about your schedule, Carol? Have you thought what your schedule might look like?"

A brief moment of panic, then an honest response.

"No, I don't know yet. I mean, I know I want to start a writing workshop and of course I'll work all the other curricular stuff around it, but I think I just have to get in there and see how it develops."

She nodded and accepted my answer and communicated that exceedingly important ingredient—*trust*. I don't think I knew how to create a realistic schedule without framing it around curricular programs. Drawing up a schedule before school started would have prevented the children and me from working out our classroom procedures together. I would have imposed a relic of the formal reading program on the vital learning processes of the children. Instead, I plunged into the school year with a beginner's knowledge of writing and reading workshops, some intuitive experience gained from working with young children, a knowledge of good children's literature, and a commitment to watching, listening, and learning with the children.

To say that I began without a schedule is not to claim that I walked into the classroom on the first day with an empty slate. I planned by choosing records and songs, preparing an art activity and a math lesson, and selecting several good children's books to read aloud. I thought about procedures for starting the writing workshop that first day and continuing every day thereafter. Most importantly, on the first day I wanted to listen to and observe the children, to talk with each one of them and get to know them.

All the research stated that writing workshop needed to be forty-five minutes to an hour each day. This seemed like a long stretch of time to a teacher accustomed to the finely segmented school day. Could six-year-olds really sustain an hour's worth of attention on one activity? I wasn't sure it was possible. When I received the schedule for special area subjects for the year, I felt another twinge of concern. There was only one hour of time consistently available every day of the week, the hour between 11 a.m. and noon. I had *always* taught reading during the first part of the morning, and I worried that 11 a.m. might be too late to engage in such a key activity as writing. My worries were needless; the children worked well at that hour. Each year since that first one, our writing workshop has begun at a slightly different hour of the morning, and I've found that the children accommodate. It's probably more important to have the *same time every day*. One year, when the schedule for special subjects forced our workshop to begin at a different time on Thursdays, the children became frustrated when the workshop hour arrived on Thursday because they were ready to write but the schedule required they wait until later in the day.

Beginning

Early into the school year the anxieties surfaced: What if this doesn't work? What if these kids don't learn to read without all those workbooks and skill lessons?

But of course they did.

I explored, made mistakes, and learned. I believe that the trust I felt filtered through to the children. I felt free to play with these new ideas about learning and teaching, to revise and clarify my thinking based on observations and reflections. For example, I thought I would use the reading program readers, but I soon learned that their sequenced approach was inconsistent with the dynamic and individual learning of my eager readers. With growing confidence, I stopped requiring that every child read every story. I was beginning to develop a more complete understanding of what I had known only in a rational way: that learning in my classroom—both mine and the children's—was an ongoing, evolving process.

On the first day of school I started children writing in small groups. By the end of the first three days every child had written something, and on Monday of the first full week we wrote together in a large group. The rest of those first days of school I let the children lead and I responded, slowly building a structure and introducing new components as the children seemed ready.

What did we do? We enjoyed art (painting, clay, construction paper projects) and music activities (creative movement to records, singing, circle games). We began our first social studies unit: comparing urban, rural, and suburban communities through observational walks, books, and conversation. And I read lots and lots of children's books! I wrote sketchy plans in my planbook each afternoon for the next day, but I adapted to the children's needs as each day unfolded. I certainly carried an overall plan—more of a philosophy, an evolving theory—in my mind, but I never regimented it into a lockstep program similar to previous years of teaching.

The year was one of the best teaching experiences I have ever had. Why? I've reflected on this question and always come up with the same answer. I had only a few basic preconceptions in my mind about *how* this writing and reading process classroom would operate: the children led the way. I listened, observed, and let them direct me in what and how to teach them next. I was developing a responsive teaching style.

I took the notion of "writing before reading" so literally that I didn't ask kids to read until mid-October. The prompt to begin a reading workshop came when I noticed several children attempting to read books on their own. Undoubtedly, they could have begun reading sooner, and in subsequent years I would initiate reading workshop during the first week of school, but I have no regrets about waiting: they all learned to read that year.

And so the children and I began together. Something intangible happened during those first few weeks of school when we *slowed down, took our time, and got to know each other*. We built a community together, and the schedule and procedures evolved to accommodate not only the curriculum but also the personality and needs of our community. By the end of October we wrote and read every day at given times. We created a daily time for reading aloud and talking about books and authors. We included times for math, handwriting, and a time each day to focus on a social studies, science, or a health topic. We established a ritual to start the day, rules for reading and writing workshops, and procedures for dealing with problems. Our routines were no longer dictated by outside authorities in the name of "covering the curriculum" but were created and managed by our own learning community. At the year's end, I knew this group of youngsters understood more about their own learning and were stronger readers and writers than any other of my prior classes. Each child—and I mean *every one*—was a literate individual!

As future school years opened, I established a similar schedule with the children. Usually, after two or three weeks of school, our basic routine was in place, providing security and comfort in its predictability. Children knew that every day at the same time they would write in our writing workshop; they knew we would read in reading workshop and listen and respond to books read aloud during our literature time. Children understood the classroom structure and the expectations for their involvement within that structure because they were involved in developing classroom procedures. I led group discussions, as the routines evolved, to find out how the children felt things were going and to get their input in making adjustments. The classroom routines became *our* routines, not *mine*—or so I thought.

When I headed to New England, I had anticipated learning a methodology, a set of practices, a new teaching program. Rather than providing a prescriptive path, my teachers extended an invitation to claim my professionalism, to *teach* in the finest sense of the word. I enrolled in the course expecting lots of answers for how to implement a workshop approach in my first-grade classroom. Instead, I took home a bundle of new theories (none of them mine yet) and rich experiences. I knew it would take time and hard work, but I was determined to nail things down, to work out the right way—to get it all under control. After the first year I felt increasing pressure (mostly self-imposed) to wrap everything up into a curriculum or a program and to justify this new approach by fitting it into the paradigm of traditional instructional practice. I think I felt compelled to articulate my teaching and the children's learning through educational jargon. Educators understood the language of curriculum and the language of programs, and these terms provided assurance for the big word looming on the horizon: accountability. Besides, there was security in knowing exactly what to teach and when and how. I didn't know that longing for security would lull me into routines that would jeopardize the heart of my teaching; it was something I would soon discover.

CHAPTER 2

The First Day
of School

For several years—six to be exact—I taught a writing and reading process classroom and each year I honed my teaching practice. Then came a day when events in my classroom forced me to confront a basic reality of teaching: maintaining the dynamic energy inherent in the teaching/learning process results not from refined teaching agendas, carefully constructed curriculum, or fine programs and materials. Instead, effective teaching is based on continuous decision making by a professional in response to the current context of the classroom. Thoughtful decisions are well informed through experience and knowledge, but they are made in response to individual children in particular settings at given moments in time. Such decision making is rarely clear but, rather, infused with tension because we are working with human beings who are as diverse as they are similar. Establishing my own set of routines became my trap. But I'm getting ahead of my story.

On a warm September morning, the first day of school, I arrive at school early, carrying the student name tags I have made and a new children's book, *Cookie's Week*. The room doesn't *need* another book to begin the year but I do. No matter how many September "first days" I go through, I am still anxious as school begins, aware that my anxiety is matched by the apprehension the children feel. So my trip to the children's section of a local bookstore over the Labor Day weekend became a means of quelling some of the jitters. Sharing a good book with children on the first day of school always relieves some of the tension inherent in a new group coming together.

I chose *Cookie's Week* because of the brief but captivating story line of a mischievous cat and her antics on each successive day of the week. I know the children will enjoy the humor on each page as Cookie knocks over flowerpots and falls in the toilet. The line on the final page—"Tomorrow is Sunday. Maybe Cookie will rest."—brings a satisfying conclusion. The repetitious pattern of the story, the large print, the small size of the book all make it appealing for beginning readers. And the delightful pictures are by Tomie dePaola, one of my favorite illustrator/authors of children's books.

All these attributes will contribute to the children's involvement with this book. There is one more: *I* like it. I'm eager to read it to this new group of children, eager for them to like it too. The book represents a kind of connector, a material object that releases an intangible energy flow when we open the pages, read, and begin our year together.

Unlocking the classroom door, I enter and head for the windows to let in morning coolness to replace the stuffy air that has built up over a hot weekend. I begin laying out the name tags on the front table. But all the while my mind is going over the plan for the day. On this first morning of this new school year, I will begin establishing procedures for writing and reading workshops and for literature time. I've done this many times now and even wrote the story of one such first day for a chapter in *Stories to Grow On*. The procedures have worked well for me: literature time, writing workshop, reading workshop—three important components of my classroom. I want to be sure to get each one off to a good start today.

The children will come in shy and hesitant, as first graders always do, but as we begin the day on the carpet in a corner of the classroom, they will begin to relax. We'll chat informally and introduce ourselves; then I'll tell about some of the things we'll do this year. I hear myself speak to another group of children on another first day, and for a few moments I relive that time.

"Every day we will sit here and listen to stories," I say. Twenty-four faces light up. "Sometimes I'll read and sometimes you'll read. And we'll talk about what we read—what we feel or what the stories make us think about. But we'll do it every day."

As I open Marcia Brown's illustrated version of *The Three Billy Goats Gruff* (Asbjornsen, 1957), some children say, "Oh, I know that story!" "It's a good one!" I read through the book, tapping my knuckles on the bench as the billy goats trip-trap across the bridge, and several children begin to tap the bookcase and the floor along with me. When I finish they cry, "Read it again." I read again and this time some chime in with the trip-traps and the ugly troll's roar, "Who's that tripping over my bridge?" I notice that Johnson, a Chinese boy who speaks only a few words of English, watches the other children as well as the pictures in the book and taps his knuckles with them. Upon hearing the troll's roar, he giggles in delight.

When I close the book, Dustin says, "I like that troll. He's funny!"

"Do you all think he's funny?" I ask.

"No!" says Meghan. "I think he's scary."

"He's like a monster," says Randy.

"The big billy goat wasn't scared of the troll and the little one tricked him. I liked that he tricked him," says Oliver.

The children relax and drop their initial reserve about coming to first grade. They are pleasant, cooperative. Most raise their hands before they speak. As the talk about the story continues, some children participate by voicing their ideas while others listen and display their interest through nods, smiles, and giggles. The responses of the children grow from literal comprehension of the text but also from personal experiences. As they talk, each child's comments prompt further ideas in other children. Their ideas differ, but by sharing they expand their understandings of the story and make new connections. They learn together.

After a few minutes I introduce Eric Carle's *The Very Hungry Caterpillar* by asking the children what they know about caterpillars. Most understand the metamorphosis of caterpillars to butterflies, and many report catching caterpillars in jars or cans. We talk briefly about the role of an author in creating a book. I introduce Eric Carle as the author of this book and then we read.

The children enjoy the repetitious language and the food the caterpillar devours. Cries of "Yum!" come from many as the story unfolds. They do not relate to the caterpillar feeling better after eating one nice green leaf, but are still enthralled with all the tasty, rich foods he consumed earlier. My typical adult response to the caterpillar's overindulgence is, I realize, not the children's view of the story. Another day I will tell them my response, but not now. Sharing my ideas too early could stifle some of theirs and be interpreted as the "right" answer. I want them to understand that there is no one correct reading of a text, that we all bring our own ideas and experiences to a piece of literature.

Before putting this book aside we look again at the illustrations, noting the holes in the pages that indicate where the caterpillar ate and talking about the varying page sizes. Why did Mr. Carle make the book this way? The children think, speculate, and share a variety of ideas—all affirmed.

I conclude the literature time by reading a few nursery rhymes. We come back to this rug and read and talk together two more times before the first day is through. We reread *The Very Hungry Caterpillar*, dramatize *The Three Billy Goats* with stick puppets, and discover several new books. The children carry home caterpillars they make from half an egg carton. (The caterpillar art project has been a successful first-day activity in my classroom for several years.)

Later on this first morning we begin our writing workshop. In order to respond individually to each child during the initial writing activity, I work with small groups of children rather than the entire class. I select five or six of the class to meet with me at a round table. The others will color a fall picture on a ditto—one of the few I will use throughout the year—at their seats. The picture requires little thought; I want them to eavesdrop on the conversations of the group at the table so that they will begin to think about what they will do when their turn comes.

I ask the children at the table to draw a picture of something they like or something important to them. The children open their crayon boxes. Danny spills the contents of his box on the table, looks through the colors, and selects a blue crayon. He swings the bright color across the bottom of this paper and a jagged line appears.

"Tell me about this, Danny," I say.

"Oh, this is the bay," he replies.

"The bay?" I ask.

"Yeah, the Chesapeake. The Chesapeake Bay. You know."

"Right, I know. The Chesapeake Bay. You've been there?"

"Well, that's where we keep our boat and that's where we go boating and crabbing and stuff."

"You keep your boat at the Chesapeake and go boating and crabbing. Well, how do you go crabbing? I mean, I love crabs but I don't know anything about crabbing."

Danny turns away from his picture to look at me. "Didn't you ever catch a crab before?" he asks.

"Never. How do you catch them?"

"Well, you can do it two ways." Danny's voice takes on an authoritative tone and he puts up one finger as he begins to explain. "One way is to just use a string and chicken neck from the side of the dock." A second finger goes up. "And the other way is with a trap. When my dad and I go crabbing, we use a trap."

"Thank you, Danny," I say and, noticing he has begun drawing again, I move on.

Across the table Trevor is drawing a dinosaur picture. I move around and stoop down beside him. "What's this about?"

"Dinosaurs," he replies. His lips purse and he presses hard with the crayon.

"Dinosaurs?"

"Yeah, dinosaurs. I know a lot about dinosaurs. I like to read about dinosaurs." I nod. Before I can respond further, Trevor returns to his paper and continues drawing.

Jan has been sitting watching and listening. Her paper remains blank. "I don't know nothing to draw," she says as I approach her.

"Nothing? You know nothing?" I respond with mock amazement that brings a grin from Jan.

"Well, I do. But I just can't think," she replies.

"I see. Well, maybe you can think of something you really like, something you did that you'd like to do again?" I nudge.

For a moment Jan is pensive. "I like that caterpillar book you read us," she says. I wait. We exchange smiles and then Jan picks up a red crayon and turns to her paper.

I continue listening and responding to the children at the table. Each time I come near Danny he is eager to tell me more about his activities on the Chesapeake. "Danny," I say after he finishes telling about the importance of running the motorboat through the channel, "You really know a lot about crabbing and boating and channels. I wonder, could you write some of those things here on the paper with your picture?"

Danny shakes his head. "I can't spell," he says.

"That's okay," I tell him. "Writers don't always spell correctly when they start to write. They fix it later. All you have to do is say the words you want to write slowly, listen for the letters, and write what you hear." With this assurance Danny is willing to try.

After the children finish this initial writing, each chooses a journal and learns where to store it in the class file. I explain to them that we will write every day in this journal. We discuss what to do with the first pieces of writing the children have just completed and decide to put them on the bulletin board. We block off a section for each child's writing.

Before we go to lunch on this first day of school, I ask the children to choose two books from those in the room and place them on their desks. When we come back from lunch I conduct my first mini-lesson for reading workshop.

"People read in lots of ways," I tell the class. "I'm going to show you some of the ways they read." I again pick up *The Three Billy Goats Gruff*. "Sometimes people read aloud like we did this morning when we read this book. They read all the words and use lots of expression. Sometimes they read silently like this, saying the words in their heads to themselves." I demonstrate reading silently. "Sometimes people read by looking at the pictures and telling the story by what they see happening in the pictures." I begin to go through *The Three Billy Goats Gruff*, talking about each picture, describing what I see in detail, constructing a story and forming questions about possible developments. "Often when people finish a book they go back and look through it again. Sometimes they read the book again. Good readers think about what they've read—what it was about, what it means to them, why they like it or don't like it."

The mini-lesson has taken only a few minutes. I explain to the children that this is our reading workshop and now they will read the books they have chosen just as I have shown them with *The Three Billy Goats Gruff*. As they eagerly open their books I begin to circulate among them.

I stoop down to Julie's desk and notice that she is pointing to the book title and making the sound of the first letter, S. "What is your book about?" I ask.

"I don't know," she replies shyly. She points to a small black fish. "I didn't open it yet, but I think it's about a fish because there's this black fish on the cover. Only, I know fish begins with F and this word starts with S."

"I think you're right. Julie, the title of this book is the name of that fish." Julie moves her finger under the word "Swimmy." "I bet you know the sounds S and W make."

Together, Julie and I make the consonant sounds and blend them together. "Swim?" Julie suddenly says.

"Pretty close! It's Swimmy!" Julie smiles, opens the book, and I move across the room to Matthew's desk.

"Tell me about your book?" I ask. The book is closed and Matthew is gazing around the room. Matthew looks at me for a moment. "I don't know," he says. I find the first page and ask Matthew what he sees. "A bear."

"Could the book be about that bear?"

"Yeah," he replies as he looks at me and smiles. I suggest to Matthew that he look at the book's pictures to see what happens to the bear. As he turns to the book I move on.

When I come to Laura she tells me, "I know this word and this word, and these words but I don't know this word in the middle. 'Oh, a . . . we will go.' "

"This book's a song! Maybe you've heard it. Let's read together." I point to the words as we read "Oh a . . ." I make the sound of the letter H, pause, and continue, "we will go." Laura's eyes go to the picture on the page, back to the text, and then she reads " 'Oh a hunting we will go!' I got it now!" She goes back to the book. I move on.

The reading workshop continues this way for ten or fifteen minutes. When I sense the children becoming restless, I know it is time to end for now. To conclude the session I ask several children to tell the group about their books.

"I read the *Hungry Caterpillar* book," says Dustin, holding it high in the air. I am pleased that Dustin announces he has *read* the book. When I stopped at his desk he was retelling the story, his voice rising and falling with inflection, although not reading with word-by-word accuracy. What is important at this time is that Dustin sees himself as a reader and strives to form meaning from the text using a variety of resources: recall of the read aloud, clues from initial consonants, illustrations, and his own sense of story.

Now, as I come out of my reverie on this morning of another first day of school, I am ready to start another year. My procedures for the first day have worked well for several years. Each year there are differences because of the differences in children, but I have been able to adapt the same basic plan as each day unfolded. I am unsuspecting of the arduous day ahead of me.

Twenty-four exuberant children bound through the doorway in a matter of minutes. I feel their energy level as they grab their name tags and zip away for a look around the room. I hear their loud voices as they greet friends and examine books. "I had it first!" comes a shout. I see two children tugging at a book but my attention is diverted by a parent at the door to meet me. After a brief conversation the parent leaves. I look back to where the tussle occurred a moment before only to see the book lying open, facedown on the floor. Two boys have found the blocks and are rapidly throwing them from the box to a heap on the floor. Another parent arrives, introduces herself, then adds, "I can see you've got your hands full. We'll chat another time." The blocks clack and the boys' voices turn to shouts as several more children join them. I move across the room to intervene.

"How's come?" they protest. "We want to *play!*" I maintain a calm and firm voice as I direct them to put the blocks away for now but I find myself wondering, "Whatever happened to those shy first graders?"

Somehow I get all the children in their seats and we proceed through the opening of the school day, including introducing ourselves and chatting together briefly. *Briefly* is all I can manage. The children all talk at once and no one listens to anything being said. We move to the storyrug in the back of the room to start our first literature time. Getting everyone settled on the rug takes longer than usual but finally we are ready to begin. I hold up *The Three Billy Goats Gruff.*

I open my mouth to speak and hear a loud voice, "I know that book. I have that. . . ." But before the sentence is finished another voice shouts, "My kindergarten teacher read that to us in my old school." As my eyes turn from the book back to the group of children I notice that a child who was sitting at my right is now on my left. In fact, several children have changed places on the rug.

"Stop it!" someone shouts. "He pinched me."

I go over the procedures for sitting on the rug, which I established only minutes earlier. There's a moment of quiet. I quickly open the book. As the children begin listening to the familiar story they respond with initial surprise then giggles at my deep voice rendition of the troll's "Whose that tripping over my bridge?" and join in with the repetitious "trip, trap" of the billy goats crossing the bridge. Their voices are loud and after each segment of the story I find it hard to pull them back to attending to the text with me.

"Read it again!" several of them cry when I finish. But I look at the clock and see that gym class begins in a couple of minutes. We line up—another complicated procedure—and hurry up the hall to meet the new physical education teacher.

Literature time resumes again on the rug after gym, math, and recess. In addition to *Cookie's Week* and *The Very Hungry Caterpillar*, I have chosen *Papa, please get the moon for me*, also by Eric Carle. *The Very Hungry Caterpillar* will be familiar to most of the children from nursery school and kindergarten. Carle's moon book is relatively new and I don't expect the class to be familiar with it. I've read it to several groups of children in the last year and found it to be a hit.

I read *The Very Hungry Caterpillar*. "What were you thinking when you heard this story?" I ask.

Elizabeth raises her hand. "Nature," she says when I call on her.

"Nature? Tell me more about what you mean by nature," I say as I think, "Where is this nature idea coming from? Kids don't talk about books with words like *nature*. Sounds like a prescriptive answer that a child *thinks* a teacher wants."

"I don't know," Elizabeth replies. "Just nature." Her voice carries a hint of baby talk that doesn't match her height and mature appearance.

"Okay. Any other ideas?" I ask. Two more children give me the "nature" response but neither can define the term. "Did you think of anything else with this story?" I ask.

"It made me think I'm hungry," says Ryan.

"Yeah, when's lunchtime?" pipes up another voice.

"Me too. I'm hungry." A clamor of voices takes over in anticipation of lunch. I capture the group's attention again by suggesting we look at Eric Carle's pictures of the caterpillar's daily meals. The children are most interested in the conglomeration of sweets and rich foods consumed by the little creature on the final day before he makes his cocoon. In loud voices they all begin chattering about food, and it takes effort and time to draw them to the reading of the second book.

Papa, please get the moon for me has fold-out pages of the "very long ladder," of Papa climbing "higher and higher," and of the full moon. When we reach that page Brian says, "It looks like the moon's smiling."

"But I don't think he could really get up to the moon," says Greg.

"Yes he could," replies Brian. "If he had a long enough ladder he could." For a couple of minutes the children speculate about going to the moon on a ladder. Their ideas are good, but I'm bothered by the challenging, almost argumentative tone of their voices.

"What other ideas do you have about the story?" I ask, striving to put a gentle, wondering tone to my voice as a model for the children.

"Space," Jody says.

"Tell me about space," I say.

"You know, rockets and stuff."

"Oh, you like rockets and stuff," I respond.

"Yeah."

"Like what?" I ask.

"I don't know. I just like 'em."

While this conversation is going on, the attention of several of the children has drifted off. They unzip and zip again and again the velcro on their sneakers. They carry on conversations in twos or threes. They play with the long hair of one of the girls. One child has left the rug and wanders around the room. I decide to read *Cookie's Week* later in the day. We sing a couple of action songs, which serves to pull the children back together, and they return to their desks.

I begin my procedures for writing workshop. Individual boxes of crayons have not arrived and I was able to round up only six boxes with eight thick crayons—the kind toddlers use. I distribute the ditto for coloring as I have done in past years, give directions for completing it, and group the children by fours to share each box of crayons. Then I call five children up to the round table in the front of the room. I have one box of twenty-four colors that I spill on the center table.

"How's come they get to go up there?" calls out a shrill little voice.

"How's come they get them crayons and we got only these?" protests another voice. Though I've already said so, I again assure the group that everyone will get a turn at the table and explain that our crayons haven't arrived.

When I ask the children at the table to draw a picture of something they like or know about, my request is met with blank stares.

"Whatjamean?" asks Laura.

"Well, like I might draw a picture of my cats because they are so much fun and I really could tell a lot about them. They play chasing games and get mad at each other and then they make up. Or, I might decide to write about trying to get in the cold ocean on my vacation in Maine." I am not comfortable providing such a precise model because I know the children will be likely to produce several cat stories and beach pictures.

Laura looks at me for a minute more but finally picks up a crayon and draws a large circle. "I'm gonna draw my cat," she says. She adds two triangles to the top of the circle for ears. "I knew it!" I think to myself.

"Mrs. Avery, what're we suppose to do?" asks a child in the large group. Many of the children at their desks are puzzled by the purple ditto. Only a few have begun to color the squirrels on the paper. Sharing the large crayons, the coloring process, the purple ditto: all this baffles them. I go over the instruction again, then turn back to the table.

Laura adds a body to her cat. Monica draws a cat's face. Cory stands crayons on end in a curving line, domino fashion. Evan draws bands of color diagonally across his paper. Matt has now joined Cory making the crayon line. "What will you draw?" I ask Cory and Matt.

Cory shrugs and Matt replies, "I don't know."

"What do you like to do? What's fun for you?" I ask.

"I play soccer," comes Matt's answer.

"Oh yeah? Can you draw that on your paper?" I nudge.

"Ummm, maybe." I can see that Matt is not committed to this drawing, but he picks up a crayon and begins. I turn to Cory and try to start him in a similar manner, but Cory is still more interested in playing with the crayons. He grins at me for only a brief instant then continues standing those crayons on end. I feel my frustration building.

"I'm done," Laura announces. She has drawn a brown animal resembling a cat. I ask Laura if she can write about her picture. She hesitates for a moment but then slowly, deliberately writes IGNCAT above the drawing. Monica responds more easily to my suggestion to write, though she is concerned about spelling. When I turn back to Laura I notice she has erased CAT and written HRD in its place. "I changed my mind," she explains and then reads "I drew my hamster." Monica writes: I LOKe to PAey WiS BONES (I like to play with Bones). The girls go back to their seats.

Meanwhile, the occasional quiet chatter among the other children is now a crescendo that interferes with the conversation at the table. The children at their desks are not tuned in to what is going on at the large table, which is the whole purpose of the coloring activity in the first place. Several children have left their seats and are wandering around the room while the paper remains unfinished on their desks. I stop everything, redirect the children, and bring two more individuals up to the table.

Through my strong nudges (more like pushes, or even demands by now) eight children, one third of the class, write at the center table this first day. With three days to this first week of school I'm right on schedule— each child will go through the initial writing experience during the first week. Lunchtime finally arrives.

Of course lunch runs overtime this first day of school and the children come back to the room fifteen minutes later than scheduled. Several of the boys have caught butterflies on the playground during recess and now each one races to be the first to present one of them to me. Looking down into the cupped little hands I see a pair of mangled wings and a slightly quivering body, the last seconds of life for the yellow-winged creature.

"See. A butterfly. Like that book you read us. You know, about that caterpillar that ate all that stuff." Cory beams up at me as he speaks. In all, six or seven butterflies have become sacrificial responses to my reading of *The Very Hungry Caterpillar*. We put the butterflies on a sheet of construction paper on the back counter.

"Do we go home now?" someone asks. Before I can answer, the playground aide comes in to tell me that there was a lot of chasing and rough play at recess and one of my children is in the health room with a skinned knee. I talk to the class about behavior on the playground. I've planned this time after lunch for reading workshop, but we must be in music soon and the music room is upstairs at the other end of the building. So I lead the group in a couple of finger plays and then we begin the process of lining up to go to music.

When the group returns from music class we gather on the storyrug again. I begin to reread *The Three Billy Goats Gruff* but never finish for the intercom comes on early with announcements for this first day of school. *The Three Billy Goats Gruff* joins an unread *Cookie's Week* on the counter, and we prepare to go home. Dismissal is hectic, but in a matter of minutes everyone is out the door and onto buses or walking the neighborhood sidewalks to their homes.

The day is over. I am exhausted, frustrated, disappointed. I wonder what the children took with them from this day. We didn't make caterpillars from egg cartons, nor draw self-portraits, nor read poems, nor sing more than two songs. In fact, I feel as if I spent most of my day either getting the children ready to go someplace, settling squabbles among them, or stating and restating my expectations and directions. There was no reading workshop, and writing workshop was definitely *not* a positive experience for anyone! Throughout the day the children did not appear to listen to each other or to me. In fact, each child seemed to move and talk in the classroom as if he or she was the only individual there. The class behaved more like a group of three-year-olds coming to nursery school for the first time than a group of six-year-olds with some prior experience of working and playing in a group. I look at the crumpled butterflies on the construction paper and think about tomorrow and the months ahead.

The second day is better—but not much. Crayons arrive and I start the writing workshop over (hoping everyone forgets the day before). This time I abandon the small-group procedure at the table and conduct the workshop with the entire group. Though I don't get to see every one of the children to provide individual responses as they work (there are simply too many children and too little time), I do get around to most of them, and my circulating among the students at their desks keeps everyone writing— somewhat. Though I'm not comfortable with my role of policewoman or taskmaster, I begin to recognize that for a while it will be necessary.

Since listening to stories had been the only strength of the first day, I integrated more read-aloud times. *Make Way for Ducklings* holds everyone's attention and becomes destined to be an all-time favorite for the year. I introduce the first reading workshop after rereading *The Three Billy Goats Gruff* and then demonstrating how one could tell this story by looking at the pictures. I show the class several other books that we can "read" this way. I ask who would like to read this book, and when the hands fly up, I begin distributing books to the children. When each one has a book I send the children to their seats to look through their books and read them.

Although the reading time at student desks lasts only a few minutes, it is a beginning.

The children still clamor to be the first in line. At recess they fight over the playground balls and chase each other. They chatter continuously and interrupt each other all day long. And at the end of the day there are several more dead butterflies on the sheet of construction paper.

Reflections

Why did this school year get off to such a poor start? I spent months sorting through the reasons.

Schedule and Materials

Part of the hectic nature of the first day of school was the schedule. In addition to recess and lunch, the day was broken up with physical education and music classes. Sending the children off to a physical education class within the first hour of school certainly was unwise. The children and I needed that time together in the classroom. I should have canceled the class.

Trying to start a writing workshop with first graders without crayons is like trying to teach reading without books. You don't need a lot of materials to set up a writing workshop, but paper and crayons (or some other tool for drawing) are basic. For young children, making marks with color is important. To expect four children to share eight fat crayons and then pay attention to the interaction I led with their peers was naive on my part. I would have done better to have dug out the old colored pencil sets and sharpened them so that each child had a set of tools. But I didn't think of it—I had my own agenda in mind.

The Children's Backgrounds

Although not immediately apparent, as the weeks passed I realized the significance of the children's backgrounds in influencing the classroom dynamics. Within recent years I have witnessed many changes in the children entering first grade. Many teachers around the country tell me they have observed changes too. The Elementary Strand of the English Coalition, a group convened to address changes in student populations and implications for learning and teaching, identified these changes as the results of changes in society, the family, and technology (Jensen, 1989; Lloyd-Jones & Lunsford, 1989). This group of children in many ways represented a microcosm of American society as I'll describe in the next chapter.

Expectations and Orthodoxies

The beginning of each school year is always a time of come-down-to-earth reality. We carry in our heads images of the youngsters who left our class-rooms only a little over two months earlier. We think of the classroom in terms of that community and all they could do individually and as a group. We forget the September days when that class first came together. Com-pounding this phenomena for me was the fact that I was returning to the classroom after a year's sabbatical. Not only did I have more distance from the reality of day-to-day classroom life, but I also had spent much time writing and speaking about the accomplishments of my former first graders. I had formed expectations for these new students when I really needed to be open to seeing and listening and learning from them.

In a talk titled "The Enemy Is Orthodoxy," reprinted in *A Researcher Learns to Write,* Don Graves (1984) reminds us how easily we can slip into formulas for teaching. Certainly we need to plan and develop strategies to manage our classrooms. But there is always the danger of creating a method-ology that becomes written in stone, that becomes another program to be applied to all children. The beginning of writing workshop in my classroom went smoothly for several years. The success created an orthodoxy for me and I lost sight of the fact that it was not particular *procedures* that enabled the children's movement into writing so much as it was my own *observations* and then my *responsiveness* to them individually and as a group. I was in too much of a hurry on this first day of school and did not allow for waiting and observing. For a while I forgot that I, too, was a learner in this classroom who needs to keep growing. I neglected to be a reflective practitioner.

The lesson learned is that I can write no blueprint for teaching or learn-ing that will be successful for every class of students. Though I had left the basal reading program behind, I had in effect created my own program. The dynamic learning I had experienced with the children in past years occurred because we worked in an *unprogrammed* manner. As architect of a new classroom community each year, I must always revise my plans and procedures in response to the students before me. I cannot force students into *my* mold of how the classroom will be run, but rather we must negoti-ate together.

Although I adhered to this belief in the past, I did not understand it as completely and profoundly as I do now. My role as a teacher is identified in my students. I ask students how and why they do things as they work in the classroom. I listen to what they tell me and observe not only the results of their labors but the processes they engage in as they read and write and talk together. As I listen and observe in the classroom I continu-ally formulate my own theories concerning the learning processes of each of my students and our interaction together as a group. I plan instructional strategies based on my theories. And I test and revise those theories as children grow and change. The children are theory makers, too. Theory-making, I believe, is a basic way we all learn.

"Theory into practice" is a much touted phrase in educational circles. Often this phrase is interpreted to teachers or by teachers themselves as meaning theory—the "best" or "right" notions about teaching and learning as professed by researchers or experts—is to be applied by classroom teachers, thus producing the "best" or "right" practices. I once believed this myself. When I removed programmed instruction from my classroom I began seeing—really *seeing*—children learning and I began *thinking* about my teaching. I realized that the children taught me and I learned from them just as much as it was the other way around. Practice changed in response to children. The work of outside theorists certainly informs my teaching. However, I came to believe that rather than theory *applied* to practice by classroom teachers, the theory of educational researchers is *transformed* into practice within the classroom setting and results in *new* theory—that of the classroom teacher. A significant change took place for me when I realized that the experts in my classroom were the children and myself and that we need not be tied to the traditions and theories of others. We could make informed decisions through thoughtful consideration of the ideas of others, balanced with our own needs.

This book is not a prescriptive formula of how to set up and teach a whole language classroom, or a process-approach classroom, or a literature-based classroom, for no formula will work for everyone—or anyone. However, I think we teachers learn by glimpsing the experiences of other teachers. We see and then make adaptations to our particular contexts. Rather than a chronological narrative (though at some points I find it necessary to document the evolution in my thinking in a chronological fashion), this book is a sharing of my experiences and what I've come to believe (my theories) about reading and writing and learning. This book contains stories of first graders and me learning together, teaching each other.

The year that began so disastrously did come together. The stories from that particular group of children provide the basis for much of this book. The next chapter relates stories of that group as we worked to form a community. It is the presence of community that influences—perhaps more than any other single factor—the effective functioning of this learner-centered classroom.

Environment
and Tone

CHAPTER 3

The Climate of
the Classroom:
A Community
Beginning

Every teacher knows that classroom tone is set during the first days and weeks of school and that the climate of the classroom is a critical element in children's learning. The final report of the Elementary Section of the English Coalition Conference refers to the process of creating the climate for an effective learning community.

> Climate becomes the invisible teacher in the classroom, establishing the foundation for the intellectual, social, and emotional development of the child. We believe that the most effective classrooms convey a sense of order through an environment that is predictable in its schedule and management, as well as in its tone. The security of this environment establishes the foundation for intellectual exploration and risk-taking so necessary for active learning.
>
> The classroom climate must be an honest reflection of the teacher's individual style. Effective climates occur when the teacher has given much thought and preparation to organization and implementation of the structure for the classroom. The teacher knows that there must be limitations and guidelines so that children can engage in real learning experiences, explore options, and make choices in using language to learn.

When teacher and children come together the first day of school, they begin to create a classroom climate. The perceptive teacher listens to children, observes the ways they learn, and finds a variety of strategies to engage children in learning, thus establishing a nurturing climate. Slowly and carefully, teacher and children build a predictable yet fluid structure, within which there is a sense of order as well as freedom of exploration and open interaction. Teacher and children respect and value each other in this climate, as they continually shape a community in which individuals flourish as well as participate as integral members of the group. (Lloyd-Jones & Lunsford, 1989, p. 13)

Beginning a new community each year is a challenge and a process that is unique to each group. This process involves the interplay of organization, management, and especially the interactions between teacher and children. The following stories and reflections come from the process of one classroom coming together as a community.

The Children

Laura cries as she wanders through our empty wing during lunchtime in this first week of school. At my desk, I hear her weeping and hurry to find out what has happened. She flings her arms around my hips, buries her face in my skirt, and sobs. The words heave out of her throat in desperate gasps when she finally speaks.

"I . . . can't . . . find . . . my class."

I lead her to the playground door where, spying the other children, she turns a quick smile to me and hurries off to play. She brushes the last tear from her cheek as she calls to a classmate.

Later I learn that Laura's trauma grew from a typical six-year-old's misunderstanding. Rain canceled our morning recess. Skies cleared by lunchtime and, after eating, the children went out to the playground as usual. But Laura remembered that I had said, "We can't go out to recess today because of the rain."

Laura's tears surprised me somewhat. On that disastrous first day she'd appeared confident—even boisterous. I'd chosen her to be among the first group of children to write because of her self-assurance. But as the September days passed, I saw her and the other children as complex personalities. We all strived to make sense of each other and this new group we were now in.

Being a child in first grade isn't easy—especially in September. There are places to be, teachers and other kids to meet, and so many new things to figure out and remember. Even though many attended nursery school and kindergarten, learning the ropes in a new situation is difficult. The episode with Laura is typical of the first days of school. First graders tug at your clothes or poke you incessantly with their fingertips, call you "Teacher, Teacher," or "Mom" and "Mommy" (and then blush with embarrassment), and sometimes "Hey!" or "Hey, what's your name? I forgot."

At 9:30 they want to know when it's lunchtime and by 11:00 they're yawning and asking, "When is it time to go home?"

In the middle of a math lesson they say, "Guess what? We're going to Hershey Park this weekend." or "Do you know my Uncle Bill?" or "My Mom might have a new baby. But it's a secret."

They forget where the bathroom is located, don't know that there are different bathrooms for boys and girls, or forget they *have* to go to the bathroom or don't *know* they have to go to the bathroom until . . . oh, ohhh.

They count on their teacher for everything: supplying tissues (including a reminder that they *need* a tissue), bandaging skinned knees, fixing leaking thermos bottles, braiding hair, finding a sweater that was stuffed inside a bookbag earlier.

And they try to be subtle, as did one hungry little boy who, thinking of the snack Mom packed, said, "I think my banana bread must be rotting over there in my lunch box."

First graders can be enchanting and charming, and also puzzling and exhausting. During the first days of school they seem to move in their own little worlds, oblivious to others and unaware that they are part of a group. I watch them, listen to them, and think, "I've got to teach these kids to *read?* "

Classes generally have fewer students than the ones a generation ago (a friend remembers a first grade with forty-five children). Yet, ask any teacher—in any grade—about teaching today. He or she will tell you that teaching has become more difficult. Why? The kids are different. Creating a classroom community seemed easier when the children came to school with similar experiences and values. A national news program on a September evening in 1988 reported that in 1948, 90 percent of all Americans lived in what is considered a traditional family home. In 1988 that percentage dropped to 40. The report cited that more people live alone and more children live in single-parent families. Even more startling was the statement that in 1988 one million homeless children lived on the streets of America, and this large figure did not take into account runaways. A teacher friend in a small town in central Pennsylvania told the story of a child in her classroom living in a car with a family of five. When the situation was discovered, the family vanished.

My school district is considered by many as the home of the wealthy and prosperous in Lancaster County, Pennsylvania. Yet each year I increasingly encounter children dealing with major problems. The most pressing difficulties result from the obvious changes in society and family structures. Technology, especially television and television games, influences all of the children in varying degrees. The effect of technology seems to be moderated by the amount of parental involvement with the children. But the changes in society and family structures profoundly affect the lives of children.

In my class are children from well-schooled professional families and those whose parents did not complete high school. Some come from wealthy homes and others live on welfare checks. They reside with both parents, or a single parent, split their time between the homes of two parents, or live with a substitute parent. They tell stories of drug and alcohol abuse in their own homes, of theft to support these habits, and of good times on family weekends at cabins in the mountains or along the river. Typically, over half the children have moved to the area since their birth. And in each year for the last several, the group of twenty-five or so children entering my classroom in September has included at least one child who has been the victim of child abuse. Frequently, there is at least one child whose first language is Greek or Chinese or Spanish.

A standardized intelligence test administered to the group produces scores that range from 72–145 with five children scoring below 80. I don't give much credence to IQ testing, especially with young children. But I think the scores reflect the diversity among the children and provide an indication of the way each child might function within the traditional expectations of a school setting. In this instance, the children with scores in the very upper end of the range come from homes of advantage. Every one of these children owns books, knows the experience of being read to regularly, and has been well fed and cared for since birth. The parents in these homes talk to their children and involve them in a variety of family activities. Each of the children at the very lowest end of the range come from unsettled home situations, homes bearing various ills of society: child abuse, substance abuse, unemployment, etc. In several cases the parent or parents are conscientiously committed and involved in reconstructing a shattered family life. In other cases the child is one more problem the struggling parents face. The test does not reveal intelligence so much as it reflects experiences—the higher scores correlating with a student's potential to readily move into and adjust to the school setting.

Among the children in this particular group are:

- a child who tells me that after school he must unlock the door and watch TV until either the mother or sister come home ("When do they get home?" I asked. "Around 5 o'clock," comes the reply. The child leaves school at 2:30.)
- a child born in a distant part of the country who has never known his father and now lives with his mother and younger sibling

- a child who by court order no longer lives with the parents; the six children in this family are separated in different homes
- a child who recently has been hospitalized for injuries resulting from a parental beating
- a child of up-and-coming professionals; both parents put in long hours and take frequent business trips
- a child representative of the typical first grader of the past—each morning one parent escorts the child to the door of the classroom and says "Good morning" to me; the parent does not linger, but simply makes a connection with this part of the child's life

Some children, like this last one, come to school from homes that have provided a secure structure in their preschool years. In writing workshop, this child will write about taking karate lessons with his dad and fishing at the river with his mom. When classroom squabbles arise, this child rarely is involved but seems to rise above such incidents. The child presents a model of a confident, self-assured first grader that is not typical of most of the children in the class. Children like this one easily move into the routines and structure of the classroom. They have developed self-control and self-awareness that provides them ready access to their talents and enables them to focus on school activities.

But in contrast, many children coming to school today have spent their early childhoods in confusion, trying to make sense out of an environment that changes daily or even hourly. Adults in their lives spend little time with them. One set of parents told me that their work schedules permitted only one night a week when the entire family was together. Little in life for these children is secure or dependable. They project distrust and are continually on guard and constantly in motion, ready for the next unexpected encounter with the world. They are excitable, tense children. Such is the diversity of our classroom.

We once used the term "melting pot" to reflect the diverse backgrounds of the American citizenry, but in recent years I've heard "salad bowl" as a metaphor that retains the integrity of the individual elements. At the English Coalition Conference, Shirley Brice Heath (1987) described American society as a "rich mosaic." I prefer her metaphor—both for society and for today's diverse classrooms. In a mosaic every piece is visible and beautiful in its own right and every piece is essential for the mosiac to be complete. The mosaic image portrays most classrooms across our country today; no longer can teachers expect groups of children from similar backgrounds but, rather, classrooms of unique individuals with widely differing characteristics and experiences.

During the first days and weeks of the school year the children and I begin to know each other. I listen and try to help them feel comfortable as we work out the procedures for the classroom. We can't hurry; building this community takes time. Years ago I read in *Freedom to Learn* by Carl Rogers (1969) that learners need "unconditional positive regard." Over the years, my experiences with children confirm this concept. So I try to communicate my unconditional positive regard to every child, and hope in the process to demonstrate this attitude for peer interactions. It's important that every child know they are a valued member of this community.

Recalling Shared Experiences

"Remember when Ian got his haircut and you didn't recognize him?"

"Yeah," says Ian, "I got my hair spiked and you didn't even recognize me, Mrs. Avery. I thought you might not let me back in our class 'cause you didn't know who I was."

The twinkle in Ian's eye and the grin on his face tell me he's continuing the playful interchange we had one Monday morning in mid-September when he arrived at school with his newly spiked hair stiff and glistening with hairdressing gel.

"Who's this?" I had gasped. "Do I know you?" In a split second Ian had picked up the playful tone and returned it. "It's Ian. Can't you recognize me?" Then he had switched to a reassuring voice and said, "Don't worry Mrs. Avery, it's Ian. I only got a haircut." And he reached out and patted my shoulder.

"Yeah, you didn't even recognize one of the people in our class," another child teases now. We've been in school a month and this morning during the chatting time that follows the opening exercises, the children and I recall incidents from our first weeks together. This chatting is more than reminiscing. As we recall shared experiences there's a sense in which each of us—myself and the individual children—invests a bit more in this class-room community. These stories are our history. Remembering helps us claim that history and serves to connect us one to another. Connections will provide a secure base for learning in the classroom. Taking time to talk about our times together contributes to building a sense of community. We are like a family that tells stories at family gatherings, stories that only family members can tell.

"I remember the day when the cat jumped in the window and we kept putting him back outside and he kept jumping in, jumping in. That was *funny!*"

"And when we went on the field trip in the woods to that—what was it called?—Gnome Countryside."

"We got to go on the rope bridge and we pretended we were the billy goats."

"And we built gnome houses out of rocks and little sticks."

"Nathan went with us. I got to be his partner and when we got back to school he read with me."

"Oh, remember how you forgot Nathan's lunch in the 'frigerator? But we all shared our lunches and then he had a *humongous* lunch!"

The children and I chuckle remembering our field trip. My eighteen-year-old son, on school holiday, had accompanied us. I was grateful for the extra adult when I took these "little squirrels" to the woods, and the children liked seeing me in the role of Mom. The day had provided us an important opportunity to engage in activities outside of the school setting.

"But some stuff's not so funny. When Megan's appendix burst that Sunday, that's a *real* important thing, and it wasn't funny," says Elizabeth.

"Yeah, she almost *died!* But she's gonna be back soon—in a couple of weeks. Our cards probably helped her get better quicker."

"I remember another thing not funny: when I said 'Fatty' to someone. I didn't know that wasn't funny, but *now* I know. I remember Mrs. Avery said, 'We will always be kind . . .' " Adam recites my exact words with my precise inflection, from that morning of the second day of school. Now he nods, acknowledging the gravity of that situation. I'm always a little awed when I hear a child repeat words I uttered some time—often a long time—previously. Frequently the words are ones from the first days of school, reminding me of the importance of those first interactions. Adam also addresses his comments to the group and not just to me—a good sign. I've been working to encourage classroom conversations to be an interchange among the children—student to students, with occasional teacher comments; not a pattern of teacher to student, student to teacher, with *my* talk interjected between each child's comment.

"What do you remember about our school work so far?" I interject now in an attempt to shift the conversation slightly.

"Writing!" Several voices chime in with the same response.

"Writing. I really like writing the best." Unanimous agreement on this. I'm not surprised. Writing workshop has been embraced by every class. But I nudge for a reason.

"Why do you like writing best?"

" 'Cause we get to draw and I like to draw."

"I like it because we get to decide what we'll write about. Only sometime it's a little hard when you can't think of what to write."

"I like when Mrs. Avery comes around and we tell her about our writing."

"I like the sharing part, when we read our writing to everyone and show our pictures and then people comment and ask questions and stuff." The child's voice trails off wistfully.

Every year the children love writing workshop. If an assembly program intrudes on the schedule, they protest, "You mean we're not going to have *writing?*" I can imagine them responding in a similar manner only if I announced that we were skipping lunch. Why is this writing so important to them? I believe it's because writing workshop provides opportunity for the children to write about themselves and their interests and to share that self with the rest of the group. It's the element of *choice* (Veatch 1964, 1966) that is critical to the children's investment in learning. This is true not only the writing but also to the entire classroom. Giving children choices within the structured framework of the classroom communicates trust in their capacity to make responsible decisions and become responsible learners. In addition, we've learned a lot about each other through the writing, and there's a nonjudgmental acceptance of each individual that emerges when we share the writing and the interest in each person's topic.

"I like math too," a child remarks as the conversation continues.

"What do you like about math?" I ask.

"It's real easy."

The children are right; math's been real easy, filled with review of counting and number concepts—things these children have understood for some time.

"I like literature time and all our good stories you read us, like *Red Riding Hood* and *Corduroy* and *Rumpelstiltskin*, and the puppets we made."

"Like our Corduroy bears. We put them up because they're so neat." The children admire the construction paper teddy bears on the bulletin board, which we made together after reading Don Freeman's *Corduroy*. The activity was a traditional, teacher-directed art project, but as we cut and pasted circles together I learned about the children's prior experiences with art tools. I could see that for some this would be an instructional lesson in using such tools. I was reminded once again of a basic supposition to bring to teaching: *presume nothing*.

The conversation continues as the children look around the room. We note the twelve birthday cake posters and recall the day everyone put a candle with their name on the appropriate month. We see our bulletin board on communities and the list we compiled on characteristics of urban and suburban life. We pause to recall favorite books as we look at enlarged illustrations from *Charlotte's Web* and posters of a few favorite picture books. We admire the first-day photos of each child that now are mounted in their blocked-off sections of the bulletin board. I am about to conclude this class conversation when a child notices one more thing and we recall one more story.

"There's your monkey poster about mistakes, Mrs. Avery. 'We all make mistakes.' Remember when you took us to gym class, and we all sat ready for the gym teacher, only we were there too early?"

They look at the poster of the little monkey behind bars, and Stacy jumps up, points to the words, and reads, "We all make mistakes."

"Yup, we all make mistakes," comments another child.

About a week into the school year, when the office buzzed me for the lunch count I didn't turn in, I had brought out my old poster and talked about error. I want the children to understand that error ("making mistakes" in the language of the children) is a natural part of everyone's day-to-day life. So many children arrive in school believing they must strive for perfection, or that doing well in school means making few (if any) errors. These attitudes hinder children in maintaining the natural risk-taking behaviors that they exercised as learners in their preschool years. I remember Chris's comment when I asked one group of children what important things I should tell teachers in a workshop I was leading on the teaching of writing: "I think the most important thing is that we all make mistakes and if you don't make mistakes you won't learn."

The Classroom: Learning to Work Together

The first days of the school year—especially with this group—were challenging ones for all of us. The children talked all the time, they clamored for my undivided attention, and, unaccustomed to a full day of school, they tired easily. We needed a relaxed pace and a playful tone to create a healthy classroom climate. The procedures don't all come together at once. In fact, I spent most of my energy in the first few weeks establishing routines and a *tone* that would help build a trusting community.

Writing Sets the Tone

After the frustrating first day of school I decide to drop the procedure of writing with small groups in the beginning, which had worked so well in previous years. The children are seated on the rug after I finish reading to them on the second morning. We sing a couple of movement songs for a brief stretch break, and then I gather them close on the rug again and begin my instructions for starting writing workshop.

"Our new crayons have arrived," I say in a hushed tone. "And right now we're going to use them for the first time."

Several children clap their hands together rapidly but quietly and exchange enthusiastic looks. One little boy scowls and another says, "What if you don't *want* to color?"

"Well," I respond slowly. Turning to this little fellow, I look him in the eye and maintain the visual line between us as I speak. "This year we will do a lot of things together because we are a group, and this is one of those things. You may use your pencil instead of crayons if you wish, but during writing workshop, we all write." I listen to my tone: quiet firmness, I hope. I can't allow the choice of not participating. This is not a do-whatever-you-please environment. Freedom of choice comes within the framework of meeting one's responsibilities within the group. As I finish the child nods and quietly says, "Okay." The scowl on the other face fades. I'm glad for the opportunity to make this point clear. I expect participation. I expect children to follow group procedures.

"I'll give each of you a piece of paper like this one and a box of crayons. Then you may take them to your desk and draw. What will you draw? Well, that's for *you* to decide. Maybe you'll want to draw something you really like or something you like to do. What you draw is *your* choice. As you work, I will come around and you can tell me about your drawing when I stop at your desk."

Some children began to stir as soon as I utter the first sentence. By now, a few stand and reach for paper. "Hold it," I say. "There's no hurry. We'll *all* work until the big hand on that clock gets up to the twelve. So take your time and think about what you're doing as you work."

The children take a sheet of paper and crayons and move to their desks. Their chatter subsides as they began drawing. This first mini-lesson for writing workshop wasn't terrific due to the impulsiveness of many of the children. I've noticed already that as a group they seem in a frenzied hurry—always moving on to the next thing, never quite listening to everything that's said. Getting them to slow down will be a major accomplishment. I wonder how much the children understood from my directions. I'll determine tomorrow's mini-lesson by the way today's workshop goes. Normally, the second writing workshop starts with a reminder to the children of the procedures with an extension of those procedures: directions about using only one side of the paper, writing one's name and the date on each piece of writing, etc. (Giacobbe, 1982). At this point, who knows if that sequence will follow? I can decide only after today.

As I move among the children, randomly stopping at individual desks, I see a diversity of topics and hear a range of stories. I catch my first glimpses of the differences in their approaches to writing, hints of their individual learning styles. Lisa works quietly and spends a lot of time on the drawing of herself taking her pet rabbit for a walk. She includes details such as eyelashes, barrettes in her hair, and a leash wrapped around her wrist that connects to the harness on her pet bunny. Natalie looks confused initially, but when she looks at Monica's paper and sees her drawing the beach, she proceeds with her own beach picture. Darren becomes frustrated with his drawing of a bike and converts the entire sketch to a house by drawing over it with black crayon and then drawing another bike, one that pleases him more, below the black house. One child fills the page with erratic scribbles. Another uses every crayon to make a design of sorts.

I stoop down next to each desk, point to the child's picture and say, "Tell me about your writing." Giacobbe had taught me that using the word "writing" defines the child's work—the drawing, scribbling, sprawling letters—as written communication. When each child speaks I listen, maintain eye contact, and nod to indicate I understand. Occasionally, I ask a quick question to clarify something I don't quite understand, but mostly I just listen, then respond with a sentence statement summarizing what the child relates to me and concluding with "Okay! Thank you." I try to match my voice tone to the child's tone as another way of communicating understanding and encouragement. When Natalie speaks with eagerness, I respond enthusiastically. When Darren expresses frustration, I try to acknowledge it through an empathetic tone. To encourage each young writer to want to write again, I must delight in their first efforts; it's important to value designs and scribbles with the same interest and enthusiasm as detailed drawing and wording (Giacobbe, 1982).

I don't linger with any child during this writing workshop so as to see as many children as possible. The children spend about a half hour writing—not long enough to see each child, though I do speak to twenty. At the conclusion, I announce that I will look at all their writing after school and tomorrow will see the children I didn't see today. I won't read everything the children write this year, but for the first few days I try to look briefly—no comments or marking of papers—at their work at the end of each school day. This procedure helps me get to know the writers and also assures them of my interest.

Many children draw pictures, but I want them to consider adding writing to those drawings. So, after listening to them tell about their drawing, I make a gentle suggestion to some of them. I ask Adam, "Could you write any of that story you just told me?" (Giacobbe, 1982)

Adam flashes a broad smile and says, "Yeah! Sure! I can do that. 'Cause last year we did writing—we drew pictures and we wrote about them."

Several other children respond to my invitation to write about their pictures. Later, when I examine their work, I notice that many wrote complete thoughts in sentence form. Ten years prior to this only a few children in a first-grade class accomplished sentence writing at the beginning of the year, and I recognize the reason for the "advanced" development in most of the children's writing: the majority of children had written in their classrooms the previous year. In public and private kindergartens, and in transitional first-grade classes, the children now write. Only one or two

Figure 3–1

Jody's writing: "My model train."

children, who moved into the area over the summer, had not experienced writing in school.

Jody is one who hasn't written before. But he watches the children around him, listens as they pronounce words and write the letters they hear in that audible scripting, and then imitates their behavior. When I ask him about his work he looks at me and says, "My model train. That's what it says."

"Could you point to the words and read it?" I ask.

He reads again, hesitating momentarily after reading "My" as he points to MI and then moves his finger back to the letter M, thus using it twice for the reading, and continues, "model train" (M I T O T O R A N). (See Figure 3–1.)

"Thank you, Jody," I say, smiling as I get up.

"I think I forgot an 'M,' " he suddenly says.

"What could you do about that?"

"I don't know."

"No sweat. Think about it. We'll talk about that another day." Jody returns my smile as I walk away.

I really don't have time to stop and address this issue with Jody today. Doing so would rob other children of interaction with me. But I do want Jody to know that we can and will confront this problem. Even more important, I want Jody to understand that he can work out solutions for dilemmas such as this without me, and that I trust his ability to think and discover his own strategies for learning. I hope my playful tone and spontaneous comment raise these possibilities.

Jody giggles and repeats my words as I leave his desk. "No sweat. Think about it. She said 'No sweat. Think about it.' Okay, I'll think about it." He turns to the child seated beside him (who has listened to our conference) and repeats my words again. Jody looks at his writing and smiles. Then he begins talking again, this time to nobody in particular. Jody talks all day long. It's as though every thought that goes through his head must be verbalized. I'm coming to see that talking is a significant part of Jody's learning style. Children *need* to talk as they work. My classroom is rarely silent. Talk fosters learning through both the social interaction with others and the dialogue with oneself.

I learn a lot from Jody in this writing workshop: his fascination with trains, his capacity to learn quickly from his peers, his problem-solving ability, his willingness to take risks, his concepts about written language and how it works. In just one writing workshop I've learned a lot about all of the children. Seems amazing, but it's true and fairly universal. One of the first things teachers tell me after beginning writing workshops is how well they know their children.

We end writing workshop that day by gathering again on the rug. Unlike the literature time earlier, when the children clustered at my feet as I read aloud, this time they sit on the perimeter of the rug so that every child can make eye contact with each member of the group. I introduce this large-group sharing time (which we would call *sharing*) by going over rules that I learned from Judy Egan, a second-grade teacher in Atkinson, New Hampshire, when Graves and his associates researched children's writing. I have written these rules on an 8-by-12-inch card with a sketch to help the children read the meaning.

1. Look at the person who's talking.
2. Keep your hands still.
3. Be very quiet.
4. Listen carefully.
5. Think of any questions you have.

I go over these guidelines the first few sharing times. After that, I reinforce by holding up the card in the direction of an offender. This gentle reminder generally resolves the problem. Later in the year the children take over the reminding. Inevitably, in every group there are one or two children who take on the role of enforcer of class procedures. That's okay—so long as they learn to do it tactfully. Shelly, for instance, assumed that role; she followed my model and held up the card to the offender, but never said a word. It worked, and probably better than if I had continued to do it.

Figure 3–2

Adam's writing: "The Statue of Liberty. I took a cruise around the Statue of Liberty."

I decide to ask Adam and Jody to share their work in this first large-group sharing time. Each boy seems confident enough to be able to sit in our author's chair, show his work to the class, and receive comments from the group. But just in case either feels uncomfortable, I check with each one privately beforehand.

Adam begins by reading, somewhat haltingly, "The Statue of Liberty. I took a cruise around the Statue of Liberty." Then he holds his picture up for the group to see (Figure 3–2).

"What do you see? What did you hear Adam read? Raise your hand and tell him," I said to the group. "Adam, you may call on people who raise their hands."

Adam proceeds to call on a child.

"I see the Statue of Liberty in your picture."

Adam nods. Silence. I see apprehension on Adam's face, reticent, cautious looks on the faces of his peers. "Any other comments?" I ask. More silence. Thinking of the words Adam read and looking at the boat in his picture I raise my hand. Adam calls on me (gratefully?) and I ask, "You took a boat ride around the Statue of Liberty?"

"Yeah, we went to New York and we took a boat ride around the Statue of Liberty." Adam smiles, directing his answer to me alone. I look around the circle of children and Adam follows my model. A hand goes up hesitantly and he eagerly calls on this child.

"That's a good picture of the Statue of Liberty."

"Thank you," Adam replies. I look around the group. Another hand is up and Adam calls on this child.

"Is that the boat you went on?"

"Unhuh." Adam smiles.

"It's a good boat." Adam nods. Then another question comes and I'm struck by the authentic ring to it. The child asks about something he doesn't understand: "What's that black circle thing?"

"Oh, that's the life ring. They have these lifesaver rings, so in case anyone falls in the water you just throw it." Adam's voice takes on energy as he explains.

"Oh yeah, I know what you mean," replies the questioner.

"Oh, I see, that ring is a lifesaver. I didn't know that. That's very interesting," I acknowledge and looked more closely at the picture. I had overlooked this part.

"Yeah. They have them at the Statue of Liberty, so in case anybody falls in the water."

"I see. Okay. Thank you, Adam. Boys and girls I think we might clap for Adam's sharing of this good story with us," I say and then we applaud. Adam beams. Everyone had tuned in to the brief exchange about life preservers. We'd ended at a good moment when interest was keen. Jody shares his writing in a similar manner and the first sharing time ends.

There are a lot of wiggles when the children sit on the rug during this sharing time, as one would expect from a group of six-year-olds. Yet the interest in Adam and Jody's work holds their attention. Each boy carries off the sharing with grace and composure and each leaves the author's chair radiating confidence.

This first sharing time was tentative, halting, and, examined out of context, might seem trivial. In a matter of days, the sharing of writing will become a significant part of building community. The experience this day was particularly good for Adam. While coming in from recess earlier in the day I had overheard Adam call a child "Fatty." I had stopped cold and gone over to him, stooped down to below his eye level, took both his hands in mine, looked him straight in the eye, and said, "In this classroom we will *always* be kind to each other. That means that we can never call anyone unkind names," in a soft but emphatic tone.

Adam had looked at me a moment and the room suddenly was hushed. Then he nodded gravely and replied, "Okay." We resumed class activity but everyone had heard and everyone knew where I stood on this matter. Selecting Adam to share at the end of writing workshop this day showed the children that I valued the individual even if I was intolerant of some behaviors.

Although the first full writing workshop was a little ragged, with the children not quite sure what to do, we keep working at it each day, revising, refining, polishing. I direct my mini-lessons to procedures that enable the children to work together without confusion, and we talk regularly about what goes well and what we need to work on.

One day I pull out three rules for workshops that I've used with other classes and ask this group what they think.

1. We work hard.
2. We work on writing or reading. (Meaning writing in writing workshop and reading in reading workshop.)
3. We use soft voices.

The children agree with these rules and we post them in the room.

The basic format for writing workshop is established. Daily writing will be central to the classroom routine, the development of a nurturing classroom community, and, ultimately, the growth of each individual. Here, everyone is the most vulnerable and takes the most risks. Through their writing the children share themselves with the group and receive responses that affirm, validate, and nurture.

Janet Emig (1983) uses the term "enabling environment," and in her essay "Non-Magical Thinking," lists four implications for presenting writing in school:

1. Although writing is natural, it is activated by enabling environments.
2. These environments have the following characteristics: they are safe, structured, private, unobtrusive, and literate.
3. Adults in these environments have two special roles: they are fellow practitioners, and they are providers of possible content, experiences, and feedback.
4. Children need frequent opportunities to practice writing, many of these playful. (p. 139)

Though Emig refers to environments for activating the natural process of writing, I believe her words are also appropriate when defining the climate of *learner-centered classrooms*. The interactions of our writing workshop will set the tone for the classroom and the remainder of the school day.

Routines Build a Secure Foundation

The routines of the school day begin to fall into place. We hang a calendar, learn how to read and write the date, and incorporate calendar activities into the opening of the school day. We also start Word of the Day (a word-play activity described in Chapter 19), devise a sign-in sheet for recording attendance and lunch count, and develop procedures for sharing within the large group. The opening activities contribute to our sense of community. Each morning we come together again and connect to each other through both the rituals of daily routines and conversational sharing. An important part of this opening is the reading aloud of a children's novel. We begin with *Charlotte's Web,* the first of a dozen or more children's novels I will read aloud to the class this year.

Scheduling reading workshop after lunch works well. Coming in from the playground after lunch recess, the children are ready to settle down and read. Fifteen-minute blocks of time—even longer—aren't at all unreasonable in September, and soon the class reads for a half hour without any difficulty. As in writing workshop, I move randomly among the individual children and ask them about the books they are reading during this time.

Helping each child focus his or her energies and become successful is part of my task during the first workshops. I must set aside the traditional instructional role and focus on the individual child, helping that child discover a rightful place in the classroom community. For the child having difficulty writing, I encourage and wait; I try new angles to approach the child until I find what works. There's no one formula, but time and the child's capacity to learn are my allies. Building class routines and helping children work within them play a significant part in community building.

By early October, the children and I are settled into routines that provide the security of a structure we all trust. We've spent the last few weeks getting to know each other and working out a classroom climate that is becoming predictable and organized. The children helped put up the displays of their work on the walls and they've taken over tasks such as lunch count, attendance, and housekeeping chores. When they arrange the books along the chalkrails and the counters, the alignments they devise look somewhat peculiar—sometimes they stack the books in neat piles, sometimes arrange them according to colors on the cover, or line them up in step-fashion according to size. But if I ask for a particular title, any number of children can quickly locate it.

Among the many items on the back counter are Indian corn; rocks from the playground with "real gold" in them; an assortment of walnuts, acorns, crumbling dried leaves, and withered dandelions; a program from a Phillies game; and tiny cars. The butterflies from the first day remain. When I look at them now I think of the eagerness of the boys to please me, to present gifts and win the favor of the ruler of their new kingdom.

The role of ruler does not appeal to me. Certainly I must lead and provide direction (there is someone in charge here!), but I'm not interested in establishing an autocratic reign in this classroom. If I set up an authoritarian rule where I continually give directions and dole out assignments for students to complete, turn back, and receive my assessment, I will rob students of the right to develop responsibility for their learning. I'd prevent them from making an investment in the classroom community.

In an autocratic, teacher-directed classroom the teacher becomes exhausted creating activities to keep the children busy. I struggled with that model for years: I designed, the children completed, I graded. I spent more time on their work than they did! I plowed ahead, covering the curriculum with minimal input from students or little regard for their thinking. Children made minimal investment in either the classroom or their learning. I believe such an environment arouses anger in students, or indifference, or cultivates attitudes of "let's figure out what she wants so we can get it done." Such responses come when the teacher holds the controls, limiting or blocking children's natural curiosity and desire to discover more of the world.

I've been the benevolent dictator in the classroom, one loving the children, concerned about their welfare. However, I still held the reins of command, and the model was still one of teacher as authority, as expert pouring knowledge into the receptive vessels of children's minds. Communities developed in these teacher-directed classrooms, but frequently the community was one of children united in waging a "cold war" against authority. From time to time hostilities broke out, and I directed considerable energy into maintaining control—otherwise known as discipline.

Now, I direct my energies toward listening to and observing children, toward striving to understand their intentions and responding to their efforts to learn (Harste, 1984). I can do this only in a well-structured classroom that invites teacher-student and student-student interactions. I cannot rule as an authority, nor pretend to be a peer, but I can be a sharer of information and a validator of experiences.

Even the way I talk plays a part in setting a tone that invites interactions from students and in building relationships that are the heart of any community. I avoid referring to myself in the third person when I speak—"Mrs. Avery wants . . ." or "Bring the paper to Mrs. Avery." I need to address six-year-olds just as I would any other responsible individual and I believe that the artificiality of third person talk serves to remove *me* from the interaction. I want to encourage the children to express their own ideas. I want to speak in ways that communicate respect for children's expertise. I strive to keep the tone of my voice subdued—soft and even, avoiding a shrill or imperative tone. I attempt to convey honest responses in a manner that is neither coaxing nor demanding.

Literature Connects the Community

A popular time of day for the group is our literature time, a time when I read aloud several children's books (mostly picture book format), and we talk about those books and authors and illustrators. Like writing and reading workshops, this time plays a major role in establishing the tone of the community. By the end of September the children form a repertoire of their favorite titles, ones they ask for again and again. During literature time on a day in late September, I ask the children to tell me their favorite books. They quickly come up with a list.

King Bidgood's in the Bathtub, by Audrey and Don Wood

The Grouchy Ladybug, by Eric Carle

Cookie's Week, by Cynthia Ward

The Three Billy Goats Gruff, illustrated by Marcia Brown

The Giant Jam Sandwich, by John Lord

Little Red Riding Hood, illustrated by James Marshall

Rumpelstiltskin, illustrated by Paul Zelinsky

Jack and the Bean Tree, by Gail Haley

Why these particular books? They've heard them several times and many of them have repetitious and predictable story lines. The children have favorite lines and they listen for them and chime in when we come to those lines. They also enjoy the delicious sense of naughtiness conveyed by the characters and story lines in many of these books.

Ian says, "I like the part in *Red Riding Hood* where the grandma says it was so dark [in the wolf's stomach] that 'I couldn't even read!'" The class agrees and then Jeff adds, "And the part when the wolf says, 'Your delicious—er, *delightful* granddaughter.'" They all like the line from *Rumpelstiltskin,* when the title character guesses the name of the baby and, stomping his foot, shouts, "The devil told you that!" At recess the children stomp their feet on the playground and say, "The devil told you that!"

The books become common ground, a part of the language and history of our community that we all know. The words live for us because of the talk surrounding this read-aloud time. Ian recalled a bit of history when he said, "Remember the day when you were reading *Henny Penny* to us and you turned the page and Ryan said, 'Uh-oh! They're gonna be supper-lupper!' We all laughed. That was really funny." The children and I remember and laugh again.

One day during the third week of school, Elizabeth brings in a copy of *Jack and the Bean Tree,* autographed by author Gail Haley. Elizabeth's mother, a second-grade teacher, bought the book for Elizabeth when Gail Haley spoke at a local reading conference. The book is rather long to read aloud, and the rich language of an Appalachian storyteller makes it difficult for the children to follow. However, their familiarity with "Jack and the Beanstalk" and Haley's outstanding illustrations support the children's comprehension as we read. But most of all, their fascination with Elizabeth's explanation of how she got this book and that it had the *author's* name in her own handwriting sparks their interest. Creating awareness of authors and their writing processes is an important goal of our literature time. However, authorship takes a backseat this day as the children's reactions to *Jack and the Bean Tree* take us in an unexpected direction.

I read the description of Jack's hand opening, finger by finger, to reveal the magic beans. I see a couple of children, including Ryan, clench their fists and then open them finger by finger in response to the words they hear. A page later Jack's mother learns he has sold the cow for those beans and threatens to give Jack "a good whuppin'!"

"She's really mad," comments a child.

Then Ryan says, "I know what I'd give him. I'd give him the finger," and his hand goes up, middle finger extended, to demonstrate his point.

"Oooooh," comes a low moan sounding like ghosts sweeping through a lonely room. Several children look at me, watching for my reaction, but I say nothing. My mind races. Now what? Ryan looks innocent. I bet he has no idea. Wait. See what happens. Maybe it will pass without anyone needing to discuss it further. But no such luck.

"You'd get in trouble," says one child.

"Troub-BULL!" A small chorus of comments surrounds Ryan.

"My brother does it," replies Ryan. A tone of innocence rings in his voice, as he looks to me for support.

"It's okay Ryan," I say. "But, I need to tell you that these kids are right. You probably would get in trouble if you did that. Most people think that to do that is rude or unkind. But I don't think you knew that did you?"

Ryan shakes his head in astonishment as he says, "Un-uh."

"I bet a lot of people here didn't know about that. But now we do, so I don't think it's something we want to do in here, any of us. Do we all agree?"

"My mom said that's not nice."

"Yeah."

"But we need to understand that Ryan didn't know. Now he does. We all do."

The tension diffuses, we continue the story. I have a feeling that the children might discuss this issue later among themselves, but I trust them to handle it on their own. I have made the point I needed to make, and I think Ryan survived without humiliation.

A few pages later in the book the class chimes in with the giant, "Fee, fi, fo, fum . . ." When the giant demands food from his wife, Monica says, "You can't order people around like that. My mom wouldn't do it either if my dad talked like that. But he would never talk like that."

For a few moments we discuss what would happen if we talked to people this way. Some children say they would be in a lot of trouble if they spoke to others—especially parents—this way, while others think they could get away with such talk. We listen to each other. I listen too and refrain from commenting on their remarks. My role is to encourage them to respond.

By the time we finish the book we have spent more than forty-five minutes reading and talking together. When I began reading *Jack and the Bean Tree*, I wanted to take advantage of the opportunity to contrast it with other versions of the folktale and point out how Gail Haley introduces her version through the image and voice of a storyteller. As soon as I read the opening pages this day, I could tell the children missed the storyteller aspect. I had planned to talk about storytelling, about how we all tell stories, and that we can write them too. But it wasn't appropriate to go back and make this point after we finished reading, so I told myself I'd do it another day. Elizabeth left the book in the classroom until the end of the year. We reread it a couple of times, but I never returned to my original intent. Somehow it didn't matter.

Recess: Learning to Play Together

Not many days of school pass before problems develop at recess. During the first few days we talk about recess procedures. Then, as the children become comfortable on the playground, the tattling begins.

"Lisa won't play with me."

"Courtney fell." (I can see an uninjured Courtney jumping rope.)

"Jason pushed me."

"I had a ball and Jimmy took it and now he won't let me play with it."

Tattletales weary me. In some cases I sense that the tattler craves my attention, while other times I feel that the tattler is seeking to vindicate herself from any wrongdoing. What exhausts me is being set up as the all-knowing, all-wise Solomon, the judge doling out verdicts.

It might be easy to step in, to be seduced by these imploring innocents into summoning the accused, sorting out the problem, and pronouncing a judgment. I might even arrive at a reasonable and just solution. But I would create future problems: I would have established a procedure that would eventually back me into a corner and deny the children the experience of working through their own problems together. I would become a rescuer.

It looks like this: Jeri reports that Kyle took the ball from him. I talk to Kyle, confronting him with Jeri's accusation. Kyle denies guilt. I'm stuck with the word of one child against another. Frequently in these situations information lies hidden beneath the surface, which I can't easily uncover, and there's no way to determine justice. I'm in a stalemate situation. To decide in favor of either child is to make a judgment based on incomplete knowledge. I could be wrong. To abstain only provokes anger over the injustice from one child and promotes irresponsibility for actions in the other.

If Kyle acknowledges he took the ball, I'm faced with providing retribution to Jeri. The standard teacher solution goes something like this: "Well, don't you think you should apologize to Jeri and give him back the ball?" or "Do you boys think you could share the ball? Now Kyle, what do you think you should say to Jeri because you took the ball away from him?" So Kyle mutters a weak "I'm sorry" and the boys go away with one child feeling vindicated, superior to the other. But both boys have learned that eliciting teacher intervention can lead to a power payoff.

How well I know these responses. I've heard myself and my colleagues come forth with them automatically, as though they were written in a teacher's manual. Yet I always felt that these procedures were ineffective because they lead children through the motions of solving problems but fail to address the underlying emotions of the children or help the children understand the interactions.

One day after recess several years ago, the class and I sat down to talk about all the tattling. "I'm feeling very frustrated with this," I told them. "I can't solve all these problems for you. And besides, I'm never sure exactly what's happened. Sometimes it's pretty hard to tell." The children acknowledged that this was true and they were quite aware of unjust decisions made by teachers. "How could we work this out?" I asked.

After considerable discussion we decided as a group that reporting a problem to the teacher on recess duty was appropriate if someone was injured, but that the person himself ought to go to the teacher if possible or that the reporter ought to check with the injured person first to decide if help was needed. The person with the injury was to be in charge of deciding whether or not to tell the teacher, unless, of course, that person was seriously hurt. When there were troubles with another child, we decided that *both* people ought to come to the teacher together, but that they should try to work out their problem first. We just couldn't go to the teacher with *everything*. We had to make some decisions about what really needed teacher attention. If one person in a dispute was unwilling to involve the teacher, the other person could, but that person had to think first and decide if it was really important. For my part, I agreed not to step in and solve problems on the spot, but to listen and try to help people think about the problems so they might work them out themselves.

Of course, this discussion did not put an end to tattling. It did, however, start children thinking and taking responsibility for some of their actions. Some children easily adhered to the guidelines while others had more difficulty, but the number of tattles diminished.

I found children telling tales on others when they were so agitated they *had* to say it to someone. I started responding to such reports with statements to reflect the child's complaint and to acknowledge their feelings: "He took the ball away! You're pretty angry about that!" Often the child responded, "Yeah!" and walked away, the anger diffused. I realized that sometimes tattling was only a way of expressing intense feelings and that when those feelings were validated a child could drop the issue. Other times I turned the problem back to the child with a comment such as, "How could you solve this?" or "What do you want to do about this?" I hoped such comments would carry the underlying message: This is your problem, not mine. I began to see results. One day two boys ran up to me, both of them shouting.

"He lost my car! I'm gonna kill him!"

"I didn't mean to! I didn't know it was his."

"Stop!" I shouted as I physically intervened to keep blows from landing. "Each of you tell me what happened. You go first. And you, you listen. You may not interrupt until he's done! Then you tell me and he can't interrupt you."

The story unfolded from each child, though I had to stop and remind each boy "No interrupting!" during the other's telling. By the time they finished, tempers had cooled somewhat. Suddenly the offending child spoke up. "I'm sorry. We could go look for it if you want." I'm sure my mouth gaped in shock at that moment.

"Well, okay. We're gonna go look. Okay, Mrs. Avery?" answered the other boy, and they left. I was stunned. What had happened? Listening? Talking? Being heard? All of these I thought. But what struck me most was the depth of sincerity in that apology. It was not the shallow apology that followed our usual teacher directives. This apology came from understanding someone else's distress and taking responsibility for one's own part in that distress. Because it was based on honest feeling, it was authentic. The honesty healed the wounds.

Now when first graders come up and begin talking to me simultaneously, I stop the talk with, "Wait, I can only listen to one at a time and I want to hear each of you. You speak, then you, and then you. No interrupting. We will all listen while each person takes their turn to talk."

Going through this routine one day, it became Max's turn to speak. "I forget what I was going to say 'cuz I was listening—I mean I got so interested in what these guys were saying I just forgot." Then he turned and started talking to the child beside him, a response to that child's talk. The two walked off together, leaving me forgotten in their wake.

Every year the talk about tattling and managing interactions with others on the playground becomes part of the important class conversations during the first weeks of school. The playground is that part of school where the children rely least on routines established and monitored by others. The playground activity is the underground curriculum of social interactions. The tone of the playground will carry into the classroom through the children's regard for others and through their own problem-solving abilities. And, like a recursive spiral, the tone of the classroom will be reflected on the playground.

One incident reinforced the recursiveness of this connection between playground and classroom. My mother's generation would have described Cory as "all boy." Tough, extremely active, and ever aggressive, he soon gained a reputation with the other children as a bully and a troublemaker despite his small stature. I began receiving reports of Cory knocking children down on the playground and then running away. "Thank you, I'll watch for that," I commented, but I had a difficult time seeing an infraction occur. Finally, another teacher saw Cory run up behind a child, fling his arms around the child's legs, then get up from the pile and run on. Cory wound up at the time-out desk in the principal's office. I walked in to hear a tearful Cory protest to our principal that he didn't do anything, he was only playing.

I knelt beside Cory and asked him to tell me exactly what had happened.

"I was just playing."

"Tell me *exactly* what you were doing," I said ever so gently. I counted on the slim threads of trust that had begun to run between Cory and myself to bridge our communication now.

"I was playing football. I just tackled him, that's all."

I nodded and maintained eye contact with Cory. He looked at me with a penetrating gaze that searched for understanding. And I searched—seeking a connection to help Cory understand and to get us both out of this confrontation. Then the idea came.

"Cory," I began, "when football players play football, like Nathan does, they learn how to tackle. (My son, Nathan, plays football, and on our field trip Nathan took charge of Cory. Cory speaks of Nathan with awe.) But there are only certain ways they can do it. And they have to practice a lot, and they have to wear special equipment, and then they learn to do it so that people don't get hurt. They have *rules* about how to tackle. They only tackle in an official practice or a game. And the reason for all of that is so that people *don't get hurt*. We can't practice football on our playground because we can't do all those things that have to be done. People could *get hurt*, Cory, if we play football here."

As I spoke the tears stopped. Cory looked at me intently. I knew I had connected with him, though I was not exactly sure how. I was also unsure of my football theory. From everything I saw in Friday night games, those guys were out to tear each other's heads off. But I decided in this situation my interpretation of tackling would do.

Cory went back to the classroom to find his classmates anxiously awaiting his arrival. "What happened?" they asked.

"Nothin'," he replied. "We talked about football. That's all."

"Cory was confused about what we could do on the playground about tackling. But I think he understands better now," I added.

Cory smiled at me. "Yup," he said.

It was Cory's smile, not a smart-alecky "I won again" smile, but a genuine, grateful smile that prompted me to say, "Do you want to tell them, Cory?"

A brief pause. "Okay. See, I didn't know about not playing football on the playground. But Mrs. Avery told me about it, how Nathan does it and you gotta do special things. So now I know I can't do that. We can't play football at recess." By the end of his speech Cory's voice had taken on a confident tone, the tone of one teaching the class new rules about playground behavior.

Then a child in the room said, "We were worried about you, Cory. We thought you were really in trouble."

"I was. But I'm not anymore." Cory smiled.

Children are always quite aware of those among them who cause problems for the group. Yet singling out any one child for misconduct can threaten the community. The children identify with that individual: this could happen to me. Cory came through this incident with his dignity intact and at the same time he began to acknowledge the inappropriateness of his behavior.

Cory was still a handful, both inside and outside the classroom, but the frequency of reports of his roughhousing diminished. I think the key in reaching him was discovering *Cory's* perceptions and *his* intentions, without jumping in with assumptions and judgments of my own. It's taken me a long time, and lots of errors on the side of injustice, to come to this realization. When I initiated writing workshops in my classroom, I learned that withholding judgments, waiting and listening, working to understand the child's intentions, were key concepts in creating a responsive, nurturing atmosphere for writers (Harste, 1984). The same principles hold true for other parts of the school day. Everything I say and do throughout the day sets the tone for the classroom.

Working through problems to resolutions that everyone can live with brings strong cohesiveness to a group and contributes to a tone that makes a class work. A couple of weeks after the playground incident, Cory sat at the center table and hesitantly read a book, the first complete book that he had attempted to read. A number of children noticed and gradually they clustered around as he read. When he finished they clapped spontaneously. "Good job!" "You're a good reader!" they proclaimed. Cory beamed at his classmates, then turned and beamed at me. This community was coming together.

Shared Rule Setting

At the end of the third week of school in one of my early years of teaching, I asked the children to come up with the rules for our class—the ones we would follow throughout the year. They talked through and dictated the following:

Our School Rules
1. We raise our hands for quiet.

2. We look at the person who is talking.

3. We don't bang on the soap in the bathroom.

4. We use only one paper towel.

5. We walk quietly in the halls.

6. We do not call people unkind names.

7. We don't kick, push, or fight on the playground.

8. We don't waste food.

We hung these rules in the classroom, but we rarely referred to them. The talk to arrive at them seemed more important than the rules themselves. I could trace the source of each rule to specific incidents or to directions given to the children. Rules three and four related to the principal's talk to the class about problems in the boys' bathroom. Number eight came from an aide in the cafeteria. I was struck by how quickly and with so little thought the children came up with rules that mirrored adult edicts. Since then I've come to understand that while children need adult input, they also need to shape rules from their own experiences and have a voice in creating the rules.

Shirley Brice Heath, anthropologist and linguist from Stanford University, has done ethnographic research with inner-city children for whom traditional structures such as the family have broken down. These children are finding mentors for themselves and seeking out structures for their lives through community programs such as those sponsored by church groups, YMCAs, and other organizations. When asked what they need, these young people specified two basic premises for operating their community structures:

- Minimum rules with maximum consistency
- Nobody gets hurt (not even "play-hurt")

Heath tells about youths setting up structures for a gym program, for example. They formulate basic rules: Leave this place the way you found it; no one gets hurt here. Other rules become necessary as situations arise and the youths take care of them by posting notices: Dirty towels go in the bins; put the basketballs back where you found them; take your sneakers with you (Heath, talk at CCCC convention, Chicago, 1990). When I reflected on Heath's work I recalled how often I had carried into each class all the rules accumulated from previous classes.

Now I try to keep rules at a minimum and develop those rules or guidelines with each group. I think of my own first-grade teacher, Mrs. Kearney, who gave us one rule when school opened: the Golden Rule. She posted it at our eye level, below the chalkboard. That rule pretty well took care of everything for us. I remember her referring to it from time to time when she discussed a particular incident. I only recall her adding one other rule all year long: "Never say ain't." I shape a classroom around the basic rules: We are kind to each other and we work hard. Actually, working hard takes on a light tone, a connotation usually not associated with work. The reason: We work together; we are a community.

Reflections

I've watched learning communities develop, and for some time I wondered when, and if, this class that started with such an ominous beginning would come together. I pondered this throughout September—and October and November and periodically throughout the year. This group came together in intermittent spurts at first, more slowly than most, but it did come together.

Working out our schedule and structure was one part of building a community. The children and I both needed to know *how* we would function and *when* we would do things. I took time to develop routines, making sure the children understood one part before I added more. Within the structure I made sure children had choices, as both Graves and Gia-cobbe advocate. True community requires that children be recognized as individuals and respected and valued as equals, people with rights, not as puppets to be controlled or manipulated. Choices for children—about important things such as topic selections for writing, book selections for reading—communicates respect as well as trust.

Talk was a big part of forming this community. Along with the talk was listening. Don Graves has said that if there is one thing he would change within classrooms it's *listening*. And he's not referring primarily to the children listening! *I'm* the one who needs to do the most listening. I worked on listening nonjudgmentally—listening to understand and taking it seri-ously. Children's talk is profound. I tried to replace pronouncements as to right or wrong with respect for children's thoughts. Through this kind of listening and talk, we negotiated problems, learned about each other, and came to accept and value our differences.

First grade is a child's first encounter with serious academics, or at least the time when school is taken with absolute seriousness by the significant others in their life. However, children need positive, affirming responses to their efforts. Learning must be enjoyable and have a playful tone, not be drudgery, burdensome, and terribly serious. I want an environment that takes school seriously but is also relaxed enough for risk taking and laughter.

A critical element for this learning community was *trust*. Trust is valuing the learner as a human being, as one who has much to give, much to demonstrate, much to teach others. Trust is esteeming the learner so that self-esteem is enhanced. Trust is believing that all children can learn to read and write and that all children strive continually to make sense of the world. A trusted individual becomes a risk taker, and to engage in learning is to engage in risk.

A classroom community is never really in place, even though it may seem to run itself later in the school year. A community continually evolves throughout the year. Like a forest, a complex ecosystem, it grows and changes with each organism gaining sustenance from those that surround it. And like a forest, growth is indiscernible on a daily basis; we notice it only over stretches of time. No two classroom communities are alike. We come together a group of strangers. We get to know each other, accept our strengths and weaknesses, and ultimately make a commitment to one another. Some years the commitment comes early and we know within a few days or weeks that this will "be a good year." Other years we struggle together. We are slowed by those who are reluctant to make a commitment, to trust the others. The development of community is a group process influenced by the tone of trust I set through all my actions and responses.

A community, however, is finally shaped by *all* the individuals in the classroom. I cannot mandate it nor dictate its terms. It grows out of the relationships between me and individual children and among all the children. Community begins on the first day of school as we begin working and playing together, gradually developing a cohesiveness that helps create a nurturing learning climate.

CHAPTER 4

Preparing the Learner-Centered Classroom

On an August evening perhaps two years after I began teaching first grade, I stopped at school with two friends, one a visitor from out of state. We walked through darkened hallways breathing the smell of new floor wax. I unlocked the classroom door and flipped light switches. As though I had waved a magic wand, a medley of bright colors and shapes appeared before our eyes. Catchy phrases, posters, and pictures flashed from bulletin boards covered with brightly colored background paper. My favorite children's books lined the chalkrails and countertops. A listening center—a record player with connected headsets—featured H. A. Rey's *Curious George.* Disks of color, designed to resemble balloons and labeled with the color words, hung from the lights. Only one part of the room remained undecorated: a section of bulletin board set aside for the self-portraits the children would draw on the first day of school.

After nearly two weeks of unpacking, arranging, and decorating, I had my room ready for the arrival of twenty-eight first graders. My preparations for the opening of school were akin to those of an expectant mother preparing a nursery and, like a mother-to-be, I was eager to show off the results of my efforts.

My out-of-state friend gazed around and then, very gently, said, "Gee, I think if I was a first grader coming here, I'd feel a little scared. I mean, there's so much to look at, so much I've gotta learn."

"Really?" I answered. "I guess things have changed since you and I went to school."

"I guess so. I *never* had a classroom that looked this way."

"No," I mused, "I guess I didn't either. But, school's different now. We all do this—get our rooms ready for the opening of school."

"It's all very attractive. It's just that there's so *much.*"

Looking back, I realize that the glitzy appearance of my classroom rivaled the fast-paced stimulation of Saturday morning television cartoons. I took room preparation seriously and sweltered for hours in the August heat to create that riotous display. I thought the definition of "dedicated teacher" depended on both the time invested and the elaborate appearance. Sometimes parents, administrators, and fellow teachers complimented my results, but despite all the effort I expended every year, no *child* ever commented on any aspect of the room's appearance.

My lovely room remained neat for a couple of weeks. As September waned the room became messy and the displays tiresome. I became involved in managing lesson plans for several reading groups and in applying my energies to creating imaginative seatwork activities as respite from the doldrums of the reading program—and to keep my students busy. There was no time to create new fancy bulletin boards. To decorate the room I relied on the children's projects from art classes or bulletin boards from previous years, which I pulled from the closet. Posters and displays from educational supply companies filled in the gaps.

Looking back, I recognize that all the preparations for school focussed on establishing a classroom that belonged to *me*. Once in a while a child made a suggestion. I'd listen and then, regretfully, explain that we probably wouldn't have time to do that—but it was a nice idea anyway. It was true. I didn't have time to allow children to plan and carry out their ideas. And certainly first graders could never produce results as lovely as mine. Anyway, I was in the groove of seasonal and monthly classroom decor and a child's idea might not fit in. Still, I hated when the end of the month or a holiday was over and it was time to change the room. But I was the teacher and I believed the room decor was my responsibility.

When my out-of-state visitor indicated that perhaps my room was a bit overwhelming, I rationalized away the remark because I certainly didn't want to make changes in my perfect room at this late hour. But the next August I remembered her comment and decided to cut back on the decorating—I hung nothing from the lights! Change came slowly.

Getting Ready for School

My preparations for school have certainly changed in recent years. I want the classroom to be warm and inviting when the children arrive that first day, but not overwhelming. I've discarded the visual bombardment of laminated colors and shapes, the teacher-made games, posters, the cutesy quotes, the oversized characters that once filled the walls. Except for the strip of bulletin board above the chalkboard where I tack the children's names, the bulletin boards are empty. In a few weeks these bulletin boards will display pictures of authors, children's art work, a mural painted by some of the group in response to *Charlotte's Web*, a collection of litter from our ecology study, and charts recording the children's ideas on urban and rural communities. Although these bulletin boards may not look as polished as those I spent hours crafting, they mean more to all of us. I admit that the first year I decided not to decorate the room for the opening of school, I was nervous! Like a child asking permission, I sought out the principal to discuss my decision. He had no problem; the anxiety was mine.

I decided to simplify, to eliminate clutter from the classroom. Fully achieving that took time. Every summer I tossed out more of the accumulated "teaching aids" that filled the closets: teacher-made learning centers and games (the kids never really liked them anyway), dusty manipulatives from discontinued reading and math programs, laminated teacher-made theme decorations. As I planned a learner-centered classroom, I moved from interior decorator to professional decision maker. Now I prepare for the opening of school by anticipating what the children and I need for smooth operation of our learner-centered classroom. (I am one of the learners there too, thus I prefer the term *learner*-centered to *child*-centered.) Before school begins I do essential tasks that free me to focus on the children during those first critical days, leaving as many tasks as possible for us to do together. Everything that goes in this classroom must contribute to our purposes: learning and literacy development in a supportive community.

In planning a learner-centered classroom, I've found it helpful to consider decisions in three categories: *physical environment, academic environment,* and *social climate.* (The following is nonessential reading. Teachers know this stuff, but I include it to take the mystique out of setting up a process-approach classroom. Please skim and scan to suit your purposes.)

Physical Environment

I consider the materials and supplies we need and then plan the room arrangement.

MATERIALS AND SUPPLIES: *Tools for writing.* I sharpen pencils, write names on crayon boxes, and set out unlined white paper for writing on the first day. I've found that lined paper frustrates young children's writing efforts because some kids feel compelled to use the lines but have difficulty. Unlined paper serves both drawing and writing purposes and creates a more natural and relaxed writing experience. It also allows me to see how children manage the blank space as they place letters on a page: left to right, right to left, top to bottom, helter-skelter. We'll mount these first pieces of writing on the bulletin board. On our September parent night they provide a glimpse of the writing of all the children in the room.

I borrowed an idea from Mary Ellen Giacobbe and made blank books of forty pages (8½-by-11-inches) for the children to use during the first few weeks of writing workshop (see Appendix A). These books certainly aren't essential but by using them, the children and I avoid struggles to manage several sheets of paper, to use the stapler, or to start a writing folder during the first days of school. In the past I made fancy books with wallpaper covered cardboard, but now I give children oaktag to design their own covers and put together books with brads.

I set up five small cardboard file caddies—the kind that are purchased flat and ready for construction—to hold the children's writing. Once I used a plastic milk crate, but twenty-five or more children crowding around one container to retrieve and put away their writing books became chaotic. Assigning several children to each caddie eliminates confusion and also provides convenient units for me to peruse the children's writing from time to time by going through one caddie an evening.

Gradually, we will establish a writing center, a place to keep the paper and tools for writing, but the books of blank paper, crayons, and pencils are enough to start the school year. Eventually the writing center will hold a variety of paper: unlined, lined, paper with lines on half of the sheet and a blank space for drawing on the other half, construction paper for covers. The center will include tools for writing and editing: pens, colored pencils, tape, scissors, white-out, staple remover.

Classroom library. From the first day, children's books saturate the life of our classroom. So, when I set up the room, a major focus is displaying lots of children's books. I've become very particular about what I put out. I weed out old, shabby, or dull texts and strive for quality literature presented attractively. When children choose books to read, they initially go for attractive books and they will spend tremendous energy learning to read these books. I want them expending their efforts on quality material.

The genres of children's literature I display at the beginning of school include:

- Folktales and fairy tales—stories familiar to many children. I choose several versions of favorite fairy tales with a variety of illustrative styles.
- Wordless picture books—books that invite children to "read" the pictures, to tell their own stories.
- Predictable books—those with repetitive language or plot sequences that encourage children to join in during an oral reading.

- Songs and chants in picture book format—the text in these books is already familiar to children and they can "read" the words easily.
- Poetry—lots of poetry from Mother Goose to "easy-to-read" collections, anthologies, and small volumes on specific themes.
- Modern classics—traditional favorites that are popular with children year after year, such as Sendak's *Where the Wild Things Are* or McCloskey's *Make Way for Ducklings.*
- Child Authored Books—ones written and illustrated by children in previous classes during our writing workshops. At the end of the year, each child leaves one book for future classes to read. Sometimes it takes several months before a new group of children will read these books and some groups never want to read the books from other classes. That's okay. Each class eventually will build its own library of child-authored books and these will become some of the most favored and significant reading materials in the classroom.

Not all of the thousand or more books that I've collected will be available in the classroom on the first day; I will set aside some titles to bring out as the year progresses. And undoubtedly I will purchase new titles as the year goes on, for the arrival of new titles fuels our continuing interest in reading and in good books.

Art supplies. I distribute scissors, paste, and crayons to each child during the first days of school. I also store art supplies in a cupboard where the children have access to them. I include crayons, colored chalk, scissors, paste, clay, construction paper and drawing paper, paint, and brushes. Gradually, I add an assortment of other items for creative construction: toothpicks, empty cardboard rollers from paper towels, buttons, lace, and fabric scraps. From time to time I share directions for constructing simple art projects, such as puppets.

Drama props and puppets. For imaginative play I gather a few items: hats, a telephone, a wig, a magic wand, aprons, etc. There's also an assortment of puppets. Children need very little to stimulate ideas; with imagination, a Raggedy Ann puppet becomes a fairy godmother or a witch.

Games, building blocks, puzzles. The games I choose for the classroom (such as checkers) emphasize thinking rather than chance. I've collected an assortment of blocks and other construction toys, and I have a few puzzles (the kind that become group projects over a period of days or even weeks).

Media equipment. A lot of options are available. Though a record player, tape recorder, and headsets for a listening center are the only items in my classroom all the time, I make use of filmstrip and movie projectors, a video player, individual filmstrip previewers, television, a camera, and a computer during the course of the year. For the opening of school, I put out the record player and some favorite records for sing-along and creative movement, and I set up an audiotape of a reading of a children's book, connect it to individual headsets, and add copies of the book for the children to follow along as they listen.

ROOM ARRANGEMENT: To set up the classroom, I work with the space I have to incorporate the following areas:

- Writing center—a place for writing supplies and for the children's writing.
- Classroom library—shelves, tubs, chalkrail, a paperback book rack; I put books everywhere in the classroom, many with their covers showing.
- Designated places—for blocks, games, art supplies and a work area for art, drama props, puppets, etc.
- Large-group gathering area—a place where the class can convene for read alouds, for sharing writing, etc. A 12-by-15-foot rug (our "story-rug") designates this area in our classroom.
- Small-group conference area—a round table of child height serves for small-group meetings for writing or reading conferences.
- Places for children's interests—a counter to display the treasures and discoveries they bring to the classroom and bulletin board space for each child; a sectioned-off area of a large bulletin board provides each child with a display space (photos taken of the children on the first day and stapled in the corner of each space identify its owner).
- Student space—individual student desks meet a basic need to provide each child a private space for storing supplies.
- Teacher space—my desk, a private space for my things. Like the student desks, it's off-limits to everyone but the owner. I've considered removing my desk to gain floor space, but I need a place for *my* things and to say, "Put it on my desk."

When I plan where to put all this in the classroom, I usually start by arranging student desks. Placement of desks is restricted by the placement of the chalkboard and the windows. Many teacher-directed lessons, brief as they are, use the chalkboard, so desks must be arranged so children can see it easily. Usually, I set the desks in two semicircles facing the chalkboard and centered around a round table that serves as a small-group conference center and a place for me to work from when the children are convened at their desks for large-group instruction. I've had anywhere from eighteen to twenty-eight students when school opened, and fitting a large number of desks in two semicircles has been tricky. Sometimes—depending on the width of the room, which determines the open space in the semicircle—I begin a third circle with two or three desks in the center. The semicircular arrangement allows the children to make eye contact with others during our class discussions, a definite plus in building a community. I first saw this seating arrangement in my own first-grade class; Mrs. Kearney, in the 1940s, unbolted those old iron and wooden desks from the floor and fastened them to two-by-fours so we could move them around. She was years ahead of her time when she broke up the "little house on the prairie" schoolroom arrangement in favor of one that took the focus off the teacher in front of the class and shifted it to individual members of a group.

Later, I may move student desks together in pairs to facilitate the natural talk surrounding reading and writing that is so helpful to children's language development. Or we may move desks to "top secret positions" for private work, such as a testing situation. And for some activities, we put three or four desks together in a table arrangement. But to start the year, I keep the desks separated. In September, first graders don't tune in to large-group talk when they sit with a partner. With some classes, the move to pair seating occurs pretty quickly; other years it takes months before the children can manage pair seating. It depends on the individual kids and the tone of the class. Some groups never work well with seats pushed together.

I sit beside the round table as I read a children's novel during the opening of the day or during large-group discussions. Years ago, when back problems prevented me from standing all day, I began sitting whenever possible. I discovered I enhanced communication and changed the entire tone in the room by leaving a stance representing authority and moving to a position that invited natural conversation between the children and myself. Such a little thing, yet how different from the edicts I remember from teacher training and administrator observations during my first years of teaching!

With student desks in place, I set up the rest of the room: unroll the storyrug carpet in a corner, organize space for games, puppets, art supplies, and move my teacher desk to the side and behind the children's desks. Then I unpack my books, collect others from the school library, and display them around the room. Children need to see the covers of the books, not just the spines on shelves. I stand books on chalkrails, window ledges, counters, and shelving, and fill a paperback bookrack. The books project a welcoming appeal; the children and I will decide together what else to display. When tempted to do too much I remember Lisa, a first grader from years ago who one day in late March pointed to a word taped to the window and asked, "Mrs. Avery, why's that word on the window?" The word: window. I'd taped it there in August and Lisa had no idea what it said or *why* it was there. The children must understand the *purpose* of everything in the classroom and so now what goes up are items connected to classroom learning usually created with or by the children.

I've included diagrams of two classrooms to show the total room arrangement (see Figures 4–1 and 4–2), but these are only two of many possible arrangements. Critical to room arrangement is *accessibility*. Accessibility means the room is designed and introduced to the children so that they know:

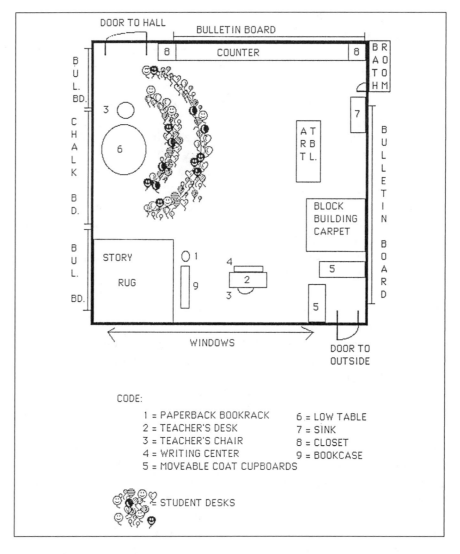

DOOR TO HALL

BULLETIN BOARD

COUNTER

B U L. BD.

C H A L K

B D.

B U L.

BD.

8

8

3

6

STORY

RUG

○ 1

9

4

2

3

A T R B T L.

BLOCK BUILDING CARPET

5

5

7

B R A O T O H M

B U L L E T I N

B O A R D

WINDOWS

DOOR TO OUTSIDE

CODE:

1 = PAPERBACK BOOKRACK
2 = TEACHER'S DESK
3 = TEACHER'S CHAIR
4 = WRITING CENTER
5 = MOVEABLE COAT CUPBOARDS

6 = LOW TABLE
7 = SINK
8 = CLOSET
9 = BOOKCASE

= STUDENT DESKS

Figure 4–1

Classroom Floor Plan #1

- where things are
- how to locate and use items in the room and the appropriate time for use
- the purpose of using all class materials
- how to make decisions for using class materials to enhance learning

I want children to use the classroom to the fullest. I want them to develop responsible and independent ways of using materials. They don't have to wait for me to get what they need or to get permission. They need access to books, paper, art supplies, puppets, games, etc. But to accomplish these goals, I take time in the beginning to introduce everything and discuss procedures for use.

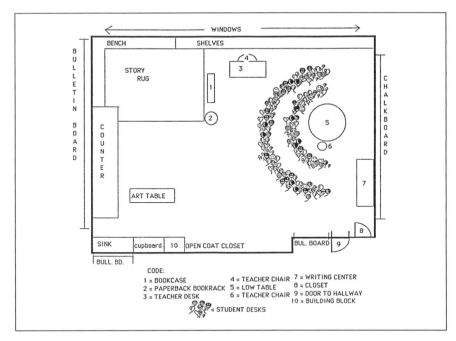

Figure 4–2

Classroom Floor Plan #2

Accessibility is more than being able to get to materials in the room. In setting up the room so that children have access to supplies, I am simultaneously clearing the way so that we are accessible to each other: child to child, teacher to child, child to teacher. Materials, supplies, programs serve us, are under our control, rather than the other way around. Learning in this type of classroom emerges in the context of human interactions, sometimes involving materials, but never removed from relationships with others.

The appearance of the room will change in the days and months ahead, but for now it is ready. I turn my attention to the sequence of activities for this first day of school. I know that taking our time is crucial. The underlying idea is to get to know each other and also begin the procedures that will structure our school day. The exact pacing will depend on the children.

Academic Environment

The decisions involving the academic environment include: time and scheduling, curriculum requirements, teaching strategies, record keeping—always taking into account each learner's needs.

TIME AND SCHEDULING: Each year the principal distributes schedules of the times classes go to lunch and to special area subjects. The rest is up to the classroom teachers. I've learned that it is essential to provide chunks of time for the curriculum basics rather than splinters of time to address a fragmented curriculum. Each day I incorporate a block of time for:

- Writing workshop—time when we write, develop the skill and tool of writing.
- Reading workshop—time to read, develop the skill and tool of reading.
- Literature read aloud—time when I or children read to the group and we talk about the books we share.
- Math—time to develop concepts and practice math skills.
- Content areas—time to focus on science, social studies, and health. I can't incorporate all three into each day, but I designate a time for content area studies and then focus on a science unit, then a social studies unit, etc.
- Free play or individual choice—a structured time when children choose from established options; choices include art, puppets, reading, writing, puzzles, games, etc.
- Opening of the school day—a beginning that brings our community together and starts our day. Beyond the traditional opening activities, our beginning includes a word-play activity and reading a chapter in a children's novel.
- Handwriting—not a daily activity, but a part of the curriculum I address with two or three fifteen-minute, teacher-directed lessons a week.

Identifying these parts of the school day, I map out the schedule (see Figure 4–3 for a sample schedule). An important feature of the schedule is that it is both stable and flexible. I don't adhere to a hard and fast timeframe every day. If reading workshop is going well I'll extend the time, knowing that another day I'll move to social studies earlier than scheduled. The exact time I move from free play into our opening each morning depends on the children's activity and the demands of a particular day. And while the schedule blocks out chunks of time to focus on particular areas, I've found that the various parts of the school day begin meshing one into the other. In literature read aloud, we read about science and social studies topics and we talk about authors and their writing processes. Reading aloud before writing workshop often establishes a natural connection, and there may be a writing mini-lesson embedded during the talk about literature (e.g., a strong lead) enabling writing workshop to begin with a brief, focussed reminder of something discussed only moments before. Children's choices in reading and writing workshops emerge naturally from books and topics discussed during other parts of the school day.

I've found it a definite advantage to teach in a heterogeneous self-contained classroom (one where all the children stay with one teacher all

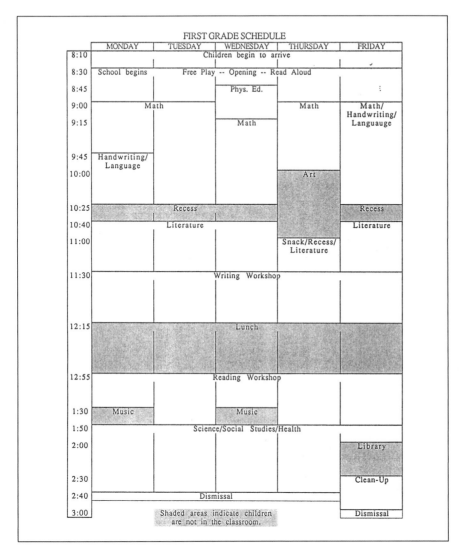

Figure 4–3

First Grade Schedule

day except for music, art, etc.). Learning connections naturally develop with ease and almost effortless grace. I can teach meaningful wholes instead of dissected parts. I save time. I avoid the hectic pace that is so much a part of ability-group tracking that schedules teachers with different groups of children each day. I can establish a community of learners who know each other well, understand and *value* each other's contributions. *All* children learn much from their peers in such an environment.

CURRICULUM: When I initially planned for a process-oriented classroom, one not using any packaged programs, I consulted the district curriculum guides, the scope and sequence charts from the programs adopted by the school district, and the assorted lists of skills considered appropriate for the grade level I taught. I compiled a list of all the concepts and skills I planned to cover during the course of the school year and referred to the list as a means of checking on myself. Was I covering the curriculum? Soon, however, I internalized the list and taught by responding to children, by demonstrating specific content and skills and strategies as they were needed. Of course I am still responsible for addressing the areas of the curriculum adopted by our school board. To do anything less would be to function as an irresponsible teacher—or a brazen revolutionary! But as the professional in the classroom, I am continually making decisions as to *how* to present curriculum. One result of a responsive teaching style is that curriculum in my classroom became integrated (see Chapter 21). But integration, I came to understand, was not merely connecting subject matter through teacher-planned units. Full integration occurred within each learner, as that learner constructed meaning from the experiences in the classroom. Facilitating this internalized integration required my expertise and knowledge of content and a keen awareness of the children and their individual needs. I needed to know the wide range of strategies that readers may employ while reading, be aware of techniques writers use to refine and craft writing, and stay abreast of new releases in children's literature. I had to be informed of new discoveries and attitudes about the content areas I taught. Understanding curriculum is more than following a list of concepts, skills, and subskills: Maintaining one's expertise on particulars related to curriculum is essential to being a professional.

TEACHING STRATEGIES: The way I prepare for teaching is quite different now than when I taught packaged programs that required organizing activities and paperwork for children. I observe and listen to children and continually offer them options of ways to learn through demonstrations and invitations. Certainly I present teacher-directed lessons. But most of these are short, focussed, and in response to a specific need. Children work with skills in the context of their learning and for meaningful purposes. Evaluation is an ongoing process, and skills are not taught for the purpose of testing (see Chapter 20).

RECORD KEEPING: Before school starts I make up two folders for each child, one for reading and one for writing (color-coding the children's names designates writing or reading). Inside the reading folder I staple a sheet of paper labeled "Anecdotal Records" and one labeled "Reading Record." The Anecdotal Record is a blank sheet to write observations of a child's successes, comments, and interactions with books, while the Reading Record (see Figure 4–4) is a simple form (with room for five entries on one page) to take notes when a child reads a book to me. Stapled in the

READING RECORD Name_____

Date_____Title_____
Observations:

Reader Comments:

Future Plans:
Date_____Title_____
Observations:

Reader Comments:

Figure 4–4

Reading Record

Figure 4–5

Writing Record

WRITING RECORD Name_____

Date_____Title of piece_____
Strategies/Skills Addressed:

Observations:

Writer Comments:

Plans:

_____

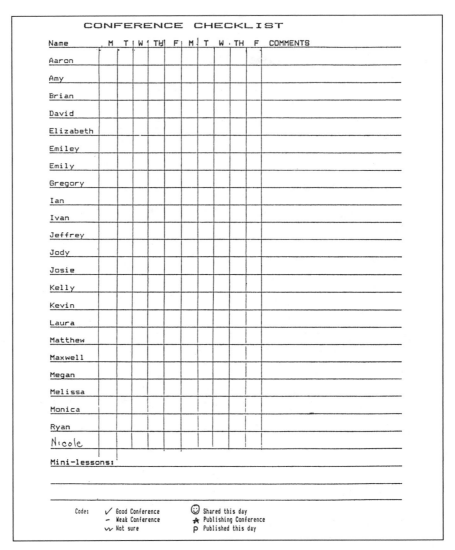

Figure 4–6

Conference Checklist

writing folder is an Anecdotal Record sheet and a sheet labeled "Writing Record." This form is designed to record notes from conferences (usually held with a small group of children) that I conduct when a child prepares a piece of writing for publication (see Figure 4–5).

In addition, I draw up two record sheets to use with the entire class. One is a grid with children's names down the length of the sheet and days of the week across the top, forming a daily checklist that lasts two weeks. I carry this paper with me on a clipboard as I move among the children during writing workshop as Giacobbe advocated. A key indicates the various markings I use to indicate my perceptions of the child's engagement in writing as I talk with that child during a writing conference (see Figure 4–6).

The second record sheet is simply a piece of unlined 8-by-11-inch paper sectioned off into blocks, one for each child in the class. I use this paper to record anecdotal notes as I confer with individual children during reading and writing workshops.

I label three more folders to hold these group records: one for the conference checklist and one each for the anecdotal record for both writing and reading workshops. I photocopy all these record sheets, arrange the children's folders alphabetically by first names, along with the group reading and writing record folders, in a small cardboard file caddie placed on our conference table where it is easily accessible. My record-keeping system to start the year is ready.

LESSON PLANS: I use a loose-leaf notebook as my planbook, adding pages I redesign each year to fit my schedule. I make a master weekly class schedule on two sheets of paper, filling in as much as possible. For example, under writing workshop I write: "Mini-lesson" and leave a space to fill in the topic later. I duplicate the lesson plan pages, punch three holes in them, and place them in the notebook so that an open spread shows an entire week. I write a mini-lesson topic into the plan the day before I teach it. Planning any further ahead would defeat the responsive nature of the instruction. There's space to write notes for any particular part of the day—plans for a publishing conference, for instance. The prescriptive format for lesson plans recommended by the school district did not fit a responsive approach to teaching. I answered my principal's questions on this issue by explaining with specific examples how plans for workshops accommodated the diversity of learning styles in the classroom.

In addition to the plan book, I keep a folder in my desk for substitute teachers that contains a two-page description of the classroom and how it operates. I describe how writing and reading workshops are conducted, suggest a couple of mini-lessons the substitute might use and explain the workshop checklists and record keeping. I've found that substitutes have no trouble working with the procedures and the children capably maintain the structure.

Social Climate

The organizational planning I've been describing is necessary, but alone cannot determine the effectiveness of the learning environment. The key to a strong learning environment is the tone of the classroom, the relationships among the group, and the type of community we establish, as I discussed in the previous chapter. The social climate in my classroom is one that allows for interactions between student and student, teacher and individual student, and teacher and groups of students or the class as a whole.

Structure in a Learner-Centered Classroom

All the careful planning and preparation does not necessarily create a classroom structure that responds to children's natural learning processes. Donald Graves has often spoken about a classroom structure that is predictable (Graves, 1983, p. 268). Sometimes I hear teachers interpret predictability and structure to mean adhering to a tightly and carefully orchestrated schedule and set of procedures. Traditionally, we in education have perceived a structured classroom to be one where the teacher is visibly in control, talking to children who sit quietly listening and following the teacher's dictates. But I think Graves speaks more of an invisible structure than a visible one. The structure lies in the flexible operation of the classroom that is worked out with the students and in which everyone has an investment. The predictability inherent in this environment enables children to learn how to make responsible decisions and to engage in purposeful learning. Learners work together but not necessarily on the same task.

The teacher role in this structure is different. Recently, a teacher in a workshop reminisced about the way she began teaching. "I was forever trying to catch errors," she said, "an octopus reaching out to grab hold of everything my students did wrong and stop it because I knew the right way. My role now is far more compassionate and, therefore, I believe more helpful." The role of teacher is changing. We use words such as *facilitator, nurturer, coach.* I hope to provide the security that there is definitely someone in charge in the classroom, someone who plans, negotiates, and continually shares expertise, but who is also a learner who is questioning, reflecting, and growing. That's a far different role than I experienced with many teachers in my own formal education.

One day a visitor in my room came up to me and said, "How do you operate without any structure?"

"Tell me a little more what you mean." I replied.

"Well," she went on, "the children move around the room. Everybody's writing something different. It just seems so chaotic. And when do you collect their papers? How can you manage all this without a structure? This must work for you, but I just don't see how."

Another visitor commented, "What incredible structure you have here. There's so much *organization!* I talked to every child and each one told me *exactly* what they were doing."

The two visitors observed the same group of children on the very same morning.

Children need a structure. So do I. We need to know that every day after lunch we will read, that in the late morning we will write, that each morning there will be time to chat and share together. We need to know that we will receive responses to our work and that we will make choices throughout the school day about what we read, what we write, and how to proceed in our learning. We need to understand that we will make mistakes and know that this is okay because mistakes are a natural part of learning. We need flexibility.

As I plan and, more importantly, as I establish the classroom structure, I've got to remember that learning is a messy, nonlinear, idiosyncratic process. If I look honestly at the children this fact is obvious every day! But maybe it is precisely because I spend my days in the classroom surrounded by the chaos of a couple dozen children working and playing together that the temptation arises to organize, sequence, and manage learning. I think this pull is part of the tension inherent in being a classroom teacher, and I keep it in mind and allow for it as I set up the classroom. I keep things simple.

On the Saturday before Labor Day, a friend and I leave the classroom we had just prepared for the opening of school. It took us only a few hours, in contrast to the days I once spent at this task. We pause at the doorway and look around.

"It's mostly books," she says.

"Yes. Without them it'd be pretty bare," I admit and flip the light switch. The September twilight catches the long shadows of books the children and I will read together over the year ahead.

First Encounters

The night before school begins, I phone all the children to introduce myself to them, chat briefly, and ask them to bring a favorite book to school the next day. I reach only two-thirds of the class. When 8:45 p.m. arrives, I make one last dial to those who have not been home and then stop. This task is time consuming but very worthwhile. One mother told me weeks after school started of the importance of this phone call: "She went to bed with a smile, eager for the morning. Before you called she had worried all day about going to school."

The phone conversations with the children are fun and fascinating. I ask how I might recognize them tomorrow and they eagerly tell me of their new clothes and their physical descriptions.

"I have a cute suit that's black and a white-striped shirt with black."

"I got all new school clothes: new stockings, new jeans, new underwear, and a new slip."

"I'll tell you one thing. I have dark brown hair and light shoes."

"I have freckles and blond hair and blue jeans."

"I'll have a dress on and I'm Ben's sister."

"I don't know what I look like. I'll have to ask my Mom."

When I ask about books, the children respond quite candidly.

"I got a whole pile of books up in my room."

"I already got one in my bookbag."

"I'm learning to read, but I can't read yet."

"My Dad reads to me almost every night, except when he doesn't."

"I do a little books. I'd rather play Nintendo."

"I can tell you my favorite book. Storybook."

"I think I'll bring *Pinocchio*. But I might change my mind."

"Favorite book. I don't know."

"I don't have no books, not really. I watch TV."

"I don't want to go back to school—just kidding."

When I ask one little girl to bring a book to school, her shy voice changes tone and she cries out, "Okay! I'm going to pick one out right now!"

When I hang up from the final call, I too am eager for the morning.

Writing

CHAPTER 5

Learning to Manage a Writing Workshop

It was Monday morning of the first full week of school, our fourth day together. This was the first year I had introduced a daily writing workshop into my classroom and I was a novice. The children settled into the workshop that morning, engrossed with new crayons and clean, white paper. All except Maggie. Maggie had arrived at school with a new set of colored markers and asked, "Can I use these when it's writing time?"

"Sure," I glibly replied, remembering that all writers, even young ones, have a preference for particular tools. When the workshop began, Maggie opened her markers instead of her crayon box. I felt a bit uneasy when I stopped to confer with her for she was obviously as absorbed in the markers as she was in the picture she drew. A few minutes later I looked across the room to see Maggie turning pages of her writing book and making sweeping circles and jagged lines on each page. I quickly moved to her desk. By now blood-red scribbles dripped from over half the pages in the book.

In an attempt to have Maggie confront the natural consequences of this action, I made some comment like, "This book is for your writing for the whole month of September. What will you do?" An undaunted Maggie twisted her mouth, rolled her eyes, then proposed several solutions: gluing in more pages, or maybe erasing the red marks, or finding a new book "somewheres." A day later I discovered Maggie with open paste jar and blank paper attempting to add pages to her writing book.

When I approached her, she looked up from the paste jar and said, "I wanted to put more pages so I'll have enough."

"Good idea," I responded, "want some help?"

"Yeah, 'cause I'm having trouble. These won't stick too good." So Maggie and I worked with paper, staples, and glue and managed to insert several pages into the writing book.

During the first three days of school, I had taken children through their initial writing experience in small groups. I began the first whole group writing workshop with a carefully thought out mini-lesson addressing procedures for the workshop.

"Every day we'll begin by talking about writing—how we work in our writing workshop or something about good writing—and then we'll all write. While you write, I'll come around to see you. When I'm at your desk—when it's your turn—you may tell me about your writing. I want you to tell me what you're writing about and what you're planning to do next. I'll try to see everyone and I'd like you to wait in your seat until I come to you." I held up one blank writing book and explained that I wanted them to write on the first page only that day. Tomorrow we would turn to a new page. (I knew what some first graders might do when handed a book of blank paper and a box of crayons. Plus, I wanted to avoid the hurried, slapdash "I'm done" approach many children tended to use.) I reminded the children of the writing they had done in small groups the previous week and that now hung on the bulletin board and said, "We'll do this writing in the same way but at our own desks instead of coming to the front table." The nodding heads and the fingers eagerly opening crayon boxes told me the children understood and were ready to begin.

That was when Maggie threw a kink into my preplanned organization. Absorbed in her new markers, she focussed on the flowing brilliant colors and neglected the writing task. When other children saw her move beyond the first page, they wanted to do the same. I realized that the children needed firm guidelines from me to get the workshop started.

So, the next day I announced that we would use crayons and pencils for writing workshop, but for now no markers. I reminded them to write just one page a day. When the children thought they were finished, they were to look back over their work and think how they could make it better. Maybe something could be added to the drawing or some additional letters could be inserted. "Take your time," I urged them.

The children slowed down. Flowers appeared around houses and vapor trails behind airplanes. Maggie pouted about markers for a moment when I privately told her my decision before school started, but she happily used crayons when it came time to write. Selecting writing topics each day was choice enough for these six-year-olds; they didn't need to face decisions this early about kinds of paper, markers, crayons, or pens. By limiting choices for a while, I hoped to focus the children's attention on the writing and build their investment in the process of writing every day. Gradually, I would add options and guide children in making more decisions.

My idealized notions of student choice had led me to believe that I'd squelch creativity or infringe on ownership by denying Maggie her markers. However, sometimes I needed to step in, to offer suggestions, even to make decisions for a child. Tom Newkirk wrote about giving children choices: "It is not simply choice that we're after, but wise choice or intelligent choice" (Newkirk, 1989, p. 184).

Of course, limiting the writing to one page in the writing book soon presented another dilemma. Within a few days Jason drew a picture on one side of facing pages and filled the other with sprawling letters. "Can I turn the page?" he asked. Obviously, he had more to write and needed the space. "Sure. That's fine," I replied. Then the child next to him hurried in order to turn his page. I stopped to talk to this child, to affirm his work—and to slow him down and prevent a potential bandwagon. This responsive management style wasn't easy!

Such is the tension of rules, procedures, and guidelines: There are always exceptions; nothing is engraved in stone. Rules and procedures provide a flexible structure to support the children's development, to encourage involvement and risk taking. To be effective they need to be fluid. As each class of children and I move through the first weeks of school, we establish procedures for writing workshop to meet both the needs of individuals and the welfare of the group. Though there are similarities year to year, each group takes on its own character.

Every year, however, I use a workshop timeframe similar to Giacobbe's that includes:

1. mini-lesson (5–8 minutes in length)
2. writing, with teacher conferring with individuals (approximately 20–30 minutes)
3. large-group sharing, where two or three children read their writing to the group and receive responses (10–15 minutes)

The total time runs approximately forty-five minutes. In the beginning of the year this may be shorter, and later the time may be extended to an hour.

Initially, everyone writes in his or her own large book of unlined paper. The book contains forty pages and, conceivably, could last each child for forty days of school. However, Lori's story about Halloween spilled over to four pages in two days, while Chris's piece on a visit to the zoo was carefully executed on one page in three days' time. The way in which the children work—the pace and style—is a function of each child's personality. Writing in blank books at the beginning of the school year offers several advantages. The book provides a sequenced record of a child's writing during the early days of the school year, which is helpful to me in getting to know the child and also in communicating to parents. With management tasks minimized, the children concentrate on putting their thoughts on paper, and I focus on responding to these young writers. After just a few days, the children's stories become longer as the young writers incorporate details and additional information into their pieces. They experiment with spelling. I show them how to line-out rather than erase when they wish to make changes. These six-year-olds begin to experience the craft of writing.

For a number of years the children and I called these blank books *journals,* and on the front cover I neatly labeled each child's name (e.g., "Greg's Journal"). Eventually I changed the cover title from "journal" to "writing" (e.g., "Greg's Writing") because of the connotations that began to be associated with journals in school. Our writing journals were distinctive from private diaries or even from journals used for reflection because the writing was meant to be shared and some of it crafted. The writing done in our writing workshop was not intended to be private, though once in a while a child wrote about a sensitive issue. Usually, I've found that children who write deeply personal pieces want to share this information with someone. In that event, I listen and acknowledge what I've heard.

One year, while writing a story for Mother's Day, Brenda wrote, "My Mommy feels sad because she says my Daddy doesn't love her anymore. He loves somebody else." I knew I couldn't let Brenda read those lines at our Mother's Day program. But that day I said only, "That sounds very sad for you." The next morning Brenda told me during writing workshop, "I lined that part out that I read to you yesterday because I think my Mommy will be sad if she heard that part." I'd been considering possible ways to lead Brenda to this decision, but she came to it on her own. We can generally trust children's sensibilities. I'm careful not to break trust with a child by discussing with others any highly personal information a child may write. (The one exception of course is child abuse, which, by law, teachers must report.)

As children become comfortable working in the writing workshop, I add options. One year in mid-October I stapled together booklets with orange construction paper covers and presented them to the class in a mini-lesson. "Authors usually write books on one topic," I explained. "Many of you have been writing about Halloween, so I made these books for you to write on that topic if you wish. You have a choice: You may write in your writing book or you may write in this book." That day all but two children chose to write in the orange booklets. A couple of days later, many had gone back to the writing books, and for the next couple of weeks the children moved back and forth between writing book and stapled booklet.

For two years I provided stapled booklets with a variety of bright covers for the children to select from the writing center. In addition, I gradually added a selection of paper each year and showed children how to staple multiple sheets together. I eventually phased out those little booklets. Even though children loved the attractive format, I spent too much time preparing them and some children started a new booklet every day. "How can we solve this so I'm not spending all my time stapling?" I asked the children. "We can do it ourselves," they told me. Now our classroom writing center has an assortment of paper and the children take responsibility for selecting paper, determining the number of sheets, and stapling. I've found that young writers, like most adults, favor smooth, clean, high-quality sheets when they start a new piece of writing. Construction paper is available for those who want to add their own colorful covers. An additional box holds staplers, staple removers, tape, scissors, and cans with assorted pencils and pens. The children have access to all these supplies (Giacobbe, 1982).

I'd like to say that this writing center is neat, organized, and well kept, but every year it quickly takes on a rather ragged appearance. Pencil cans become depositories for the lost and found crayons and pencils of the classroom. New pencils or ones with erasers soon disappear to be replaced by badly chewed stubs. First graders eat the erasers and feed the wood to the pencil sharpener. Often when they get paper they reject the top sheets, and like someone digging past the crust and first slices in a loaf of bread, they pull sheets of paper from the middle of the stack.

I once taught first graders to use a stapler in order to staple seatwork papers. Now this is a mini-lesson: line up the paper, place the stapler, squeeze gently and listen for the click-click sound. I give the lesson and everyone nods that they understand, but I know that they still need to experiment and learn from their experiences. Although I demonstrate stapling with one staple in a top corner, I'm not surprised to see a child struggling to turn pages connected with five staples placed three inches in from the edge. Some children attempt to staple thirty sheets or more and discover the task is impossible. Others take one sheet at a time as they write, returning to the writing center for each new page—and for the experience of using the stapler again. I've counted thirty staples in one piece of writing! Some children create patterns with staples; stars or triangles are favorites. The first roll of tape in the writing center lasts a maximum of two days, so we talk about the tape issue and the staple issue; the school cannot provide an unending supply of such items. The children understand and take responsibility for using supplies.

As the children use the last of the blank pages in their writing books, I phase in individual writing folders as a place for each child to store new writing (Giacobbe, 1982; Graves, 1983). Setting up folders takes several mini-lessons scattered over a period of time. First graders are not particularly good at maintaining writing folders. For every child who keeps a neat folder and records appropriate information, one or two others doodle on their folders and neglect to record information. Soon, some children's folders are overflowing, with paper extending from all three open sides. During writing workshop, a folder topples from a desk and the paper scatters. "Oh no!" says the child and I think "Not again." But I say nothing—usually. These are young children and they will learn through their experiences, even from such minor things as spilled writing folders.

We continually negotiate these management problems. In a talk about the folders, we decide to clean them out once a month or so and file old writing in boxes where the children have access to them. Sometimes, like the time the pencils disappeared and we found them in one student's desk, the initiative for negotiation comes from the children. There are days when I think it would be easier to just impose directives on the group. But then I realize that I'd be back in the role of enforcer and the children would have little investment in my decisions. So we start with a few classroom procedures and negotiate others as the need arises. The classroom becomes predictable, yet evolving to accommodate the ongoing development of the children. The structure serves diversity among the children, and I work with them according to their individual needs.

One morning after we had problems with overflowing folders, the children used free-play time to organize their writing folders. They gathered all but one or two pieces of recent writing and placed the rest in a folder made of construction paper in a box that we labeled "January Writing." We stored the box on a shelf where the children would have access to it. Periodically, as writing folders became filled, we'd repeat the same activity. Keeping all the children's writing in the classroom until the year's end is important. The children need to look back at their writing from time to time to see their own growth, and they learn to turn to old pieces of writing when they are stuck for a new topic. The accumulated writing also provides documentation to share with parents at conference time (Giacobbe, 1982).

On this morning I watched Edward, a reluctant writer in September, carefully turn each sheet in his neat stack of papers. He examined each page, smiling and occasionally talking to himself and nodding. When he had finished, he brought the folder to me and said, "Anyways, I like to write, so don't lose this because this is real important."

That same morning I sat on the floor with Matthew, helping him sort through the disarray of papers in his folder, sequencing stories that long ago lost their staples, trying to teach him something about organization. I was lost, but Matthew knew how each page fit with the others. Amazing.

"I'm a pretty sloppy kid," he smiled rather matter-of-factly.

"Really?" I replied.

"Yeah, sloppy. I said that to my mom once—about me being sloppy. Guess what she said."

"What?"

"She said that's the way I came and I always been sloppy. Guess I'll always be a little bit sloppy." He grinned broadly. His demeanor and tone revealed both an awareness and an acceptance of self. Then he shrugged his shoulders and added, "But I'm still a good writer, don't you think?"

"Right, Matt. You are a good writer." Edward, Matt, and all their classmates understood what was important.

Reflections

Managing writing workshops cannot be reduced to a how-to formula; it is an ongoing, complex task that develops differently within the context of each classroom. The pioneers in the teaching of writing wisely avoided giving us definitive directions. Graves made us aware of the importance of process. Mary Ellen Giacobbe emphasized the roles of time, ownership, and response for implementing a writing workshop. Although neither Graves nor Giacobbe meant to provide us with recipes, we teachers grasp at these terms when we reach for concrete instructions to get a handle on new teaching procedures. Tom Newkirk (1989) in his essay, "The Roots of the Writing Process," discussed the complexities of implementing and managing these new modes of teaching writing. He pointed out the danger in using these terms as absolutes.

> Too many of the ultimate terms, those used again and again to justify this approach, are simply the obverse of traditional terms. "Product" is opposed by "process." "Assignment" is opposed by "choice." The "authority" of the teacher is set against the child's quasi-right to "ownership." But "the effort of thought," as Dewey would say, "is to see these terms not as mutually exclusive choices, but as complimentary principles." (p. 187)

The challenge in implementing and managing a writing workshop is to blend new principles with traditionally sound ones, with unique results. The heart and art of teaching is applying, reflecting, and revising one's evolving beliefs (theories) in the context of day-to-day developments in the classroom.

Writing workshop is a daily time where we *work* on writing, struggle with evolving texts, develop writing skills, and learn to use writing as an effective tool for communication and learning. As a classroom teacher I'm continually caught in the tension of an incredible balancing act. To manage all these ideas within the reality of the classroom, I've learned to trust my instincts, to consider the principles of outside experts, and to listen to the children and to my own needs. I keep working at this craft of teaching, making decisions, making mistakes, and struggling and learning. And when in doubt, I look to the children. For they always know, with the uncluttered wisdom of youth, which way to go. They continue to be my best teachers.

CHAPTER 6

Writers Begin

My beliefs about children and writing are based on three assumptions: (1) young children *can* write, (2) young children *want* to write, and (3) young children possess knowledge, interests, and experiences to write about. The work of Graves (1983) on writing and of Harste, et. al. (1984) and his associates on literacy of young children professed these same assumptions, and my experiences with first-grade writers validated these beliefs. First graders may not use standardized spelling nor adhere to many of the other conventions of written language, but they do understand that created symbols communicate meaning and they are capable of communicating by placing marks on paper. All children have experiences to write about. They do not need to go on elaborate family vacations or own fancy toys to find topics. In my classroom Jody wrote about watching the trains go by his house, Megan about an old stuffed panda, Natalie about riding the school bus. The children write without assigned topics or classroom experiences designed to supply topics. I avoid measuring the children's writing against some preconceived concept of what they should or should not be able to do as writers. Such expectations handicap their efficient, natural learning styles. Don Murray often says the role of the teacher of writing is to laugh and cheer. I like his advice and I try to keep it in mind as I listen to writers talk about their writing.

In watching ten years of first graders begin to write in writing workshops, I've noticed that each one does it differently: different topics, different pace, different working styles. The stories of four children writing over the first few days of school show the diverse ways children move into writing.

Chad

Chad is blue-eyed and strawberry-blond. His father is deceased and his mother has remarried. He has an older sister and a stepbrother who is his

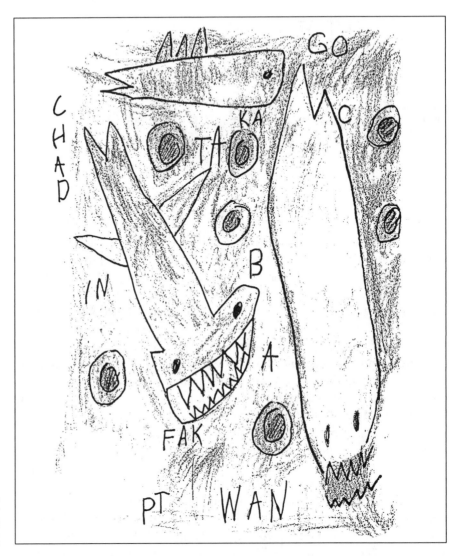

Figure 6–1

*Chad's writing:
Day 1*

age. Chad's paternal grandparents are members of the Old Order Amish community of Lancaster County. Although Chad is not an active member of this community (his mother is not Amish), he maintains close ties with his grandparents. Chad is pensive, reflective, and thoughtful. He takes his time as he works. For the first seven days of school he writes about sharks.

Day 1: In Chad's first drawing, three sharks swim amid a school of jellyfish (see Figure 6–1). At first glance, I think that either the sharks pursue the jellyfish or attempt to flee from their stinging tentacles. But when I talk to Chad I learn both assumptions are wrong. Chad gazes at me and patiently explains that men go under the sea to watch sharks. "And there's jellyfish there, too," he adds, "because jellyfish swim underwater and these sharks swam into a whole group of jellyfish. There were jellyfish in the water when we went to the beach." The men watching sharks are not in Chad's drawing but they are clearly in his mind, and Chad drew the scene not from the perspective of an outside observer but from the viewpoint of the undersea explorer.

Chad turns to read his written words. "Do you mind if I write what you read on this page so we remember it?" I ask. (In the beginning of the year, with the author's permission, I sometimes lightly pencil in children's words when they read their writing to me, not for children's recall but for mine, and also to share with parents.) Chad gives permission and begins to read.

"When people go in cages they have . . . " The words are scattered randomly on the page. To read, Chad hunts for each word, stabs the page with his finger as he locates the next word. He's stuck after reading "have" because blue crayon around the sea creatures covers the pencil marks.

"How did you decide where to write these words?" I ask.

Chad looks up, gazing into my eyes and replies, "I put them wherever they would fit."

"I see. Did you write them before or after you colored the water?"

"I did the water after I did the words." I nod. Chad is having trouble locating his words because he's covered them with crayon, but I feel no need to comment on this nor on the random placement on the page. My "teacher" self thinks about left-to-right progression, but I keep still. I want to learn about Chad and his thinking, work on building trust between us, and make sure he wants to write again. To accomplish all this I've got to set aside concerns for conventions. No suggestions, no correcting, just listening, learning, delighting.

"You know a lot about sharks?" I ask.

"Yes, I do. I think sharks are very interesting creatures," Chad replies thoughtfully, maintaining that direct, serious gaze. His words seem carefully chosen.

"I think this is an interesting piece of writing. Thank you for sharing it with me," I respond and start to leave.

"What should I do now?" Chad asks.

"Well, you could keep working on the reading, if you want, or look over the whole thing to see if there's anything you'll change. It's up to you. Don't forget to write your name, though. An author *always* puts his name." I move on to another student.

At the end of the workshop Chad comes to me and says, "I found all the words and I remember what it says." I have no time to jot down those words and by the next day Chad has forgotten them. No matter. There would be lots of writing. We would be able to see the development without reading or remembering every word.

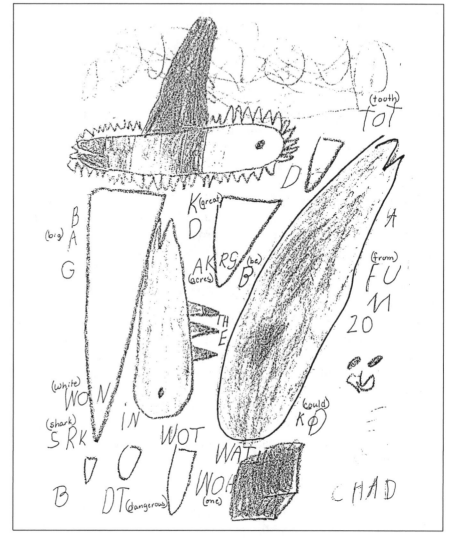

Figure 6–2

*Chad's writing:
Day 2, "One
tooth from a great
white shark might
be twenty acres
big. One shark
in the whole
world could be
dangerous."*

Day 2: Chad solves the problem that hindered his reading by restricting
the blue crayon to the top of his picture (see Figure 6–2). "I didn't put all the
blue in as I did yesterday because I thought that would help me read it more
easily today," he tells me. His pensive tone, his sophisticated speech is so
atypical of first graders. He reads the writing to me, again searching the
page for the words, sometimes pausing with comments such as "Wait a
second. I have to find the next word." Chad reads, "One tooth from a great
white shark might be twenty acres big. One shark in the whole world could
be dangerous." Then he tells about the drawing. I learn even more than
what is written on the page as Chad tells about the sizes of sharks and their
ferociousness.

Figure 6–3

*Chad's writing:
Day 3, "A great
white shark's
favorite food is
a sawfish. A
shark would know
how deep the
horizon is."*

Day 3: Chad begins by drawing the surface of the water across the top of the page, then adds various sea creatures swimming beneath (see Figure 6–3). Later in the workshop Chad reads his writing, "A great white shark's favorite food is a sawfish. A shark would know how deep the horizon is." He uses some words more than once as he reads: "shark" appears on the page only once but Chad points to it and reads it twice.

"Tell me what you mean by 'how deep the horizon is'?" I ask.

"The horizon is the top of the water. You can look out and see the horizon when you're standing on the beach. Sharks live under the horizon, in the water. They know where it is, how deep the horizon is as they swim."

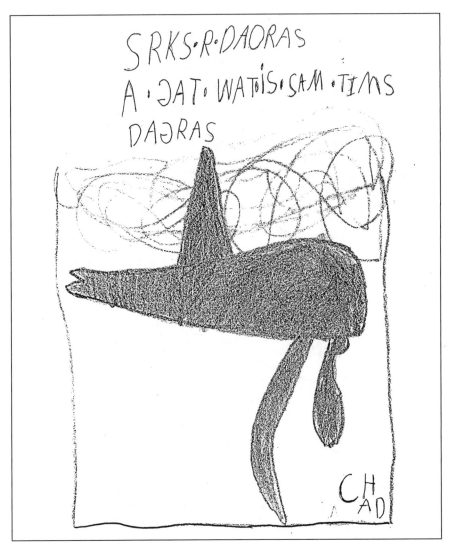

Figure 6–4

Chad's writing: Day 4, "Sharks are dangerous. A great white is sometimes dangerous."

I understand. Chad's vocabulary, like all children's, develops as he comes upon words in conversation every day. He adds those words to his vocabulary, constructing the meaning by connecting the new word to what he presently understands and making his own sense of that word. Using "horizon," even with his approximation of the meaning, was a way of playing with language, of refining meaning through use. I've regularly seen children develop language proficiency this way.

Chad continues his writing (on Figure 6–3) after I leave by adding the numeral one and the row of zeros to explain just how deep the horizon might be, and then, on the opposite page, a title: "SRKS."

WAN·A·HAMR·HAD·SRK
LAS·BABBES·AT·
CAN·LA·40·OAR·50·

Figure 6–5

*Chad's writing:
Day 5, "When a
hammer head
shark lays babies
it can lay 40
or 50 . . ."*

Day 4: Chad draws one large, black shark and the surrounding sea, then writes in left-to-right progression with invented spelling, "Sharks are dangerous. A great white is sometimes dangerous" (see Figure 6–4). He inserts large dots between the words to establish boundaries. Like many children, he develops this strategy on his own, a procedure that seems to help him write and read his own words. I can see how these dots assist his reading by helping him focus on each word. For Chad, the dots function far more efficiently than mere spaces between words.

Days 5 and 6: With the discovery of left-to-right progression, Chad's fluency develops. His next story extends to two pages (see Figure 6–5).

Figure 6–6

Chad's writing: Day 6, ". . . babies. If you caught a fish the person who killed it can be in great danger because blood brings a shark. A nurse shark is dangerous."

Chad reads, "When a hammer head shark lays babies, it can lay 40 or 50 babies. If you kill a fish, the person who killed it can be in great danger because blood brings a shark. A nurse shark is dangerous." The story continues the next day (see Figure 6–6). Chad reads, "A nurse shark is dangerous. Any person that's in the water may destruct. The person that's in the water can be killed." Chad carefully draws the pictures, correlating the details between illustrations and text. There are exactly forty "babies" beside the hammerhead. The nurse shark hovers above the distraught human, colored red—the color of blood. Above the shark and the human is a gray shadow, which, Chad explains, is the bottom of the fisherman's boat as seen from underwater.

Figure 6–7a

*Chad's writing:
Day 7, "A shark
can love each
other. When a
shark loves each
other . . ."*

Day 7: "A shark can love each other. When a shark loves each other, they make a cave that's a hut." (See Figures 6–7a and 7b). Chad reads his next piece and gazes into my eyes with the honest, straightforward, gentle look that I have already come to understand to be an extension of the honest heart that makes its way to every page of his writing.

The saga of sharks ends. The following day Chad writes a short piece about travel: "People go across the ocean. They go from California to India." Then he launches into a series of pieces about rockets. When a hurricane threatens the eastern United States, Chad writes about hurricanes for several days. In the next few weeks he writes a series on each of the following topics: robots, the ocean, playing Pac Man, stars, and clowns.

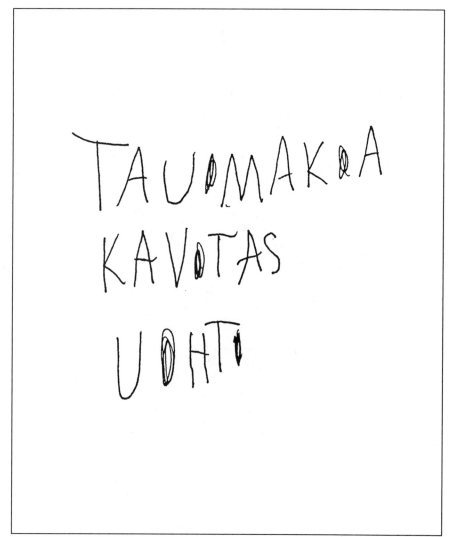

Figure 6–7b

Chad's writing: Day 7, ". . .they make a cave that's a hut."

On the day when grandparents are invited to school for lunch, Chad's Amish grandparents attend. Ten minutes into the afternoon I notice that Chad is missing. I send frantic messages to the office. A few minutes later a calm Chad appears with his grandfather. They've been touring the school. This gentleman with a white beard and dressed in the black garb of the Amish shakes my hand and bows ever so slightly. He thanks me for teaching Chad to read and to write. He tells me that he writes too. I look into his eyes and then into Chad's. I see the same gentle gaze and I understand, as never before, why our Lancaster County Amish are known as "the gentle people."

Later in the year, an illustrated *Stopping by a Wood on a Snowy Evening*, by Robert Frost, becomes Chad's favorite book. In March Chad begins to write poetry. One rainy, spring morning he hands me this poem:

Spring is dreary, dark and deep.
And lots of children play with me.
And a drafty wind sweeps the earth.
And a drafty wind sweeps the earth.

Chad says, "I'm going to be a writer when I grow up." No doubt he can reach his goal. But then, he already is a writer.

Sarah

Sarah's small size, brunette hair, brown eyes with long lashes, and creamy complexion give her a pixie look. She loves precision, which is evident in her always neat desk, her deliberate pace at everything she undertakes, and her enjoyment of math computations, each number carefully formed. Sarah's parents are divorced. She lives with her mother and younger sister in a low-rent apartment complex. Her father resides in Pittsburgh and Sarah sees him infrequently. Shy and quiet, Sarah is also one of the youngest members of the class.

Day 1: Sarah begins by drawing a band of blue across the top of the page to make sky, then a similar green band across the bottom for grass. She adds an apple tree, the sun, and a large flower. She works quietly, head down except to steal occasional glances at the child next to her. I stoop at her desk, she smiles shyly and says in a hushed little voice, "It's a tree and a flower."

"Oh, a tree and a flower," I reply in an equally quiet voice.

"An apple tree," she adds.

"Oh, and what else will you draw?" I ask.

Sarah shrugs, hesitates, then replies, "Me and my mom and my sister."

"Ahh, well, I'll be interested to see this after you do that." After school I look through the children's writing and see that Sarah penciled drawings of three people and added her name and date. She also wrote "I," a heart, "U" (the "I love you" message that many young children have learned to pen) and added heart-shaped balloons on strings (see Figure 6–8).

Days 2–7: Sarah writes, then reads the "I love you" message during the writing workshop. She spends most of her time drawing, however, and seems to add written words at the end of each workshop almost as an

Figure 6–8

Sarah's writing:
Day 1

afterthought to fulfill a requirement to write. A close look at her succession of drawings reveals an evolving development: Each drawing expands on the one before it. Sarah begins each one with the tree, flower, sun, and people she included in her first drawing and then adds to the scene. A rainbow appears on the second day, a tiny house on the third, and on the fourth day the house enlarges as though through a zoom lens.

In our conference Sarah tells me she is playing outside her house with her sister. "Could you write that?" I ask. Sarah looks at me. " 'I play . . . ' Could you write those words? Listen for the letters you hear." I repeat the words "I play" slowly, emphasizing each letter, then ask Sarah what she hears first as I repeat the words again.

Figure 6–9

Sarah's writing:
"I play."

"I?" she says.

"You got it. Write it," I answer. Sarah writes the letter "I," looks up and smiles. "What's next?" In a couple of moments Sarah has added "P A" and together we read her sentence: "I play" (I P A). "You wrote a whole sentence, Sarah," I say. She smiles shyly and goes back to coloring. On the following two days Sarah draws her house and writes "I P A." (See Figure 6–9.)

Day 10: Sarah draws a tree, a bush with flowers, the sun, sky, grass, and a person (see Figure 6–10). All these elements appeared in prior pictures, but never in quite the same arrangement. She writes, "I Y T e G r e" and reads this line: I went to my tree to get a leaf.

Figure 6–10

Sarah's writing: "I went to my tree to get a leaf."

"Sarah! All those words! And this picture—you tried some new things here," I say. Sarah smiles her shy smile and nods. Later she adds "A i e four i m," copying "four" from the chalkboard. I don't get back to Sarah to ask what the words say, but I don't need to know. I do know that this has been a breakthrough day for her.

Every day thereafter Sarah writes a different message. Her fluency increases. Only a week later she writes: I Y two B four I e e r A B two e N I r A B two I C D N I N two B N I Y N. She reads her writing, pointing to the letters as she does so, using them as clues along with her memory of her intended meaning: I went to bed. Before, my mom, she read a book to

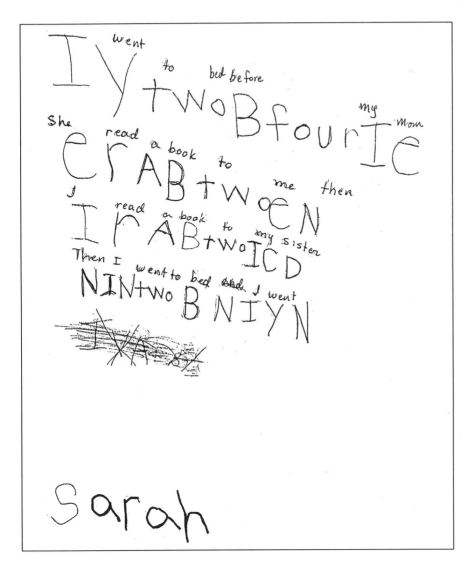

Figure 6–11

*Sarah's writing
in March:
"I went to bed
before my mom.
She read a book to
me then I read a
book to my sister.
Then I went to
bed. Then I
went."*

me. Then I read a book to my sister. Then I went to bed. Then I went. (See Figure 6–11.)

In the following days and weeks Sarah composes pieces about visiting Kennywood Park on a trip to Pittsburgh, learning to ride a bike, picking apples in a local orchard, dressing as a witch for Halloween, missing the school bus. She fills the page beside each picture with rows of letters. As she writes she whispers words to herself. She cannot always read her entire piece because she writes only one or two letters for each word and as the pieces grow in length she has difficulty remembering every word she has written. "I'll just tell you what it says," she says when she gets stuck.

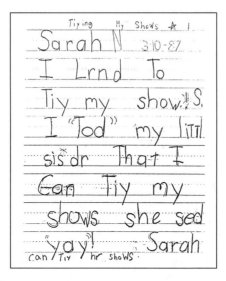

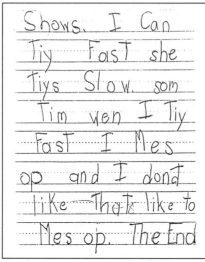

Figure 6–12

Sarah's story

Sarah works carefully and thoughtfully all year. In early March Sarah writes "Tiying My Shows" and illustrates the story with a picture of a house with Sarah sitting inside tying her shoes (see Figure 6–12). The story seems to sum up her learning process.

I lrnd to tiy my shows! I "tod" my littl sisdr that I can tiy my shows, she sed "yay!" Sarah can tiy hr shows. my Mom seaed "good" because wen I go to school av day She owes hs to tiy my shows. and she dosit like to tiy my shows. I can tiy fast she tiys slow. som time wen I tiy fast I mes op and I dont like to mes op. The End.

Figure 6–13

Tiffany's writing: "I am at the library."

Tiffany

Tiffany is one of five children. Another sibling is born during this school year and when the baby girl is less than a month old, Tiffany's mother brings her to school and permits all the children to hold the baby. This is typical of the warm, accepting, and trusting attitude Tiffany's parents give their children. Tiffy, as she likes to be called, portrays a quiet confidence as she moves through the school day, always smiling. She seems wise beyond her years.

Figure 6–14

Tiffany's writing:
"I like the hungry
caterpillar. I like
when he eats leafs
and I also like
when he turned
into a butterfly."

Day 1: Tiffy's love of color and of books comes though in her first writing. She draws the library and uses every crayon in the box on the wall of books (see Figure 6–13). She writes letters down the side and joyfully reads, "I am at the library."

Day 2: Tiffy writes about Eric Carle's *The Very Hungry Caterpillar*. She draws a smiling sun surrounded by the apples and plums, the pizza and cake, and finally the small green leaf that the caterpillar ate in Carle's story (see Figure 6–14). In the bottom corner Tiffy shows the little caterpillar hatching into a butterfly; to the left of the sun the butterfly begins to soar.

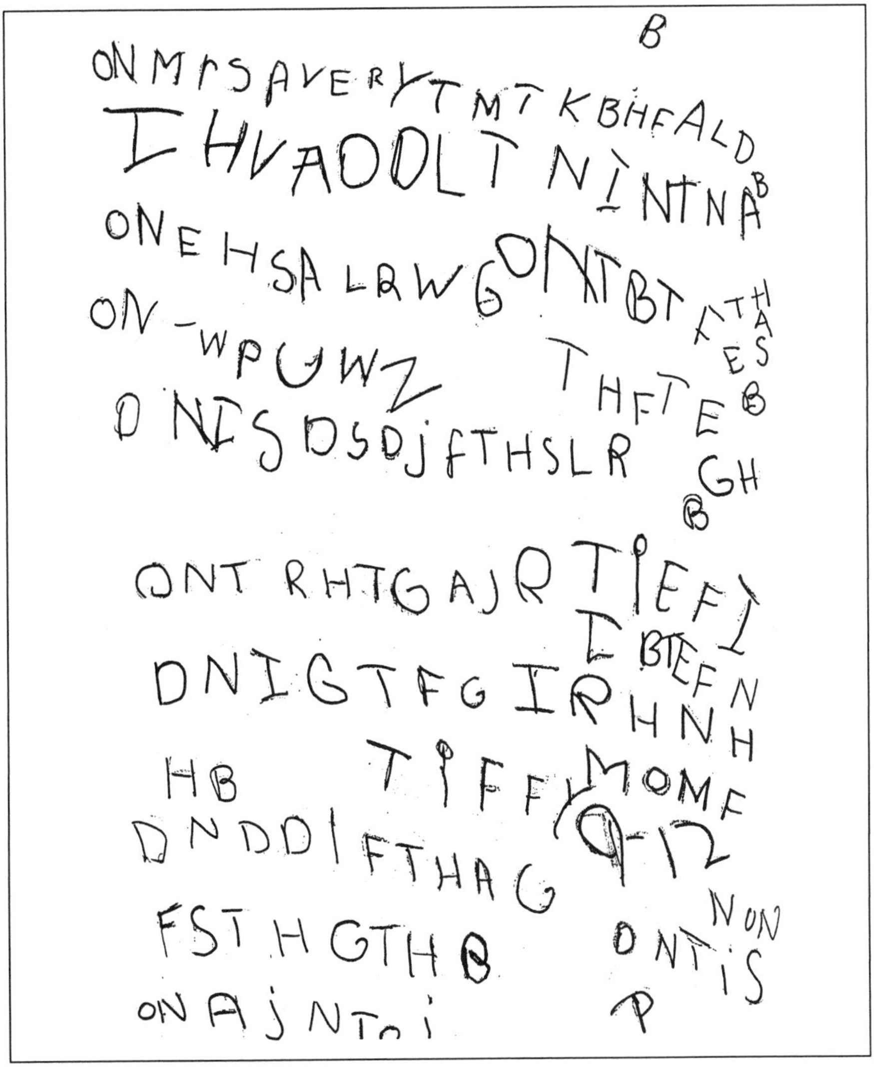

Figure 6–15

Tiffany's writing: Day 10

Moving her finger under the letters at the top of the page, she reads, "I like the hungry caterpillar."

"Why do you like this book?" I ask.

"Because I like when he eats leafs and I also like when he wasn't hungry and turned into a butterfly." Tiffy adds these lines to her page after our conference without any urging on my part.

Day 10: Tiffy focusses on the ideas she wants to write, without fretting over correct spelling or striving for perfection. Her story about a grasshopper is typical (see Figure 6–15):

I have an old lot near my house. It has a lot of weeds. I was picking out the weeds and I saw something jump from the grass. It was a grasshopper. And I ran home to get a jar and I came back. He was not there, but I saw something jump from the grass. It was a grasshopper. And I holded the jar and he jumped in it. I ran home and showed my mom and I asked her if I should bring it for show and tell and she said, "It's up to you." So I brung it and I brung it with a book. Mrs. Avery said, "You could keep it here for a little bit."

Tiffy draws colorful pictures and writes stories with ease. She enjoys writing and has no difficulty coming up with a new topic every - day. I learn about her pet bunnies and their eating habits, about losing a tooth and the tooth fairy's visit, and about the excitement of catching a big fish after reeling in many little ones. After two weeks in school her words (usually one or two consonant letters per word) fill a page every day. After three weeks of school, her stories are three, four, five, or six pages in length, continuing from one day to the next until she has told her tale. She always can read her entire piece to me.

Troy

Troy has dark brown eyes and curly brown hair. He is extremely shy, but on the playground he holds his own with the others despite being the smallest boy in the class. Troy's family lives only slightly above the poverty level. His father, who appeared at our parent conference in a muscle shirt with a bandanna on his head, is a laborer. I never met Troy's mother, or had any contact with her. Troy moved before the school year ended.

Day 1: Troy draws an underwater scene and labels the large fish with a letter "C" (see Figure 6–16). "That's for shark," he says, barely pausing to indicate the "C" as he fills the page with blue crayon. I wait. Troy continues to color.

"Are these sharks too?" I inquire, pointing to the bottom of the picture.

Troy finally pauses. He seems somewhat startled by my interest. "Yeah, more sharks."

"What else is here?"

Figure 6–16

Troy's writing:
C = shark
IG = one jellyfish
E = eel
V = starfish

"Oh," Troy replies in an offhanded tone, "starfish, eel, turtle, clam. A jellyfish." He goes back to coloring. He has not yet made eye contact with me.

"A jellyfish?" I reply quickly to keep his attention.

"Yeah." Troy keeps coloring.

"Will you write anything about the jellyfish or these other animals?" Troy glances up. I keep talking. "Jellyfish. What letter do you hear in 'jellyfish'?"

Figure 6–17

Troy's writing: K means "all these catfish."

Troy shrugs, then softly says, "Jellyfish." Pause. "G?" he suddenly asks, and picks up his pencil and writes "G." As I leave Troy's desk I see him write "E" beside the eel.

Day 11: For the next ten days Troy draws underwater animals and labels the pictures with the initial consonants, each day adding more and more letters to his work. Then one day he writes only one letter, a large "K," on his picture (see Figure 6–17). At first I think Troy has regressed or decided to rest from the steady growth. I am wrong. Troy tells me that he "made a

Figure 6–18

Troy's writing: "The archer fish is trying to catch the catfish."

big K for *all* these catfish." Instead of regressing, Troy is experimenting with writing and language, playing with concepts to figure out how language works.

Day 14: Troy abandons picture labeling and writes a string of letters, which he read to me: The archer fish is trying to catch the catfish. (See Figure 6–18.) Without ever making eye contact with me, Troy tells about a family fishing trip. He describes his cat sitting on the bank watching the fish (upper right-hand corner of the drawing), the catfish (on the right), and the archer fish (on the left) with a butterfly under it. I ask Troy why the butterfly is in the water and he explains that the archer fish has caught the butterfly by spitting at the butterfly to shoot it down. I am slightly puzzled even after asking Troy again, and I conclude that fantasy and reality mingle in his mind.

Two years after Troy left my classroom I looked at his writing and my notes from that day. Tracing his work onto a transparency for a conference presentation, I mused about the archer fish and decided to look the term up in my dictionary. I learned the archer fish has "the capacity of ejecting drops of water from its mouth at insects resting on objects over the water, causing them to fall so that it can capture them." I looked at Troy's drawing. A line extends from the mouth of the archer fish to represent the stream of water. My knowledge, not Troy's, was incomplete and my assumptions about his thinking were wrong. Troy continued to be my teacher two years after he left my classroom.

Reluctant Writers

Occasionally, a child comes to the classroom who is reluctant to write. This problem often doesn't surface immediately, for the child will draw and write something—a house, a rainbow, a design—during the first days of school. Soon the writing stagnates. For days and days the child draws rainbows or designs or just sits and stalls. Many factors influence classroom attitudes and performance; a child's life in the classroom can't be separated from the environment of his home, the interactions with others in his life, or his physical well-being.

Ben drew designs and wrote very little in the writing workshop. He often seemed puzzled when I stopped to talk to him. Although he was agreeable and pleasant and even nodded in acknowledgment when I made suggestions, there appeared to be little progress. Ben drew more and more designs. Occasionally, if I sat beside him, encouraging him while he worked, he drew a truck or a car. Eventually, Ben's parents and I considered his frequent ear infections, had his hearing tested, and uncovered a hearing loss. Ben did not follow through with tasks because he heard only snatches of classroom talk. He certainly didn't hear sounds in order to write corresponding letters. Fortunately, Ben's hearing problems were correctable, though it was late in the school year before the physical problems were cleared up.

Carol Zartman, a first-grade teacher and an exceptionally good observer and listener, told the story of a little boy who struggled every
day to write. "I just didn't know how to help this little guy. I didn't
want to step in and take over, direct him in what to write, because I
knew he'd never get involved. One day I wrote his dictated story and I
saw how many ideas he had in his head. He just couldn't get them
on paper. Then another teacher, who was visiting my classroom, suggested I give him a 'secretary,' a peer who would write down his stories
and get him started. It worked." The designated secretary not only
wrote the boy's words but also showed him how to get his ideas
on paper, both through demonstration and explanation of how she
wrote. For a period of time the child secretary started the boy's
writing each day, then turned it over to him to complete. He patterned
his writing after hers and, after a time, began writing on his own without her.

Anyone who writes knows about stalling tactics. There are times
when I'll do just about anything to avoid writing, including major
household tasks, ones I'd usually avoid. Children do this too. Joey
sharpens his pencil, chats with Craig, pauses to browse through a
book, and generally avoids getting down to work. I watch and wait
and finally choose the time to confront him with a matter-of-fact
reality. "You have a choice," I say. "You may write now or later at
recess." It's amazing how many young writers decide to use the workshop
time.

Sometimes emotional factors block a child's ability to write. Marcy
cried silently every time the class did something new, whether it
was writing or removing pages from the math workbook. She whispered
only "I can't" when asked what was wrong. During writing workshop
she stretched bland topics out for days. One day I presented a mini-
lesson demonstrating brainstorming to find a topic. Again, the silent
tears rolled down Marcy's face. I stooped in front of her desk and she said,
"I can't."

"Do you live alone?" I asked in a no-nonsense voice.

"No."

"Who lives with you?"

"My mom."

"Write it down," I said. Marcy wrote "Mom."

"Anyone else?"

"I have a brother."

"Write it down." Marcy wrote her brother's name.

"Anyone else?"

"My cat." Marcy wrote "cat" without my direction.

Then she looked up and said, "I used to have a dad, but he died when I was a baby."

"Oh yeah?" I replied, barely audibly. Marcy started telling the stories of her dad, stories she had been told over and over again about the father she didn't remember. I listened. A few moments later, she wrote about her dad and at the end of the workshop, shared her story with the class. The tears stopped that day. Marcy confidently participated in *all* the class activities, especially writing.

However, more times than not the emotional baggage children carry continues to hamper their involvement in classroom activities—especially writing—all year. Rich drew designs and wrote only a few words. Occasionally (with a lot of one-on-one urging and support on my part) he wrote a narrative. The only piece all year that I saw him initiate and become truly involved with was a story of his Christmas trip to Florida with his Dad. A custody battle between Rich's divorced parents was brewing. Even though the issue would not surface for several months, the strain affected Rich's classroom performance and was evident in his rather cursory involvement in classroom activities, especially writing.

Marcy and Rich remind me of the vulnerability of all writers no matter their age. No writer knows what will emerge when she brings pencil to paper. Writers need environments where their first tentative explorations on paper will be not only accepted but also valued. Writers need to experience safety in that environment. Reluctant writers perhaps sense the vulnerability. They know instinctively that writing can be risky.

There's no one strategy or set of procedures for reluctant writers. I try one approach after another, hoping to find something that works. These children remind us of what all children need: honesty, space, caring, and our continuous efforts to help them help themselves.

These brief stories of children moving into a daily writing workshop are a mere sampling of the diversity I've observed in child writers. Just as no two children write identical stories, even on the same topic, so no two children move into the writing process in the same way. In ten years of observing first-grade writers I can attest that every child has been different. This was the central finding in Graves's research on children's writing. It is precisely the diversity he observed that makes this teaching so invigorating, so demanding, and so rewarding. I find it difficult to respond to questions such as "What do you do about the child who . . . ?" because the solution that enables one child is likely to fail for another despite similar characteristics. I want to avoid categorizing and labeling differences between children. If I slot children into pigeonholes, I recreate the blinders that hide each child's dynamic learning process, the blinders that existed under programmed instruction. My job is to listen and understand, to coach and encourage, but also to remain open to the unexpected. My responses must be as fresh and new as the wonderfully diverse stories the children create.

CHAPTER 7

The Mini-Lesson

By the third week of September, most groups of children have enthusiastically produced longer and longer stories to accompany their drawings. However, I've learned not to be lulled into complacency by the rose-colored memories of previous classes. The histories of former classes remind me of what is possible, but I must always respond to the needs of a new group and the individuals within that group. One year the children became initially involved in the writing workshop, but after three weeks produced little actual writing. Even the strongest students added only a brief sentence to accompany their drawings, and they quickly wrote this sentence during the last few minutes of the workshop. They rarely, if ever, reread the words they wrote despite my strong urging. I knew these children could do more; yet my encouragement and strong nudges (which by now were verging on imperatives) produced no results.

On Friday Amy told me that her mom was signing her up for "writing lessons." Later that day I learned from Amy's mom that the writing lessons were, in fact, art lessons. Could it be the children viewed drawing as "writing"? Had I inadvertently communicated this concept during the first days of school? True, drawing forms a large part of young children's writing and can serve as a rehearsal for writing, but the research on early literacy by Harste, Woodward, and Burke (1984) demonstrates that by age three children know the difference between writing and drawing. How could I get more writing from these youngsters?

I mulled over this question throughout the weekend. On Saturday I heard Glenda Bissex deliver a keynote address at a Connecticut conference. Glenda talked about reading/writing connections and about teacher as researcher—learning in one's own classroom. Our classrooms are our texts, she reminded us, and teachers look for the anomalies, those puzzlements when things don't quite follow the expected plan. Anomalies provide us with opportunities to grow by learning from our students.

Her talk jogged my thinking and got me considering my classroom in a new light. On the flight home I thought again about my current anomaly. The children dutifully completed their drawings in writing workshop—just as they had learned to churn out many products in nursery school and kindergarten. But they lacked investment in their work. They regarded writing workshop as another school activity for the purpose of doing another paper for the teacher (of this I was sure). Glenda had expressed concern that students may write to produce something to be corrected rather than something to be read. It occurred to me that possibly these first graders did not think of their drawing/writing as *communication*, as something meant to be *understood* by others. In prior years, children had quickly recognized that their writing held meaning to be shared with many readers. This group was different. These children, I theorized, probably did not write the ideas they talked about or incorporate suggestions from either me or their peers because they lacked a sense of audience other than the teacher. Subsequently, they made little investment in either the process or the product. What had I done or neglected to do that contributed to this? I had no idea, but I began to see that the essential reading/writing connection was missing.

How to jar them out of this rut? How could I help them experience their own writing as something to be read, which needs to make sense to the reader, to anticipate audiences for their writing and, in turn, invest more in their work? After some thought I decided to write a story in front of the class and involve the children as a responding audience. This would be Monday morning's mini-lesson.

The term *mini-lesson* is rather new to education. Lucy Calkins (1986), who first used the term, finds that "the ritual of beginning every writing workshop with a whole-group gathering brings form and unity to the workshop" (p. 168). Mini-lessons do that in my classroom; they get us started each day and direct the attention of writers to some aspect of writing. Lucy also speaks for the "simplicity and brevity of a good mini-lesson." Simplicity and brevity are essential; a student teacher in my classroom once presented a mini-lesson that lasted thirty-five minutes, leaving the children overwhelmed with too many concepts and only ten minutes remaining to write.

Most of the mini-lessons for our writing workshops are brief—sometimes only a minute in length and rarely over five minutes. I present focussed information concisely and directly. Good mini-lessons also respond to the writers; the content grows out of daily observation of the children and helps the community work together or nurtures their development as writers. Because of this responsive quality, I can't plan mini-lessons days ahead of time. Like the lesson I was planning now, the purpose emerged from the context of my classroom at a particular time. Because a mini-lesson in which I write is likely to run longer than other lessons, I decided to start the workshop a few minutes earlier than usual. Also, I drew a picture of an airplane in a night sky before class began because drawing in front of the children would consume too much time and because I wanted to downplay the significance of the drawing.

On Monday morning I taped my airplane picture to the chalkboard and began the mini-lesson by describing the sketch: the plane, the stars and moon to show it was nighttime, the black earth below with lights resembling glowing campfires.

"You drawed a good airplane," someone remarked. I could sense that the children felt I was finished. Their response confirmed my prior assessment of the situation: drawing a picture was enough. Now to take them forward.

"Thank you. Now I'm going to write my story," and I turned to the paper taped to the chalkboard and wrote: I WT N A ARPN

As I wrote, I spoke each word, stretching it out, listening for the sounds to determine which letter to write, just as the children did. When I came to airplane I commented, "I know *airplane* begins with an *A*. I've seen that word in lots of books." I wrote the letter and continued. By talking as I wrote I let the children hear my thinking and I demonstrated ways to determine what letters to write: connecting letters to sounds or remembering letters from words I've seen. I reread the completed sentence, pointing to each word as I encouraged the children to do when they read their own writing, then turned to the class and said, "Do you like my story?"

For a moment there was silence. A child commented again on my drawing. But I wanted the focus on the words. "What do you think of my *story*? Does it make sense? Is there anything else you want to know?" They looked puzzled. "Let me read it to you," I said. "Writers read their writing, you know, in order to decide if it makes sense or if there's anything they left out." I read the sentence again.

"Where did you go?" someone asked.

"To Connecticut."

"When did you go?"

"On Friday night." I assumed the role of a child answering only what was required without elaboration. I waited for the question that would open up the story.

"I went on an airplane to California once," came a response from Greg, setting off comments about airplane trips from several children.

"But about my story," I interjected, "I want to know if there's anything else I could put in it."

Jeff raised his hand. "What is it like to fly on an airplane?"

"Fun! I liked it." I was so much into my role right now that I replied with a typical child answer even though Jeff asked a leading question, one I could feel cracking into my writer's caution. His question was one that I had been asking in writing conferences: What was that like for you?

Jeff paused momentarily but then came right back. "Yes, but what was it *like* to fly on the airplane?"

Something in the way Jeff asked his question this time, not a routine question but an imploring, genuine question, coming from someone who really wanted to know, caused me to search for the best answer I could give. In my mind's eye I sat again in the seat awaiting takeoff, and I described the moments I now relived. When I finished Jeff said, "Ahhh. Now I know."

"Should I write that? Do you think this would make my writing better, more interesting for someone to read?"

Jeff shrugged his shoulders. "I don't know. I guess. Yeah, why don't you write it."

I suddenly felt the choice I was forever turning back to writers. This was risky. But I decided. I turned to the board and wrote:

WE FASTN R STBLT The Pln
WT TO the rNWayThn it srtd
to GO FST I CD FL the Wels
going rNd We rcd dN the rNWay
and TN We WT up up up. I CD
FL My Ers popt SO I SWIlod hd.

I continued writing with invented spelling in order to maintain the connection with the children and their writing. Also, I wanted to be careful to avoid a perfect spelling since I was just getting some of the children to set aside their worries about spelling correctly as they wrote. When I finished writing I reread the entire piece then turned to the class and said, "Is my writing more interesting now? Do you think it's more interesting to listen to and for someone to read?"

"Yes!" came a chorus response.

I stepped back into my teacher role and asked, "When I read this piece, could you get any picture in your own head of me or the airplane?"

"Yes!" The group teemed with energy.

"I could see that plane go up, up, up!" commented Greg as his hand imitated the plane's ascent, and he punctuated his sentence with the sound of an airplane's zooming takeoff.

"Good writers try to include information so that readers will know just what it was like to ride in a plane, or play football, or whatever it is they're writing about. To do that, they think about the time they're writing about and put down the things that they can see in their heads, so then when readers read the writing they will get those pictures in their heads too. You could do this in writing—add information so that other people will know what it was like, so they will get pictures in *their* heads." The lesson was done. It had taken just under fifteen minutes.

In part I had paraphrased Peter Elbow (1973) describing "movies of the mind," a way to explain how writers communicate meaning (the movies in their minds) through effective writing that allows readers to construct movies in their own minds. "Words," wrote Elbow, "don't transport the contents of my head into yours, they give you a set of directions for building meaning, we end up with similar things in our head—that is, we communicate" (p. 152). We cannot hope to *tell* our meaning to others through words, we must *show* meaning through words that create images.

The focus of the mini-lesson had developed into "showing not telling," one characteristic of good writing. More important, this lesson had been "showing not telling" too. Many mini-lessons are directive, *telling*, but this one was an active demonstration to *show* the children, to provide an experience with writing and audience. When I began the lesson I didn't know what I would write. My writing emerged in front of the children and with the help of their questions. Their genuine interest encouraged me, the writer. I felt the power of an affirming, responsive audience. I became involved in writing about the plane flight and I actually wanted to continue this piece of writing and share it with these children. I hoped the children would begin to anticipate audiences for their writing and expand their pieces.

That morning Greg wrote about his airplane trip to California, a piece he continued for two days. The mini-lesson marked a breakthrough for this writing community. Even though the only change evident at first was in Greg's writing, I could sense the children understood something new about how writing worked. The mini-lesson provided a context that I referred to as I conferred with children in the days ahead. "Could you add that to your piece? You know, like I did in my airplane story?" At last, energy emerged within this group of writers.

On Tuesday morning I decided to return to the airplane story for the next day's mini-lesson. I started by reading what I'd written the day before. "Writers can get into their writing by reading what they wrote yesterday," I explained. While reading the story, I experienced the plane trip again and, at that moment, remembered a previously forgotten incident. I quickly taped a new sheet of paper to the chalkboard and wrote:

Wn MN STD to gt of beks he ws
on the wrg plN. So the plN wnt
bk to the gat and he gt off.
Thn we had to wat to tk off.

I read my addition to the class and added that the man wanted to go to Rochester, not Hartford, but the captain made the announcement to the passengers after the man left the plane so as not to embarrass him. "I forgot to put that part in," I said. "But when I read this I remembered this whole part I didn't put in yesterday. I don't know why. I just forgot. That's the way writers work."

The children nodded and one child added, "You could still probably add that if you wanted to." Things were looking up in this writing workshop. Two days later a child asked how my plane story was coming. For Friday's mini-lesson I taped the three-page story to the chalkboard, read it, then noted that the last part was out of order. I reread and asked the children to help me find the spot where the incident about the man fit. They easily located it just before the part where the plane started to go fast. I drew a large star at that place, circled the section about the man, and explained that when readers came to this star they should go to the circled part and read it next.

Not one child picked up on moving information within their own pieces. However, the class had been exposed to the idea and, when sequencing information came up in editing conferences two months later, the experience of this day provided a background for understanding the process.

The focus of each of the mini-lessons on the airplane story was very specific: showing not telling, adding information, sequencing information, reading one's own writing as part of the writing process. And writing in front of the children demonstrated tips for their writing. A few I addressed indirectly were:

- spacing between words
- listening for sounds and using invented spelling
- using drawing as a starting point for writing
- beginning to put periods in when the writing pauses
- recognizing words we can spell, such as *we, the, so, to*
- including details, specific information
- recalling visual spelling (*A* in airplane)

Each of these items might be the focus of a future mini-lesson at some time. I covered many issues in passing as I moved through the piece, but to point out and reinforce all of them would overload the children and confuse them. I know the children will observe and learn from the entire demonstration, not just the focussed issue; they intuitively soak up many other concepts. Children learn from *all* the demonstrations by the others around them, both the formal and the informal ones that occur all day long. They take what makes sense to them, what touches their interest or needs at a given time, and incorporate that experience—*as they perceive it*—into their growing understanding about the world. In many ways, this mini-lesson contained something for everyone. But precisely what each child took away from those ten minutes, I will never know. The central issue of this mini-lesson, however, had been the connection between reading and writing as creative communication processes. Stimulating an awareness of the vital and dynamic relationship between these two aspects of written language would serve all learning in this classroom.

My airplane story broke the logjam. By the second day, a few children followed my model and began writing more than one sentence. Others began when I reminded them during a conference: "Do you plan to add those things you've just told me to your writing—like I did in my airplane story?" "Oh yeah, I think I will." Still others watched their classmates, and when they saw them attempting to include more details in their stories, they drew inspiration from their peers.

In the days that followed, the children's growing involvement with writing opened up possibilities for more mini-lessons. Two weeks later I wrote in front of the class again, focussing on information gleaned from observing the children writing. By now most of the children attempted to add to their writing, but since they did not always reread what they wrote, repetitions, sentence fragments, and gaps in information appeared in their compositions. The writing was incoherent.

I imitated their writing with my own brief story:
"I went to Park City. I had fun. I like Park. I think. We had fun. My son Nathan too. I had fun." Then I faced the group and waited.

"Aren't you going to read it?" a child asked with the same outrageous teasing tone I'd heard myself use with them.

"Oh, should I read my story?"

"Of course," everyone agreed, so I read my story, pointing to every word as I went. I could hear them suppress giggles behind me.

"It doesn't make sense."

"And there's too many *funs.*"

"Well, what would you want to read in this story?" I asked.

"We could ask you questions and then maybe you'd get some ideas," someone suggested. The class quickly produced a series of questions that brought information: What store did you go to? Did you buy anything? Did you go to lunch? I acknowledged that there was a lot more I could include in this writing.

I concluded the mini-lesson with a summary statement. "To write something for someone else to want to read, the writing has to make sense, be interesting, and have good information. One way that writers work on this is by reading the writing and thinking about these things as they read."

A couple days later I asked the class why they read their writing as they worked on it. They produced the following reasons, which we listed on chart paper in their words:

1. so I will remember it
2. to see if I want to revise it (change anything)
3. to see if I left anything out and to see if it makes sense
4. so I know how to read it in sharing circle

In the next week I saw children reading and rereading their writing and adding details to enhance their stories.

Then I noticed children writing the same line twice. I watched carefully and realized the repetition resulted from the reading. A child wrote, stopped and read, then continued writing by repeating the last few words, the ones freshest in memory. To nail down the exact word that comes next could be very difficult! Time for another mini-lesson. I wrote a very quick story one Monday morning.

"My son Nathan broke his hand broke his hand at the football game. Someone stepped on his hand." (I chose not to use invented spelling in this lesson because I wanted the lesson to focus on the repetitious line.) Of course, the children quickly noticed the repetition when I read the story. I demonstrated a way to deal with this by drawing a line through the unwanted words.

When I stopped to confer with Max during writing workshop he said, "I had some extra words—ones that were in here twice—so I lined them out like you did."

That same day Amy commented, "Oh, it doesn't make sense. They won't know *why* my dad was there." She added clarifying information to the end of her story which, of course, was out of logical sequence. I chose to ignore this fact; Amy's accomplishment was sufficient. To now ask her to move the information might have overloaded and discouraged her.

This series of mini-lessons, which occurred over a three-week period, nudged the children into writing beyond drawing, expanded their writing, involved them in rereading their words in anticipation of an audience, and established an investment in writing as communication. I can't pinpoint the precise moment when the children became invested in writing; the process emerged over time. But I knew that true involvement would make the difference in writing and reading development in this classroom. I had presumed a reading/writing connection that did not exist in the minds of these children. Mini-lessons provided the mode to create and nurture this basic concept. But golly! Process-approach teaching can be complex.

Learning About Mini-Lessons

One of my first concerns the year I began daily writing workshops was the mini-lesson. Could such short lessons be effective? How would I come up with topics? Hearing that lessons would come from teacher observations in the classroom wasn't much assurance. Certainly, I could see some topics for mini-lessons—but something for *every day?*

During the first two years in writing workshops, I frequently found myself at a loss for mini-lesson topics. I heard myself repeating lessons on punctuation or capital letters or topic selection or minor revision strategies (mostly how to insert words or move information around). I felt woefully inadequate at teaching my students how to write.

Don Graves reminds teachers that children direct their attention to the concerns the teacher addresses. If mini-lessons deal primarily with the traditional skills, children will be concerned first with correct mechanics. But if we deal mostly with content, with qualities of good writing and with strategies to develop writing processes, children will work on these issues. I remember an exchange with Chris during the first year I used the writing workshop. In the first days of school I showed the children how to use a caret to insert letters, words, or chunks of information. I also talked about leaving spaces between words. Chris read his work to me when I stopped at his desk.

"I am near a pond and there is a duck and it caught a fish." (See Figure 7–1.)

I responded to the content then looked at the writing. Puzzled, I pointed to the written line and said, "Tell me about these zig-zaggy lines."

"That's—what did you call it—'celery'? You know, like you did on the board when you want to put something in."

"Oh, you mean carets."

"Yeah, carets. I put those in because it means put a space here. Like you told us to do."

"Like you told us to do." Those words still ring in my head. Two things happened with Chris: He experimented with a strategy by overusing that strategy and he followed his teacher's directions. If the teacher liked these little marks, he obviously reasoned, then she was sure to be pleased with an abundance of them. Chris helped me see that young writers will focus on teacher priorities. If I was to help writers I would have to learn more about good writing and shift my emphasis there. Writing is more than a neat, skill-perfect final product. I had a lot to learn. I still do.

Slowly, the realization dawned that I wasn't really teaching children how to write in the traditional sense but, rather, creating a climate where they could develop as writers and mini-lessons enriched this climate. I began emphasizing the content of the writing, showing children strategies to try. Most children did not immediately pick up on the strategy that was the focus of a mini-lesson. Sometimes days went by without a sign that anyone had heard a word I said. Then out of the blue a child would say, "See I did this like you did when you were writing the other day." Many of

Figure 7–1

*Chris's writing:
"I am near a
pond and there is
a duck and it
caught a fish."*

these comments referred to the mini-lessons in which I wrote in front of the class. I don't believe that the majority of mini-lessons ought to be the teacher writing in front of the group. The effectiveness would diminish and the lesson would consume too much time. I suspect that the children remembered those lessons because I presented demonstrations based on concerns or needs I saw as these young writers worked. The lessons were not prescriptions planned days ahead of time but connected to issues writers were experiencing at the time. I suspect the lessons were effective also because I wrote as a writer struggling with her material, not as a teacher performing for the children.

I could not always come up with daily mini-lessons during those first couple of years, but the children survived and still developed as writers. In fact, I've often thought that because I presented a mini-lesson only when I had a strong focus in mind, the children tended to take heed. They remembered the less frequent but focussed mini-lessons. Don't misunderstand. I'm not advocating that teachers downplay the importance of mini-lessons but when I began daily writing workshops so much was new to me, I needed to be easy on myself. Forcing a mini-lesson just to have one every day wasn't helpful to me or the students. As I became more experienced with writing workshop and learned more about the qualities of good writing, the muddied water cleared (somewhat) and I saw new ways to help my students.

Where do the topics for a mini-lesson come from? Graves, Giacobbe, Calkins all tell us to follow the lead of the children. I understood the concept logically, but I had to experience observing and listening to children for myself in order to discover mini-lesson topics embedded in the writing workshop. Now, when I see children wanting to add information but abandoning the idea because the page is full, I recognize the possibility for several mini-lessons on strategies for adding to a piece. When children rush to get paper or line up to use the stapler, I know I need to address procedures for managing materials. When children are stuck, not knowing how to proceed with a topic, I know that the time is right to present ways that writers deal with this situation, such as abandoning a piece and moving on, or setting it aside for a few days, or talking with another writer, or rereading the piece. When a child incorporates conversation for the first time, I see the opportunity to share this new technique with classmates. Gradually, potential topics for mini-lessons become easier to recognize.

To help writers, I also had to hone my own writing skills and my awareness of good writing. My background in English studies and teaching English in high school helped some, but most of the schooling in English studies revolved around literature. Grammar books that accompanied writing courses weren't much help. I had developed my own process of writing, and I had some ideas about good writing, but I hadn't a clue how to help these first graders develop as writers. I had work to do! Here are some of the steps I took.

1. I began reading about writing starting with books Giacobbe advocated. Don Murray's books, *A Writer Teaches Writing, Learning by Teaching, Write to Learn*, and William Zinsser's *On Writing Well* helped me articulate qualities of good writing and the craft of teaching writing. I found it helpful to read these books *while I was working on a piece of writing* rather than studying them while preparing to write. In Zinsser, for example, I read about educational jargon, and when I turned to my writing I did so with a new desire to write more clearly.

2. I began to take notice of techniques authors used, such as strong leads, the structure of a piece of writing, word choices. I found myself talking about them with other readers and writers. A friend lent me Harry Crews's book, *A Childhood, the Biography of a Place.* The next time we met, both of us were eager to talk about the opening line of that book: "My first memory is of a time ten years before I was born, and the memory takes place where I have never been and involves my daddy whom I never knew." Wow!

3. I worked on my own writing. I tried out strategies and techniques gleaned from points one and two above, and I got helpful responses from someone who knew more about writing than I did. I continue to learn from editors and responders who make refinements in my pieces after I've taken them as far as I can. I'm grateful to the writer friend who wrote "Choose one or the other" when I used two verbs when one would do, and reminded me to "get out of the passive voice" when I'd slipped into old writing habits.

4. I listened to and observed the children in my classroom and paid attention to what and how they wrote and what they said about writing. I shared what I was learning about writing with the children and we talked about writing as fellow practitioners.

I don't think I could have learned how to teach writing from a book or from a scope and sequence program. I had to get inside the writing process myself, through my own writing and through talking and thinking about writing. Once this happened I saw topics for mini-lessons all the time. I also understood that mini-lessons are not just objective lessons to be presented once and considered done ("covered," in school curriculum jargon). They are far more than skills. Mini-lessons help writers develop and craft writing in order to become skillful writers.

A Sample Mini-Lesson Topic: Leads

Writers strive for effective leads to begin their writing, ways to capture the interest of the reader and pull the reader into the writing. First graders tend to begin their stories the same way every day. Each child quickly falls into a pattern for starting the writing: "I went . . ." "I am . . ." "I like to . . ." "We are . . ." The children chance upon these beginnings during the first days of writing workshop and stick with them.

I begin addressing leads by pointing out the variety of ways authors begin their writing. The natural opportunity for such discussion occurs as I read to children. We notice how authors begin books and how those opening lines set the tone for what follows. Writers hook the reader, I tell the children. Like a fisherman, the writer offers inviting bait, enticing the reader to read on. The concluding lines in books get readers off the hook, leaving them with a sense of completion. We notice ways authors craft their work through leads and endings.

The playful tone in the opening lines of Walter Piper's *The Little Engine That Could* sets the scene for this story about a little engine, and the famous concluding statement brings closure: "Chug, chug, chug. Puff, puff, puff. Ding-dong, ding-dong. The little train rumbled over the tracks. . . . I thought I could. I thought I could. I thought I could."

There are endless examples of leads that hook and endings that unhook.

- *Ghost's Hour, Spook's Hour,* by Eve Bunting: "When I woke up it was really dark. Something went Wooooooo outside my window. . . . I held his warm paw and Mom's hand and counted moon shadows on the ceiling till I fell asleep."
- Byron Barton's *Machines at Work*: "Hey, you guys! Let's get to work. . . . Let's go home. More work tomorrow."
- Eric Carle's *The Very Busy Spider*: "Early one morning the wind blew a spider across the field. A thin, silky thread trailed from her body. . . . She had fallen asleep. It had been a very, very busy day."
- And the opening and closing lines from *Teammates,* Peter Golenboch's picture book about Jackie Robinson and Pee Wee Reese and the integration of major league baseball: "Once upon a time in America, when automobiles were black and looked like tanks and laundry was white and hung on clotheslines to dry, there were two wonderful baseball leagues that no longer exist. They were called the Negro Leagues. . . . 'I am standing by him,' Pee Wee Reese said to the world. 'This man is my teammate.' "

When we read folktales and fairy tales the children noticed that these stories began and ended in similar, somewhat predictable ways. Paul Zelinsky's version of *Rumpelstiltskin* opens with, "Once there was a poor miller who had a beautiful daughter." It ends, "And he was never heard from again." James Marshall's *Red Riding Hood* begins, "A long time ago in a simple cottage beside the deep, dark wood, there lived a pretty child called Red Riding Hood." The book ends with the line, "And she never did."

When we read a book for the first time, our first and most important purpose was always the enjoyment and the meaning we took from the book. But when we reread, as we did with nearly every book, we looked at the author's techniques. Having our literature time just before writing workshop turned out to be a boon. We read and talked about books, about authors and their writing, and then moved into writing workshop.

I often discovered mini-lesson topics for writing embedded in the literature time, and it took only a few seconds at the beginning of the workshop to remind students of a particular writing strategy we'd discussed recently. The first mini-lessons on leads were reminders such as this. Other times a mini-lesson connected more directly to the children's writing. On the morning after our field trip to Pumpkinland at a local farm market, I wrote an opening sentence about the trip similar to what the children would write: "We went to Pumpkinland." Then I asked the children for ideas of other ways to begin the writing. They produced the following list:

Our class went to Pumpkinland.

Both first graders went to Pumpkinland in our school.

Once upon a time I went to Pumpkinland with my class.

Mrs. Riddle's and Mrs. Avery's first-grade classes went to Pumpkinland.

We went on a hayride.

The children were beginning to stretch their concept of beginnings. Though I still saw lots of "I am . . ." and "I like . . ." in their writing, I also saw them considering other options.

Periodic mini-lessons on leads continued throughout the year. Once I wrote two leads of my own, one a boring statement and the other a vivid description of the same event. I asked the children which was better and why. "The second," they agreed, "because it has more information," and "we can get a picture in our heads." ("Picture in our heads" became a familiar term, one we used to talk about good writing that "shows not tells," that created images for readers.) Another day I read several leads from books familiar to the class and we noted the differences in the ways the authors started their books. We had talked about these leads before, but taking a few minutes to look at them again renewed the children's thinking about improving their own writing.

One day in February I began a mini-lesson by writing three beginnings to a story about a skunk that went through our backyard the night before. I composed the lines in front of the class by thinking back to the experience of the night before and describing it from three different approaches:

1. A warm fire made the room cozy. A strange smell suddenly filled the air.
2. "What's that smell?" I said.
3. I sat in the chair. For a moment I wondered what the smell was that filled the room this cold February night.

Then I turned to the class and said, "These are three different ways to start any story. I wrote the first by thinking of my senses, how I was feeling: warm and cozy and then the smell. The second starts with what I said, a quotation. And the third tells what I was doing and thinking. All are about the same moment but they're just different ways to describe that moment."

After discussing the three leads I concluded by saying, "Sometimes writers think about a good beginning when they start writing. Sometimes they come back and write a better beginning when they revise."

The children's writing demonstrated their growing awareness of good writing. In April, Chris, who had been concerned about carets and spaces, began his book about his mother: "Do you know what I think the best thing in the world is? It's not Disneyland or the movies. It's my mom!"

When I look back at the leads and endings of the children's books, I can see their involvement and the crafting of their work. Amy's "There's a Cat in the Bathtub" begins (after Amy experimented with three opening sentences): "Splash! Patches fell in the bathtub! The water was very deep." The story ends with the lines, "Mommy said, 'It is time to go to bed.' I kissed Patches goodnight and I went to sleep." Ellen followed the model of folktales when she wrote her own fairy tale, "The Very, Very Hungry Princess." Like a folktale, her story begins and ends with the predictable pattern: "Once upon a time, there lived a very, very hungry princess. Her name was Chickie. . . . And she has never been seen again."

Atwell (1987) described similar lessons with leads with her eighth graders. Topics such as leads come up naturally when we write ourselves, become aware of how writing is done, and work with writers in classrooms.

Mini-Lessons to Pull It All Together

Sometimes I use the mini-lesson to compile group-composed lists of what children have experienced through their writing. This kind of mini-lesson helps them articulate their growing knowledge about writing. In late fall, when Kristin published a book which the entire class loved, I asked them to tell me what Kristin had done that made her piece of writing effective. As children contributed their ideas I wrote them down on a chart.

Kristin's story had:
1. good information
2. clear sentences
3. a title that fit the story
4. an interesting lead
5. a good ending
6. answered the question words—who, what, when, where, why, how

The chart hung in the room all year, providing a checklist for writers. When I unroll this chart now, several years later, I'm surprised by the last line on question words because I haven't used this phrase in recent years. At that time I used an old teaching strategy of reminding children to address these questions as they wrote. I've dropped that procedure because the children and I have learned to listen to writers and ask authentic questions: what we need to know to make sense of the writing. I no longer need the structure of question words.

Through the years I've asked children periodically to list the attributes of good writing. My most recent group came up with this list in early March.

Good Writing

1. has a good lead (hooks the reader)

2. makes sense

3. has a good ending (gets the reader off the hook)

4. makes the reader feel a response (happy, angry, sad) or think about something

5. has a good title

6. has strong information

7. has a focus

A group from the previous year produced a remarkably similar list despite many changes in my teaching.

What Makes Good Writing:

1. good lead—get the reader hooked

2. good information—to make it interesting

3. makes sense

4. clear—so the reader can understand

5. gets the reader off the hook at the end

6. interesting words

7. good editing

First-grade children can craft their writing and they can articulate that craft. I had underestimated their capacity to understand, to assess, and to really work at making their writing better. They talked about the crafting process when I conferred with them. Lori said, "I don't think I did so good on my picture of people sitting down, but I really like my lead." And then she read, "One morning, bright and early, my mom and I went to breakfast. We went in and sat down. The waitress said that I looked cold!" Lori looked at me and said, "I spelled 'waitress' wrong. I put a D but it's supposed to be a T." She crossed out the D and wrote above it T R. "There that's better." These young writers could juggle several concerns simultaneously. As writers and thinkers they could keep up with the best of them.

Types of Mini-Lessons

Mary Ellen Giacobbe (1988), based on Atwell (1987), categorizes mini-lessons into four areas:

1. Procedures: operation and management of the writing workshop

2. Strategies writers use: techniques for writers that facilitate the writing process, such as discovering topics

3. Qualities of good writing: considerations to improve the writing, such as using a strong lead, ending effectively, using conversation, eliminating clutter and excess words, using adjectives and adverbs sparingly, selecting pronouns, focussing the writing

4. Skills: conventions of English usage that are important to help readers with meaning

Traditionally, writing instruction in school has emphasized the skill component and skills became the thrust of many mini-lessons during my first couple of years with a writing workshop. Eventually, the dominance of skill lessons diminished; I present them now as I see writers needing a particular skill. A skill mini-lesson is short, easy to plan and manage, and less likely to lead to other mini-lessons. I often prepare a couple lessons of this kind and leave them in the substitute teacher folder.

Procedural mini-lessons are scattered throughout the school year but concentrated during the first few weeks of school. Often I feel a tension during the first days of writing workshop as I try to balance procedural lessons with lessons addressing writing itself. It is important to establish workshop procedures early, but getting children thinking about good writing early in the year sets a standard for a writing classroom. Throughout the year, most mini-lessons deal with strategies writers use and the qualities of good writing.

By studying Graves, Giacobbe, and Calkins and through classroom experience, I've learned that effective mini-lessons are:

1. Short: usually under five minutes; if I anticipate the lesson going longer, I make accommodations accordingly.

2. Focussed: even though several issues may be apparent, I don't emphasize them all in one day.

3. Gentle in tone: light, informing, with humor and playfulness; these lessons are invitations, not mandates.

4. Responsive: the content is determined by the needs of the writers in the classroom.

What follows is a list of some of the mini-lesson topics I have used during a particular school year. This list is neither inclusive nor exclusive, but is included here to provide an example of the range of topics addressed in a primary grade writing workshop.

Possible Mini-Lesson Topics
Procedures:

- writing the title, author's name, and date on writing
- establishing workshop rules
- defining the structure and sequence of the workshop (mini-lesson, writing with conferring, large-group sharing)
- using only one side of the paper to facilitate revision
- managing time in the writing workshop
- identifying ways to respond to writers
- using a writing folder
- suggesting procedures for editing one's writing
- establishing procedures for illustrating a published book

Strategies Writers Use:

- choosing topics
- using books as inspiration for topics
- saving all writing and using it as a resource for future topics or revision
- considering genre and strategies for writing: poetry, biography, autobiography, nonfiction, how-to books, fiction
- reading a journal (kept on a trip) and listing possible topics
- reading old piece for possible revision or new topics
- choosing topics by hearing other writers' pieces (e.g., sleepovers, birthdays)
- rereading for clarity and completeness
- sequencing information by cutting and pasting
- lining out to make changes rather than erasing
- strategies to correct spelling
- inserting information by circling a section and drawing arrow to indicate relocation
- inserting information using an asterisk or caret
- reading one's writing and having a writing conference with oneself
- determining the focus of the writing
- writing from another point of view
- foreshadowing—providing hints of what is to come
- avoiding plagiarism
- reading old pieces

Qualities of Good Writing:

- writing to get "pictures in your head"
- adding information for clarity

- describing a situation through "show not tell"
- deleting information for clarity and conciseness
- focussing writing—too many stories in a piece
- writing effective leads
- writing effective endings
- considering connections between leads and endings
- omitting extra "thens"
- omitting extra "ands"
- eliminating sentences connected with "and" or "then"
- eliminating excessive adjectives (for first graders the word "very")
- writing effective titles

Skills:

- managing space: words too big (only two or three to a page), words too little (run into each other)
- using left-to-right, top-to-bottom progression
- inserting spaces between words
- using capital letters to start sentences
- using captial letters for proper names

- alphabetizing a list (in a glossary, for example)
- using picture dictionaries
- using exclamation marks
- using question marks
- inserting quotation marks
- changing "me and my friend" to "my friend and I" (compound subjects)
- using antonyms
- using synonyms
- using homonyms to refine spelling
- form for writing a letter
- using possessive ('s)
- using plurals (s and es)
- using consistent verb tense
- using "ing" endings
- using "ed" endings
- using commas to separate items in a series
- using comma in greeting and closing of a letter
- inserting punctuation at end of sentences (not at end of lines)
- using a colon
- using nouns as antecedents for pronouns
- using contractions

Even as I categorize these topics (all of which I've addressed with first graders) I realize that they are not focussed, that each topic can be broken down to several parts for the purpose of addressing it in a mini-lesson. Topics also overlap and every topic (with possible exceptions in the proce-dural category) is addressed in several mini-lessons throughout the year, though never in the same way.

Ways to Present Mini-Lessons

The variety of ways to present mini-lesson topics is endless, but I offer some samples.

Direct Presentation

In these types of mini-lessons I convey information by telling the group in direct, concise fashion: "This is your writing folder where you will keep all your writing from now on . . ."

Role Play

I notice individual children procrastinating during writing workshop. I perform an exaggerated role play of their behaviors by opening a writing folder, sifting through the papers, dropping the folder, picking up the papers, going to the pencil sharpener, stopping to talk to several people, sitting down and hunting through paper again, breaking my pencil, heading to the pencil sharpener, until suddenly writing workshop is over and it's time to share. "Oh-oh, I didn't write." The giggles break out midway through my mini-drama, and when I'm finished the children quickly identify with the point of the lesson.

Or I might use a role play for a lesson on punctuation. Children smack a period down at the end of each line on the page so the right-hand margin sports a string of dots down the side. I want to break the pattern quickly. I display a page of my writing on newsprint. "Now, I'm going to put in periods," and I read aloud and stab a dot onto the end of each line.

"No," they cry.

"What's the matter?" I ask in mock horror.

"You've got to *listen* to where the words stop, not just put it at the end of every line. It doesn't make sense," they tell me. I play the inexperienced writer, allowing them to be the experts who teach me. A playful tone and humor helps me make the point. None of them will correctly punctuate their intricately constructed pieces of writing by the end of the year, but the lesson helps them work on punctuation.

Demonstration by a Child

Marlene learned about placing quotation marks in her writing during the publishing process. She taught the class about quotation marks (with a little help from me) by using colored chalk to correctly insert quotation marks in her own sentence, which I had written on the chalkboard, and explaining why she used quotation marks. Marlene was a far more effective teacher for her peers than I would have been.

Compiling Lists from the Group

Like the lists of good writing discussed above, the class periodically participated in brainstorming ideas or knowledge from their experiences in writing workshop. In one mini-lesson we began listing some of our strategies for topic selection, producing a review in chart form that we posted in the classroom.

1. Draw until you think of something.
2. Go to the list of "Ideas" in your folder.
3. Brainstorm a new list of topics—accept anything.
4. Look at your old pieces of writing—you might find something you abandoned that you can revise or write again because you know more about the topic now.
5. Talk with a friend (limit of five minutes).
6. Think of ideas other people wrote about, like birthdays or going to Hershey Park. Write *your* story about this topic.
7. Read one of your published pieces and see if it reminds you of another idea to write about.
8. Look around the room at the books and think of what they reminded you of when we read them.
9. Read a good book for a few minutes (ten-minute limit).
10. Just write "I don't know what to write today because . . ." until something comes to you.

The list prompted children to suggest other strategies they use to keep from being stuck. Mark told us that he made little notes at home or when he went on trips to help him remember things he would want to write later. Jonathan brought in his journal from his trip "up home." (When children go out of school for family trips I staple a dozen sheets of paper with a construction paper cover, title it, for example, "Jonathan's Vacation Journal," and send it along with the child as the homework parents so frequently request when they take their child out of school.) Jonathan read the journal of his trip to the class and later, during the discussion of topic selection, we went through it again and Jonathan came up with ten possible topics he could develop. Five minutes into writing he announced, "I just thought of another—seeing my old cat."

Teacher Writing in Front of the Class

I addressed the issue of focussing writing with this kind of approach. I composed a brief draft of two stories obviously connected together. One year I wrote about a family vacation in Maine and about taking Nathan to college after we came home. The children understood that the two incidents were really different stories and that a good writer would separate them. The children began to observe during the sharing circles: "I think you have two stories in this piece of writing."

Telling Past Classroom Experiences

I tell the children about the boy in my class several years ago who wrote about visiting his sister in Colorado. The piece began when the family got up in the morning, continued as they loaded the car, drove to the airport, got their tickets, boarded the plane, and flew to Colorado. But he wasn't done there. The story went on and on and on, telling about skiing, going to the movies, his sister's apartment. " 'And then . . .' 'And then . . .' It got so boring," I tell the children, "because he told everything about his trip to Colorado! And when he was done even he didn't care about it anymore."

I still remember how this youngster finally learned the concept of focussing. All my efforts to dissuade him from telling everything about his trip had failed. When he got ready to publish it, he insisted the entire story be published. As a last resort I sat him down with two of the more patient students in the class and asked him to read the piece to them. It took him a half hour! Meanwhile, I moved on to confer with other students. Once in a while, one of the listeners caught my attention and rolled her eyes with an "I don't believe this" expression. I smiled an acknowledgment and, when he finished reading, joined them at the table.

"Well," began one student somewhat hesitantly, "it's a little long." I nodded. The other peer continued.

"I thought so too. I got tired of listening. I'd probably get tired of reading. It's longer than I can read!"

Then we talked about choosing some information and focussing the piece. The young writer went back and eliminated whole sections of his story. He saved them for possible future stories, but for the publication of this writing, he pared the writing down considerably. This child talked to the class later about this process and laughingly told everyone throughout the year about the time he wrote "everything into a very boring story."

Earlier that same year, a child from an upper grade came into our classroom to read the book he had authored. Patiently, we sat and listened as the story moved from one incident to another. My first graders had become fidgety as they listened and looked to me to stop the reading. Good writing resembles a string of pearls, graded and carefully put together so that each blends and leads to the next to form a beautiful whole. The writing we heard that morning seemed more like someone picking up one bead after another, telling us a little bit about it, and then putting it down only to reach for another that only slightly resembled the first. That experience had a connection to the Colorado story. The author recognized the connection, laughed at himself, and revised. He became our authority on focussing writing and eagerly reminded the others of the problems encountered by writing too much. I tell this story year after year (without identifying the young writer). It makes the point.

None of the pioneers—researchers or teachers—who opened the doors to the teaching of writing provided us with prescriptive lessons. None of them has produced a book of mini-lessons. They know, because they truly understand the nature of the writing process, that such a book would become a formula written by an outsider unfamiliar with the diversity and uniqueness of the writers in a specific community. On some days I wished for such a book; now I'm grateful I didn't have one. What I did have were the demonstrations of expert teachers and an invitation from these innovative educators to develop an expertise with my own students, to learn about these children and about writing from these children.

My teaching is rooted in responding to writers. I doubt if I'll ever use the specific format of the lessons I've described in this chapter again. The stories of these mini-lessons belong to classes of the past. New groups will require their own lessons. The children will write new stories; I must present responsive lessons that are just as new. I share these lessons as examples that may evoke new lessons from teachers of other groups of children. Also, sometimes I find it helpful to look back at what I've done in other situations. Through reflecting on past solutions in present situations, I come up with new ways to tackle the present. Robert Frost said, "I am not a teacher, but an awakener." I liken the teaching that goes on with mini-lessons to Frost's statement. I am not teaching so much as awakening within young writers the stories they have to tell and providing demonstrations of ways to write those stories effectively. The writers in a literate community teach themselves, each other, and their teacher.

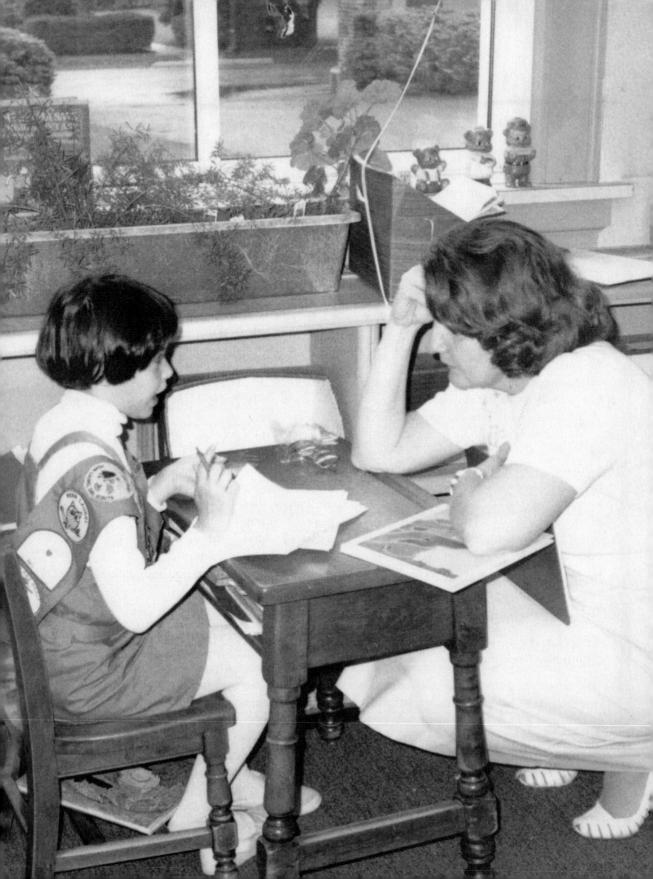

CHAPTER 8

Listening and Responding

A district administrator steps into our classroom and looks around. With a hint of alarm he asks, "Where's your teacher?" I sit on a tiny chair beside a child's desk in a sea of classroom activity. I'm listening to a writer. The six-year-olds find the incident amusing, and when the visitor leaves they bat the question back and forth in exaggerated outrage. "Where's your teacher?" "Where'd they think she'd be? On the playground?" This event is usually repeated every fall, but after the first occurrence each year the children deal with the issue. The next time, the child answering the knock graciously addresses the visitor before the question comes. "My teacher's over there. But she's busy having a conference right now. Would you like to wait?" The children know writing conferences are important.

I spend most of writing workshop moving around the room, sitting so I can look directly at the writer—not hovering over a child, looking over her shoulder, nor even looking at the writing. I look the child straight in the eye and listen as the child tells me about the current piece of writing.

Around us the other children work on writing. Some begin a new piece; others continue a topic they've been working on for several days. One child, preparing to publish a piece, searches for spelling in a picture dictionary. Two or three pairs of children sit together, one child reading and the other listening to the child-authored writing. A child or two moves around the room to sharpen a pencil, get more paper, or just to move about because he feels restless. There's a quiet hum of "working noise."

Moving away from the orderliness of a quiet classroom was hard at first; I feared unleashing chaos, opening myself up to criticism from colleagues and administrators. Some days that "quiet hum" became downright loud (especially with some groups of children) and I kept the classroom door closed—even on the hottest of days. I worried about the principal's observations. Would I be criticized if my children were out of their seats, if they were talking? I had reason for concern. At that time, these factors were noted on teacher observation reports. A quiet classroom indicated a well-managed classroom where everyone industriously worked "on task." I know better now and so do our administrators. And we understand how crucial movement is, and especially how important all that *talk* is.

Vygotsky (1978), the Russian psychologist recognized as a pioneer in developmental psychology, stated: "The most significant moment in the course of intellectual development, which gives birth to the purely human forms of practical and abstract intelligence, occurs when speech and practical activity, two previously completely independent lines of development, converge. . . . A child's speech is as important as the role of action in attaining the goal. . . . The more complex the action demanded by the situation, the greater the importance played by speech in the operation of the whole. Sometimes speech becomes of such vital importance that, if not permitted to use it, young children cannot accomplish the given task" (pp. 24–26). Vygotsky concluded that "children solve practical tasks with the help of their speech, as well as their eyes and hands" (p. 26).

I watch children in the classroom. They talk when they build with blocks, when they mark the check-in board in the morning, when they manipulate counters in math class, and when they gather their things to go home. They talk to themselves, to each other, to me. A few never seem to stop. In writing workshop they talk softly to themselves as they draw, or sound out words, or reread their writing and determine what to write next. They spontaneously speak to someone—anyone—near them (or across the room) as a particular thought comes to mind. And they talk to me as I move among them during the workshop.

All that talk contributes to the children's development, and the writing flourishes. Mini-lessons demonstrate strategies and skills for writers, but the heart of the writing workshop is the thirty minutes or more when children write and talk and I listen and respond (Giacobbe, 1982; Atwell, 1987). An energy develops in that time and that energy spills over to other parts of the school day. I believe that the talk surrounding writing is vital.

Learning to Listen

In the early days of writing workshop in my classroom, the children wrote and wrote and I responded. I set aside concern for convention (correct spelling, punctuation, grammar) and responded totally to content. Ignoring errors opened up the children's writing and they fluently wrote one piece after another. About this time I began using a hand-held tape recorder as I conferred with the children because I felt a need to understand just what occurred in writing conferences. When I played back the tape of those conferences, I heard myself doing most of the talking. Although the children began conferences, I soon took over. I interrupted at the slightest pause, made strong suggestions, asked many questions—one right on top of the other. I ignored the children's intentions and shifted their thinking to my perspective. *I* knew what was best and *I* held the answers. After all, I was the teacher. My heavy-handed approach, I realized, robbed them of the thinking that goes with writing. In professional presentations on implementing writing workshops I'd heard Don Graves say, "Shut up, listen, and learn." I needed to "shut up, listen, and learn."

I kept using the tape recorder. The knowledge that later I would listen to myself, and feel that agonizing embarrassment, kept me quiet. I'd worked on wait time and questioning techniques for years beginning with a self-paced inservice course I'd taken in the early 1970s. Listening to tapes of conferences helped me refine these techniques. It took us a while, but soon the children began talking. They began anticipating my time with them and the questions I would ask. They started talking as I approached them and they continued: "And you want to know what I'm gonna do next? Well . . ."

Children began using the writing conferences to think and to consider possibilities for their writing. I stopped groping for the right questions to ask and just listened. When I did ask questions, I asked genuine questions—ones that came naturally to my mind because I felt confused or wanted more information. Instead of supplying answers, I turned issues back to the children by asking: What do you plan to do about that? How will you solve that problem? Given the opportunity to talk with a more patient and authentic listener, the children came forth with wonderful ideas that amazed me with their rationale, thoughtfulness, and creativity. First graders had astounded me with their accomplishments as writers; now they demonstrated an incredible ability to be thinkers and problem solvers.

Roving Conferences

Early March. Writing workshop. The room bustles with a quiet hum. I close the notebook where I write during the first minutes of every workshop, pick up the conference checklist where I keep a record of the children I see, and begin moving around the room. I stop at Sonja's desk.

Sonja has recently moved to our school and writing workshop is new to her. She is a capable student. For two days she's been writing a fictional piece about "robbers" and the "other people," whom she referred to on another day as the "good guys." Her story moves from incident to incident; she hasn't had the benefit of our class discussions about focussing writing or of our read alouds and talk about how stories are constructed. After listening, I confirm my understanding of the story so far and then try to help her manage the writing by asking about her plans for the ending. As we talk, I sense that the wandering plot is literally developing on the spot. When I hear some energy in a phrase ("brave enough to look") I repeat the words for her to hear before I leave.

> SONJA: I'm reading it over and after I read it over I'm gonna put in that the police took the people to jail and how they had to stay in jail.
> MRS. A: Now, this is the story about the people who had robbed the other people's houses and now they're caught . . .
> S: Yeah.
> MRS. A: . . . and now they're going to jail.
> S: Yeah.
> MRS. A: Have you thought how you're going to end this story?
> S: I don't know. Not yet.
> MRS. A: OK. All right. You remember we talked about how sometimes fiction stories kids write—or even grown-ups—get going and keep rambling on and on and on . . .
> S: Right.
> MRS. A: . . . and they don't end when they should end.
> S: Yeah. Well, I think that after they get out see, they're gonna go back home and they're gonna live happily ever after. Then I'll put "the end."
> MRS. A: Who's gonna go back home?
> S: The people who were in jail.
> MRS. A: Okay. What happened to the people who were robbed?
> S: Well, the people who were robbed weren't in jail. And the people that were robbed were not in jail and the people were not, got out.
> MRS. A: [I'm confused and seek clarification.] The robbers went to jail and what about the other people?
> S: You mean the people that were in their houses and were scared?
> MRS. A: Uh huh.
> S: They were brave enough to look. And then after they looked, they called the police and police came looking for them.

MRS. A: "They were brave enough to look."

S: Yeah.

MRS. A: I like that phrase. Okay. Thank you.

Tara rereads her writing and tells me about two revision strategies she is implementing. The energy in her voice tells me she's involved in this piece.

TARA: I'm writing about my birthday still, and you know how you said all that stuff up there you don't need? [Tara refers to the mini-lesson where I wrote and included extra phrases such as: This is the problem. Now I will tell you the problem.] I read this over and I found some of that and I just took it out.

MRS. A: Really? You found some of that?

T: Yeah.

MRS. A: That happens a lot—writers find stuff like that.

T: Yeah. And you know where I put the check marks where I didn't put things? I looked around my house and I found out some things my mom and dad got me.

MRS. A: Oh, so at certain places you put check marks because there was more information but you couldn't remember what it was.

T: Yeah, I found out what it was.

MRS. A: So now what are you going to do?

T: I'm putting it right in. I'm reading over so I can see if I have any of that stuff still in and then when I come back to this page I can put it in.

MRS. A: You have a lot of plans don't you.

T: Uh huh.

MRS. A: Okay. Thank you.

I move on to Nickolas, who slouches in his seat. He chews the end of his pencil and appears to be daydreaming. His voice lacks enthusiasm when the conference begins. When I ask him a question about a part I don't understand, he sits up in his seat and speaks in a decisive tone of voice.

NICKOLAS: I'm still writing about, uh, ah, my hamsters, you know. And now I'm putting what we did to play with them. We made circles with our legs and that's what I'm putting now. [His voice trails off as he speaks. He only glances at me and stares at his paper.]

MRS. A: You put—I'm sorry, I didn't hear. You made a circled coop?

N: We made a circle with our legs.

MRS. A: You made a circle with your legs?

N: Yeah. Then we put the hamsters in the middle for a while.

MRS. A: You put the hamsters so they could move around in the middle of this circle between your legs.

N: Yeah. And [pause] we watch them on the spinning wheel.

MRS. A: Who sits and makes this circle with your legs with you?

N: My friends.

MRS. A: So you—I'm not sure about this—you put your feet together?

N: Umm.

MRS. A: Tell me, how do you do that?

N: We put our feet together and we have like about five people and
you put your feet together and make a circle.

MRS. A: Ohh, it's not just two of you, it's five of you—a huge circle.

N: Then you need to put your hands down here [he stuffs his hands
behind his knees] so they won't get out. Because then they can't
go underneath your legs. So you have to put your hands here so
they can't get out.

MRS. A: I see. So you're writing all this. You're describing all this
now?

N: Yeah.

MRS. A: You're putting all that in so that people will get that picture.

N: Umm hum.

MRS. A: Okay. Thank you.

Kelsie stands behind her desk, holding her papers. She's been reading to
Amy seated beside her. Kelsie's a confident writer and always open to
suggestions to improve her writing. She also is comfortable rejecting suggestions that she finds inappropriate. Today she's writing a letter to author
Arnold Lobel. In the conference I try to nudge her to think of her letter as
more than a string of questions.

KELSIE: I'm starting a letter to Mr. Lobel and I've asked the question
that we're stuck on—the question that all our class was wanting
to know. Then I'm asking what's his favorite book is and how he
likes it.

MRS. A: So—read that question. I'd like to hear the question.

K: Okay. "I don't understand why you don't put if they raked the
leaves in *Frog and Toad All Year*, in 'The Surprise.' "

MRS. A: Oh. So now you're asking about the end of that story
because we were puzzled and now you're going to ask him what
his favorite . . .

K: Favorite things are.

MRS. A: Is there any information you want to *tell* him?

K: Well, I already put in that my teacher likes his books. And uh, I'm
gonna put in that I like his books too, and what was his last book
to make.

MRS. A: You know what Kelsie?

K: What?

MRS. A: I think he might want to know *why* you like a particular book.
[Amy has listened to the entire conference and now she adds, "I think
    so too."]

K: Oh yeah. OK, I might put that in too.

I move past a few desks and stop at Terri's seat. Terri was labeled Learning Disabled when she was a toddler. I've learned that she writes best if she verbalizes her ideas first. Rarely does she include information that she hasn't talked about. Conferences are critical for her.

TERRI: I'm writing about when I went to Chris's birthday party. And
    I'm gonna put in more information about it.

MRS. A: You're gonna put in more information about Chris's birth-
    day party.

T: Uh hum.

MRS. A: Tell me. Tell me what is going to be the most important
    information you . . .

T: Well, I got him a wheelie—a car that goes on its back wheels and
    the car does a wheelie, whatever.

MRS. A: The car goes on its back wheels and does a wheelie and that
    was your gift to him?

T: Uh huh.

MRS. A: So you're going to put that in the story?

T: Uh hum.

MRS. A: Is there anything else about . . .

T: I'm gonna put who he invited. I know all the guys—there were no
    girls except for his sisters. The party was mostly boys.

MRS. A: The party was mostly boys and the only girls were his
    sisters. OK—and you!

T: Yeah, I'm not one of his sisters. I'm just his friend. But Christy and
    Chad didn't went. Christy can't go and I don't know what hap-
    pened to Chad.

MRS. A: So, where are you in this story right now?

T: Well, I'm gonna put we played musical chairs.

MRS. A: You played musical chairs. And then, what are your next
    plans?

T: I'm gonna put then we got our prizes. I got a tablet and pencils.

MRS. A: You're gonna put about the prizes. You have to put in this
    part about the gifts.

T: Yeah, I do. And somebody's names and . . .

MRS. A: OK. Thank you.

Bobby sits next to Terri. Usually I would move to a child seated farther away, but Bobby's face is contorted in frustration. He often is tense and nervous, but he loves to write and comes up with unique topics. Like Terri, hearing his own words helps him get them onto paper.

BOBBY: I'm writing a story and it's about a forest and it rains about . . . maybe—let me think—a couple of months and then it turns into a flood.

MRS. A: A flood?

B: Uh huh.

MRS. A: A flood. It rains a couple of months and then the forest turns into a flood. Where did you get this idea, Bobby?

B: Well, [pause] I don't know.

MRS. A: No idea? [Bobby shakes his head. He still hasn't made eye contact with me.] How is the story starting?

B: Well, it's gonna start "Rabbit walked out and took his umbrella and he was soaked the minute he walked out because it was starting to pour."

MRS. A: He was soaked the minute he walked out . . .

B: Uh hum. [Hearing his own words, Bobby finally looks at me.]

MRS. A: . . . because it was starting to pour.

B: Uh huh.

MRS. A: That beginning really makes me want to read more. Thank you.

Bobby started writing as soon as I repeated the first sentence, and so I concluded the conference. In second grade Bobby will be labeled Learning Disabled.

These six conferences have taken ten minutes. Even though I spoke directly to only six children, I know others overheard our conversations and picked up ideas for their own writing. Amy gave her undivided attention to Kelsie's conference. The eavesdropping is not always obvious, but it occurs all through the roving conference time. This is why I move around the room randomly rather than by seating or any other order. Mary Ellen Giacobbe calls learning by overhearing the "Dumbo effect," after the baby elephant with the big ears.

Both Graves and Giacobbe gave me suggestions for conducting conferences. Long conferences leave the child with too many concerns to keep in mind. Long conferences prevent me from seeing as many children and build a backlog of writers with whom I'm loosing touch. Several strategies help keep conferences short: The writer begins the conference (thus eliminating the "hi, how are you?" small talk) by telling me the topic, where she is at the moment, and what she intends to do next. This information requires writers to keep their process in mind and provides the groundwork for my responses. Most important, the procedure allows the *child to do the talking in the writing conference.* By talking, the child thinks. By thinking, the child develops.

Thoughts About Conferences

Keeping three procedures advocated by Graves and Giacobbe in mind helps me keep conferences running effectively:

1. *Listen* to what the child has to say.
2. *Tell* the child what I understand.
3. *Ask* the child to clarify or expand on what I don't understand.

Individual writing conferences function to keep the writer going, or in Lucy Calkins' term, to "nudge" them along. Questions help a writer discover for himself what he knows.

Author, poet, and teacher, William Stafford (1986) says, "I never assess a whole paper or judge a person. Puzzlement in places, yes. Curiosity about further information, yes. Quirky, alive reactions, any time. . . . I want the students to know I am with them, that I do have reactions. But my reactions are only those that a friend would have during a conversation. . . . My way to be accountable is related directly, simply, honestly, nonthreateningly (and nonpraisingly) to my individual student" (pp. 93–94). Responding to first-grade writers is no different.

In these short, frequent conferences with children, my goal is to help the writer. So I respond to the writer, not the writing, and trust that if I help the writer, the writing will come. Sometimes I make suggestions, but I don't require that writers follow my suggestions. I don't have a list of questions in mind as I come to the conference. Still, when I listen to tapes of my conferences, I hear the repertoire of questions that have evolved for me. When trying to find out the writer's purpose I ask questions such as: What's this writing about? What's the best part of this piece?

When trying to discover how things are going for the writer, I'll ask: Where are you right now? What's the best thing you've written so far?

To help the writer nail down a direction for the writing, I may ask: What will you do next? What are your plans for this piece?

To help the writer articulate the experience she is attempting to communicate, I'm likely to ask: What was this like for you?

The most demanding hours of teaching I've encountered have been listening to and responding to writers. Listening means hearing the words, reading the body language and voice tone, being aware of the child's behavior throughout the workshop, knowing the history of the current piece of writing and the child's process with this piece as well as past pieces, and connecting all this to the present moment. The context informs the moment. Often I find that I'm listening for the words that aren't said or yet written. Meaning, I know, is within the writer. A response may be a smile or a nod. Sometimes I can respond to a writer as I pass by the desk and we exchange glances and I know and the writer knows we've communicated—no words necessary.

My conferences with children are only part of the conferring that goes on during the writing workshop. Children naturally turn and chat with each other as they work on their writing. The conversations are natural sharing and learning—which is what conferences are all about. These exchanges are as important as the talk with me. Usually, after a few weeks of school, I announce one morning as we begin to write, "If you need to talk to a teacher about your writing and this teacher (I point to myself) is busy, you could ask the teacher seated beside you. There are many teachers in this room. If one is busy we can find another." (Giacobbe, 1982). The children nod. I'm merely confirming what they have already experienced. Some years we've designated areas of the classroom for children to meet and respond to each other's writing. The designated areas provided a place for this more extended talk without bothering other writers.

Once in a while the children begin to use the opportunity of talking with a peer to avoid writing. We address the problem in a class meeting, and the children usually solve it themselves. But one year this sharing became so intensive that the writing was falling by the wayside. Children talked until there was little time to write, and then the next day they'd start out by talking with a peer again. To break this cycle I taped sign-in sheets in the sharing centers and required children to record the time they arrived and left the area. I never checked those sign-in sheets; but they thought I did, and the problem cleared up.

Record Keeping for Conferences

I maintain a record of conferences to help me respond to writers. The easiest is my conference checklist (see Figure 4–6). At the bottom of the checklist I write the key to the marks I use so that a substitute teacher can use the form. This key provides a code for marking the box beside a child's name on a given day. *The marks note the child's engagement with the writing process at a given moment.* I'm not evaluating the writing. Nor am I assessing how well the child articulated her writing process. I want to remember how the writing is going: smoothly, struggling, charging ahead, needing help.

My code is simple.

✓ —Everything is going well.

✓+ —The child is sailing ahead, has plans, and the writing is surprising the writer and me.

‿ —The writer is struggling, things aren't going well.

∿ —I'm not sure how things are going. They may be okay, but I want to keep in touch.

Ⓢ —The child shared in large-group sharing.

The checklist helps me keep track of who I've seen or not seen during a workshop. I also can look back and quickly recall the tone of the conference from the day before. Knowing who has shared recently is important in selecting each day's sharers. When it comes time to choose sharers, first graders clamor to read to the class. (I hear lots of "I didn't share in a long time" statements—even from yesterday's readers.)

In the ten minutes of conferences with children at the beginning of this chapter, I noted the following on each child:

Sonja— ✓(She's involved with writing and the conference seemed to help her.)

Tara—✓+(Tara knew what she was doing and why.)

Nickolas—∿(Nick seemed to move into the writing at the end of the conference, but his uninvolvement a moment before leads me to keep a close eye on him.)

Kelsie—✓ (Writing going well, though I've seen better days with Kelsie.)

Terri— ✓(A typical day for Terri.)

Bobby—∿ (I'm not sure how Bobby's doing—he may need another conference soon or he may take off.)

Looking at the conference checklist over a stretch of a few days alerts me to possible concerns. Take this example of Charles's checklist over a two-week period.

Charles	∿	✓	∿	✓	∿	A	‿∿	∿	∿	✓Ⓢ⁺	

During the first week, the notations for Charles alternate between checks and squiggle lines; on Friday I talk to him twice during the workshop. The following Monday he is absent—significant because now he has been away from his writing for three days. Tuesday shows a dash and a squiggle line—two conferences and I'm getting concerned. On Wednesday and Thursday I record two squiggle lines. I feel out of touch with this writer and I sense he's struggling though I can't put my finger on the difficulty.

On Friday I spent a longer time than usual with Charles. We talked about HO trains, a hobby he shared with his dad. He knew a lot about this topic but writing all the information was difficult. I suggested he manage his topic by writing about the engines on one page, including everything he could think of about them, then on another page writing about the caboose, and so on, and then we could see what to do next. The strategy worked. Charles shared the writing with the entire group that day. The writing evolved into a "Dictionary of Trains" and Charles successfully alphabetized the typed pages, each one a different topic related to trains, by laying them out on the floor and following the alphabetical sequence from the alphabet posted in the classroom.

An alternative form of record keeping for writing workshop is an anecdotal record sheet. This record has a block for each child in the class, with space to write brief notes as I confer with him/her. At the end of the conference I write down the child's topic and notes to remind me of this particular conference: the intentions, a strategy the child used, the child's plans. I didn't use this record-keeping procedure during the conference session I've shown earlier, but if I had I probably would have made notes similar to these:

Sonja: Robbers. Rambling??? Plans: people to jail . . . happily ever after. "brave enough to look."

Tara: Birthday. Plans: Lining out "extra stuff." Checked at home and adding info. Used checkmark to add.

Nick: Hamsters. Plans: describing circle with legs, play with hamsters.

Kelsie: Lobel Letter. Ask Mr. L ?'s—why didn't he tell if they raked leaves in "The Surprise." Shared with Amy. Plans: Ask favorite things. Sugg: tell about *why* like books.

Terri: Chris's B-day. Plans: wheelie present, guests, prizes. Next: musical chairs.

Bobby: Forest—flood. Told me lead then began to write. Plans: ?

These notes provide quick day-to-day reminders of the children's writing. I inform the class of the record keeping I'm doing. By telling the children that I'm noting their plans, they tend to remember those plans better themselves and take responsibility for carrying them out.

Responding to Problems

In roving conferences during writing workshop, I encounter writers dealing with a number of problems. The following examples demonstrate ways the children and I together address problems.

The Writer Is Stuck

Being stuck looks different with different writers.

Ray was stuck. I watched him gather and staple paper, chatting with friends the entire time. He sat at his desk, went to the pencil sharpener, returned, and then wrote a few words. He flipped pages, looked around the room. I was pretty sure of the problem: he was beginning a new piece of writing and although he had his topic, he didn't know how to start. This was a pattern for him. I stopped to talk.

RAY: I'm gonna write when I went to my friend's. My title's "Sleep Over Night."

MRS. A: Are you making a title page here with the title and your name and date?

R: Yeah.

MRS. A: It's about sleeping over at your friend's house?

R: Well, we stayed up until midnight.

MRS. A: You stayed up till *midnight?*

R: Un huh.

MRS. A: What was that like, Ray?

R: Well, uh, well he, well, when it was time to go to bed, well, uh, we were looking for ghosts—we were just staying in bed—and, uh, and it looked like there was a ghost at the door when we were going to sleep.

MRS. A: You were looking for ghosts and you thought you saw a ghost at the door when you were going to sleep.

R: Uh huh!

MRS. A: How did that feel?

R: And John . . . well, we . . . we, we were scared. John and me were sleepin', well John um . . . [Lots of stammering around. I've thrown him off track by my question. He stops to answer but now searches to recall his original train of thought.] I mean me and my friend were sleeping in the bed and John was sleeping on the floor. So, um . . .

MRS. A: So there were the three of you. Another friend and John.

R: Uh huh, and when me and my other friend were in bed the ghost was just standing there and we were so scared we were hiding our pillows behind us.

MRS. A: Oh my gosh! Is all this going to be in there? How you were hiding the pillows and saw ghosts and all this business.

R: Uh huh.

MRS. A: You won't forget any of it?

R: No.

MRS. A: Should be an exciting story.

Ray began writing about the sleepover. Talking got him going.

Mandy knew she was stuck. She'd been stuck for two days and she said so when I stopped at her desk. In this conference we struggled together to find a topic.

MANDY: I'm stuck.

MRS. A: Is this the same story you were stuck with yesterday?

M: Yes [a big sigh].

MRS. A: Mandy, I have an idea. See what you think about it. You seem to be stuck on this piece. What if you put this piece away for awhile? Just put it in your folder, and you can come back to it after you've thought about it. Get out another piece of paper and just start writing and see if you can write about something else. You could write about something from your vacation journal.

M: Well, there's one thing I know about my birthday. It's funny.

MRS. A: Yeah?

M: And I hate my birthday being in April because there might be, you know, there might be a shower in April. And then May, that's a good time for birthdays because flowers grow.

MRS. A: Yes.

M: Lots of flowers. [Mandy's thoughts ramble and one topic leads her to another and another. The temporary inability to focus may contribute to the sense of being stuck. I try to get her to think about one idea.]

MRS. A: Yes. Okay, so what about your birthday would you like to write?

M: Well, it's very close to April Fool's . . . [Mandy continues to ramble. After several attempts to get her to focus, I determine that the birthday topic is going nowhere. I try another path in an effort to help.]

MRS. A: Okay [pause]. Okay, what do you want to write about now? What about Christmas? What did you do over Christmas?

M: Well, I didn't get lots of things.

MRS A: What was your favorite thing?

M: I didn't have a favorite thing.

MRS. A: Um. You didn't have a favorite thing. Did you have a good time?

M: Yes, but there's something I just remembered. [There is sudden energy in her voice. Her eyes and her whole body perk up.] I got a record player from Grandma and my Aunt Snookie and the little needle—it broke off. Daddy had to buy a new one and he put, he put the needle that he bought back on, on the record player and now it works.

MRS. A: Could you write about that? The record player? And getting it fixed?

M: I think I will.

The story of the record player worked out for Mandy and eventually she published this writing. Selecting topics continued to be a problem for this child, although once she had a subject she worked for days drafting and refining the writing. She maintained high standards for herself, which probably contributed to her dilemma in choosing topics. Each choice had to be a good one. Conferences helped her learn to seek out her own topics, although she always weighed each choice long and hard.

Jared sat holding his head with one hand and his pencil with the other. I'd been aware for the last several minutes that he'd run into a problem. He'd begun the workshop writing up a storm, but now, suddenly, he was stuck.

JARED: Um, um, um, I'm writing about the USFL and I wrote all the teams but I'm figuring out um, um, what Washington's last name is.

MRS. A: Ohhh. You can't remember that. You've been sitting here thinking.

J: Uh huh.

MRS. A: I'm wondering, Jared, if it would help if you went on and left a space for that, and then when it came to you, you could sit down and finish it—come back to it. What do you think?

J: Um hum. [He hasn't looked up from the paper and the tone of his response tells me he's not sure this will work. I try again.]

MRS. A: What part is going to come next?

J: Um, um. [long pause] Who played um, in the game. Like um, Philadelphia played Denver and um, New Jersey played Los Angeles.

MRS. A: Who played the first games . . .

J: Yeah.

MRS. A: . . . on the first Sunday.

J: Yeah. [Suddenly Jared begins writing, turning his attention totally from our conference to his writing.]

MRS. A: So you know where you're going now.

J: Uh huh. [He never looks up. I leave.]

Jared needed to talk to discover what he knew in order to continue writing. He didn't pick up on my suggestion to leave a space for the information he couldn't recall. When I asked him what part was going to come next he got back into his topic again.

Most of the problems writers confront revolve around getting stuck in one way or another. In the writing conference I listen to their struggles, ask questions, possibly make suggestions, but allow the writers to make their own decisions in working through the problem. The experience of that process is as important as the final product. I need to remember that I'm there to respond to the writer, not the writing.

The Writer Copies Other Writing

Eventually plagiarism comes up with every group of children. A child picks up a book and copies word for word. I ask why they decided to do this and have to marvel at the underlying problem solving. Usually the child tells me with honesty and even pride how they figured out a good story to write. It's easy to just write the words in the book. I inform the child that this is something writers must never do and I bet he didn't know that. As I explain, the children react in amazement, and sometimes with a bit of chagrin. But the issue is critical for writers and we need to address it. Later, the child may join me in talking to the whole group about plagiarism. A significant discussion always ensues with the "experienced" child in a teacher role.

Sometimes child writers fall into retelling stories from television or movies. Eileen attended a local children's theater and was eager to write about the experience. She had loved the play, but when she wrote she discovered she couldn't manage the material. In an attempt to explain the parts she enjoyed, she got bogged down in retelling the play. It was October. I suggested she set the writing aside until a later time or that she just write about attending the theater without getting into the details of the play. She chose to go on to another topic. Months later she pulled this writing from her folder and said, "I think I know how to write this now. I'll just tell a couple parts I liked and why I like them because I can't write the whole play!" And she laughed at her earlier attempts.

The Writer Borrows from Popular Culture

In September, Thomas wrote superhero stories day after day. Was he copying the television tales? "No!" he insisted, and the other children confirmed that these stories were original. Thomas borrowed the superhero characters and their unusual environments for his stories. The other children loved the stories and Thomas would have nothing to do with personal narrative, the genre favored by most of the class. Thomas and I both had difficulty reading his writing because he reversed many letters, neglected to leave spaces between words ("I just had my mind on the *story*," he'd explain), and frequently wrote left to right for a line then right to left for the next line. However, he could always retell his stories, finding words here and there in the written text for prompts. But I felt uneasy as the days went on because I could find no way to help Thomas. I waited for a change. Finally, I could stand it no longer.

"Thomas," I said one morning, "I'd like you to find another topic to write about today. I can't help you with your writing because I don't know enough about superheroes. And my job is to help you when you write."

"But Mrs. Avery," Thomas wailed, "I have this great story in my head today. I've gotta write it down."

"But what can we do? I can't help you and you have trouble explaining it all to me."

"How 'bout tomorrow?" he suggested. "Tomorrow I'll write something else."

It took two days before Thomas switched to his new topic: dinosaurs. He wrote about dinosaurs for weeks and became our dinosaur expert. I became captivated by the wonderful imagination he brought to these compositions, and I understood why his superhero stories had so enraptured his classmates. Superheros opened the door for Thomas to write; I was glad I hadn't slammed it in his face through a premature response.

I've been tempted to banish television cartoons or movies as topics for writing, but I know I'm dealing in a gray area. Although I don't encourage these topics, I refrain from making an absolute edict. Sometimes children write their reactions to these stories—why they like them; sometimes they begin with a story and then take off with their own plot. Personal narratives are more manageable, and most children write personal narratives in the beginning of the year because that is the model I've provided as we initiate the writing workshop.

The advent of video games brought about another problem situation. One little boy, a delightful child and a solid student, received one of these machines and the accompanying games for Christmas. The effect was so gradual I didn't notice it at first. He began writing about Christmas and his presents and soon was into the games. The writing made no sense to me and, like the games, it never ended. When I talked to him he spoke only of the games. One morning his mother stopped in to drop off bookcovers she had made for us and I briefly expressed my concerns. A week later I noticed a definite change. This child began talking about playing soccer and getting ready for Valentine's Day. Weeks later I learned from his mother that the parents had limited use of the video game machine to two hours on weekends. I was amazed and thankful. And I was keenly aware that the daily conferences allowed me to notice the situation.

After this experience I decided to ask children to eliminate video games as writing topics. "I'm not sure that writing about these games helps you as a writer," I explained, "and I don't know how to help you write these pieces of writing." I anticipated grief and complaints; instead I got agreement. "Those video game stories are sorta boring, anyhow," commented one child. "Boring to write and boring to read," said another. Group consensus. Why had I waited so long? Because we all needed to wait that long in order to come to this realization.

The Writer Produces "Shocking" Content

Do I ever censor children's writing? Yes! I've never allowed fictional blood-and-guts stories. Even first graders are capable of producing shock-laden material. The six-year-old of the nineties is far more worldly than counterparts of earlier generations. When this kind of writing comes up I simply respond similar to Giacobbe and Atwell, "I am offended by reading that kind of stuff and so in this classroom, we will not write pieces like this." Most of the group sighs in relief. I also ban profanity, though most youngsters know instinctively that such language is not allowed in school. Usually the issue doesn't even come up. But then, sometimes it does.

Alex moved into our class in January. Such a bright child! Soon his writing provided a model that inspired the others to try new topics and new techniques. Alex enlivened writing workshop through the sheer inspiration of his presence. One day in March, individuals from the Pennsylvania Department of Education came to videotape our workshop. Our principal, two fellow teachers, and an official from Harrisburg observed, for the tape was to conclude with a conversation among the adults.

All went well through the mini-lesson and the roving conferences. I had stopped to talk with Alex early and noted he was into an interesting piece about his dad mowing the lawn. When it came time for the group sharing I selected the children to share to represent a range of writing within the group. I chose Alex. When his turn came he read the lines I had heard during our conference. The next part was to be about the lawnmower breaking and how his dad fixed it. Alex told the story all right. "Then my dad said, . . ." and Alex quoted a string of words to turn a sailor blue.

Suddenly, every child's eyes were on me. My eyes connected with Kevin and with Beth, then I looked back to Alex. Murmurs rose from the professionals seated in the back of the room. Then quiet. The camera's red light glowed indicating it was recording every moment. All the while I looked at

Alex who, after he read those words, turned and looked at me, awaiting my reaction. The entire room awaited my reaction.

"Continue. Is there anything else?" I said.

"No, that's all I wrote," Alex replied.

"Okay, boys and girls, do you have any responses for Alex?" I knew I had to say something. The children probably wouldn't touch it, but as usual I would add my response—whatever it would be—after they gave theirs. I knew my response probably carried more weight, but I'd found that embedding it with the responses of a group allowed the writer to accept or reject it with grace.

Tentatively, Kevin raised his hand. He looked at me, not Alex. Alex called on him and Kevin began to speak, looking over to me to check for affirmation as he proceeded. I nodded ever so slightly, not knowing what Kevin would say but deciding to trust his response.

"I, um, I don't, um I think that, well, you wrote this book, but if you published it, if you made it into a book for people to read, well, um, I wouldn't be able to take it home because my mom won't let me say words like that. So I couldn't read it." Kevin's voice started hesitantly, but as he spoke his back straightened and his voice gained strength. He looked at me and I nodded as he finished and settled back on the rug. Alex made no response except to call on Beth.

"I'm not allowed to say those words either. I really don't like to hear words like that," came her quiet comment. Now several children raised their hands and each child affirmed Kevin and Beth. A landslide was underway and I didn't want Alex to be buried, so I interrupted.

"Alex, do you hear what these children are saying?" He looked at me intently, striving to maintain his dignity. "I think they are saying that the words in this writing offend them and they don't want to read them. In fact, they'd be in trouble at home if they read them. Sometimes, Alex, grown-ups write words like this in their writing and then people have to make a choice about reading it. That's part of an important freedom in our country. But I think these boys and girls are telling you that in this class-room they don't want that writing. Their moms and dads don't want to hear it and they're not allowed to read it or even say those words."

Alex nodded. "I can line them out," he said.

"Yes, you can," I replied. "You have an important choice to make."

"I think I'll probably line them out or I might just start a whole new piece," he answered.

The community provided the response. I believe that Alex knew exactly what he was doing and chose to test the limits of his new environment. But the structure was in place. The children knew how to respond even though we had never talked about this particular concern. Children's sensibilities can be trusted, and sometimes the most appropriate response is to wait.

Gold Star Addiction

"I'm done. Mrs. Avery, I'm done." Samantha stood beside me, lightly tapping my shoulder as I conferred with Mark during our writing workshop. I tried to ignore her but she wouldn't go away.

It was mid-March and Samantha had been with our class for a little over a week. Although writing workshop was new to her, she was a capable student and was catching on quickly to daily writing. At first her stories portrayed fantasy adventures that I guessed to be spin-offs from children's television shows, but Samantha paid close heed to the writing of the other children and, in her second week with us, began to write narratives based on more personal experiences. Despite her progress, she frequently appeared at my elbow throughout the day, interrupting conversations with other children, smiling, presenting her schoolwork, and awaiting my approval. As the days passed and I attempted to wean her of the need for continuous affirmation, she became more insistent and demanding. Samantha was addicted to praise.

"Excuse me, Mark. I'll be back," I said, and turning to Samantha I took her hand, met her expectant countenance with a direct gaze that did not return her smile, and led her back to her desk. "Now, tell me what the emergency is," I said. Her smile, which had briefly turned to puzzlement, returned. She presented her writing to me saying, "I'm done. Did I do a good job?"

"What do you think?" I asked. Her smile evaporated.

"*I* don't know."

I pondered her reply a brief moment. She was right. She didn't know.

Tiffy, a quiet observer at the desk adjoining Samantha's, spoke up. "But, Mrs. Avery wants to know what the *emergency* is." Tiffy recognized the most immediate problem: interrupting a writing conference.

Samantha looked puzzled. Tiffy's eyes met mine with a look that communicated she understood the issue that had initiated today's incident.

"Help me, Tiffy. Can you explain to Samantha?" On several occasions I had attempted to address the interrupting with Samantha. No change resulted. As with many issues in the classroom, I knew that a peer might communicate far more effectively than I could. It was no accident that I had placed Tiffy's desk beside Samantha's. The children regarded Tiffy as a peacemaker—pleasant, kind, and fair—qualities highly valued by first graders. I knew Tiffy would facilitate Samantha's adjustment to the classroom. I could not plan nor mandate such interactions, but only provide the setting for them to take place when moments such as this arose during the school day.

Tiffy responded to my query with a smile and a modest shrug as she said, "I don't know. I'll try." Then, turning to Samantha she explained ever so gently, "See, when Mrs. Avery is listening to someone talk about their writing no one's suppose to interrupt, not unless there's an *emergency*. Remember the other day when she said, 'Only if someone's throwing up or bleeding to death' and she hasn't noticed it? At the beginning she told everyone that and sometimes, at first, we forgot. I forgot and once Jason forgot."

Hearing his name, Jason looks over and grins. We all remember the day in September when Jason persisted in interrupting the writing conference until I turned and in a greatly exaggerated horror said, "I certainly hope someone's bleeding to death or throwing up or there's some other emergency that I haven't noticed!" Jason had retreated quickly in momentary embarrassment.

Later, in a large-group talk, we had discussed my reaction and the children, including Jason, all felt comfortable with the basic rule about not interrupting teacher/student conversations, understanding that we needed this for the smooth operation of the whole school day, including writing workshop. The children began seeking ways to work on their own without my constant input. Although on the surface I established the rule for management purposes, the embedded intent was to develop independence in these first graders, both as writers and as learners. The outrageous tone of voice I used that day became a legacy, a tool I employed throughout the year to communicate a point firmly, while still maintaining an underlying humor. Voice tones became part of the communication history of our classroom, which we all knew and understood. But Samantha was new to our group. There was much about our communication, procedures, and tones within the group that she did not understand.

Tiffy instinctively knew this as she continued talking softly. "What she means—what I think Mrs. Avery means—is that when someone's talking with her about writing, it's real *important* and she might not be able to listen so good if people interrupt her. You have to wait 'til it's *your* turn and then you can talk to her."

Samantha looked at Tiffy and then at me as she gave this matter thought for a moment. One could almost see the wheels turning in her head. "Oh," she finally said, slowly. "Well, what about when I'm done. Aren't you going to read it?" she asked me.

Before I could reply, Tiffy answered. "Mrs. Avery can't read *everything* we write. You gotta choose your best pieces to put in the basket for her to read and then you can publish that piece maybe. If you finish one piece, you just put it in your folder and then start another one. You read your writing and when you do—while you're reading it—you *think* if it's good or not and if it makes sense. Sometimes, if you read it on the next day, then you can decide if it's good and you might want to fix some parts to make it better."

Samantha looked at Tiffy, then at her writing. She turned to me and said, "Well then, what should I do now?"

"Well, you could read this piece to see if it makes sense, like Tiffy said, or you could start a new one and come back to this another day," I replied.

"She could read it to me, if she wants, and I could help her some," suggested Tiffy. Samantha looked at me, checking this possibility out.

"What do you think?" I asked.

"Okay," Samantha replied. "I'll read it to Tiffy."

I returned to Mark. Later I overheard Tiffy say to Samantha, "See you don't need to always ask the teacher if it's good. You can figure it out yourself." A puzzling concept for Samantha, I thought.

The contrast between Samantha and the rest of the children in the classroom at that point in the year struck me vividly. These young writers wrote for themselves, not for grades, gold stars or stickers, or teacher praise. They understood the highs and lows, the ups and downs of a writer. They had developed an ability to assess their own progress and the quality of their own writing.

Samantha, on the other hand, worked for the goal of completing a task and submitting it for the approval of others. She was dependent on feedback and, since she was quite capable, she was accustomed to regular doses of glowing accolades. She lived under the illusion that she did everything she tried well—even outstandingly. In this classroom Samantha was experiencing withdrawal from gold star addiction, a dependency that teachers foster in students when they heap rewards and praise on all the students' efforts.

One reason for gold star addiction is that we tend to give praise too liberally—too much, too often, too indiscriminately. Children come to believe that all of their efforts are "great," "wonderful," "super," and that they need do only more of the same. A child easily might resist risking new ways of thinking about or attempting a task because of the fear of error and the subsequent loss of reward. Indiscriminate praise tends to require escalation. The child becomes accustomed to stickers or stars or superlative comments and we lock ourselves into giving rewards regularly. When a piece of work comes in that is of slightly less quality we are trapped. What do we say? Do we give a sticker or not? The young child's perception is more than likely that reward means success, lack of reward means failure. We discourage the child (who may have put forth his best effort) because we determine we cannot give the reward this time, or we continue—albeit uneasily—with the hypocrisy. On the other hand, when a child shows improvement, we provide the reward even though it may not accurately communicate the growth we observe. "Too much praise in the profession is diminishing and manipulative of the child," warns Donald Graves (1983, p. 215).

I recall watching children pull papers from the classroom mailboxes many years ago at the end of a school day. "Oh a sticker! Look!" cries one child while another hurriedly stuffs a stickerless paper into a bookbag. I remember feeling uncomfortable with both responses—the gloating and the shame—to my subjective judgments. I've given up putting stickers as rewards on children's schoolwork. First graders love stickers and I still give stickers. But I'll hand one out to every child in the room, not as a reward but simply as a gift.

As with all addictions, the substance that provides the glow, be it stickers, stars, or superlatives, becomes the essential end for the recipient. I've heard teachers say, "Kids will *kill* for a sticker." (And the statement that frequently follows is, "I can get them to do anything when I promise stickers.") Soon, however, the glow fades and we teachers become trapped into increasing either the frequency or the sparkle of the reward. We give two stars instead of one, hand out scratch-and-sniff stickers rather than plain ones, pile on the superlatives: "Wow! Terrific! That's great!" Children shift their focus from involvement in the learning task to striving for the reward, thereby increasing their dependence on us, the suppliers of that reward, rather than developing the appropriate independence as individual learners that comes through realistic recognition of their own talents.

In *Children's Minds,* Margaret Donaldson (1978) states, "There is now a substantial amount of evidence pointing to the conclusion that if an activity is rewarded by some extrinsic prize or token—something quite external to the activity itself—then that activity is less likely to be engaged in later in a free and voluntary manner when the rewards are absent, and it is less likely to be enjoyed" (p. 121). Over and over, I've seen young children strive for and delight in the accomplishment of learning tasks without the promise of either rewards or punishments dangled before them. I think of Lori saying, "I wanted to read *Charlotte's Web* because it's such a good book but it was pretty hard for me. I kept practicing and practicing reading and then one day I picked it up and then I could read it." I remember Traci racing in from the playground to report, "I just learned to jump rope. I jumped ten times without missing!" I see Jenny throwing her hands up in glee during a writing workshop and saying, "I did it! I wrote a whole sentence! I didn't think I could, but I tried, and then I did it." As their teacher, I encouraged and provided demonstrations, provided honest and helpful feedback, and when they succeeded, celebrated with them.

Responses to children are never neutral. They are biased by my own experiences, interests, and knowledge, even my state of mind at a given time. But by listening and giving as honest a response as possible I believe children will trust the response and also their own process. If we heap mounds of praise on children, they will feel the shallowness of this praise. In every group of children I've worked with, every child has been able to identify the strongest reader, the most talented artist, the most gifted mathematician in the group. Children know each other's talents and they have a healthy awareness of their own strengths in comparison. By providing specific responses to children we confirm what they already know, validate that awareness, and demonstrate our own respect and valuing of each child and the talents he/she has to give.

Reflections

Learning to respond to writers meant learning to listen to children. I think this listening/response is the heart of good teaching. I sure didn't do it well when I began teaching, and even after years of working with children I still come out with some awful comments in response to what they've said. Usually it's because I've jumped to conclusions about their meaning or intentions. When I started writing workshops with children, listening and responding became a necessity. It's more than a skill, more than an approach. I think it's an attitude or classroom lifestyle, for it spilled over from writing to every other part of the school day. One day I wrote a list of reminders for responding in a writing workshop—things I'd learned from Murray, Graves, Giacobbe, Calkins, Atwell, and others, and from my own classroom experience. With only a little imagination, each point on the list could be stated to apply to all of my classroom practices.

1. Keep conferences short.
2. Listen and learn from the children, allowing them to do the talking.
3. Tell the child what I've understood, and ask questions to find out what I don't understand.
4. Give encouraging and genuine responses, avoiding a lot of praise.
5. Keep the conference focussed by talking about only one or two issues.
6. Maintain efficient records that inform future conferring and help develop knowledge about each writer.
7. Drop the traditional teacher agenda to "teach" in each conference and trust the child's capacity to learn from the entire context of a literate community.
8. Look at what the child can accomplish rather than focussing on the deficiencies.

9. Use the conference to gently nudge the writer, to keep the writer writing.

10. Relax and enjoy talking with the children.

Some final thoughts. Although I've moved away from a teacher-centered classroom, the nature of school gives me considerable influence. As manager of the classroom, influence helps me keep things running smoothly but, as a facilitator of learning, I must be cautious of my power. If I use a heavy-handed approach—one where I am always the expert and final authority—I could crush children's curiousity, intrude on their thinking, and interfere with learning. By sharing power with the children, we become a team and can relax, laugh, marvel together over what we discover, and we can learn. Sharing my expertise is basic to the teacher role. But *how* I share that expertise and the *timing* for sharing must be in response to the children, both individually and collectively. Determining how and when to "teach" creates the dynamic tension in good teaching and the precise reason why teaching can never be reduced to a set of procedures, practices, and plans. I've found that I must begin by irrefutably trusting the children's desire to learn and their ability to do so; I must respect children and try not to judge them. Trust and respect become the foundation that enables me to listen and then respond to the children with authenticity and a light touch.

CHAPTER 9

Large-Group Sharing

"Can I share?"

"Can I? I didn't ever yet—well, almost never."

A clamor of voices bombards me with requests as soon as I ask children to gather for the sharing time that ends every writing workshop. My conference record sheet helps me choose a child who hasn't shared recently. I also try to call on a writer who has had a particularly good day or one who has tried something new. Sharing time contributes to the supportive nature of our writing community and also provides a time for specific instruction.

During the workshop this day, a month into the school year, I've asked Amy and Darren to share. Amy has included direct quotations of conversation in her writing. Darren has happened upon a way to use the sides of his crayons. I've seen this technique before but Darren's blending of colors creates an unusual visual experience. Darren is delighted with himself and his work today. Sharing his drawing will enhance his status in this community. I look at my checklist to select a third sharer and notice that Erika hasn't shared for a while.

"Erika, do you want to share that piece about horseback riding?"

"Okay." As we move to the storyrug, Erika confides that she's not sure she can read all her words. I assure her this will be okay, to just read what she can and tell us about the rest. Erika could tell me her intended meaning in our writing conference, though she was unable to read every word in her writing. I'm not concerned. Erika uses letter and context clues along with her memory of the content to read what she has written. Her writing fluency expands each day and she's developing reading strategies.

In turn, the writers take their place on the author's chair. Ellen Blackburn Karelitz gave us the term *author's chair*. She described it as the place where either she or a child reads to the class. In the research Donald Graves and Jane Hansen (1987) conducted on the connections between reading and writing in Ellen's classroom, "author's chair" came to symbolize the relationship between reading and writing. "Readers who are also writers develop a sense of authorship that helps them in either composing process" (p. 183). We actually have two author's chairs in this room—two small captain's chairs decorated with handpainted Pennsylvania Dutch motifs that are characteristic of Lancaster County, Pennsylvania. I didn't plan for two chairs; the need for two developed out of the collaboration that occurs between two children in reading and writing: sometimes two children share a piece they've co-authored or a book they've learned to read together.

The children know the procedures for sharing at the end of writing workshop.

- The author reads, shows illustrations, then calls on responders (children or teacher) who have raised their hands.
- Responders begin comments with "I" rather than "you."
- Responders avoid using the word "should." (Both of these guidelines allow the responder to take responsibility for his or her comment on the writing. "You should . . ." or "You did . . ." imply that the responder knows the best way, which the writer has yet to figure out. Using "I think . . ." "I wondered . . ." "I didn't understand . . ." the responder takes responsibility for her opinion and allows the author to accept or reject the responder's idea.)
- Responses are to tell the writer as specifically as possible what we liked or learned in the piece by quoting words or phrases if possible. (Comments such as "I like your writing" are too vague to help writers.) Also, responders ask questions about parts of the writing that are unclear or about which they want more information.
- Individual sharing sessions end by applauding the writer.

Erika shares first today. She begins reading hesitantly.

ERIKA: One time I went with my dad for a ride and we—I'll tell you this part. It says, it says here we rode a horse—it was fun. I wanted to say giddy-up and they said to get down then. This is my picture of me riding a horse.

E: Karen?

K: I learned that you went with your dad for a horse ride.

E: Un-huh. John?

J: You wanted to say giddy-up but they said you had to get down then and . . . did you get to ride the horse?

E: Yes. I said that in the writing. Stacy?

S: How's come you *told* us some parts instead of reading 'em?

E: I c . . . well, Mrs. Avery said it was okay just to tell it if I didn't—if I wasn't sure exactly what it said.

S: Oh. [Stacy nods and smiles, acknowledging her understanding.]

MRS. A: Sometimes we have trouble reading what we wrote. So I told Erika to tell us because she knows what it's about. It takes practice to learn to read anything. It's one of the things you work on when you write—reading what you wrote. [The children nod.]

E: Darren?

D: I like your horse, and, um, I like your horse. You drawed good.

E: Thank you. Anyone else? Jody?

J: Well, what's that circle thing in the top of your picture? Is it a railroad or something?

E: That's a track where you can ride the horses only we didn't ride there. We just went on this path because the track is where they go fast but we couldn't go fast. So we didn't go on the track.

J: Oh, 'cause I thought it was a train track. Trains have tracks, too.

E: Mrs. Avery?

MRS. A: A track for horses and a track for trains. Two kinds of track, humm. Interesting. And I was wondering if you've ever ridden a horse before or if this was the first time?

E: No, I've ridden—well, this wasn't the first time I ever roden a horse but it was the first time we ever went to this place.

MRS. A: I see. Well, what's it like to ride a horse? Probably some people in here haven't done that before.

E: Well, it's sorta scary at first and you're really high up and I can't get up myself. My dad helps—he lifts me up so then I can get on and you have to hold the reins. But at first my dad just held the reins and I held the horse's hair—the mane. I held the horse's mane.

MRS. A: So it feels scary because you're high up and someone has to hold the reins, and at first your dad did and you held the horse's mane.

E: Yeah, but then I held the reins. Josie?

J: Maybe you could put that in if you wanted to.

E: Yeah. Greg?

GREG: I was wondering why you decided to write this piece? Was it because you like horses? 'Cause I remember you were reading that book—what's it called? *All the Different Horses?*

E: *All the Pretty Horses.* Yes, and because we went to ride a horse.

MRS. A: Thank you, Erika. [Applause]

Amy sits in the chair and reads.

AMY: I just learned how to ride a two-wheeler. This is the story. [Amy looks up from reading and comments. "I put that part— I wrote that in later. That's why it's so tiny a writing. I didn't think it would make sense if I just wrote the next part without that." She continues to read.] I was over at Josie's house and she just learned how to ride a two-wheeler. And she asked me if I could ride a two-wheeler. I said, "No, but I'm going to try." So I got on the bike. And then she said, "That is bumpy." So I went the other way. Then I said, "I did it, Josie. I learned how." Then she said, "Why don't you ride Emily's bike?" So I rode Emily's bike. Josie's bike was small. Emily's bike was the right size for me.

A: Laura?

L: I heard that you learned to ride a bike and you learned to ride Josie's bike.

A: [Nods to Laura.] Monica?

M: I heard you read that you rode Emily's bike and I wondered, "Who's Emily?"

A: Well, Emily is Josie's sister. She's in second grade.

M: Oh, I see. And I was confused at the part when you said it was bumpy. I didn't get what you meant.

A: The *road* was bumpy the way I was going, so I went the other way.

M: Oh, now I get it.

A: Elizabeth?

E: I liked when you said, "No, but I'm going to try." And then you said, "I did it, Josie."

A: Thank you. Mrs. Avery?

MRS. A: I like that part, too. Amy, could you tell the group how you wrote those parts.

A: See, I was reading it over and then when I talked to Mrs. Avery she asked if I put that part in—the part that said, "I did it, Josie" and I thought that was important for people to know that I did it and so I wrote it and I put circles and arrows like Mrs. Avery showed us. ["Ohhh" and nods from the group.]

MRS. A: Any questions? Amy revised her writing by putting information in that she forgot the first time she wrote it—just as we talked about in mini-lessons. This writer also did something else. She included *conversation*. She thought of the words she said and wrote them, and I think it made it more interesting than if she'd just *told* us she learned to ride the bike. Don't you?

GREG: Yeah, you can *hear* her talking in her story. You know, like we talked about seeing pictures in our heads. Well, here we can hear people talking in our heads.

MRS. A: I like that. I hadn't thought of it quite that way before. Putting in conversation is something you could think of for your writing, so readers can hear the words in their heads. Thank you, Amy. [Applause]

Darren is next. Writing has been difficult for Darren. He strings tiny, neat letters across a page but he can't read a word of it. If I sit beside him while he composes, I am able to read some of his writing later, but I also notice that his mind switches from one topic to another and so does his writing. He loves drawing and carefully produces trucks, tractors, bikes, and buildings. One day he expressed frustration at not being able to reproduce the correct perspective on a barn. I provided him with illustrations and spent some time during free play showing him how to draw only two sides of a building instead of three. Today he holds up his work in sharing circle: reds, browns, yellows, blues, oranges, a blended spectrum that fills the art. Darren's work is unique. The exquisiteness of the page causes the children to suck in their breaths.

"How did you do that?"

"It's *beautiful*!"

"Neat!"

"I like them colors!"

"Wow! Darren, you're an artist!"

Darren beams. So far he hasn't said a word. The children seem to sense he's not ready to take charge of his sharing session and they respond without waiting for him to call on them. Yet they maintain order. I marvel at their instinctive ability to manage situations with such grace. But I want to draw Darren in so I prompt him.

MRS. A: Darren, can you tell them how you did this?

DARREN: I just, ah, ah, I, um, with crayons.

MRS. A: With what part of the crayons, Darren?

D: The sides.

MRS. A: Can you tell us more?

D: I just, um, I used the sides—with no paper. Well, see, the paper all come off my crayons.

MRS. A: Ah, no paper on the crayons. Do you see, boys and girls?

VOICES: I did that before—but not like Darren.

What's the picture at the bottom?

D: A farm.

VOICE: Oh, it's a farm.

D: My granddad's farm. I go to my granddad's farm.

VOICES: I like the trees.

I like the sky! All those colors. That sky's really neat.

It's probably a sunset sky.

MRS. A: Can you tell us about the sky or the trees, Darren?

D: The leaves, um, they're all colors.

MRS. A: The leaves are all colors?

D: Un-huh, 'cause it's fall and that makes the leaves all colors.

MRS. A: Fall makes the leaves all colors. And you like those colors, Darren?

D: Um, I like the leaves all colors.

Darren squirms. His restlessness tells me he's done enough for now. We applaud Darren and get ready for lunch.

The group sharing circle, another procedure learned from Graves, Giacobbe, and Calkins, is a ritual to end the workshop just as the mini-lesson is the opening. The children seem to appreciate the closure procedure as well as the opportunity to hear their classmates' writing. One day when a change in the school schedule required that we omit the sharing the children protested, "But we didn't have sharing!" In the first weeks, I take a strong leadership role in the sharing to establish the procedures and the tone. Gradually, I work into a more backseat role—one where the children listen and take the lead in responding. Basically, through my model, I'm trying to teach children to listen to a writer's meaning, to ask questions to clarify that meaning, and to examine the techniques the writers use to effectively convey meaning—all the while affirming the writer.

On this day, the sharing time provided an opportunity to expand writing skills, to enhance the sense of community, and to encourage and affirm writers. Some of the topics that arose in this particular session were expanding the children's understanding of a word (track), adding description, including conversation, inserting information, rereading one's writing for meaning, learning to read one's writing, connecting writing ideas to books, and using crayons differently. We didn't discuss every concept, but participating in the group sharing contributed to the bank of experiences that enrich the children's growing sense of themselves as writers and of their writing processes.

Sharing time also needs to nurture the writer. I supported Erika after she fielded Stacy's question about telling the story instead of reading it. In Darren's session I spoke a lot because Darren hadn't become comfortable leading the sharing session. He would gradually develop this ability, and I would remove my support in proportion to his ability to take over for himself. The critical encouragement for Darren as a member of the community came from his peers.

During the sharing I usually select a particular point to emphasize to the group. We can't address everything; to do so would overload the children and frustrate their progress. In Amy's sharing, for instance, I could have responded to the question "Who's Emily?" by pointing out the writer's responsibility to consider if the reader will know what the writer knows. Instead, I chose to comment about Amy's inclusion of conversation, which Greg so beautifully described for us. The class would come back to his phrase "hearing talk in our heads" again and again during other discussions of children's writing. Stressing Amy's accomplishment provided opportunity for everyone to learn. There will be moments in the sharing when a problem in a piece becomes just the right time to address a specific writing technique—a time when children are ready and will grow from the discussion. The writer must never feel embarrassed or uncomfortable. In fact, often the writer helps with the teaching by expressing in natural language a way to improve the writing.

Learning to hold back and ignore opportunities to address a skill was probably the hardest part of making the writing workshop a time for children to grow. In the end, the responsive approach covers more than any sequenced approach ever did. But with this responsive approach to teaching, I am continually making choices as to what to respond to and the appropriate timing. My decisions are informed not only by curriculum and my own knowledge, but also by my awareness of the children. As the professional in the classroom, I must respond to those "teachable moments" in a way that helps us all become excited about learning.

More and more as the year unfolds, the children listen, respond, and manage for themselves. In February Chris wrote a fiction piece entitled "Patrick and the Elf." He shared the story in progress with the class.

Chris read the title, turned to the first page, and continued with a somewhat choppy rhythm, a natural aspect of reading a rough draft. "There once was a little boy named Patrick. One day Patrick wanted to go to his friend's house, but his mother didn't let him go. Wait a minute . . ." Chris interrupted the story, paused, then reread, "but his mother didn't let him. He got very mad and said, 'No one is fair in this house. No one is fair. It would be better if I lived alone.' So he packed his clothes and went on his way."

Again Chris paused as we worked to locate the words on his messy draft. "On his way he met some bushes that were shivering. 'Now how do you think those bushes are shivering?' he muttered to himself. Suddenly a hat popped out. He was shocked but curious. He got a little bit closer. Suddenly a voice stopped him. The voice said, 'Don't you take another step closer or I will shoot you dead.' Patrick was scared but still curious. He sneaked over to the bushes. This was what he was an expert at. Patrick peeked through the bushes and . . ."

Chris came to the end of the written words but he continued speaking. "I stopped there because that's when you said we had to stop. I'll tell you what I'm going to write next because it's like it's going to be an elf and he's going to find out and then he says, 'It's an elf,' and a gun's pointed at him and he says, 'Don't be hasty little elf.' And then he started walking backwards and the elf says that. And then they make friends and they start living. And for supper they have raw fish and beets. And he didn't like it." Chris grinned as he told this part. His classmates sat in rapt attention, hanging on to every word and itching to share their responses. Chris continues. "He goes, 'Aahhh!' And then he doesn't eat it. He only eats some of the beets and then they start like having a new life together."

The hands flew up the second Chris finished. He looked around and called on Eileen.

"I think you have a very good story going," said Eileen. Chris nodded an acknowledgment, then called on Danny.

"I *love* that story. It's *so neat!*" The words rolled out of Danny's mouth; his tone emphasized his enjoyment of the story. Chris smiled and nodded.

"Becky?"

"I like when you said, 'Don't take another step frontwards or I'll shoot you,' " said Becky, and Chris's face suddenly brightened.

My hand was up and Chris called on me. I picked up on Becky's comment, "I think you chose some excellent words. I liked when you used the word 'curious' and said the 'bushes shivered' . . ."

"And 'muttered,' " Chris interrupted, relishing the word as it exploded from his lips. Then he added, "I like the one about don't be hasty!"

"I like that one, too," I replied. Then I turned to the group and said, "Don't you think that the choice of words that he uses makes his story interesting?" The children agreed in a chorus of affirming comments.

Chris called on Jason, who said, "I like when you said, 'Don't be hasty little elf.' "

Then Missi commented, "I think you can make that into a book because it's so *long.*"

"I do. I want to," said Chris, "because some of the pictures I really want to draw because I know what to do."

At this point I commented, "I sense, Chris, that you really feel in control of this writing. You really know where it's going and what you're going to do with it."

"Yes," Chris acknowledged. His smile confirmed the confidence. He called on Jason again.

"That's a good book and I think that if you were a grown-up and you wrote that book you could turn it into a published book that people might read." Jason paid Chris a strong compliment by telling him that his writing would succeed in the grown-up publishing world.

One final question came from Kevin. "Do you want to publish that book?"

Chris knew his writing process well enough to defer such a commitment at this time and replied, "I might." We ended the sharing session with our customary applause. The energy in that session spurred Chris to continue his writing and prompted other children to try fiction and to consider effective word choices. The momentum of that session, which grew out of all the sessions since the beginning of school, continued into the days and weeks ahead.

Sometimes we lose this momentum or have trouble developing it. One year during the first week of school I watched Lauren during the share circle. She held her hand poised to fly up the instant the reader asked for responses. Sure enough, up went the hand and Lauren gave the first response. "How did you get the idea for this piece?" she asked.

The question startled me because I'd never heard one of my first graders ask such a question during the first days of school. Their natural inquiries usually centered on the drawing with questions such as "What's that yellow thing at the bottom?" Lauren's question surfaced again and again and I noticed that she paid little attention to the answer. I waited for the right moment to ask Lauren the question that burned in my head: "Lauren, where did you get the idea for that question?"

"From last year when we did writing. I always asked that question." I understood. Lauren had participated in a writing workshop in kindergarten in another city. She had learned a formula, a routine complete with rote questions. She asked questions without thinking, without listening to the writer, without really wanting an answer.

Group sharing occasionally hits this snag. The children fall into a pattern of repeating questions they've heard me ask and spitting them out like robots. The sharing time loses its responsive nature, and subsequently its effectiveness. Questions lacking authenticity produce answers lacking authenticity.

Q: How did you get the idea for this story?
A: I just thought of it, or Because I like my dog.
Q: What will you do next?
A: I don't know yet. I might add more or I might not.
Q: How do you feel about this piece of writing?
A: I like it.

Children participate in a meaningless dialogue of routine questions and answers. What's more, they supply bland comments such as "I like your story," "I like your picture," "I think you have a good piece of writing." Programmed questions, answers, and comments lack the thoughtfulness of genuine responses and the sharing circle disintegrates to a useless ritual.

I've confronted this development off and on in writing workshops over the years and struggled with the children to improve questions and responses. I knew that we needed to provide writers with specific responses rather than generalized ones, but I never could identify why these ineffective patterns developed. Lauren showed me. Her question was blatantly formulaic and unresponsive to the writer. It helped me understand that our central role was to *listen* to the writer and ask questions and comments based on what we heard. It was as simple as that.

I had inadvertently developed my own set of questions, which turned into another orthodoxy for teaching writing. I had become concerned with modeling good questions so that children would know how to question and internalize questions for themselves. What I needed to do was model good *listening*. To nourish the momentum of effective group sharing, I needed to listen and enter into the writer's space at that moment. Then I could provide thoughtful responses. It boiled down to just plain hospitable conversation. When I listened, so did the children and they responded authentically. They also learned over time to develop effective questions and to internalize those questions for themselves. Listening led to thoughtful responses, ones that help writers.

Most first graders are eager to share their writing with the class. Only one year did I encounter a child reluctant to read her writing. At first I thought it was because she was unsure of being able to read what she had written. But as I watched this child I realized that she was genuinely frightened. She clearly communicated that no, this was not for her. I gave her time: time to trust the environment, the children, and me. In March I tried once again by asking her at the beginning of the workshop to share that day. She shook her head. "How about tomorrow?" I pressed. Reluctantly she agreed. But the next day she put me off until yet another tomorrow. On the third day I reminded her that today she had agreed to share, and throughout the workshop I stopped by her desk to encourage her. As she took the author's chair I reminded the class that this was her first time to share her writing and that I was sure they remembered how scary it was for each of them to share for the first time. The children listened and gently responded. At the end the writer smiled at them. Though she never volunteered to share, this young writer henceforth accepted my invitations to participate in the group sharing. The precise reason for her fear remains a mystery.

My role in the writing workshop fell into a pattern that worked: I started with a mini-lesson, circulated among the children listening and responding, participated in the group sharing, and eventually published the children's writing.

I suppose I could have gone for years this way—establishing, reflecting, revising, and administering a writing program in my classroom. Then one day in November, after I'd left all the programmed instructional materials behind, an incident in my classroom changed my perspective on learning and teaching.

I returned from the NCTE convention in Washington, D.C., on the day before Thanksgiving, buoyed by all the stimulating presentations of the previous days. As the children settled into writing that morning, a tall, strawberry-blond, and rather shy boy came up to me and said, "Mrs. Avery, you always *tell* us about your writing, but you never *write* when we write. How come?" With the imploring honesty of a child straight out of Dickens, Chris stood before me, looked me straight in the eye, and awaited an answer.

I looked away briefly, then back to Chris and replied, "You're right, Chris. I'll write today." I vaguely remember turning to the whole class and announcing that Chris had asked about my writing and therefore I intended to write today, too, rather than circulating around the room. With no idea of what might come, I picked up a pen.

The night before I had driven my car around the mall in Washington searching for the newly dedicated (and as yet unlighted) Vietnam War Memorial. Dusk fell. I stopped to ask directions. Finally I parked my car and headed on foot, alone, into the darkness, away from the safety—if even uncertain safety—of big city streetlights, into the unknown to search out this new memorial. Suddenly my feet sank into soft earth, and in a moment of horrified realization, I knew I'd walked on the newly tilled earth of the memorial itself. I was above The Wall, trespassing on the gravestone of long dead friends and peers. Turning, I made my way along the monument's edge to ground level, and there in the darkness met several veterans who lighted matches so that, together, we might read the names on the narrow point of that angling marble. I walked deeper into that cavern of scooped out ground and touched a rose lying beside a votive candle. Moments later, I walked back through the darkness to my car to head home. My heart and thoughts were a wild collage of war and death and friends and struggles and life.

Now, the next morning during writing workshop, in this first-grade classroom, I said I would write. When I put my pen to paper, the words that came described the experience and intense emotions from the night before that still enveloped me. I wrote. Several children moved past me. One or two smiled or nodded, but no one spoke to me. They seemed to respect my need not to be interrupted, that what I was doing was important. I continued to write far longer than I initially had planned. When the time came to share a child said, "Mrs. Avery's going to share her writing today." Panic.

"No, that's okay," I said. "I don't need to share."

"Yes," they chimed in. "You share."

"We want to hear your writing."

"You have to share, too."

I took a breath. "Okay, but I don't think it's anything you'll understand."

"That's okay," they replied and I heard buzzings of "Mrs. Avery's gonna share." "It's her turn." As we gathered on the carpet I thought that perhaps they might forget by the time my turn came. Of course they didn't. I began to read slowly, hesitantly. The children were hushed and perfectly still. When my voice cracked, Eileen slipped an arm behind me. When I struggled again to keep reading, Marlene lightly touched the hand that held the paper. I finished the reading. The hands went up and I proceeded to call on children for responses.

"I liked the beginning when you said the part about 'soft squishy mud . . . around your feet.' "

"I think it was scary the way you walked in the dark and you could see the lights only they were far away."

"This writing made me feel spooky and sad both."

"I think this is a good piece of writing and that it was hard to write this."

"Yeah, I'm glad you shared it with us."

I knew that my writing was filled with words and phrases that the children could never define if they encountered them out of context. I had not written the story planning to share it with anyone, let alone anticipating the children as an audience. Yet they had understood. The responses, verbal and nonverbal, from this gentle audience left me wanting to continue this piece of writing and wanting to receive their responses again.

I walked with the children to the cafeteria and then came back to my desk, my head reeling and my heart raw. Finally I began to write. I wrote to record what had just happened—the children's responses, how I had felt, now felt. I wrote to begin a reflection process on being a writer and a teacher of writing that would continue for weeks and for months. I had just experienced one of those moments in teaching, an anomaly, that surprises us, teaches us, invites us to change, to outgrow ourselves.

Prior to this I had been amazed by what the children could achieve, but my amazement had been restricted to their academic accomplishments. I delighted in the ways they experimented and played with language. I marveled at their ability to transcend errors with grace, to use error as a natural path to further learning. I admired the energy of their learning, surging and receding again and again, yet always moving onward. But now I understood, because I had experienced through them the source of that energy—the heart and humanity of being a writer in a community. The children had taken me into that community in a new way. They taught me that academic behaviors are important, but that they develop best out of an intangible, unmeasurable essence created out of relationships.

CHAPTER 10

Revision and the Publishing Process

Years ago, before writing workshop days, I gave first graders story starters. Some of these prompts were pretty silly, such as the one I used to conclude our science unit on dinosaurs: "If I had a pet dinosaur . . ." For a winter unit I led the children through a creative movement activity and then asked them to write by finishing this opening line: "If I was a snowman melting in the sun . . ." After the children wrote I corrected and they recopied the brief pieces. I'd "taught" writing and integrated it into curricular areas to boot.

In November every class wrote about Thanksgiving. Instead of a cute story starter, I asked the children to write about *their* Thanksgiving—anything about their Thanksgiving. Here are two examples from that assignment from years ago.

"I had a turkey. I had a nice dinner. I had giving. I had potatoes. I had gravy. I had corn."

And: "On Thanksgiving for dinner I had turkey, potatoes, stuffing, cranberry and we had corn. It was delicious. Yum!"

This second story was one of the most interesting in the entire class. The words "delicious" and "yum" set it apart from the others. When I read these stories today (I had been so pleased with the children's writing that I saved much of it), I notice that every child wrote about Thanksgiving dinner. I suspect that I had "motivated" by talking about food and dinner and the children had figured out what I wanted. Even by the end of the year, when the children wrote about their mothers for Mother's Day, their stories still sounded similar. The following example is typical.

"I like my mom. My mom likes me. We like to go places."

In this batch of Mom stories, perhaps the strongest voice emerged in a piece about the birth of a baby brother.

"When I went to the hospital my mom let me stay and see Michael for a long time. And he was so so very so cute. He was adorable. I loved him. When my dad said it was time to go I said, 'Okay.' The End."

Reading through the accumulated writing from former classes, I notice development in spelling and mechanics for most of the children as the school year moved along. Certainly these skills ought to have improved. After all, every set of papers bears the marks of my colored correction pen and a brief comment about the content (e.g., "Outstanding story" or "So nice. Mom will like it."). There's not much development in the content though. Once in a while a child hit on a strong topic such as the baby brother story above. The saddest observation I make as I peruse these papers is that all of the most interesting stories—and I do mean *all*—come from the kids in the top reading group. Did I believe more in them? Encourage them more? Take more interest? Just expect more from them? And as a corollary, did I expect less or give less to the other children? I cannot escape the fact that grouping for reading quickly established a tracking system in my old first-grade classroom that spilled over to other areas of the curriculum, including writing. Also, I see that I was not really teaching writing, just correcting mechanics.

When I began trying some of the suggestions for teaching writing coming from Don Graves's research, encouraging invented spelling and self-selected topics, delighting in the content and ignoring initially the mechanical and grammatical errors, the content of the children's writing began to improve and the disparity between children in the leveled reading groups began to dissipate. In January of the year when I first began playing with this approach to writing, when children wrote as part of their seatwork, one of the children in the lowest reading group wrote the following:

> Long, long ago there were strange creatures. Their name was dinosaur. When they stepped their footsteps were like lightning. Some of them ate plants. Some of them ate meat. Soon the volcanos killed some of the dinosaurs. The scientists think a meteor hit there. The water sunk in the sand. The dinosaurs didn't have enough water. They died. The alligators are related to dinosaurs.

At the same time, a child in the top group wrote this fictional story entitled "The Brave Dog."

> Once there was a brave dog. He had no home. He had to make his home. His home was in the forest. His name was Freddy. He is a good dog. He saved a cat. The cat's Mommy told the owner, "This dog saved

my cat." The owner said, "I'll let the dog stay." The dog had a home. The dog had food. The dog had love.

I could no longer connect the children to their reading groups by looking at their writing. The barriers between the school-imposed homogeneous groups had begun to dissolve. Writing played a major role in bringing down these walls.

In the end, it was children's voices emerging through writing that hooked me on these new approaches to teaching writing. I remember one child writing "Did You Know That My Mommy and Daddy Got Divorced?" and recall his process: coming to me as I taught a reading group, waiting patiently until I could pause, then reading the words, looking for the acknowledgment of being heard, then going away to write more. The story emerged.

> Did you know how my Mommy and Daddy got divorced? My Mommy and Daddy fought a lot. They fought about money. So finally my Mommy and Daddy got a divorce. My Daddy didn't want to go because he knew he would miss us. He's fixing up a house. I live with my Mom. I couldn't have lived with my Daddy. My Mom takes me places to make me feel better but it never works. I feel happy about it because then they don't fight. I feel sad about it. I miss him. I miss going sledding with him. My Dad feels sad but he doesn't show it. My Mom feels angry about the divorce. My sister feels sad about the divorce. But I still like to go to my Dad's house. My Mom and Dad really aren't divorced yet. Did you know that my Mom and Dad were divorced? I hope you like my book.

This child had been one of the "reluctant writers" in the classroom, beginning many pieces of writing but rarely completing any until this piece. After this story writing became easier for this young writer. On the last day of school, he handed me the published book saying, "Here, you keep it for me. I don't need it anymore." The power of writing was emerging within my classroom. But, to be honest, at the time I was still focussed on the publication part of the process.

The publication of little books with the child's own words neatly typed pleased everyone: the children, their parents, and me. We delighted in the charming and touching stories the children wrote. More than that, products provided proof of achievement and I needed that tangible assurance. So I typed after school, before school, and in the evening at home to bring out volume after volume of child-authored stories. I required nothing of the children in the way of revision and editing (I didn't believe first graders could manage much of this part of the writing process). The children simply wrote and handed the writing over to me for typing and making into a book. I also spent lots of time cutting paper into various shapes and creating fancy covers (also in a particular shape) for shape books—cute books in the shape of a particular topic on which I had all the children write. All of this was part of *my* development, stages I needed to go through. I was breaking new ground and I really had found no other model to follow from my own classroom experience, teacher training, or through reading about other classrooms. Although I gave the children choices about most of their writing topics, with few exceptions I maintained control over the publishing by deciding what to accept and reject for publication and by editing (I called it correction) as I typed the children's drafts.

Gradually I became weary of this bookmaking process. My student writers could dash out stories faster than I could produce bookcovers and type their pieces. Something had to change or we would burn out. After participating in the Giacobbe workshop where I wrote myself, I began to understand that process and product were reciprocal elements of writing. Final products in attractive formats encouraged my young writers. But engaging in the process of writing, with all the struggles along the way, requires an involvement from the writer that makes the final product ever more meaningful.

Don Murray (1982) defines writing as "the process of using language to discover meaning in experience and to communicate it" (p. 73). In the beginning there is only blank paper, says Murray, and at the end of the composing process there is a piece of paper that has found its own meaning. "This process of evolving meaning motivates writers" (p. 18). Participating in a writing workshop rather than just learning *about* the teaching of writing helped me realize that in prior years my first graders were "doing writing," producing a lot writing, but they were not really engaged in the *process* of writing. The procedure had been: they draft, I revise and publish. I took over and did most of the work, robbing my students of meaningful engagement as writers. In order to develop as writers, the children needed to experience the process of using written language "to discover meaning in experience and communicate." We needed both process and product, and my responsibility now, I realized, was to involve the children in revision and editing.

Beginning Revision

Revision of writing begins the first day of school when I say to Josh who starts to erase, "If you change your mind or decide you want something different in your writing, just line out the part you don't want and then keep on writing. All writers change their minds. I don't know of a writer who gets his ideas down just the way he wants them the first time." Josh gives me a dubious look but then flips his pencil around and follows my direction. Later I talk with the entire class about revision by repeating what I've told Josh. "All good writers revise. In here this year, we'll all do lots of revising as we write. Sometimes writers remember things they forgot to put in or they decide to take some things out or to change the words. I'll help you learn how to do these things. We've just talked about one way: lining out and going on when you change your mind about something you've written."

During the first weeks of school I show children how to reread their writing and then line out repetitious words or how to change letters or words by lining out and then writing in the new letter or word. I show them how to use carets to insert missing words or phrases. These first strategies help young writers view their writing as evolving texts, and it's crucial to establish this attitude early in the year. The point is not just to correct mechanical errors but to have the writing make sense or say what the writer wants to say. My conferences with children focus on meaning in order to help them develop this attitude. These young writers begin anticipating readers who want to understand what they have written.

Six weeks into the school year of that first year after taking the Giacobbe course, a boy named Jon showed me how important responses were in the children's processes of clarifying meaning in their writing.

"Will you read my writing?" Jon asked at the end of the writing workshop, "I think it's a really good piece."

"Sure. Tell me why this is good, Jon," I replied.

"I don't know—'cuz it's long and it's about our vacation."

After school I read Jon's story. (See Figure 10–1.)

When I finished reading I wrote Jon a brief note: "I like your story about Hilton Head. What was the best part of the trip?" The next day Jon read my note and immediately started writing. He brought me the piece again. "I wrote some more about Hilton Head," he said. Figure 10–2 shows the addition to his story.

At the end of that workshop Jon read his story in group sharing. The children were confused. Because Jon had added the new information to the end of his first writing, the chronological sequence of events was missing, making it difficult for readers to follow. Jon had no idea how to move information in a piece of writing. I explained to Jon and the children that writers sometimes make big changes—more than just a few words or letters—so that their writing makes sense to readers. I told the group that I would help Jon move some sentences in tomorrow's workshop and then he could show them what he did. The next morning I asked Jon to read through his piece and locate the place in the story where the added information actually occurred. Jon went off and a few minutes later came back to

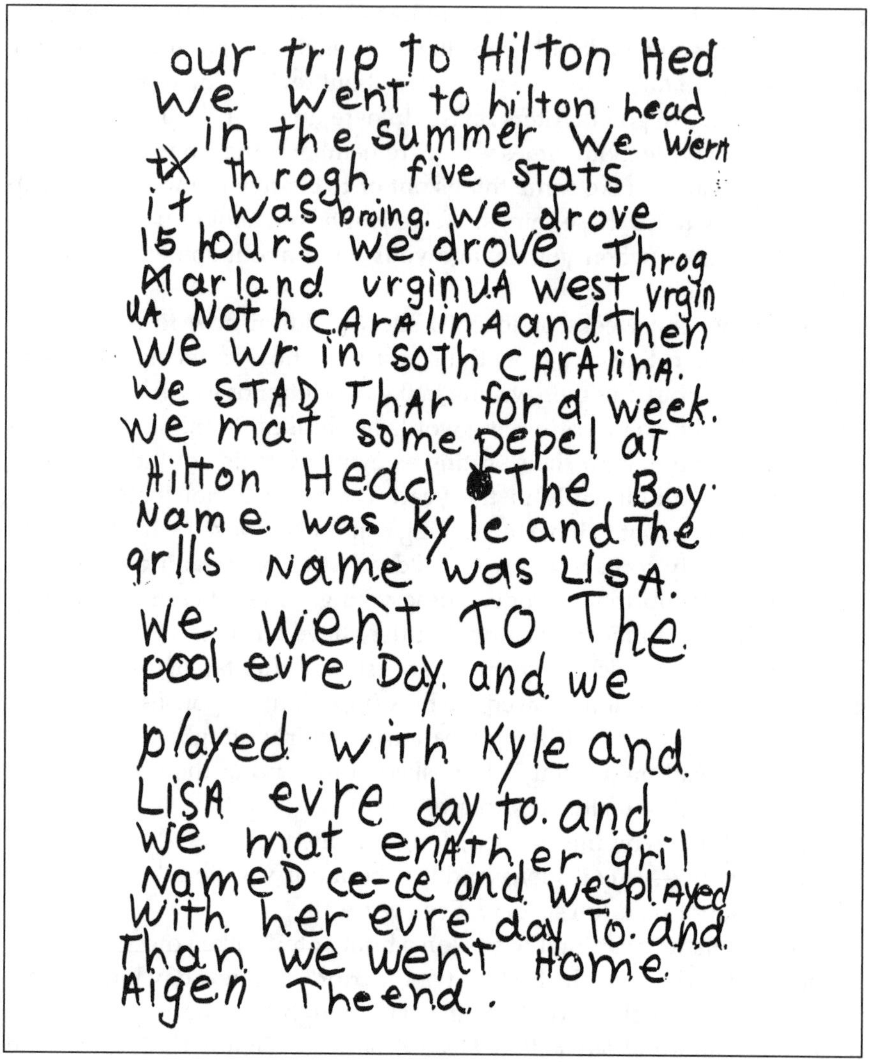

our trip to Hilton Hed
We went to hilton head
in the summer We Went
tX throgh five stats
it was broing. We drove
15 hours we drove Throg
Marland vrginuA West vrgin
uA Noth cArAlinA andthen
We wr in soth cArAlinA.
We STAD ThAr for a week.
We mat some pepel at
Hilton Hedd The Boy.
Name. was kyle andThe
grlls Name was LISA.
We went To The.
pool evre Day. and we

played with Kyle and.
LISA evre day to. and
We mat enAther gril
NameD ce-ce and we played
with her evre day To. and.
Than we went Home.
Aigen Theend..

Figure 10–1

*Jon's original
story.*

show me a large dot he had placed in his draft. Together we read his words,
shifting to the ending section when we came to the large dot. Later, Jon and
I showed the entire class this procedure. In front of the group we cut the
first section apart at the dot and taped the insertion in place. When Jon
reread the newly constructed piece, the children commented that two lines
didn't seem to belong. Jon agreed with his classmates and eliminated the
lines. As a final part of the writing I taught Jon how to put commas between
the states he listed at the beginning of his piece. The typed book became the
first published book in the classroom.

Jon's revision in his Hilton Head vacation story marked a milestone for
me. I saw how a child's writing could open up with one simple question.

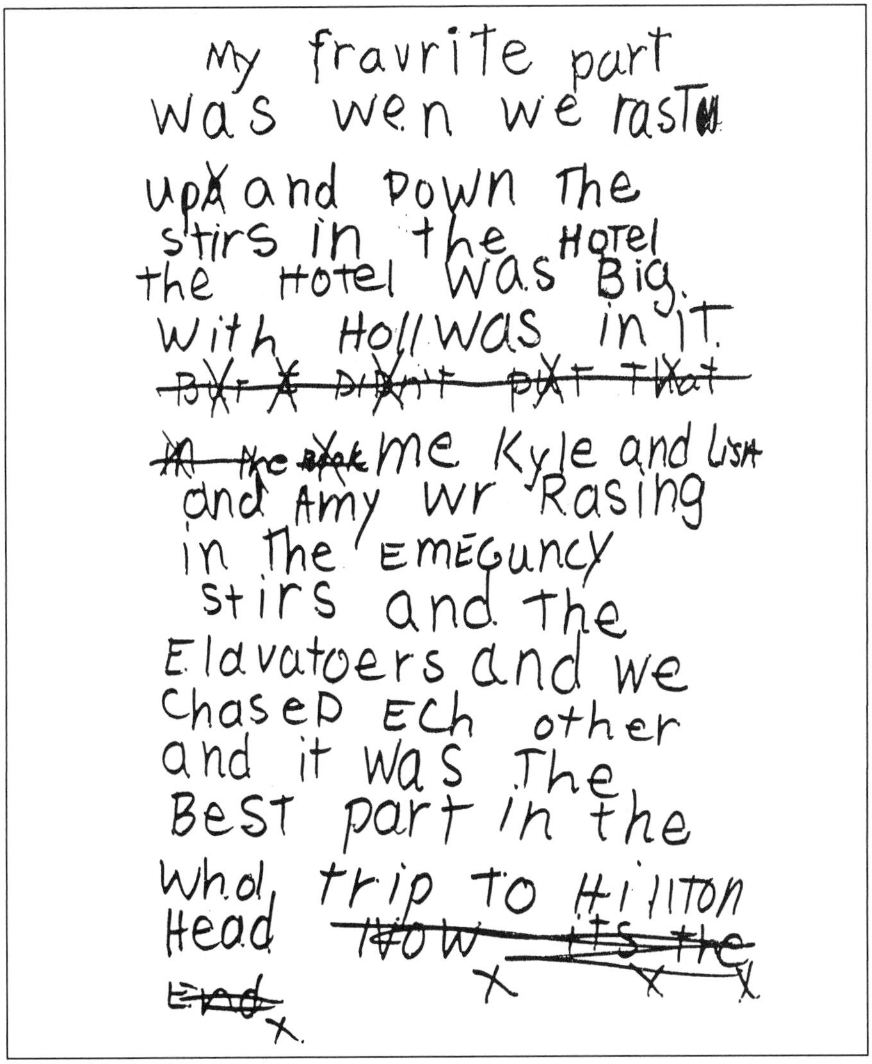

My fravrite part
was wen we rast
up and Down The
stirs in the Hotel
the Hotel was Big
with Hollwas in it.
~~But I Didn't put That~~
~~in the stor~~ me Kyle and Lisa
and Amy wr Rasing
in The Emeguncy
stirs and the
Elavatoers and we
Chased Ech other
and it was The
Best part in the
whol trip to Hillton
Head ~~Now its the~~
~~End~~

Figure 10–2

Jon's addition to his story.

That question, "What was the best part of your trip?" hadn't been calculated or carefully chosen to evoke more writing from him, but rather asked because it had come to mind when I read his story. Jon's answer surprised us both. He was quite involved with this new information—as though he'd remembered something that he'd forgotten. Now I understood what I had previously heard Giacobbe say: that *all* writers, children no exception, know more than appears on the page they draft. Part of the intrigue of writing is getting in touch with lost or forgotten experiences, putting them into written language, and communicating to others. After that, I discovered frequent opportunities to encourage children to add information as they talked about their writing.

When Kelly wrote about going to a local farm to pick a Halloween pumpkin I heard an energy in her voice that had not yet emerged in the written story. Trying to get at just what was really important to her I asked, "Kelly, what was this like for you?" She paused, looked off a brief moment absorbed in thought, then turned back to me and said, "Well, I'll tell you. It looked just like someone took a huge bag of orange balloons and dumped it all over that field. That's what I kept thinking the whole time I was there." It wasn't choosing a pumpkin that Kelly remembered from that day so much as the sight of the pumpkin field. Kelly's added description brought energy to her writing and the orange balloons became an example for other students of how to write description. To this day, when I pass a Lancaster County pumpkin field in autumn I think of Kelly's image. Those pumpkin fields *do* look like someone spilled a big bag of orange balloons on them!

Questions such as What was the best part? What will be the best part of this writing? or What was that like for you? have not only helped writers consider the focus of a piece of writing, but also enabled them to uncover the point of the entire piece. I hope these questions aren't becoming formulaic. I realize that I must always guard against becoming prescriptive. I hope to help the writer get in touch with what he or she knows, then to help that writer discover options for the direction of the piece.

The children began thinking about their topics in more depth, and this thinking often led to revision, usually by adding information. I was turning more control of the writing over to the children. The emphasis on product diminished for both the children and me, and I realized that publishing meant more than making lots of little books. The function of publishing was to enhance the central purpose of writing, the process of making meaning.

First Publications

After the children have become comfortable with the procedures of writing workshop and have developed a degree of writing fluency (usually in the late autumn), I help them publish their writing in book form. Book publication provides important reading material for beginning readers and also takes children's writing out of the school and into the homes of families and friends. Its most important function, however, is deepening the engagement of writers by requiring them to probe their individual meaning-making processes even further, as Giacobbe also found.

Beginning to publish student writing takes some planning. Giacobbe's model helped me shape my procedures for a publishing process. If I announced one day that we were all going to select a piece of writing for publication, I know I'd soon be overwhelmed with the workload and both the children and I would become frustrated. I can't manage a whole class of first-grade children revising and editing their publications at the same time. So I create a routine that allows me to respond to individual children. I start with a couple of children, helping them rethink, revise, and edit a piece of writing, and then gradually involve more children in the same process. This pace allows me to respond to individual needs, to establish a publishing procedure that will serve us for the remainder of the year, and, by beginning with confident writers, to provide a growing number of reassuring models for the more reticent class members. It takes nearly a month to take every child in the room through the book publication process.

Monica and Greg

On a morning in late October I approached Monica and said, "You've done a lot of writing since school started. I'd like you to look through everything you've written and choose what you think is your best piece. I'm thinking that we can work on that piece a little more, see if there are any changes that might make it better, do some final editing, and then publish it by making it into a book."

"Okay," Monica replied. "I think I know which one is my best—my story about Bald Head Island."

"Well, look through the writing and be sure. When you've decided, I'd like you to read the piece carefully to make sure everything will make sense to people who read it. If you find things that need changing, make those revisions. Then we'll talk again."

"Okay." Monica's tone as she turned to the task was neither overly zealous nor reluctant. She proceeded with the quiet poise typical of her style in the classroom.

When I presented the same request to Greg a few moments later he replied, "All right. But, see, today I was planning to write that piece about me and my dad, the one I was working on yesterday you know? So, I wanted to do that 'cause it's in my head right now."

"That's fine. No hurry. You can do this whenever you're ready. Let me know when you've chosen something." Greg went to work on his current topic. He wrote for a while, then began reading through his writing. By the end of the workshop he had made a selection.

"Why did you choose this particular piece?" I asked.

"Because it's about our trip to *California!*" His eyes glowed with the memory of the family trip.

"So this was really an important topic for you."

"Yes! It's a good piece!" My question helped me understand Greg and his writing and also helps Greg begin to ask such questions of himself, thus developing awareness of his own decision-making process.

Monica spent much of the workshop reading through her writing. She chose the three-page story of Bald Head Island. When she came to me she said, "That was really neat reading through all my writing."

"Oh?" I waited for Monica to tell me more.

"Yeah," she mused. "I kept reading things I had forgotten about and then I kept remembering more things I did and places we went and things like that." Her voice trailed off for a moment and a pensive look came to her face. Then she looked at me and said, "It made me think about my life, sorta." In her quizzical countenance and voice tone I detected a new awareness dawning in her mind. "Do you know what I mean?" she asked.

"Yes, I think I do. Writing's like that—at least for me it is. Keeps me thinking about my life," I replied. Monica nodded. We exchanged smiles.

That evening I read Monica's and Greg's selections. I studied each piece of writing, noted how words and pictures connected to tell a story, and listened to the writer's voice speaking from the page. I saw each writer's emerging control over the conventions of language. My reading now was certainly different from my old teacher role of identifying errors. In the reading and reflecting, I felt myself understanding each writer better and saw possibilities for helping each writer in the publishing conference to be held the next morning.

PLANNING FOR GREG: Greg's invented spelling gave me no problems as I read (see Figures 10–3a and 10–3b). I looked at Greg's detailed drawing of the airplane and recalled conferring with him when he wrote this story. At that time I'd had a bit of trouble with the words "little kitchen," but Greg read them easily. He had just finished writing "it was fun." First graders write this line a lot, frequently while the writer pauses to contemplate what to write next. "It was fun" can become a sign-off, a concluding sentence when nothing else comes to mind. I had asked Greg what he planned to write next and he had answered, "I don't know." But even as he said these words his mind was going, and before I could reply he added, "We had pizza one night. I might write about that." He told me about eating pizza at the plant where his dad was working (it turned out that the trip was a business trip for Dad). He added the information about eating pizza after I left and ended his story with "it was fun."

As I read Greg's page-and-a-half of work, I could hear Greg telling me about his California visit. The energy in the writing matched his enthusiasm for the trip. An articulate boy, Greg spoke in complete sentences that communicated a lot of information. His speech and his thinking followed a logical sequence. He wrote the same way, packing his written sentences

I WAT To KA FAr UA

MY DAD PAT Me and MY MOM

AT The Ar POt

WE SAD IN A HO TAL

UrTh A LATO KIT SAIN.

with information and details. The proportion of nouns in relation to the entire piece revealed this: Dad, Mom, California, airport, hotel, kitchen, night, pizza, plant. The grammatical structure "me and my mom" or "me and my dad" was part of his speech and so naturally appeared in his writing. He spaced his words across the page from left to right, formed the letters with a firm stroke, spelled a few words correctly, and used invented spelling to approximate others.

The airplane in Greg's picture indicated the same thoughtful involvement. I marveled at the angle of the plane's wings, the inclusion of two engines and three flaps on each wing, and Greg's attempt to show the cylinder of the jet engines through penciled spiral lines. He included other

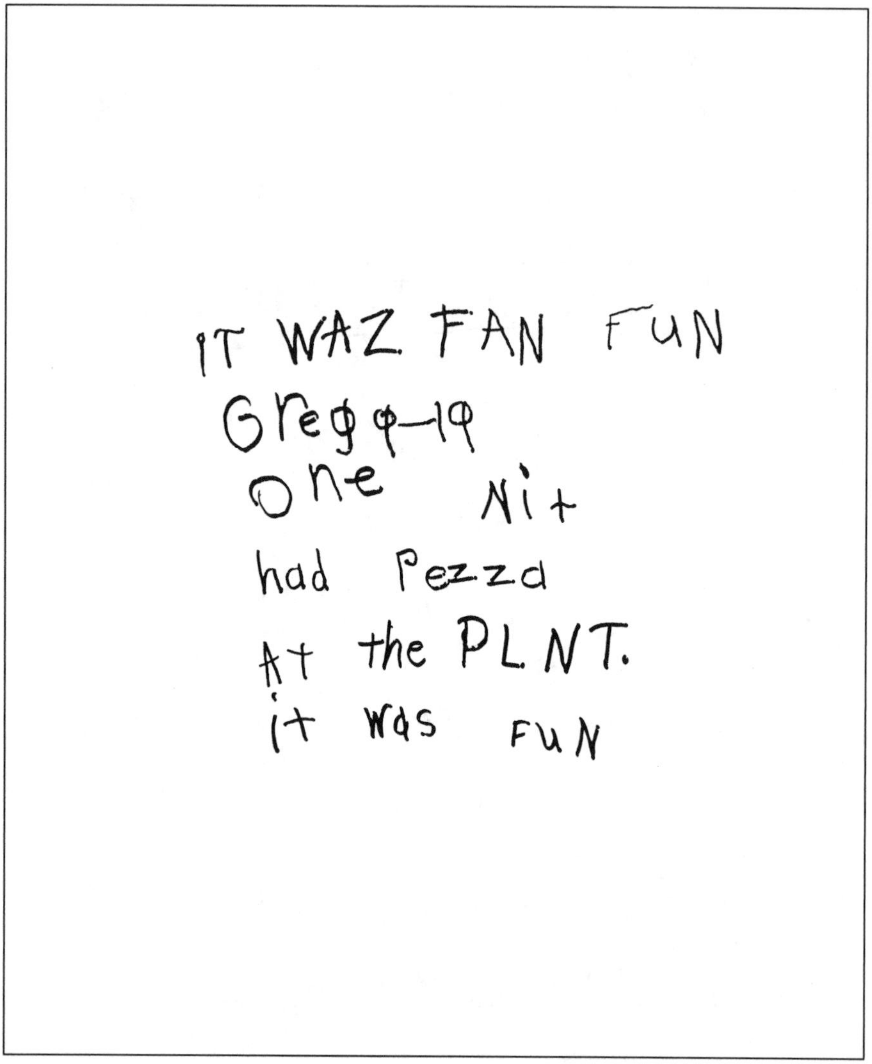

IT WAZ FAN FUN
Gregφ—1φ
One   Nit
had Pezza
At the PL.NT.
it was FuN

Figure 10–3b

Greg's writing.

details: a row of windows (one with a smiling face—probably Greg's) lining the fuselage; three exit doors, appropriately placed and marked with the letter E (I pictured Greg listening to the flight attendants before takeoff); and a rear baggage compartment filled with suitcases. The plane's tail sported an airline logo and a tail flap. Cumulus clouds and the sun—wearing sunglasses—completed the scene. I remembered Greg telling me that he drew the plane in yellow because it was the crayon "nearest to the plane's *actual* color." He had considered gray but decided it was too dark, not shiny enough.

Greg had communicated so much! Reading this writing—both words and illustration—evoked a deep respect for this young writer. Now my responsibility was to help Greg develop and polish this writing. I planned a conference involving Greg's peers where, by responding to the content, we could focus on clarity. I would come to Greg's publishing conference prepared with possible ways to help him as a writer, but I would listen to him before making suggestions. Of course, I wouldn't expect Greg to revise, edit, and correct this piece of writing to perfection. But working together to refine the piece for publication would help Greg's continuing development as a writer, a goal far more significant than developing a perfect product. Like all of writing workshop, *the underlying premise for the publishing conference is to help the writer rather than the writing.*

To plan for this publishing conference I noted possibilities for revising the piece. Missing words were the most obvious: "My Dad picked me and my Mom [up?] at the airport" and "One night [we?] had pizza." Readers needed these words and I was sure Greg would want them included. I could address the "me and my Mom" construction, work on misspelled words, or focus on ending punctuation. Greg placed a period after "kitchen," a clue that he had begun thinking about punctuation. All of these issues could come up during the conference, but whether we dealt with them at all would depend on Greg and his limits for what he could handle with this one piece of writing.

The first focus of this conference was to be on meaning and helping Greg clarify his intended meaning for readers, and so I read the piece and listened for meaning. I understood three separate points: the family took an airplane trip to California, they stayed in a hotel with a kitchen, and they ate pizza at a plant. Then suddenly the story stops. As a reader, I'm left hanging, wondering why I've read this story. If I feel this way, other readers likely will feel the same. I know Greg knows much more than what is on the paper. Helping him find the information that will bring the piece to a more coherent whole for readers will be worked out in the conference.

I jotted reminders for myself on a small Post-It™ note:

story stops
omitted words (up, we?)
sp. and punct.

I decided not to address "me and my Mom" but rather to introduce it in a future mini-lesson for the entire class. The Post-It™ note went on the outside of the folder I maintain on Greg's writing. I set the folder aside until the morning conference that would also include Monica.

PLANNING FOR MONICA: I picked up Monica's writing and read (see Figure 10–4).

I went on a boet it wos acshe [actually] a fare It tok os to Bohedilnd [Bald Head Island] I wnet is my Mom and my Dad and my brothr and my

I WENT ON A BOet
it . WOS AK SNLE A .
FARE It taKøs OS to
Bod he oiLNd I WNEt wis
MY mom aNd MY DAD
aNd MY BROthR aNd MY
GRiNomon aND MY iNt aNd
MY OKOL WEN WE GEt
thER thay hAD to
oNi LOWd WOt we
BROt thEN WE hAD to
GEt on the tRim thEN
that is WEN the tRim
tAKS OS to the
BECHnAWS thEN WE hAF to
oNi LOWd Are haws is NOS.

But the ILId hAS
Som hiws ore OF the
hiws iS a ViARe hiye
MY DAD WENt DAen
the hil in A GOFCRt
hE WoS A litit
SiARd I WoS EViN SiARd
WiN I WENt DAWN
oN MY BoSiKoL I
hAd to WaK the
BoSiKoL hAF WAle DAWiN
the hile. I GOt to
to DRiV the GoFCRt
aND that WoS FUN.

I JeSt WeNt
to thes BoLdhed ILId
fun New It WoS
evin BEtr I em
GoeF Krt. on the
LiKe It siMs
the I Kod dive
my theSiLF GoeF KRt OL BiY
thenAJrs LiKe But, One
or oWsr Kene 16
they ILid is dive
niYs I LiKe it Ferey It
iS fun ther.

grindmom and my int [aunt] and my okol wen we get thethy had to oni
lowd [unload] wot we brot then we had to get on the trim [tram] then that
is wen the trim taks os to the bechhaws then we haf to oni lowd. Are haws
is nos. But the Ilid has som hiws [hills] one of the hiws is viare hiye My
Dad went Daen the hil in a gofcrt he wos alitit siard [little scared] I wos
evin siard win I went dawn on my bosikol [bicycle] I had to wok the bosikil
haf wale dawin the hile. I got to driv the gofcrt and that wos fun. I jest
went to Boldhed Ilid thes somr. it wos fun new I em evin betr on the goef
krt. it sims like I kod dive the goefkrt ol biy my silf But, onl thenajrs
[teenagers] like 16 or ower kene dive. they Ilid is ferery [very] niys I like it
it is fun ther.

Monica demonstrated some of the same strengths in her writing that I had noticed in Greg's. She wrote fluently, setting aside concerns for conventions and devoting her energy to putting her ideas on paper. In her drawing the ferry skims the top of the water. I remembered the conference when she drew this picture. She told me about the beauty of that ferry ride and the sun on the ocean, but she didn't include this information in the written story. Looking at her drawing now, I see shafts of sunlight streaming between the clouds. The detail in Monica's drawing indicates that, like Greg, she is a keen observer of her world. Only the nature of the topics differed: Monica noticed shafts of sunlight, Greg the parts of an airplane.

I reread the opening line: "I went on a boat. Actually it was a ferry." Monica's voice. I could hear her say those very words. The listing of family members, strung together with "ands" was Monica too. Replacing those "ands" with commas might be something to show her in the conference, but I needed to read on to get inside her writing. I knew she chose this piece thoughtfully and that it meant a great deal to her. I listened for the story between the lines. What was important to Monica? Certainly the presence of all the family members was important and the trek to the island cabin had impressed her. But as I read on, I pictured the hills, Monica on her bicycle, and the golf cart. The story seemed somewhat disjointed but in these lines was something significant to Monica. On the Post-It™ note for Monica's folder I wrote:

golf cart—hills

commas in sequence

spelling and punct.

I was ready for the conference with Monica and Greg in the morning.

THE SMALL-GROUP PUBLISHING CONFERENCE: The next morning we gathered at the conference table. Usually the publishing conference consists of three or even four children. Today we had only two, so I asked Max to join us. A third child would add another responder and Max had demonstrated skill in listening to writers and then asking effective questions.

I explained to Max, and several seated nearby overheard: "Monica and Greg have each chosen a piece of writing that they believe to be one of their best. They've read it through to see if it makes sense. But we all know that writers miss things when they read their own writing so we're going to read these pieces in this small group and we'll all listen to see if each piece makes sense to us. Writers need readers and listeners to help them make sure the writing makes sense and that everything is clear." The children nodded and smiled in agreement. "As we listen, I'd like you also to listen to see if there's anything you want to know more about, anything that doesn't quite give you a complete picture in your head."

The children understood the procedure. Greg began to read. He inserted the word "up" when he came to that place in the writing. I noticed that the missing word fell at the end of a line on the page. As a reader anticipating the next word, he automatically read it as he began the following line even though the word did not appear on the page. When he came to "one night . . . had pizza," he hesitated, quickly noticed the omission, and pencilled in "we" as he said, "Oops, I left out a word."

When Greg finished reading he looked to Monica and Max awaiting their responses. Max spoke first. "I think it's a good piece about flying to California and all, but I was just confused about one part. When you said you had pizza at the plant—well, what is the plant. I never heard of a pizza place called "The Plant."

"No, no," said Greg. "See the plant is the factory where my dad was working. He was there for a business trip and then my mom and I joined him. We flew out there later, after he was there and we had pizza at his plant—where he worked."

Max pressed for more information. He wanted to know if everyone at this factory had pizza and what factory it was and how long they stayed in California. Monica said she was confused about the hotel with a kitchen and wondered why they didn't eat there. Greg explained that only he and his parents ate pizza at the plant, which was Armstrong, and that they stayed three weeks. He described the efficiency unit where they stayed, explaining that they only ate breakfast there. Monica observed that he had said "It was fun" two times. (We had addressed repeating lines, especially "It was fun" or "I had fun," in mini-lessons.) Greg recognized this repetition as soon as Monica pointed it out, and he quickly reread his writing, located the two identical phrases, and made a decision to line out the first one. Monica, Max, and I waited and watched. When he finished, Greg grinned and said, "That makes it much better. I don't need that *twice*." I could sense the comfortable tone in the interchange among the students. Greg didn't view their comments as criticisms, but as helpful suggestions.

"Maybe you could change some other parts and put some of the other things in that you told us—like maybe people need to know it was Armstrong," Max said. Greg agreed that he might change "plant" to "Armstrong."

All of our work during writing workshop contributed to the effectiveness of this publishing conference. In mini-lessons, individual conferences, large-group sharing, and all our talk about writing and writers, the children had learned to recognize potentially unclear areas of writing for readers. They had developed poise and sensitivity in responding to writers. Now they capably carried these responding strategies into this small-group conference. Throughout the first part of the conference, I spoke only to assist the management of the conference or to briefly help a child clarify ideas as he or she spoke. Now I entered the discussion to nudge the children in their development as writers.

"Greg, it sounds like this trip to California was really special to you. You say you stayed three weeks. I was curious about what else you did in those three weeks."

"Well, we did lots of stuff, but I didn't write all that because I can't quite remember it all. So I didn't put it all in."

"Right. Putting *everything* in would probably get pretty confusing to write and for readers to read. You really have a lot of information here and I can tell that the plane trip and eating pizza at the Armstrong plant were important parts of that trip. But I felt the piece sorta stops. You go to California and then you eat pizza . . ." I let my voice trail off.

"Yeah how did you get home?" Max suddenly interjects with a broad grin on his face.

Greg grinned back and launched into a story about a crowded airplane where the family could not get seats together.

"Could you add that?" I asked.

Greg looked at his page. "Sure, I still got some room here."

"Tell me what your plans are for this piece now, Greg?" I asked. Greg said that he planned to add the information about coming home and fix the part about eating pizza.

"Sounds good," I said. Monica and Max concurred.

We moved on to Monica's writing. I asked Monica if I might read her story so that she could hear it too. She agreed. When I finished reading the story both boys said they thought it was fine. "It makes sense," they said. I glanced at my Post-It™ note, then spoke.

"This part about the hills is really interesting. This island really had steep hills, didn't it? What was that like, Monica?"

"Well, I never *expected* that Bald Head Island would have such steep hills. I had to walk my bicycle and it was scary in the golf cart too."

"Did you get to play golf?" Greg asked.

"No, you have golf carts because they don't allow any cars on the island."

"No cars?" Greg and Max were amazed. A world without cars. Monica went on to explain that the island had golf carts, a tram, and bicycles. And she had driven a golf cart! The boys asked how and why she got to drive the golf cart since the writing said only teenagers could drive. Monica explained that her dad helped her drive a little and that she got better and better at driving the golf cart. As she spoke, I heard in Monica's voice the reason why this writing was special to her. The island was a place apart from normal life, located in the middle of the sea, with steep hills, without cars, a safe place where she enjoyed a privilege reserved for older people. Meaning went beyond the written words, the meaning was within Monica herself. The words on the page represented the significance of that time to Monica. Through writing, Monica had stayed connected to the magic of that special time.

We urged Monica to add some of the information she told us. The boys thought she needed to clarify that she learned to drive the golf cart, but that she didn't drive it by herself. Greg reminded her that her writing had some "It was fun" lines in it, too. Monica said she would add information and take out the extra lines. I suggested that the children use colored pencils to make their changes so I could see the revisions. I told them to read the revised piece to either of these group members to see if everything worked and then put it on my desk. The publishing conference ended. It had taken approximately ten minutes.

As the children left the conference table I overheard Max say to Greg, "That's a neat plane." Greg explained all the details on the plane, including the red dots, which were the lights on the outside of the plane. I had missed those when I looked at the illustration.

We hadn't dealt with any of the editing skills (the items involved in traditional correcting of student writing), even those I had listed on my notes. Each writer had enough to deal with for the moment. I stuck the notes inside their folders, knowing that we'd get to these items later.

Greg inserted "up" and erased "we," replacing it with "me and my mom and my dad." He changed "plant" to "factory," then later erased and changed "factory" to "Armstrong." (Since Armstrong World Industries is a major employer in our community, the name is a household word, making this term the most specific for his audience.) And he added four sentences at the end (see Figures 10–5a and 10–5b). He also wrote a dedication—Dadakcan to Dad and Mom—and circled the line to indicate that although it was written at the end of the piece, it belonged at the beginning.

Monica lined out both "It was fun" sentences. In small print she inserted the words: You rid in the foef kart be cos they are no crs a lawd on the Ilid. She lined out "I kod" and replaced it with "I now haw to," thus clarifying the writing as her audience had indicated in the conference.

When the writing came back to me again I brought Greg and Monica together and said, "One of the last things writers do when they finish a piece of writing is check for correct spelling and punctuation. Now, of course I don't expect you to be able to spell all these words correctly, but I would like you to do some work on that. Remember at the beginning of the year when I said we'd work on spelling later? Well, now is that time. I want you to go through this writing and underline three words that you know are spelled correctly. Then I want you to find three words that you know are misspelled but that you think you know how to spell and can correct, or that you can figure out how to spell by yourself or by finding the correct spelling somewhere. Can you do that?"

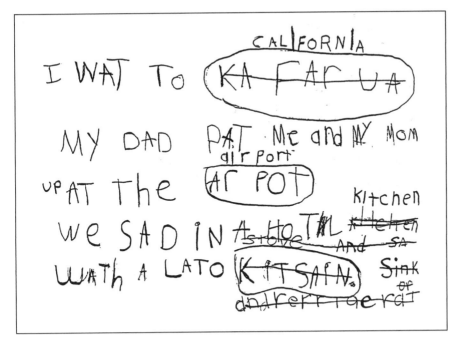

Figure 10–5a

Greg's revisions.

Both children attacked this task with confidence and enthusiasm. Greg underlined the phrase "me and my mom and my dad" and circled "arpot," "kitsain," and "Kafarua." He located "airport" and "kitchen" in the small picture dictionary he (and every other child in the classroom) had in his desk. "California" presented a more difficult problem, and he came to me for help. I handed him the "C" volume of the *World Book Encyclopedia*. In no time Greg found the correct spelling. Monica underlined "the," "one," and "went." She identified "dawn," "wak," and "gofkrt" as incorrectly spelled. "Down" and "walk" presented no difficulty; she found them in the picture dictionary. "Golf cart" was more challenging. I could think of no resource in the classroom where she might easily locate the word, so I asked her if she knew anyone who might know how to spell "golf cart." "Probably my mom or dad," she answered. She wrote a reminder note for herself that read, "I ned to no haw to spel gofkret i ned to asesk my mom." The next day she came in with a slip of paper on which she had correctly printed "golf cart."

There was one final step for Monica in preparing her piece for publication. With the changes she made, the sentence "I jest went to Boldhed ilid thes somr" became an obvious interruption to the section about the golf cart. I met with Monica, read that part, and asked her what she thought. "I don't think it fits," she said. "Can I just take it out?" She lined through the words. We reread the section again and agreed on the improvement (see Figures 10–6a and 10–6b).

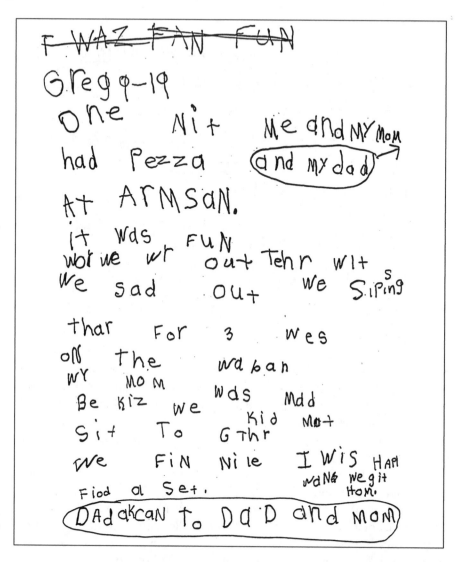

Figure 10–5b

Greg's revisions.

Greg's piece needed one final revision too. When he corrected the spelling of "kitchen," Greg had added "with a stove and a sink and a refrigerator." The words were all spelled correctly, leading me to suspect that the picture in the child's dictionary inspired the line. Greg probably liked writing those words. But when he read the revised piece to Monica, she told him that every kitchen has a stove, sink, and refrigerator and that she didn't think he needed to put that in. Greg lined out the words before the piece came back to me.

The children's writing was ready for the typist. Both Greg and Monica had expended a great deal of energy, an indication of their investment in the writing. They cared about these topics and wanted them polished for

Figure 10–6a

Monica's revisions.

readers. But I sensed that they had reached the limit of willingness to revise and edit. They had taken their stories as far as they could and it was time to let these pieces go and move on to the next.

The children sat with me as I typed their books, a possibility that semester because a student teacher worked in our classroom. The child read the manuscript and I typed. As each page came out of the typewriter I handed it to the child to read back to me. We folded a piece of lightweight oaktag around the typed pages and fastened the edge with a row of staples. The typed draft was now ready for the child to illustrate. I allowed each child one writing workshop to work on illustrating. Experience has taught me that writers will procrastinate and some children will take days illustrating to

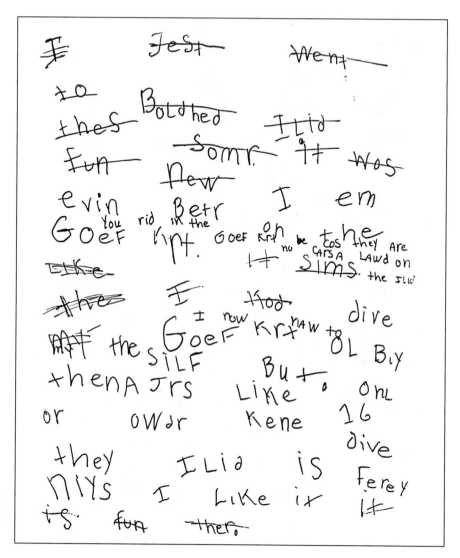

Figure 10–6b

Monica's revisions.

avoid going on to a new piece. Allowing one day validates the importance of the illustration process and provides time for the writer to think about the next topic. (After that, children can complete their illustrations during the school day: the morning free play, or indoor recess.) When the drawings were done, I used rubber cement to glue the completed story into a wallpaper and cardboard book cover (see Appendix A: Instructions for Bookbinding).

Before Monica and Greg finished the final editing of their writing, I started three more children on a similar process. Gradually over the next month, all of the children chose a piece of writing for publication, met with a small group to consider ways to revise their writing, and then made changes to clarify meaning for their readers. The nature of those revisions depends on the individual child, but the first issue addressed always revolves around meaning. Don't misunderstand. Certainly I am concerned about teaching children the conventions of written language. But I know that the key to developing writers is giving primary attention to the ideas one wishes to communicate to an audience. Writers who are truly involved with clarifying the content of their writing become very particular about the mechanics.

Each year there are children who come to the classroom with so few experiences with written language that the publishing process with small groups is inappropriate. I usually work with these children on an individual basis to help them develop a piece for publication. Michael and Darren were two such children.

Michael

Nearly a month after Greg and Monica published their stories I asked Michael to select a piece for publication. He beamed and said, "This one." He pointed to the paper he had stapled only a few moments earlier. Several trees covered the page. He had written his name, the date, and "FAIHOT." "Fort," he said, pointing again. "Fort?" I repeated, puzzled.

"Unhuh," he smiled, showing the black cavities in his teeth. "Me 'n Kevin buil-a-fot." The words slurred together in the mumbled baby talk intonation I'd gradually come to understand.

"Ohhh, this is about the day you and Kevin built a fort. I remember." I recalled the boys telling me about their fort a few days earlier. Michael nodded, grinned, and turned the page. "What will you do here?" I asked.

"Umm. The fort." Michael began to draw.

"I see, you're going to draw your fort and then you will write about it?"

Michael nodded and went to work. I left but I checked back with Michael several times during the writing workshop. He could not always read his writing if too much time passed, so I wanted to catch those words while they were still fresh in his mind.

When Michael moved from out of state and came into our classroom in late September, he had just turned seven. We'd all had trouble understanding him at first. In fact, he'd talked very little and looked away when any of us spoke to him. But Michael loved school. He loved the children, loved listening to stories, and loved writing. He spent the first week or so in writing workshop drawing or watching the other children work beside him. I moved his desk next to a couple of confident students, and they naturally included Michael in their conversations as they wrote. Soon Michael started adding letters to his drawings, and then I noticed that he began matching those letters to the sounds in words. His cooperation and charm quickly earned him a place in the classroom community.

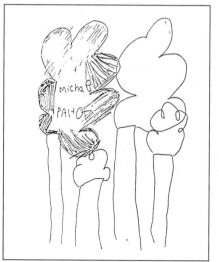

Figure 10–7

Michael's writing.

Michael completed two pages of writing during workshop that day. Above the drawing of the fort he wrote four lines, which he read to me word by word, pointing to each word and looking up to me for acknowledgment before he continued. "The day me and Kevin built a fort this is a fort." On the next page, he drew hearts and wrote four words. At first he had trouble reading them to me. We pointed to the words and I suggested he skip the first word and go on to find a word he knew. "Hearts! Stars!" he blurted out. "Now I know. There were hearts, stars" (see Figure 10–7).

"Okay. Now let's read it all again." And so Michael and I read through his entire three-page, seventeen-word story (including the title). I told him

Figure 10–8

Michael's revisions.

I'd read it that evening and we'd talk about it more tomorrow. When I looked again at the writing, I noticed that Michael had put commas between many words; we had been talking about commas in the classroom. He correctly spelled "the," "me," "this," "a," and "day." I knew where "day" came from. Each morning we wrote the day of the week on the chalkboard and all the children knew the d-a-y spelling. "This" had been on the chalkboard. I couldn't be sure about "the" and "me." Perhaps Michael remembered them himself. The "si" spelling of "is" gave me a clue to his visual memory for spelling. But I was confused by the story itself. I understood the part about building a fort, but how were hearts and stars connected? I'd have to ask Michael.

Figure 10–9

Michael's revisions.

In conversation with Michael, I learned the answer. Kevin and Michael built a fort, and then they crawled inside and put heart and star stickers on paper. I helped Michael determine the placement of this information in the story and he added a line to the page with the fort picture: "Me and Kevin put stickers on paper" (see Figure 10–8). "Raor" appeared twice because the first time Michael wrote he left out the word "on." When he read the sentence, he realized there weren't enough words and added another "Raor," though the "r" closely resembled a "p." After reading the entire story to me again, Michael added another sentence at the end by writing it down the side of the page beside the heart: "We put stickers on papers in the fort. I went home. Kevin went it home" (see Figure 10–9). Prior to this

Michael had made few revisions in his writing. By spending a few minutes with him each day *as he wrote,* I better understood his writing process, his story, and his intentions. I could then help him take the writing further in ways appropriate for Michael. By the end of this process, I knew Michael had ventured into a lot of new territory as a writer. I wasn't about to require that he seek out words to correct for spelling as Monica, Greg, and some of the other children in the class had done. There was plenty of time. This was early December. Michael had been writing for just two months.

Darren

Darren wrote about visiting his mother's place of work. Like most of his writing, the words conveyed a jumble of thoughts, incoherent to any reader including Darren himself. I sensed that Darren wanted to publish his writing as he saw the other children doing, but he shrugged the idea off when I mentioned the possibility. "No, I can't, don't, I can't do that. I don't know how," he said. I sat beside Darren and together we read the piece by using Darren's vague recollection of the ideas he tried to write and the clues gleaned from the letters he'd written. We unraveled the meaning as far as we could and then Darren told me what came next—just one sentence.

"Write that," I said. "Okay," he replied and then earnestly put the words on paper. I returned a few moments later and, with my help, he read what he had just written. He told me the next part and we followed the same strategy. Gradually, sentence by sentence, the written story emerged (see Figures 10–10a and 10–10b). I read it to Darren. We both agreed that it made sense. Darren heaved a big sigh and said, "I done a lot didn't I?"

"You sure did!" I agreed.

"I think I spelled 'my' right, didn't I? See, here I spelled it 'mi' but I changed it. I changed it to 'my.'" I could only infer that he had become aware of correcting spelling from observing his classmates work through revision and editing.

"Am I done now?" he asked eagerly.

"What do you think?" I asked.

"Yeah, I think I'm done because I did a lot."

"When I read your story it makes sense and I think other people will think so too. I think they'll like reading about your mom's work."

"Yeah, I did a good job," Darren said.

This process was a milestone for Darren. The support I provided for Darren and Michael was similar to that for Monica and Greg as they, too, worked with their stories so the writing made sense to readers. The major

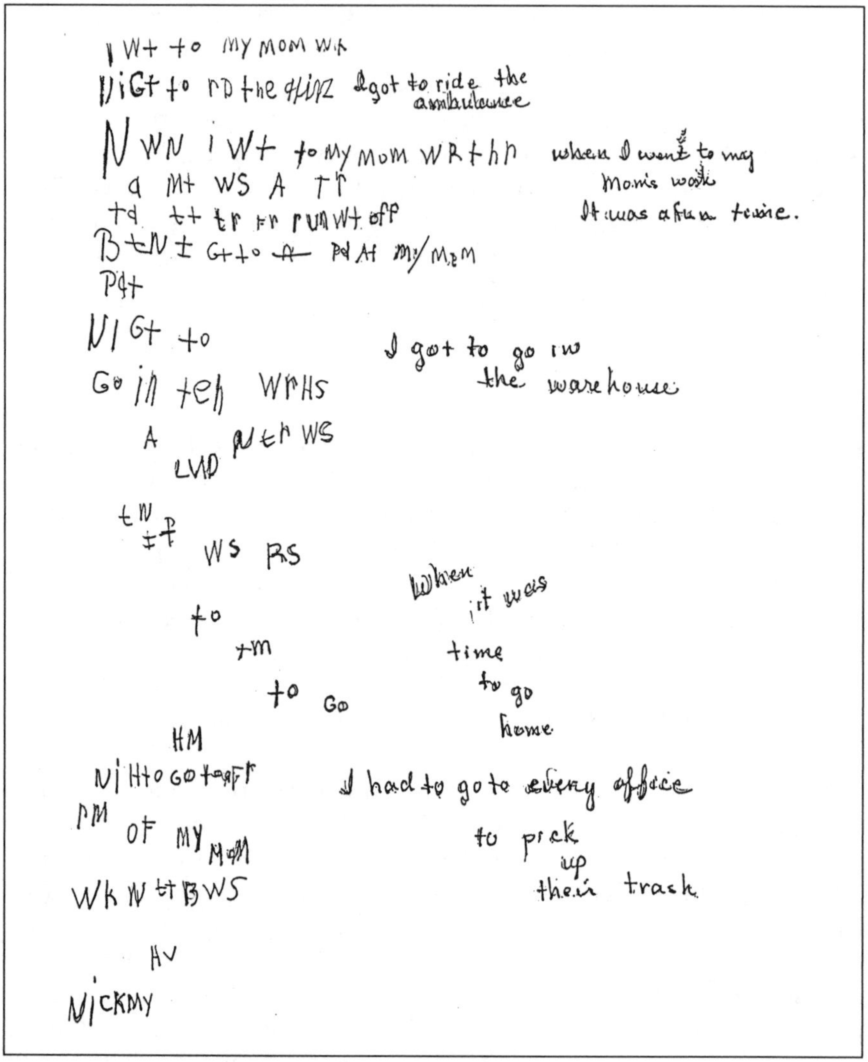

Figure 10–10a

Darren's writing: "When I went to my mom's work I got to ride the ambulance. When I went to my mom's work it was a fun time. I got to go in the warehouse. When it was time to go home I had to go to every office to pick up their trash."

difference was that I stayed close to both Michael and Darren to assist them through this process.

Later, Darren sat with me when I typed his book. Every sentence was connected to the next with "and." I suggested that as I type I take some of them out and reminded him of a recent mini-lesson. Darren nodded and said, "I put words and then when people tell me I believe them." His comment seemed particularly significant. Later I thought about his statement and realized Darren was telling me that he "put words" when he wrote but was aware that the story might not be clear to others. He counted on responses from other people and trusted that what they told him improved his writing.

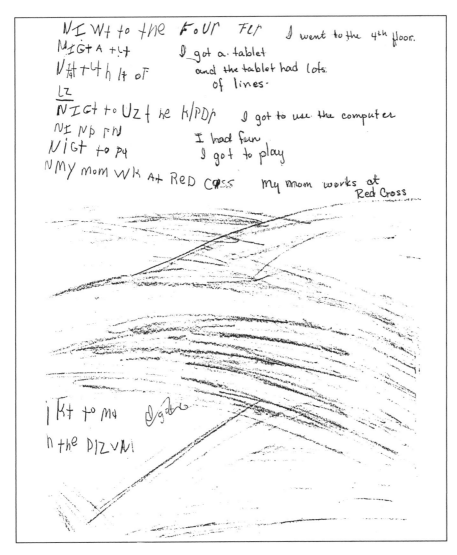

Figure 10–10b

Darren's writing: "I went to the 4th floor. I got a tablet and the tablet had lots of lines. I got to use the computer. I had fun. I got to play. My mom works at Red Cross."

The Publishing Process

Preparing a piece of writing for publication requires students to reread and rethink the piece and to make changes that refine the piece for their audience. I can't expect children to produce perfect pieces of writing; even the best authors need good editors. As part of the publishing process, just before a piece of writing goes to the typist, I ask each child to do some editing. Sometimes I work with the child, especially if this is the first time the child is attempting a new skill. More often I ask the child to go through the piece of writing and do the best job possible. Early in the year, the task might be inserting periods and capital letters, but I don't expect perfection from first graders. Punctuating sentences in our English language is a very complex skill. If we wrote all the time in simple sentences, problems would be few, but complex sentences and phrases trip us up. We tell children to listen for the stops and to insert a period, but the phrasing of our sentences does not always lend itself to easily accomplishing this.

By their second or third publication, all the children do some form of editing, if only approximating a particular skill such as inserting periods or correcting one or two misspelled words. As Atwell also did, during one school year I maintained a list of editing skills the children used.

- determining the end of sentences and inserting periods
- determining the end of sentences and inserting periods and capital letters for first words in new sentences
- identifying questions and inserting question marks
- identifying direct quotes and inserting quotation marks
- inserting commas to separate items in a series
- capitalizing the first letter in proper names
- adding "s" for plurals
- adding " 's" to indicate possessive nouns
- identifying a few correctly spelled words and a few incorrectly spelled words and then finding correct spellings (The number of words varied in response to the child's ability to manage this strategy; usually, a maximum of six words was the most any child tackled with one piece of writing.)
- leaving spaces between words
- leaving spaces between lines
- using legible handwriting

While these last three items could not easily be corrected on a draft, we discussed them in publishing conferences when writing became difficult to read. Students saw the necessity of not crowding writing on a page and worked on this with subsequent pieces.

The most significant work during the publishing process involves modifications to the content of the writing: refining and shaping the ideas to improve the final communication. Initially the children wanted to write their stories and be done with it, and in September I couldn't have asked them to make major changes in their writing because they lacked experience as writers and the writing community was undeveloped. We needed to establish a trust level before we plunged into the high-risk activity of revising content.

Revising writing requires sensitive responses from readers who communicate first that they are interested in the writer's ideas and in helping the writer communicate those ideas as clearly as possible. When the responder cares about both the writer and the writing, the writer trusts the responder. Even so, the writer is not going to make every change suggested to improve a piece of writing—especially when the revision process is a new concept. The kind of changes I've found that children will make when they first begin rethinking and reshaping writing include:

- adding missing words (usually they've been left out by accident)
- adding information to clarify the total content
- adding a title
- using arrows to move information to another part of the page
- using an asterisk or star to indicate where to insert information
- adding a title page
- adding a dedication page

With more experience, young writers wade a little deeper into the waters of the revision process and are willing to try changes and strategies such as:

- eliminating "then" or "and" at the beginning of every sentence
- brainstorming several possible titles and selecting one
- brainstorming several possible opening sentences and selecting one
- considering the ending (does the story just stop or does it need more information) and then revising that ending
- adding conversation to show not tell
- adding description to show not tell
- removing "and" and replacing with commas or periods
- adding an author's page (to give biographical information)

In the last months of the school year these young writers are totally immersed in the process of drafting, revising, and editing their writing. Then, as throughout the year, the children work at various aspects of their individual writing processes on any given day. This might seem like a totally chaotic environment. Not so. In fact, it's this facet of writing workshop that enables the workshop to function so smoothly. Everyone comes to count on responses from peers and from me to help them make their writing the best possible. The community establishes a repertoire of strategies, and children try out new ways of writing and revising that they observe within the community. Some of the more sophisticated practices they easily incorporate include:

- planning effective beginnings to hook the reader
- connecting endings to beginnings to get the reader off the hook
- revising a multi-focussed piece into one that tells a single story
- removing irrelevant information (They labeled this the "junk writing" that needs to be thrown out, to go into the garbage can.)
- separating sections into "chapters" (which is really a form of paragraphing for first graders)
- supplying antecedents for pronouns or eliminating indefinite pronouns
- reordering information
- choosing different words for effectiveness or variety (for example, substitutes for the overworked "said")
- including a table of contents
- including and alphabetizing a glossary

These skills emerged from the children's writing. I addressed them with the children because each skill was necessary to develop effective communication. I've come to see that a prerequisite list of skills (such as a curriculum might provide) can be artificial, restricting what children can and need to do as writers.

During the typing I corrected all spelling and inserted correct punctuation so that the final product presented a perfect model for reading. I explain to the children that final pieces that are going out of the classroom to readers must follow the conventions of written language. "I will help you do as much as you can and then I'll fix the rest when I type."

"Yeah, 'cause we can't do *all* that!" a child comments.

"Not yet. But as you write you will learn to do more and more of these things for yourself. However, I think it's important for you to know that every writer needs a good editor, and so it's always a good idea to have somebody else check your writing when you've finished with it."

The children learn from seeing the correct spelling of their words. More than once I've heard a child say, "Oh, so that's how you spell the, t-h-e. I thought it was t-e-h." Children invariably pay close attention to the details of their own words in print. Usually I leave the child's language, particularly grammatical structures, as in Greg's "me and my mom . . ." At times, when I've corrected errors of this type, the child reads the writing and says, "Mrs. Avery, you made a mistake. This is suppose to say 'me and my mom.' " Or the child misreads the correction, substituting their own language for the corrected form. Valuing the child's language is important, and I also want the child to read words that correspond with actual words on the page. This does not mean that we don't work on developing grammatically correct language. The language-rich environment of the classroom—

lots of talk and lots of reading aloud—gives children experience with standard English. I'll present mini-lessons on these topics too. Some children will understand and begin to make the shift in their speech and in their writing and some will not. But like many mini-lesson topics, I'll present this topic several times throughout the year. Knowing the children well and observing their language development influences the corrections I make. When I typed a story by Josie I changed "me and my sister" to "my sister and I" because I knew Josie's speech and I'd heard her correct herself when she talked. I showed the corrected version to Josie explaining, "I think this is what you meant." "Oh, yes!" she answered. The decisions on correcting grammatical structures, like so many of the decisions to assist writers, are always based on the context of helping a particular writer at a particular time.

In the days before writing workshop, when I corrected errors in the children's writing, I effectively took the pencil out of the child's hand and imposed my authority on the writing. Urging children to develop their own writing required a new role for me: placing the authority for their writing in the children's hands. When I did, the children experienced what it meant to be a writer.

The Authors' Party

The children stand in a line outside the classroom door. Their bodies wiggle with excitement but their voices are still. They know that seated inside on little classroom chairs are their parents, awaiting the special reading about to begin. Each child clutches a self-authored book. The last parent arrives, the two children who stood in the doorway to greet guests and hand out programs move to their place in line, and then the children file into the classroom and seat themselves around the edge of the storyrug just as they had practiced the previous afternoon. They all maintain a dignified poise. This is a special occasion and they've worked hard as individuals and as a community to come to this moment. The authors' party is ready to begin.

Nearly two weeks earlier we began planning for this event to present the first published books to parents. Together we composed an invitation and wrote it during a handwriting lesson. The RSVPs started coming in. The children practiced and practiced reading their books to each other and to me so they would read "with expression," not just "dumb boring reading" as Stacy put it. One child wrote an invitation to the principal, another to the reading teacher, and then everyone added his or her signature before these special invitations were delivered. We decided on punch and pretzels for refreshments. I typed a program listing the titles of the books, and the children signed their names beside the appropriate title. We composed a greeting for the mistress of ceremonies to read and chose Elizabeth for this role since her mother would be unable to attend. And on the day of the program we rearranged the room, shoving child desks to one end, arranging chairs for the audience, and setting the author's chair on a small raised platform. We set up a microphone to project the young voices.

Elizabeth moves to the center and warmly welcomes the parents. "Welcome to our authors' party," she begins. She announces the first reader, who takes the author's chair and begins to read. I've warned the children that grown-ups may laugh at parts that they don't think are funny, but to pause for the laughter before continuing reading so that everyone gets to hear the entire book. Sure enough, ripples of laughter break out from the delighted audience. One little girl catches my eye and shakes her head in amused, tolerant disbelief. The children read books with titles such as "The Karate Test," "I Went to My Mom's Work," "Catching Caterpillars," "Trick or Treating," "The Tree House." Michael reads "Fort" and remembers to keep the book away from his face so we can hear his words.

Cory takes the author's chair, holding "We Catch Butterflies." He looks up and grins at his audience and for a moment seems to forget what he's to do. Then he reads loudly, clearly, stopping to grin broadly at the audience after each page. I hear this story and remember that Cory was one of the boys who brought me butterflies from the playground that first day of school.

"Me and Michael went in the woods to scare my friends. Then we saw a butterfly. We caught it. Then we looked for more. We found pretty ones. We caught some of them, but we let them go again. Then we went to the park." When Cory finishes he looks over to me and smiles that broad grin, then looks back to his indulging audience. He takes a couple extra seconds, savoring this moment, before he realizes that he's done and it's time to move back to the rug.

The readings are nearly done when Elizabeth's mother slips into the room. Elizabeth's face sparkles when she spies her and she turns to me to check that I, too, have noticed. After Elizabeth reads her book, the final volume shared this day, she thanks the audience and extends our invitation for refreshments. Parents and children mingle, munch pretzels, spill punch, and then go home carrying the published books to share with their families.

The children will return these published books to the classroom tomorrow. Each book has a library card and pocket in the back. After the initial sharing at the author's home, the book becomes part of the classroom library for the remainder of the year. The children learn to read each other's books and teach each other how to read them. When they can read a book to the author (the authority on the book), they can sign it out for one night. The children become very particular about their book being read accurately, and I've overheard comments such as: "I think you need more practice before you sign this out, but I'll help you if you want." Class librarians take charge of carding the books each morning and reminding the forgetful; this classroom library is run by the children. I set up the procedures and then stay uninvolved unless specific problems arise. Through the years only one book has ever been lost. The children hold these books in high regard.

From now on, as the children's writing is published in book form, we'll hold much smaller authors' parties. The children will be the audience and two or three books will be presented at a time; we will conduct such an event perhaps once every couple of weeks. Publication brings deep satisfaction to a writer who truly engages in the writing process. But we don't need to publish everything that is written, nor do we need to publish in abundance. My first graders publish fewer books now than earlier classes, but their engagement as writers, and subsequently the quality of their writing, is far greater than that of other groups.

CHAPTER 11

How Do You Write?
Why Do You Write?

Chris returned from Christmas vacation, wrote and published a book entitled "The Wise Owl." Then he went into a slump. He sat in writing workshop, writing only a sentence or two each day: "Jason is my friend. We play
at recess." "David is my friend. We like to play." When I'd stop at his desk
he'd say, "I don't know what to write" or "I'm thinking." By this point in
the year I knew Chris to be a serious student and I took him seriously. "Can
I help?" I'd ask and he'd shake his head. I waited. For two weeks. Then one
day he began "Patrick and the Elf." It took over a month to write, revise,
edit, and publish this piece of writing (see Figure 11–1). Here is the finished text.

> There once was a little boy named Patrick. One day Patrick wanted to
> go to his friend's house. So he asked his mother. His mother said, "No."
> "But Mom."
> "No buts!"
> He got very mad! And he said, "No one is fair. It would be better if I
> lived alone!" So he packed his clothes and went on his way.
> On his way he met some bushes that were shivering. "Now how do
> you think those bushes are shivering?" he muttered to himself. Suddenly
> a hat popped out. He was shocked but curious. He got a little bit closer.
> Suddenly, a voice stopped him. The voice said, "Don't you take another
> step closer or I will shoot you dead!"
> Patrick was scared but curious. So he snooped over to the bushes. This
> was what he was an expert at. He peeked through the bushes and saw an
> elf with a gun pointing right at him! The elf started to walk frontwards.
> "Don't be hasty, Mr. Elf."

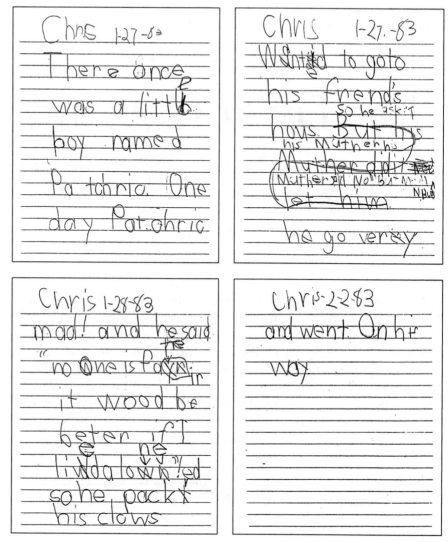

Figure 11–1

*"Patrick and
the Elf"*

Suddenly, Patrick hit a tree.

"So your name is Patrick," said the elf.

"Yes, it is," said Patrick.

"Now come along," said the elf.

Patrick and the elf started towards a little hut. They went in the elf's hut. The elf said, "Would you like some raw fish?"

"No, not really," said Patrick.

Patrick took his backpack and took some cookies and took a thermos out, too, and poured some milk into a little cup.

After they had supper they went to bed. In the night his Mom and Dad were worried about him. So they called the police to find a lost boy. So they searched the city but they couldn't find Patrick. They searched the forest but they didn't find Patrick.

The next day the elf woke up early for a special reason. He was going to the farm to get some eggs and he was going to milk the cow for some milk to go with the eggs. He went back to the hut. Then he started a fire. Patrick woke up. They had their breakfast. Then the elf got a safe preserver.

Patrick said, "Why are you taking a safe preserver?"

"Because we're going for a swim!"

"All right!" said Patrick. So they went to the pond and took a swim. THEN PATRICK SAW HIS MOTHER AND FATHER!

"Quickly," said Patrick, "I must go and get some dry clothes and I will catch up with my mom and dad and tell all about what I did with you. I won't forget all of the fun I had with you. Even every holiday I'll take a visit. Bye now!"

THE END

As Chris was in the process of illustrating "Patrick and the Elf," I interviewed him about writing this piece.

MRS. A: Tell me about this writing, Chris.

CHRIS: Well, this boy named Patrick, he goes away and he meets this elf.

MRS. A: What's your favorite part?

C: Well, right here when the police try to find him. [Chris reads the part.] And at the end there's an author's page and I'll read it to you."Author's page: Author's family—Dad, Mom, two sisters, and one small brother who is sometimes a brat. Chris's hobby: His hobby is collecting rocks."

MRS. A: How did you go about choosing the words that you used in this story. I liked the part when you said "the bushes were shivering . . ."

C: And "don't be hasty Mr. Elf." Well, my friend said "Don't be hasty" a lot to me and I'd like to write about that and so I wrote that. And I heard about "muttered to himself" and I'd like to write that too. Sometimes in the book you'll see sloppy letters. That means I was not feeling so well and I was getting a little bit grumpy and I didn't want to write and I just wrote sloppy letters. [He points to examples in the text.]

MRS. A: So sometimes you made sloppy letters because you didn't feel like writing that day?

C: Umhum.

MRS. A: How do you feel about the book now?

C: I really want to publish it and I just have some pictures to do and I'll be done. [He indicates the drawings in the typed book.]

MRS. A: Okay. You didn't draw pictures with your first draft on this piece?

C: No, I just wrote the letters and sentences.

MRS. A: When did you think about the pictures?

C: When I was writing the book. I just pictured them in my mind when I was writing and I thought, Well, I can put them in this draft when you had finished typing.

MRS. A: Why are these lines on these words? [I indicate line outs in the draft.]

C: Well see, I'll read it to you. "*Then* he went back to the hut. *Then* he started a fire. *Then* Patrick woke up . . ." I crossed some of those out because it went: then, then, then, then! Too many.

MRS. A: I see. Too many thens. Tell me about this. [I indicate words in capital letters.]

C: Well, I wrote it in capital letters because it's the exciting part. It would be like an exclamation point would be after every letter.

MRS. A: So you wrote them in capitals because it's suppose to be real exciting?

C: Umhum. [We turn to the last page of the draft.] Here's me saying "The End" and I'm saying "Whoosh" because I'm all tired out.

MRS. A: You were all tired out when you finished this piece?

C: Unhum.

MRS. A: I notice you put quotation marks in. When did you do that?

C: In the starting I did them but I forgot them in the exciting part because I had my mind on *that*, and so I fixed the quotation marks after I wrote it. If you read it over, you can find out the parts you left out and you put the parts in and make it so you won't get confused. Now I have just to make the pictures and I'll be done. And I think this is my best piece of writing.

MRS. A: Why do you think this is your best piece?

C: Well, it was so long to write it and because it was about my friend and it was about an elf and I like it so much that I say it is my best piece of writing.

MRS. A: Tell me what you think about writing.

C: Well, I think that writing is sharing about your life and when you share about your life, it could keep going on and people could get some ideas about their life and they'd keep writing it down and keep it a long time and other people could read it and find out what you were like.

Chris has articulated his process of writing "Patrick and the Elf." I heard comments similar to his from many children. The children learned to get in touch with their processes because I continually asked *how* and *why* they made the decisions they did as writers. Sometimes we did this in a large-group setting, a procedure that helped everyone learn to reflect on the process of writing.

One year in mid-November I asked the children how they wrote. Only a little over two months earlier they had referred to writing as drawing, been concerned about spelling, chose general topics. They had progressed rapidly and now I wanted them to articulate their perceptions of writing as a means of solidifying progress and of helping me understand their perspective on writing. In a few moments they produced the following list. I recorded the children's words on chart paper as they spoke.

How We Write:
1. I sound out the words, like h-h-here. You try to see what letters are in it.
2. You think of the things you've done and think which one you want to write and make a story out of it.
3. You have to make spaces and make titles at the beginning.
4. I think of what I did and choose the longest story to write it.
5. You have to write your best—like your pictures are your best.
6. You can't just write one letter and say "I'm done." You write more letters and words.
7. You have to want to do the book. You have to *want* to write.
8. I know most of my words and you sound out words when you read it.
9. I write first and then draw pictures and read it over and see if it makes sense. It has to make sense to make a story. Then you could line out and write a different word that would make sense.
10. You have to *think* and sound out letters and write it down.
11. I always write first and then I do a picture if I have room.
12. You have to concentrate on what you're doing.
13. You put periods whenever you think the sentence would end.
14. I always make a picture so I don't forget what I'm going to do.
15. You can't write one sentence. It wouldn't be interesting.

Most children understood the process of putting information on paper by drawing and sounding out, and they had begun to think about broader issues: making choices, ascertaining that the writing made sense, realizing the commitment of a writer. Throughout the year we continued to talk about writing and how we wrote.

In May I asked the same group of children, "What do good writers do?" Two or three hands flew up. I called on these children and as I recorded their comments on chart paper several more hands went up. One comment stimulated another and I went for more chart paper—four times! The children produced the following list.

Good Writers . . .

1. know how to "spell" without being perfect (on first drafts)
2. write the words down (their thoughts) before they "go out the window"
3. think about things to write; think of a story when they're going somewhere or doing something so they won't get stuck and get out of the habit ofwriting
4. think about what will make sense to other readers
5. don't write a 1000 pages to be good because long doesn't mean it's better
6. have to make a good beginning and a good ending
7. don't write lies (When Matt contributed this idea I stopped and asked him to tell me more. He explained that a writer can't just make things up because nobody will believe him—a writer's got to write what he knows about, like what he did or "stuff like that." We added a second sentence: "They write what they know about.")
8. have to make it interesting; they make choices to put in what readers really want to know about
9. make decisions—you can't write about everything in one story
10. look at the pictures to figure out the words if they can't read their writing
11. number the pages to keep them in order so the reader isn't confused
12. put in lots of strong information
13. use their own ideas; they don't copy other authors' writing
14. think of a good title, one that hooks the reader; one that matches the story, like Stacy's golfing story
15. keep their writing because they know all their writing is important
16. draw pictures that go with the story (In *The Trouble with Tyrannosaurus Rex* the author didn't match the pictures with the words. She forgot where to put the animals.)
17. put their name and date so they know when they wrote it
18. line out instead of erasing in case they change their mind and want it back again

19. revise after, before, and during the writing as they write to make sense and to make it clear and interesting

20. think about what they could do with their story to make it better

21. read their writing to see if there's missing words or ideas

22. read other authors' writing

23. choose good words that make the writing better

24. write everyday

25. don't publish everything they write—some stuff is boring, junky— and they don't revise everything either

26. READ all kinds of writing: good books, poems, fiction, nonfiction

27. make spaces between words; use periods and commas, quotation marks, question marks

28. work hard!

29. read their writing to other people to see if it makes sense and to revise it

All of these points came up during our writing workshop during the year as the writers gained experience writing. These children learned what writers do because they wrote every day. This list represented more than behaviors; it reflected understanding about the process of a writer writing. At first I asked the class, "What makes good writing?" Though this question was worth thinking about, when I asked "What do good writers do?" the children had more ideas and contributed more thoughtful responses. The latter question proved to be more effective because it focussed on the writer rather than the writing.

Do all of the children like to write? Most do. But every writer in the room experienced days when they didn't want to write. Courtney commented, "Writing is very hard work on days that you don't know what to write about. But on easy days it is easy because I know what to write about." Jeremy said, "All it is, is time and hard work! Sometimes it's easy, but lots of times it isn't. But I still like to write." Most of the children learned to push through the barriers that made writing difficult by sticking with the writing, learning to trust that the words would come. Kelly commented at the end of one workshop, "Yesterday I only wrote a couple of words. My mind just wouldn't get thinking. But today I kept writing and writing and writing! I didn't even know it was time to stop when you said it was sharing time." Some children had more trouble. Jody usually spent a day of restlessness when he finished a piece before he could begin another one. Cory said he liked to write, but if he missed a day or two of school he had a hard time getting back into his writing, and I sensed that without the discipline of the daily workshop, writing would easily drop out of his life. Darren loved to draw in writing workshop and he loved the *time* the workshop provided for him to dream and imagine and "live in his own world," but he consistently said that he didn't like to write. I suspect that his difficulty getting coherent thoughts on paper contributed to his feelings.

Still, every class of children has loved writing workshop. The children protested if workshop was shortened, let alone eliminated for even a day. I don't think this is because they found writing fun, easy, and enjoyable day in and day out. Part of the appeal, I'm sure, grew from having access to each other with the potential for learning and building relationships together. But there was something more. I think the children found writing to be satisfying and rewarding because it tapped something deep within them, an innate desire to learn, to know, and to understand. After writing about China, Leslie said, "I thought I only knew a little bit about China but I found out I know lots of stuff. I just forgot I knew some of it." Oliver talked about writing about his brother's birthday: "I just had to write all the birthday things down so I could stop holding them in my head and then we could always remember them because I wrote them down. And when I started writing I wrote some things that I forgot about!" We write to learn and to discover. We write to forget and we write to remember.

The children frequently referred to imagination when they talked about writing. They were able to tap into their imaginations far more readily than I've seen many adult writers do. During a mini-lesson in January I referred to a book by Ruth Brown entitled *Our Puppy's Vacation* and discussed the way this author told the story from the point of view of the puppy rather than just telling the story of a family going to the beach. I mentioned that Ruth Brown used her imagination to think what the vacation was like for the puppy. Near the end of the workshop I talked with Monica. She had come to me earlier and asked if she could read her writing to me when she finished. I had said I'd see her just before sharing time. Then she read her story, "Over the Rainbow," which had nothing to do with point of view, the focus of the mini-lesson, but had everything to do with the purpose of writing.

> I wonder. I do wonder, what it would be like over the rainbow. Would it be another world? Would it be the same? Would there be little people? Would it be a forest? I would like to walk over the rainbow. And when I would get to the top, I would like to slide right down it. But! before I got to the bottom, I would stop, look, and if there was a pot of gold at the bottom, I would slide right into it. I really do wonder.

By the end of the reading, her voice had taken on a tone of awe and wonder. When she looked at me I saw a deep pensiveness in her eyes. I felt us encircled by a quiet sense of mystery and magic, which the writing had tapped somewhere deep within this child. "Tell me about this. How did you write this?" I asked quietly.

"I don't know exactly. It's really strange. When you said how writers use their imagination . . ." Monica interrupted her thought to respond to my puzzled look. "In the mini-lesson—you said writers use imagination." I recalled my passing comment, nodded, and Monica continued. "Well, I started thinking about that—about imagination—and I've been wondering about rainbows a lot and so I just used my imagination and I really got into it and the words just came out of my head. I didn't know I had those words. They just kept coming out. I keep thinking and thinking about it."

Janet Emig (1983) wrote:

Literacy is not worth teaching
if it doesn't provide access;
if it doesn't sponsor learning;
if it doesn't unleash literal power;
if it doesn't activate the greatest power of all—
      the imagination (p. 178).

I think Monica and her classmates understand. They write.

Children's
Literature

CHAPTER 12

Beginning Engagements

From a shelf at a used book sale I pulled a thin, well-worn version of *The Story of the Three Bears*, an identical copy of the first book I remember owning. Opening the cover, I found familiar faces of large-eyed bears and a Goldilocks with Shirley Temple curls. I smiled at crayon scribbling on the pages, knowing that those marks were not a sign of disrespect but represented a child claiming a cherished possession. Later at home, I read aloud and relived early childhood moments. I remembered my mother's arms encircling me, the smell of her almond-scented hand lotion, the sound of her voice fluctuating from falsetto to gruff as she read "little, small, wee bear," "middle-sized bear," and "great, huge bear." Her tone had helped me make sense of the words, and the repetition of lines had allowed my mind to catch up with the flow of the story. I had been confused because the picture of little bear's broken chair appeared two pages after the written part of the story, but she had listened to me and then reread the words and showed me the matching picture. She had explained that porridge was like the oatmeal we ate for breakfast.

Closing this book, I could recall other moments and specific books and discussions from my mother reading to me. When she read *The Three Pigs*, she explained a butter churn by describing her childhood chore of churning butter. She often drew a picture of an animal after we had finished reading about one. The oldest child of Scandinavian immigrants, my mother could not speak English when she herself started school and endured taunts from other children: "Sweda-buck, Sweda-buck, stuffed full of straw. Can't say nothing but 'hee, hee, haw.'" She learned English (which she always referred to as "American"), brought it home to her immigrant family, and eventually loved its sounds and rhythms enough to save her high school poetry book (during the days of the depression students purchased their own texts). When she read to me she passed on her enjoyment of language and of stories.

Finding this particular version of "The Three Bears" evoked memories so vivid that I knew my teaching practices, in regards to children's literature, were as rooted in personal experiences as in formal teacher training. My reading to children in the classroom echoed my mother's reading—times filled with talk, laughter, and the sheer delight in good stories.

When I went off to school in Waterville, Maine, every teacher read aloud to us every day, and they read everything from the Bobbsey Twins to the classics. When the teacher finished a book, we all clamored to be the first to read it for ourselves. The memory of my teacher's voice accompanied my own reading, enhancing meaning, adding expression, and filling in unknown words. In third grade Mrs. Howard read *Tom Sawyer*, and to this day I carry images of Tom whitewashing a fence, of Tom and Becky lost in a cave, of Tom, Joe, and Huck prancing into church to attend their own funeral. Mrs. Howard explained key words such as "whitewash" and how it differed from paint. When we read *Lassie Come Home*, she clarified "licking his chops." Through school read alouds I met Meg, Amy, Beth, and Jo in a book I would read over and over again. The highlight of a childhood trip to the Boston area was seeing Louisa May Alcott's grave and realizing the woman who wrote this special book had actually lived. She had once been a girl like me, and I believed, were she still alive, that we would be best friends.

Remembering school read alouds, I am struck by the realization that no teacher ever bombarded us with questions, follow-up activities, or book reports. Our teachers read; we read. Our teachers kept pointing us in the direction of good books while we gossiped about the "best parts" of the books we read, played one-upmanship by boasting about our latest reading, checked out books from the children's room of the town library, and saved our allowances to buy a few precious books of our own. The pervasive message about reading from our teachers was "keep reading and enjoy it." We did. Not until seventh grade in another school, in another state, did a teacher ask for a book report, which I remember as a dull, rather purposeless activity compared to the lively engagement I'd been experiencing.

When I became a mother I read to my sons, Tim and Nathan, and I learned that children differ in their responses to books. Tim was not a child to sit for a story. However, *Richard Scarry's Best Word Book Ever* was published when he was two and Tim became absorbed in the intricate ink-line drawings. We spent lots of time (in short spurts) talking about those pictures, especially his favorite pages of cars, trucks, and red fire engines. One day, when he was not yet four, Tim constructed a three-dimensional truck with his paper, scissors, and paste and the open book spread on the floor beside him. He worked patiently and became frustrated only when the awkward shapes he had cut and pasted to the sides for wheels would not turn. At about age four when Tim began sitting for stories, his favorite books had ink-line drawings like the Scarry book. He liked *Giant John*, an early book by Arnold Lobel, and Maurice Sendak's *Where the Wild Things Are*. As he had with the Scarry book, he poured over the pictures. Recently I asked Tim (now a mechanical engineer) what he remembers from his first books and he answered, "I remember the book about those monsters—the wild things." *Where the Wild Things Are* was the first book he purchased for his infant daughter.

Nathan responded entirely differently to books and reading. He loved stories and board books were favorite crib toys. Throughout his childhood he went to sleep surrounded by books that he would browse through after our reading aloud time. There were many he enjoyed: *The King, the Mice and the Cheese*, by Nancy Gurney, Dr. Seuss's *How the Grinch Stole Christmas*, Leo Lionni's *Swimmy*. But like his brother, his favorite was *Where the Wild Things Are*. However, unlike Tim, he relished the language as well as the illustrations and frequently read along with me. Where Tim had studied Sendak's monsters, Nathan talked about them, asked questions, even told stories about them. Tim and Nathan, though brothers, displayed different personality traits from birth and their responses to books were only one manifestation of those differences. Today, Tim reads technical engineering journals, materials on do-it-yourself projects, and mysteries. He requests a "handy handyman's book" for Christmas. Nathan reads novels and poetry and readily recites poems from collections he has read over and over. They share a common interest in material on sports topics. Each son has a different literacy, one that serves his own interests and needs and that has been evident since the earliest years of their lives. If such differences existed between two brothers, I could only imagine the diversity within a classroom of children and the implications for helping those children develop as literate people.

When I became a first-grade teacher, I brought not only my history as an elementary librarian but also a personal heritage with children's books, and I read to my class—a lot! Like my teachers in Maine, I read from a children's novel to begin the school day and I read lots of picture books. Even so I felt uncomfortable—even guilty—spending so much time reading aloud. Later, when I gave children's literature official sanction by allotting forty-five minutes in the schedule every day to read aloud, I was into revolutionary stuff. A teacher who responded to the curriculum I wrote for state department requirements wrote, "Reading aloud every day is unrealistic." An administrator coming to observe the class while I was reading announced, "I'll come back when you're teaching." These responses, while disconcerting, turned out to be helpful because I began considering just *why* I was reading every day and what was going on during that time that could be justified as educationally sound.

Educational research in recent years has validated reading aloud. In an examination of literature-based reading instruction, Tunnell and Jacobs (1989) found that regular "reading aloud seemed to be a must. Daily reading aloud from enjoyable trade books has been the key that unlocked literacy growth for many disabled readers" (p. 475). In *Awakening to Literacy*, Teale (1984) cites numerous studies supporting the value of "storybook reading." Holdaway (1979) advocates "shared book experience."

Gordon Wells, in his longitudinal study of children's literacy development (1986), found that of all activities that gave children an advantage for school education, the "sharing of stories" became the most important. Children who succeeded in school had heard many stories in their early years. Jonathan, in Wells's study, came to school having heard over a thousand stories while Rosie had heard relatively few. Jonathan easily moved into school learning while Rosie struggled; those patterns continued through the conclusion of the study, when the children were in fifth grade. Wells believes that stories are particularly important because:

1. In listening to stories read aloud . . . before they can read . . . children are already beginning to gain experience of the sustained meaning-building organization of written language and its characteristic rhythms and structures. So, when they come to read books for themselves, they will find the language familiar.
2. . . . through stories, children vicariously extend the range of their experience far beyond the limits of their immediate surroundings. (pp. 151–152)

We can no longer dismiss reading aloud to children as a peripheral activity. This time spent reading aloud is more than just my voice bringing life to the words on the page, as Jane Hansen enabled me to recognize when, years ago, she asked, "What do you do when you read to children? I know you do more than just read." I couldn't answer Jane's question at the time, partly because I was unaccustomed to giving much thought to what I actually did or why. Jane's question stayed with me, and after considerable time examining my practice and reflecting on what I saw, I realized that what I did other "than just read" was *talk*. I read to children and we talk. We talk first to make sense of what we read. We talk to connect reading to our individual lives, to make connections to other books, and to extend our understanding of stories. We talk about books, authors, and illustrators. We talk about reading and writing processes because conversation about meaning and about books and about their creators naturally leads to such talk. This talk follows no curriculum, adheres to no plan for literary analysis nor integration with other topics, nor is it geared to any preplanned questions gleaned from some literature guide. It doesn't even stay on the topic all the time, but rather veers off on tangents and sidetracks the way natural conversation among people has a way of doing. In my classroom, I read and the children and I talk about what was read, both to understand and to enjoy. The result, I am convinced, influences the children's reading, writing, and thinking and strengthens our classroom community thinking.

Literature time is the term that's evolved to denote the daily chunk of time devoted to this reading and talking. In addition to literature time, I read a children's novel to the class as part of the opening each morning and I read poetry throughout the day. We easily spend an hour each day reading and responding to children's literature. Reading aloud and talking about the reading is a key structural component for learning in my classroom. The benefits spill over to every other aspect of the school day, weaving an intricate web connecting every aspect of the curriculum.

Starting Literature Time

Literature time begins on the first day of school. The children gather on our storyrug and I read several books. We'll read three or four titles during this time every day all year long. The children listen and talk and talk. It's not long before they have favorites. They love Robert McCloskey's *Make Way for Ducklings* and listen with unfaltering attention as I read it again and again. They notice every detail in the brown and white drawings. The boys make the screeching sounds of cars coming to a halt as the ducklings cross the street. They all giggle at the rhyming names of the ducklings, not because they rhyme but because "their mother must get them all mixed up when she tries to call them." I show them photographs of the little statues of Mrs. Mallard and her ducklings in the Public Gardens in Boston and tell them about seeing children sitting on the ducklings and talking to them.

"I'd talk to them too," says Matt. "I'd tell them I like their book. And do those ducklings ever go in the water?" His questions unleash a crescendo of voices as children speak simultaneously.

"Wait!" One at a time." I struggle to make myself heard through the din. During these first days of school it seems I'm forever working to get the children to talk one at a time and to listen to each other's comments. "Everyone may talk," I explain, "but one at a time. You begin, and then you, and then you. No one may interrupt and I want you to listen to each other." After a child's comment I ask, "What do you think about that idea?" and listen to one or two peer responses before I continue. We begin to establish ways to listen and respond. In the beginning the pattern of talk is teacher-child-teacher-child. Slowly that pattern shifts to child-child-child-teacher, with my input receding each day. Eventually the children respond to each other in group conversations and my role drops back to a few occasional questions or comments to nudge thinking or to assure that everyone has the opportunity to speak.

One McCloskey book leads us to another and another. When we read *Blueberries for Sal* I stop at the words, "Kerplink, kerplank, kerplunk," McCloskey's language that imitates the sound of berries falling into an empty tin bucket. I say, "Listen to those words. What do they sound like, I wonder? How do you suppose Mr. McCloskey thought of them?" The children listen to the words, enjoy the sound, but are puzzled. Plastic has replaced metal buckets and they have no experience of picking berries. I explain about metal buckets and their imaginations take over.

"Oh, I get it," says Max. "It's the sound of the berries hitting the bucket. Neat!" As the story continues the children giggle at the plight of Little Bear and Little Sal and understand the mixup with mothers before the characters do in the story.

When we read *Mrs. Wishy Washy* the second time, the children chime in with the repeating "wishy washy, wishy washy." They request a particular version of *The Three Billy Goats Gruff* because they like the picture of the troll. "He's more like a monster," says Jody. The group agrees. When we read Robert Munsch's *Love You Forever*, they laugh uproariously at the role reversal of the son rocking the mother. When I finish reading the book Aaron says, "It keeps going on like the other book, like *Henny Penny*. It keeps going on and on."

"Yeah," says Jeff, "she'll grow up and then he'll get old and then his daughter will come and rock him." Aaron and Jeff caught the pattern and made connections between two books. The pondering looks, then nods among the children indicate that the boys have helped everyone understand.

I read nursery rhymes (which some groups regard as "baby stuff") and let these rhymes lead us into poetry. Sometimes children respond with blank stares when I first read poetry, but after a couple of rereadings of lyrical or humorous verses faces light up and they cry, "Read it again!" Judith Viorst's "Mother Doesn't Want a Dog" is always a favorite as is "A Thousand Hairy Savages," by Spike Milligan. I begin reciting it as the children line up to go to the cafeteria and the class chimes in. Later we'll do the same with William Carlos Williams's poem "This Is Just to Say" for this lunchtime ritual. The children also love e.e. cummings's poem "Maggie and Millie and Molly and May." We don't talk about the alliteration, but I know it's the sound and feel of those words falling off their tongues that the children find playful and intriguing.

Popular books are ones with repetitious lines or books that are songs. After reading *I Know an Old Lady Who Swallowed a Fly* to the group, I point out two different versions. The group's attitude is "So what?" I quickly dropped my plan to compare the two versions. When I read *Oh! A Hunting We Will Go,* the children sing the refrain. "You can probably learn to read this book because you already know the words," I say. Looks of surprise cross their faces and then hands fly up and the pleading requests come, "Can I have that book?" "Can I read it?" "Can I?"

During literature time I introduce books that children can learn to read, such as these predictable books or books with a strong story line told in a few words. We also read more complexly written stories, ones that children can read through retelling, using illustrations to remind them of the story. We become a community that reads together. The books—stories, poems, and nonfiction—become a common ground of shared experiences that knits our community more closely together. The benefits of literature time spill over to every part of our school day. I focus on the children's natural delight in listening to and talking about stories, and I strive to maintain the role of a responsive teacher while at the same time teaching children about genre, authors, literary conventions, and so on.

"Favorite Books": A Nice Idea that Backfired

Reading aloud was always part of my classroom. Leaving the basal behind released time to read at a regular time *every* day. Even though literature time, with its solid group conversations, developed each year without elaborate planning on my part, I felt a gnawing concern: just reading and talking seemed so simple that often I felt I wasn't really teaching. So one year I tried to launch literature time with a formalized activity. I asked each child to bring a favorite book to school and we would read some and chat about the books we owned and loved. By starting with what the children knew, our literature time would connect to their lives and homes. Soon I realized what an unrealistic, naive notion this plan was.

On Friday afternoon of the first week of school (it was the year of that frustrating first day), I finally got around to the "favorite books" I had asked the children to bring when I phoned them the night before school opened. The entire week had moved at a snail's pace, with everything taking longer than I'd anticipated. Squabbles constantly erupted among the children. Every teacher knows that it takes only one quarrelsome child to create a contentious tone in the classroom. I was beginning to identify at least half a dozen or more such children in this particular group. Ninety degree heat and humidity aggravated tempers of even the most cooperative children. When recess came, everyone was eager to leave the hot classroom. The children ran to a sultry playground and I headed to the air-conditioned office on the excuse of checking my mailbox.

That Friday afternoon the children returned from the playground with flushed faces and perspiration-soaked bodies. I shut the office door, leaving springtime air behind, and headed down the hall. It took twenty minutes for everyone to get drinks from a fountain that sprayed a limp arch of warm water, and I argued with a couple of kids about keeping their mouths off the fountain. "You're not suppose to suck the water out," I said. Cory kept sucking until I tugged him away. He shrugged and grinned that innocent, winsome grin I'd seen all week. "I should have called a room mother and asked her to get us popsicles," I thought and then remembered that I don't have room mothers yet; I hadn't gotten around to making those calls. I was glad it was Friday.

Maybe sharing the favorite books would rejuvenate us. We'd sit quietly and chat, and end the week on a positive note. When I asked the children to get out their books, a couple cried out, "What books?" or "I think I took mine home." Two or three children ran across the room to search bookbags while others began rummaging through their desks. As the group gathered on the carpet they fanned themselves with the books, twirled and flipped them, tossed them in the air, and swatted each other on the head with them. No one opened a book. No child spontaneously started talking about the story in their hands.

"I'm glad to see your books," I began. "I'm not going to read all of them aloud to the whole class (I knew that would open a can of worms I'd rather leave unopened), but I would like you to tell us about your books—why you like them, and why you chose them as your favorites. Talking about books is something readers do. Readers tell other people about books they like and why."

One by one, the children made brief, perfunctory statements. The majority of the books were "grocery store genre," with characters from television or movies. Most of the children's talk turned to television shows or movies. I felt my disappointment in their choices and my growing annoyance at all the talk about television cartoons. I eagerly responded to the few exceptions. Stacy showed her book (one I was unfamiliar with) and commented, "This is a really good *story*." She emphasized "story," strung the word out, rolled her eyes, then added, "My dad reads it to me a lot!" She chuckled and hugged the book as she concluded her little speech. Amy shyly presented a book that had belonged to her mother. "My grandmom was a teacher and this was a book my mom used to learn to read," she whispered.

Natalie proudly showed a tattered book about a unicorn. "This is my *favorite* book!" she said. "Will you read it? I like when somebody reads it." Though her book was not a television spinoff, I knew it was a tedious read aloud. Natalie kept begging; I put her off until Monday with a "We'll see. It's almost time to go home now." One or two other children talked about reading with parents or babysitters, but most seemed only slightly acquainted with books and with being read to. The books they had brought to school were not ones that most adults would enjoy reading and rereading at bedtime. The "conversation" degenerated to short dialogues between me and individual children while the rest picked and poked at each other. Lots of talk, not much listening, not much interest.

Finally the day—and the week—did end. As I straightened the room I made a mental note to work with the children Monday on end-of-the-day housekeeping and I thought about this "favorite book" activity. I'd anticipated the sharing of these books as a means of building community and of opening communication. The children would share what they liked, and I would affirm their previous experiences with books, and we would talk about reading and . . . wow, did I miss on this one. But I learned a lot. A gulf existed between the children's experiences with books and the literary expectations of school. Most of the class had been uninvolved in my activity. Some sat quietly; others verged on misbehavior. Some had books; others did not—even though I had restated my request in school in addition to the phone calls. A couple of children had picked up a book in the classroom to bring to the rug. The silence and the vacant looks on their faces now haunted me. I remembered reading about the "literacy club."

Frank Smith (1986) defines the "literacy club" as "a club of people who use written language. . . . children join the literacy club the way they join the spoken language club—with the implicit act of mutual acceptance. There are no special admission requirements, no entry fees" (p. 37). Membership in the literacy club begins before children come to school, and its membership is not defined by social or economic levels of society, nor by the criteria established by schools. But that day in my classroom, even with the best of intentions, my selective affirmations had clearly revealed to everyone the membership lines of an elitist branch of the literacy club: the literacy valued by school. I had elevated the members and exposed the outsiders. I recognized how we in schools unwittingly perpetuate "the club" as an exclusive organization even though theoretically we are appalled by the concept and believe that *we* don't do that in *our* classrooms. I felt terrible. My activity of sharing favorite books was one of those school activities that sounded good and even might have worked in another situation, but on this day it had backfired. Why? I think, unwittingly, I felt the pressure for a reading *activity* to *enhance* my teaching. The success of the activity took precedence over responding to children. I resolved to rectify the situation on Monday, to strive for "mutual acceptance."

On Monday morning Jeff walked in the door and announced, "I brung my favorite book today." From his bookbag he pulled Chris Van Allsburg's *The Polar Express.* "Let me show you," he said and, plopping the book on my lap, he began flipping through the pages, talking all the while. "This is my favorite picture. No wait, I think I like this one of Santa's sleigh, and see, you can look down like Santa does. I like how everybody looks so *small,* like they're teeny-tiny ants." He paused a moment, looked up at me for acknowledgment or to check that I was listening, and then continued. "But this is my favorite part too. See, at the end he finds the bell under the Christmas tree." Jeff proceeded to retell the ending of the story.

"Will you tell everyone about this later?" I asked.

"Yes, but I gotta take it home tonight. I can only leave it here one day," he said emphatically.

"That's fine," I answered, and Jeff carefully laid the book on a table and went off to play with blocks.

Later that morning Jeff shared *The Polar Express* as his favorite book and I read Natalie's unicorn book by telling the story. Natalie sat beside me and turned the pages so the class could see the illustrations and filled in my narrative with contributions of her own. That morning, both Jeff and Natalie shined as members of the literacy club. To be literate, children don't have to think like me, or believe as I do, or value the same books I value. Yet access to and knowledge of the "literature of school" and the "culture of school" provides mobility in our democratic society. All children deserve this access and knowledge. At the same time, they deserve recognition and valuing of their home cultures and the literacy of that culture. Balancing both perspectives has become one of the tensions embedded in my teaching. I also was reminded that my literature time had been working in previous years because it was *responsive* in tone. That meant I needed to share literature as part of establishing the environment and then permit the *children* to respond. If I attempted to shape their responses into the patter and pattern of "school responses," I was not really establishing a place where children could authentically and honestly respond to literature. By preventing such responses I denied them connections to their literary heritages.

A couple of weeks later Jeff pulled another book from his bookbag and announced, "I changed my mind. *The Polar Express* isn't my favorite book. This one is." He held up *The Ox-cart Man,* by Donald Hall.

"What made you change your mind?" I asked.

"See, my mom read this to me last night and I knew that I really liked it a lot, so I decided now that *this* is my favorite."

I've often asked the question What is your favorite book? or . . . your favorite piece of writing? or . . . your best piece of writing? Asking someone to choose their favorite or best is like asking a parent to select their favorite child or asking an individual to designate their favorite friend. The question is too restrictive; it prescribes boundaries. During the school year, when I've asked children to name their favorite book, they reply with answers typical of these that Margaret, Josie, and Jason gave.

> MARGARET: I think . . . *The Boxcar Children.* Yes, my favorite book is *The Boxcar Children* because that's the one you're reading to us now.
>
> JOSIE: I think I like *Mufaro's Beautiful Daughters.* That's my favorite for *now.*
>
> JASON: [after looking around the room] Let's see. That's a hard question. There's so many that I like. I like *The Art Lesson,* and I like *The Piggybook,* and I like *Four on the Shore.* I love James Marshall's books. I know, I think I like *Goldilocks,* James Marshall's *Goldilocks* the best. (Then he added, as his eyes roved the room) but there's some other books I like too.

The children talk the way readers talk about books: mentioning titles, favorite authors, and leaving options for further choices. Another problem with my "favorite book" activity was that the underlying question, What is your favorite book? led children to make a choice to fulfill a teacher requirement rather than causing them to thoughtfully consider possibilities. My hunch is that many teaching activities and teacherly questions provide assurance (perhaps false assurance) of student accomplishment and validate our accountability, but do little for children. Jason, Margaret, and Josie talked about books as readers because they read. Listening to literature and responding by *talking* about books enriches children's awareness of written language, which in turn enhances their development as learners, thinkers, and language users. Literature time in my classroom is a time for reading and talking—and enjoying books.

CHAPTER 13

Reader Response Theory

Sometime during the winter of the first year that I incorporated daily writing and reading workshops, and expanded the use of children's books, I noticed that echoes of children's literature began appearing in the children's writing. Words and phrases from children's books popped up regularly, and children began writing fictional stories borrowing the characters from books by professional authors. Eileen, a child in that first class, wrote "Babar's First Tooth."

> Babar was a baby elephant. He lived in a beautiful house with his brothers and sisters. Babar was the smallest elephant you have seen. Babar had no teeth.
> Babar's brothers and sisters called Babar names because he was little. Babar felt sad. Babar didn't pay attention to them at all.
> One day Babar grew a tooth. He ran inside to tell his brothers and sisters, "I grew a tooth."
> "We don't care if you grew a tooth."
> "But it's my first tooth."
> "We don't care!"
> Babar went to his room. He started to cry. His mother and father came up to his room. They said, "We're glad you grew a tooth."
> Babar stopped crying. He dried his eyes. He said, "I don't care what they say."
> Babar marched downstairs. He said, "You better quit it!"
> "Why should we?"
> "Because I said so." Babar taught them a lesson.
> "Now are you going to call me names?"
> "No. We're not."

"Well good!"

Babar's brothers and sisters are playing with Babar now because Babar taught them a lesson. The End.

I came across an old tape recording of Eileen telling me how she got the idea for this book.

"See, I was looking through some of my Babar books and I got an idea to write about Babar's first tooth. In the back of the book it was talking about how teeth grow 'cause his little boy had eight teeth and he lost one of them and the boy was sad so he got a new tooth so I thought to write a 'Babar's First Tooth.' " Then Eileen read the lines that she felt were the best part of what she had written so far (she was in the middle of composing the story during this conversation). She read, "Babar's brothers and sisters called Babar names 'cause he was little. Babar felt sad. Babar didn't pay attention."

After listening to the tape I dug out my notes from a parent conference in November. Eileen's mother had told me of her daughter's apprehension about first grade, especially about learning to read. Most of Eileen's playmates were second graders who teased Eileen, making fun of the fact that they could read and she could not. Eileen's parents urged their daughter to ignore these taunts and reminded her that soon she too would read. Eileen's story, written shortly after she began reading, was not only about a young elephant acquiring a tooth, but also Eileen's story of her own growth. Like all good literature, a children's book evoked a personal connection in the life of a reader. For Eileen, writing was the process for expressing that connection.

Eileen's story was well received by her classmates. They lauded it as "one of the best stories they'd ever read!" Good stories beget more stories, and in discussing Eileen's book, the children talked about times when they too had experienced the injustice of mean taunts by older children. This involvement with a story and meaning on the part of Eileen and her classmate was far deeper than any I have ever been able to elicit through traditional teacher questions or follow-up class activities to children's literature. It captured mind and heart and imagination of each child. *Engagement* with books such as this evokes responses that not only lead the readers back to reading again and again, but also connects readers to their communities, helps them understand experiences, and make sense of their very existence.

This engagement with language and literature and meaning began appearing regularly in my classroom. I could conclude only that these responses to literature, which made such profound connections to children's lives, came because of the environment. The children read and wrote every day. They chose their books for reading and their topics for writing. And every day the children heard lots of literature read aloud and had an opportunity to talk about that literature. During that read-aloud time I restrained myself from channeling children's thinking toward adult answers. I had dramatically restructured my classroom that year. No models of other classrooms existed and so I looked to the children to be my teachers. I established the structure and tone, then helped maintain it as it evolved, but I did so with a responsive teaching style and with a light touch. I made decisions by listening to and observing the children. I trusted their capacity to learn. They never let me down.

When Eileen wrote "Babar's First Tooth" I was unfamiliar with reader response theory, even though good children's literature had replaced the basal readers for my first-graders' reading material. After hearing the terms *response groups, reading response,* and *responding to literature* batted around (but not *really* understanding what they meant), I read *Literature as Exploration,* by Louise Rosenblatt. There I found a theory about reading that articulated the intangibles I saw as my first graders read and wrote about and talked about their reading.

The acknowledged pioneer of reader response theory, Louise Rosenblatt is a dynamic, energetic woman who, in her eighties, continues to contribute to educational theory and practice. *Literature as Exploration* was first published in 1938, and in 1978 she wrote *The Reader, the Text, and the Poem,* where she further defines her theory. Rosenblatt describes reading as an equal transaction between a reader and a text in which meaning is constructed in the mind of the reader. The particular meaning and the way in which the reader constructs that meaning is unique to each reader. Rosenblatt (1978) says:

> The reader brings to the text his past experience and present personality. . . . The reading of a text is an event occurring at a particular time in a particular environment at a particular moment in the life history of the reader. The transaction will involve not only the past experience but also the present state and present interests and concerns of the reader. (pp. 12, 20)

Readers bring to a reading event not only knowledge and understanding from previous life experiences, but also current hopes, wishes, dreams, biases, concerns, expectations, attitudes, and feelings that affect or create meaning. Certainly, readers must remain attuned to the text and responsible to what is written there, but diverse interpretations will emerge among readers due to the different emphases of different readers. And every reading—and rereading—is a unique experience eliciting a unique response. Almost anyone who read *Gone with the Wind* as a teen and reread that text again years later, perhaps at age thirty-five, recognizes that they read a different book. It is not that the text has changed but that the reader has, and therefore so has the meaning that has been constructed.

Rosenblatt uses a continuum to help us understand the range of purposes for which we read. The purpose of a particular reading experience ("transaction," to use Rosenblatt's term) will fall somewhere along this continuum according to the reader's "focus of attention during the reading-event." At one end of this continuum is *efferent reading*—reading in which the reader's attention is focussed on what will "remain after the reading," what will be carried away from the reading: information acquired, questions answered, etc. Rosenblatt provides an example of efferent reading: a mother whose child has swallowed poison reads the poison bottle for the sole purpose of discovering the antidote. The mother certainly does not pause to think, "Oh, that's awful tasting stuff. He might not like that," or "I remember tasting that once." Her concentration is only on gleaning specific information to deal with the emergency. In less urgent examples, Rosenblatt notes, we also read newspapers, cookbooks, and history books with an efferent approach. Efferent reading answers questions of who, what, when, to whom, in what sequence, and so on.

At the other end of the continuum is *aesthetic reading*—reading in which *"the reader's attention is centered directly on what he is living through during his relationship with that particular text"* (p. 25). In addition to "images or concepts or assertions that the words point to, [the reader] pays attention to the associations, feelings, attitudes, and ideas that the words . . . arouse within him" (1978, pp. 24–25). This aesthetic reading leads to more open-ended questions, such as What were you reminded of? or What were you thinking and feeling as you read? Rosenblatt says the aesthetic is a more "literary" reading of a text.

A reading experience is rarely either/or—efferent or aesthetic—for as we read, we move along the continuum. We shift our focus of attention, at times responding with an efferent stance (gleaning specific information from the text), and a moment later, a more aesthetic one (pondering what that information means to us, how we respond). We adjust our reading purposes from that of obtaining information to considering the personal response the reading evokes within us as we move through a text.

I read the newspaper, for the most part, in an efferent manner, to learn what is happening in my community and the world. I read headlines, scan and skim news stories, putting together a composite update of recent events. I could give up this reading in favor of watching television news. In fact, some days I do. However, my purpose for reading shifts as I read the newspaper. Sometimes I read human interest stories or articles about people I know or parts of news stories that evoke responses, which in turn cause me to shift my reading away from a mere gleaning of information. My reading often slows down when I come to this kind of reading and I find myself reflecting on specific details and making connections to my own experiences or beliefs. I've moved along the continuum and am reading for aesthetic purposes. For example, after the war with Iraq I recall a front-page story in the *Philadelphia Inquirer* on the plight of Kurdish refugees. This particular news story told of a mother who walked for hours with her two-year-old on her shoulders, paused to rest, and discovered that the child had frozen to death. The parents left the child at the side of the road and moved on, hoping to save their other five children. My response, as I read, shifted along Rosenblatt's continuum of reading purposes from efferent—gathering facts about the Kurds—to the more aesthetic, evoking compassion and anger and creating images in my mind. This news story stayed with me for days. I sought out more news of the plight of the Kurds in subsequent days, both in newspapers and on television. My engagement went well beyond the mere facts in the story. The facts played an important part in the experience—the story doesn't exist for me without facts (my efferent reading); without those facts I couldn't even retell the story. However, it was the aesthetic reading that captured my imagination and connected me to that mother and to the plight of the refugee children. Aesthetic reading requires *more* of readers than just a recall of text.

In the last decade the concept of reader response has gained prominence among literary theorists at all levels of education. With the momentum toward literature-based instruction for elementary classrooms, the theory of reader response becomes important for classroom teachers. However, when considering Rosenblatt's efferent-to-aesthetic reading continuum in relationship to reading instruction in schools, I feel somewhat chagrined. For the most part, reading instruction has leaned heavily toward the efferent position in all reading, one with right or wrong answers. We define purposes for readers by "setting the purpose" when we introduce a new book to a class. Reading programs and reading instruction in schools favor the *literal* reading of a text, crowding out the *literary* reading. After all, that's what we can test; we base comprehension on a literal recall of facts. We ask who did what, when, how, to whom, in what order, and on and on.

Our literal approach to reading begins early in school. We read a story to our students such as *Goldilocks and the Three Bears*, for example, and then we ask questions correlated to specific reading skills.

- What did Goldilocks do first when she went in the bears' house? What did she do next? (In our educational jargon, this is called sequencing.)
- Why did little bear's chair break when Goldilocks sat on it? (making inferences)
- Why did Goldilocks run away? (cause and effect)
- What is the main idea of this story? (I'm frequently confused when this one appears in tests and teacher's manuals. I usually have to look up the correct answer in the answer key. One preprimer test provided a three sentence story with a picture and then asked children for the main idea.)

All these questions have "right" answers (our answers, or "school" answers), and we expect children to provide those answers to demonstrate that they are good readers. Even with more open-ended questions, a notion exists of what the best answer ought to be. Indeed, the teacher's manual for the reading program provides open-ended questions and then is likely to add: Accept any answer such as . . . A brief list of answers considered appropriate follows these instructions.

One day in my own classroom I asked, "How do you think those bears felt when they came in and saw what Goldilocks had done?"

"They probably thought it was pretty funny," a child replied. The traditional teacher response to such "inaccurate" answers is to redirect the child's thinking by saying gently, but firmly, "Well, look at the picture. Do those bears look like they're laughing?" or "Would they *really* laugh if someone broke their chair?" And the child pulls back his reply and begins seeking out the one the teacher wants by searching her face, listening to her hints, and then submitting a more acceptable answer. But on this day before I could say anything the child continued, "It's just like my little brother the other day. He sat down on his chair and it fell apart just like that, and he started laughing and we all laughed because it was so funny." And then the child went on to explain that part of the chair had become unglued and so the whole chair was weak, and his brother was too heavy and when he sat down it fell apart. Maybe that happened to the bear's chair too, he proposed; maybe it needed to be glued.

This child responded to the story with a memory from his own experience. The story connected to his life, leading him to some specific speculation as to why the chair broke. It's pretty hard to talk about an aesthetic response to reading without getting into an efferent response as well. Of course, we say, we ask children *why* they gave a particular answer, but I know that in the course of a busy school day, often I haven't taken the time to explore the thinking behind children's answers. Once the majority of talk surrounding reading in my classroom, both the reading aloud of children's literature and the reading children did, focussed on answering teacher questions. These questions often boiled down to requesting obvious information or directing children's thinking to "correct" (adult?) interpretations of books. Such questions laid the groundwork for "school talk." Beneath the surface was the message: Prove to me that you read this book and understand it as I think you ought. Questioning is an effective teaching technique, but I was so concerned that children understand the "correct" interpretation of books that I funneled children's responses into "right answers" and entertained children's ideas as "cute." In truth, I paid little heed to those ideas and did not value the children's experience with the reading.

"It's the *experience* that's so important," Louise Rosenblatt said to me as we sipped iced tea on her back porch. I told her about Jeff.

"Jeff was reading to me and came upon the word 'disgusted.' 'My Mom keeps saying that word a lot but I don't know what that word means.' I asked Jeff what he *thought* his mother meant. 'I'm not sure, but I think she's angry,' he said, and his voice tone switched from unsure to definite in that answer."

"Yes!" said Rosenblatt. "That's it. That's the experience."

Jeff understood the meaning of a word based on his experience with that word and brought that meaning to the story he read. The reading experience further developed his understanding of the word. I did not refine his definition; he'll continue to do so in his own time and through further experiences with reading and talking with others. Jeff's response to one word provided me with an example of a child learning to read aesthetically. I want to help children learn how to read with more than mere decoding skills and literal comprehension. I want to help them develop Rosenblatt's aesthetic approach, to *experience* literature through personal meaning making and then deepen that experience in reading communities of discussion and acceptance. If Jeff learns to read this way with one word then he will bring broader issues to his reading and come away with a thoughtful understanding that further enhances his understanding of not only the text but his own life. This is the power of literature. It is not merely knowledge that we are after (though that is important and will develop too), but also *understanding*. Experience and reflecting on experience leads to understanding.

Schools and teachers have been accused of producing individuals who *can* read but who choose not to read. Reading instruction that focusses on literal recall with correct answers (an efferent approach to reading) may be one reason for this disinterest in reading. Mark Twain said, "The man who does not read has no advantage over the man who can't." First graders showed me that it is aesthetic reading that hooks readers. I began allowing and then encouraging their responses to reading and found that children who learn to read for aesthetic purposes as well as efferent ones become readers who choose to read because they experience meaningful connections to their lives. This was the kind of reading I'd experienced in the early years of my own life, and it was this approach to which I returned when I left behind programmed reading instruction.

For a long time I suspected that literature time was vital in the children's development as readers and writers and thinkers. After reading Rosenblatt I realized that it was more than just hearing books read aloud; all the talk that surrounds the reading helps develop the range of purposes for reading. Children talk to express *their* ideas, not to answer my questions. In the rich conversation that gradually develops, they share ideas about meaning and about the personal connections to what we read. The talk extends everyone's understanding of a particular text. It increases the children's involvement with particular books, develops their natural responsiveness to literature, and leads them further into books and reading. However, I learned that it's not always easy to establish this authentic talk—not as simple as bringing the children together, reading a book, and asking for their responses.

Learning to Talk About Books

Literature time on the first day of school usually went well. I had come to count on this time as a way of establishing rapport with a new group of children. Then came the discouraging first day I described in the beginning of this book. However, the disillusionment I felt after the literature time on that first day helped me answer Jane Hansen's question, "What do you do when you read to children?" If this group enjoyed listening to stories they kept it well hidden, but the chaos during our first literature times enabled me to examine how to build a community that could honestly and thought-fully respond to literature without heavy-handed teacher control. That first day the children had poked and pushed and jostled for position on the rug. They had responded to the reading of *The Three Billy Goats Gruff* in tones of impatience and annoyance—not delight—because they were familiar with the story. Oh, they became involved when I read the book—involved with the drama of my exaggerated expression. But I knew that I couldn't, nor did I want to, sustain that over-stated reading for the next 179 days of school.

Then there was Elizabeth's comment about "nature" after I read *The Very Hungry Caterpillar*. This wasn't child talk, the way a child really talks about a book among peers. This was *school talk,* the kind of response a child gives to a teacher in a school setting. And indeed Elizabeth had attended kinder-garten and a couple of years of nursery school. She was well versed in school talk. I could see my work was cut out for me: to show these children that rereading books was important and could uncover new ideas, and to help them take the risks of honest communication. To lead these children back to their natural and engaging talk about books took time and effort.

On the second day I read *The Very Hungry Caterpillar* again, and this time when I came to the page where the caterpillar ate through two plums I commented that I liked plums and that I didn't get them very often when I was a child because plums didn't grow in my area. The children began to voice their own likes. "Umm, I like chocolate cake," said one child, and then a succession of "umms" followed from the group with the mention of each food item. When I finished reading I said, "I really like the picture of this butterfly."

"Yeah, I do too," said a child at my feet, and I knew that she'd agree with whatever I said. But I continued, "It sorta reminds me of the butterflies that have been around our playground at recess."

"Yeah, we catched some," said Cory. And a conversation on catching butterflies and recess broke out. Greg said he knew how butterflies grow and he explained that the butterfly is first a caterpillar and then it makes a cocoon and then "hatches" into a butterfly. It was a small beginning. The children had responded to this book with slightly more natural talk and made a few connections to their own lives, thereby claiming aesthetic purposes as well as efferent ones for reading.

To help children learn to talk about books in this way I need to handle my role gingerly: sometimes offering my ideas, but quickly diminishing their importance; accepting unconditionally the children's spontaneous thoughts; asking what *they* think and then welcoming those responses; striving to understand and delighting in their ideas; and, in the beginning, being cautious about expressing my own opinions. Though my role is to be someone in charge, helping to manage and coordinate all this talk, I can't afford to be the expert with the final answer, nor the judge valuing one idea over another.

Our community grows around this literature time of reading and talking. The books become a repertoire of common experiences, and the children's responses contribute to the development of both the individual and the community. I approach the entire process of teaching literature with an attitude of trying to *understand* the children rather than attempting to change them to my views. Understanding is a funny thing. I can't set out to understand with an agenda of trying to change learners; but understanding evokes understanding in others and, as a result, I find myself changed from the community experiences of literature time. I suspect this occurs for the children as well. I found that if I concern myself with understanding the children's ideas and drop the traditional teacher role of then trying to mold those ideas to conventional school thinking, the children express their opinions more freely. I nod and reply "I see," or ask questions to help me understand. I presume that the children's logic makes sense and that if I don't understand it is *my* problem, not theirs. I continually learn new ideas from them. As part of the talk, and as a way of clarifying for myself and validating for a particular child, I often restate their ideas and then comment, genuinely, "I'm impressed!" or "I hadn't thought of that."

I began to ask questions for which I didn't know the answer, questions that arose from the situation and the interactions among the children. Those questions became very specific because they resulted from listening and asking about what I didn't understand, and they evoked thoughtful answers. Sometimes, at first, children responded to such questions with "I don't know." At one time I supplied answers to the "I don't know" responses. Then I began to suspect that "I don't know" really meant "I don't know what you want me to say, teacher." I began responding to "I don't know" with "Think about it" or "Let me know if you think of something." Often the best questions, I came to realize, are ones that can't be answered immediately and that, by leaving unanswered, allow children to mull over ideas.

Of course one could argue that some readings are "better" than others. For example, a "better" reading of *Goldilocks* recognizes that the three bears are outraged rather than amused by Goldilocks's breaking and entering. I still ask questions or make comments about a text to direct children's attention to inferences or details in the text for the purpose of helping them become better readers. We want children to read thoughtfully, analytically, and critically. However, I believe that to nurture the development of thoughtful readers, children need to spend time with books in a supporting and sharing community where they can explore their own ideas and learn through hearing the ideas of their peers. Such experiences lead to the development of sophisticated readers. By directing the attention of young readers to adult interpretations of texts we may short-circuit children's thinking processes.

While I want children to become aware of the ideas books stimulate for them, I've discovered that initially questions such as What does this make you think of? when referring to an entire text are just too broad. (That's probably part of the reason I got that "nature" answer. I asked a vague question; I got a vague answer.) The children come forth with much better responses when I pause during the reading to ask for responses or to share *my* authentic responses to a *particular* line, a *particular* character, or a *particular* situation. My comment about fruit during the reading of Eric Carle's book was specific and honest. I can't write or plan these questions ahead of time; they've got to come from within me at the moment that I'm reading to the class, for then they will be honest responses to this particular reading. The children intuitively know this. Children are very good at "reading" adults and knowing what's authentic and what's not. I'm modeling responses for them, but I think there's something more than modeling. This kind of talk is very real: genuine and of the moment. It puts me in mind of a line I read somewhere once: Honesty and openness evoke honesty and openness in return.

When I read aloud the first chapter of *Maniac McGee*, the 1990 Newbery Award-winning book, the line " . . . out the side door and into the starry, sweet, onion-grass-smelling night" always catches my breath because of the description of a spring evening and because of the ways its rhythm contrasts with the surrounding paragraphs. I come to that line and pause to say, "I just love that line. How do you suppose Jerry Spinelli thought of it?" Listeners pause, then comment with their responses. If there are no comments I continue reading, leaving the question unanswered. We take only a moment and then go on, but those moments of turning words and phrases around to savor their taste before we swallow and digest them adds to the entire experience with books.

With time, patience, and many invitations to respond, even this class, that in the beginning had been so unruly, becomes adept at talking about books. They consider possible interpretations and make sense of what they don't understand by pooling their knowledge. They move back and forth along Rosenblatt's continuum between aesthetic and efferent as we read and reread books. Knowing that it's okay to express their ideas, it's only a few days into school when the children speculate when we read *Snow White* as to how to defeat the wicked queen. "Color the apple *yellow* and give it to her," is an idea they all like. When we read Eve Bunting's line about leaves chasing each other in *Ghost's Hour, Spook's Hour,* Matt says, "Yeah, I see them playing tag. I play tag." When the little boy in this story says that his *dog* was scared, the children giggle knowingly and Laura says, "He [the boy] was too! He just didn't want to say. He's too embarrassed." It is mid-October when we read *Where the Wild Things Are,* and a discussion ensues about what the wild things will do at the end of the story.

"Max doesn't want *them* to eat dinner because they're man-eating—they'll eat *him!*"

"Why are they man-eating?"

"They have sharp teeth and sharp claws like meat-eaters."

"They won't [eat him] because they're friends."

"They'll dance all night. That's what they'll do."

"No. They don't want him to go because he trained them with their eyes and they didn't want him to go." Each child's comment reminded me of an interest or experience particular to that child: dinosaurs, good friends, and staying up late at night.

A week later they loved Alvin Schwartz's *In a Dark, Dark Room and Other Scary Stories,* but after the story where a sweater appears on a grave Lisa says, "I don't get this one. It doesn't make sense." I ask the others what they think. One child replied and started a string of responses from other children, each thought stimulating the next response.

"I think the mother died."

"Maybe he was alive in the car ride and *then* he died."

"But the Mom said in the story that he'd been dead a year."

"I think the sweater sunk up on top of the soil."

"Maybe it was spirits." The notion of spirits hushed the group and they lapsed into shudders and spooky "oooo" sounds.

In January I first read Chris Van Allsburg's *Two Bad Ants.* In this book ants discover wonderful crystals, which they take home to their queen. She pronounces them the most wonderful thing she has ever tasted and dispatches the ants to bring back more. It is on this second journey that two ants stray from the group and decide to have these wonderful crystals for themselves. The hazards these two "bad ants" encounter shape the plot of the story. On the first reading of *Two Bad Ants*, the illustrations played a particularly significant role. The children loved the unusual perspectives from the inside of a toaster, of nostrils and the upper lip of a man just about to sip from a cup ("He needs a shave," one child commented), and close-ups of ants carrying crystals. When we finished this first reading the children pronounced it a "good book." "We gotta read that one again," stated one child firmly. The class agreed. The engagement with *Two Bad Ants* and with an ongoing process of meaning making had begun.

The first reading was wonderful, but it was the second reading of this book, and the third, and fifth, and tenth, and fifteenth where the richness developed and continued developing as readers speculated, theorized, considered, talked and listened to each other, changed their minds, tested ideas and formulated new ones. Van Allsburg brilliantly weaves text and pictures together in this book without providing absolute answers. For example, we know that the ants seek crystals, but what are these crystals? Sugar? Salt? Van Allsburg provides clues but never comes right out and tells us. At one point Jody said that he was sure it was salt because he'd looked at salt crystals under his magnifying glass. "I didn't have the book with me, so I had to just remember what they looked like, but it's salt. Salt looks just like that when you look under a magnifying glass." Matt asked Jody if he'd looked at sugar too and Jody admitted he hadn't thought about doing that. The group began questioning Jody's answer, saying that you'd have to look at sugar too. "I just thought it was salt, so that's all I looked at," said Jody, and then went on to suggest that he would have to look at both salt and sugar while referring to the book.

The ants travel through a "forest" on their way for crystals. "That doesn't look like a forest," commented one child. In the discussion that followed the children concluded that what was small to us would appear large to ants, and so this "forest" was probably grass. When they arrived at this conclusion, a child noted that they should remember to look at all the pictures this way since the illustrator probably drew them all "like the ants see things." I stayed out of this talk, trusting the children to raise questions and work out possible answers through their discussion. They did. The thoughtful comment about the illustrator's perspective surprised me and reminded me to maintain a low profile in further discussions. I held the book so all could see and allowed the children to do the talking, interjecting only to help manage the conversation from time to time (for example: "I think Emily has something to say. Let's listen to her idea.") or to give an occasional nudge ("What about this part of the picture?" or "Tell me what makes you think that"). I was glad I kept quiet. I learned how important it was to leave questions hanging, unanswered with no closure. As a teacher I have sometimes fought minor skirmishes with myself to provide closure by presenting final answers, but as a learner and a reader with the children, I enjoyed turning the page and saying, very honestly, "Hmm, wow, interesting. Lots of ideas to think about here."

Van Allsburg's text says that the ants went up a wall. "I don't get it," commented a child. "It says they went up a mountain but how did they get *inside*, because I remember they got inside the house."

"That mountain's really a chimney," answered another child.

"Yeah, look. See, it's brick. It looks like a chimney," said another.

"It could be a wall."

"A wall would just get them into the yard or something," said another child.

"Or they'd run into the roof if they just went up the outside of the wall."

"Well, maybe it's a chimney."

"Chimneys don't go to the ground. They're on the roof."

"My chimney does." The discussion continued and was left unresolved. Several children checked out chimneys outside of school—on their own initiative—and reported later that some chimneys go to the ground and some are on top of houses. They considered many possibilities but were content to allow each reader to come to his or her own conclusion.

On the page where the ants enter the house there is a picture of tiled walls and a cupboard and counter of some type. What room were the ants in? The kitchen? The bathroom? The talk went like this:

"I think it's the kitchen because there's paper towels."

"Well, it could be toilet paper."

"There's a clock. So it has to be the kitchen. You wouldn't have a clock in the bathroom.

"We have a clock in our bathroom—so my daddy doesn't get late for work when he's shaving."

"Well, there's a window. Bathrooms don't have windows."

"My bathroom does."

"But you wouldn't have a plant in a bathroom."

"My mother has a plant in our bathroom."

Unanimous agreement from these six- and seven-year-olds came when one child said that this had to be the kitchen because if it was the bathroom, the window would be closed and the shade would be down!

The ants are scooped into a "boiling brown lake." What is this lake? Coffee? Tea? Soup? Gravy? Cocoa? Of course, one's answer is connected to whether or not one thinks the crystals are sugar or salt. The liquid is "bitter" the author tells us, but the children did not think that meant that the crystals had to be sugar. Rather, they questioned which liquids might be bitter.

"It's tea 'cause that's what people stir like that and tea's bitter so it's probably tea."

"I tasted coffee once and it was bitter."

"I did too and I didn't think it was bitter. Tea's bitter."

"Tea's not bitter. Not herbal tea."

"I think it's cocoa 'cause I drink cocoa in the mornings sometimes."

"You don't put sugar or salt in cocoa."

"My mother does." (Turns out there was one mother who still made hot cocoa from scratch.) The group reached no consensus. A pattern of responding to this book developed: talking about possibilities, permitting individual interpretations to stand, sometimes arriving at a group consensus—but only when the facts and inferential information seemed overwhelmingly in favor of a particular conclusion *from the point of view of the group*. For the most part, the children remained open to new information and interpretation.

The children talked about the saucer under the cup.

"It's a plate."

"No, a saucer."

"What's a saucer?"

"It's the plate under a cup."

When the ants crawled onto a disk that eventually ended up in the toaster, the children speculated as to what this disk might be. English muffins? Bread? Rice cakes? Eventually someone asked, "What is a disk shape anyway?" and I explained by comparing it to the shape of a frisbee. "Then if it's bread, it's gotta be round bread," they concluded. This illustration caused the children to notice the line drawings that Van Allsburg uses throughout the book. Were these the side of bread slices or the motion of the disk-shaped object popping from the toaster? The class recalled an art technique, line drawings, that they had worked with in art class.

The ants are caught in a "whirling storm of shredded food and stinging rain." The children were really puzzled; not one child knew of a garbage disposal. I didn't tell them. But in a couple days Amanda came in and said she had a pretty good idea. Then she described a garbage disposal and declared that it was dangerous. Her daddy had put a fork down it by accident and she was not allowed to go near it. In the following days others reported that they, too, had garbage disposals in their homes.

Near the book's end Van Allsburg pictures the ants being propelled from an electrical socket.

"I know what's gonna happen. They're gonna get electrocuted."

"Wow! They shouldn't do that. You should never go near them holes. You get electrocuted."

"Yup! They got electrocuted all right. I got electrocuted once." Then most of the class acknowledged that they too had been "electrocuted once." I explained the difference between electrocution and electrical shock and for a few minutes we listened to several stories about experiences with electrical shock.

Typical of righteous first graders, the class speculated on a moral when we came to the end of the story.

"They learned their lesson."

"They got in trouble because they didn't do what they were supposed to."

"Yeah, they didn't listen."

"They wanted to have all them things for themselves and that's how they got in trouble."

"They can't have all them things."

"They didn't share."

With every reading of this book the group refined their ideas, clarifying and supporting their individual positions during the group talk. Then one day I was out of the classroom and a substitute teacher read the book. The next morning the children pounced on me as soon as they came in the door.

"*She* said it was sugar."

"*She* said it was coffee."

"*She* said it was the kitchen."

"*She* said it was English muffins."

They were clearly annoyed with the absolute answers and what's more, they didn't want to read the book again. The magic came from considering possibilities, figuring out meaning from those possibilities, revising, refining, clarifying that meaning, and doing it all through reading and rereading of the book in a community that talked and accepted a diversity of ideas. Each reading was a new experience. With absolute answers the magic was gone. The children's involvement came through connecting the text to personal experiences and knowledge and then enriching that connection through interaction with others. Their responses required thinking and use of imagination.

Despite their protests I reread the book again that day, but reopened questions by pointing out that readers must be true to what author Van Allsburg writes. We cannot call the ants bees when he clearly writes ants, for example, and if he had told us that the crystals were salt or sugar we would have to agree. But when the author has written and illustrated his book with clues as he has, he invites us to use our imagination and figure things out for ourselves. The children once again became involved in the book. Reading with a totally efferent purpose with absolute answers was a reading they could easily give up. Reading that blended aesthetic responses along with the efferent led these young readers back to this book again and again.

The children chose this book to read on the last day of school. Jeff noticed a jar with the letters "GAR" in the corner of the picture and said, "I just learned how to spell sugar—I *think* sugar is s-u-g-a-r, but I might be wrong. But if it is the way to spell sugar, then that might be another clue that it's sugar. I don't know *for sure* that it's sugar. It just *might* be." Even during this last reading in this community the children chose to leave final interpretation open for future readings.

Meaning is within people, not in texts. We construct meaning anew with each reading. A teacher told me of comments relayed by her English teacher who studied with Robert Frost. Through the years Frost's famous poem, *Stopping by a Woods on a Snowy Evening,* has been the topic of seminars and discussions, with a focus on its meaning. Frost reportedly told his class that he had no idea what the poem meant to him when he wrote it, that he could only say what it meant to him at the present time.

Patricia MacLachlan (1990), author of *Sarah, Plain and Tall* says, "as a writer I trust fully that my readers will come to my books with their own pasts, their memories, their own views of the world. I am always delighted when readers make my books theirs with their interpretations, and I am just as delighted when my books raise questions rather than just provide answers" (pp. 220–221). The reading these authors describe is reading that creates readers who will come back to books again and again to seek meaning for their lives. They will be able to figure out answers for themselves using reading both as a comfort and a resource.

When children "make books theirs," to use MacLachlan's phrase, it's important to remember that their interpretations will not match ours. My students loved *The Piggybook,* by Anthony Browne. In this story, "Mr. Piggott lived with his two sons, Simon and Patrick, in a nice house with a nice garden, and a nice car in the nice garage. Inside the house was his wife." Mom does all the work in this household before going off to her own job during the day and continuing when she returns home in the evening. That is, until one day when Mr. Piggott and the boys arrive home to find that Mom has left. A note on the mantelpiece reads, "You are pigs." And they literally turn into pigs. Every item in the pictures takes on pig appearance: the telephone, the water spigots, the tulips on the wallpaper, and of course Simon and Patrick and Dad. Mom finally returns. They beg her to stay and they divide up the chores. The book comes to a close: "Mom was happy too." (Turn the page for the last line.) "She fixed the car." My students were puzzled by this last line on the final page.

"I don't get why the author wrote that last page. The book ends here—'Mom was happy too.' "

These children brought to the reading their experience from an era when Moms may indeed fix cars and they didn't see the twist that older readers might. Eventually I shared with the class that adults often laugh when they turn the last page and read the last line, and I explained why. The children shook their heads in amazement. "Grown-ups sure have different ideas sometimes," piped up one little fellow.

Most adults love Elsie Minarik's *A Kiss for Little Bear*, in which a kiss for Little Bear is passed along. But Emily expressed disgust. "Too much kissing in this book. YUK!" she said after she read it.

Children pick up on the specific language authors use. Jon giggles and repeats James Marshall's line in *Goldilocks,* " '. . . your delicious, er delightful granddaughter,' I just love that part. I think I know why James Marshall wrote that. I think he wanted you to know that the wolf is a tricker!"

This is the aesthetic reading of which Louise Rosenblatt writes. For these children, talk about characters and plot development and themes occurred as more than abstract analyzing or studying about aspects of literature. Such discussion developed as children became involved with literature and wanted to understand more of what that literature offered. The primary response was Rosenblatt's aesthetic, a response that connected to their lives. This response led to consideration of the facts—the details, the specifics in a piece of literature—because the children wanted to understand more fully.

Summing Up the Teacher's Role

What then is my role as teacher to ensure that children understand the reading process and adjust their reading to accommodate a range of purposes?

First, I have to establish and then maintain the tone and structure of the environment. In addition to demonstrating a nonjudgmental stance and respecting all positions that are not abusive of others, I need to moderate the talk at times so that one or two children do not dominate. "I think Alex has something to say," or "Let's listen to what Elisa thinks about this," became typical comments. In addition to moderating the talk, I provide support for more reticent speakers in the group. Even so, some children are never comfortable making contributions in large-group settings, and so I set up times for small groups, or pairs, or one-on-one with me to read and talk about books. I create a place for these alternative structures within a daily reading workshop or during the morning free-play time.

Another critical role for me is to provide both a range and a depth of quality literature and present this literature to the group. I can't presume that children know good books, and I recognize that my choices influence the children's. They read what I first read. So, I need knowledge of children's books. This does not mean selecting a list of good books or obtaining a list from some other source and reading the same books year after year. Rather, I have to seek out and read children's literature myself in an ongoing way: going to bookstores, reading journal reviews, talking about books with the librarian and other colleagues, and most of all reading. My list of books is in a continual state of revision as I add new titles, delete old ones, shuffle the order in which I might choose books. I don't need to read everything I bring to the classroom, but I do need to know what I like and establish criteria for choosing books. I read a variety of genre: folk and fairy tales, nonfiction, poetry, biography, fantasy, realistic fiction. I share knowledge about authors and illustrators and how they work, the decisions they make and why.

A third role is to provide children with other options for responding to books, in addition to the talk that surrounds reading aloud in our literature time. In September and periodically throughout the year I plan a group activity such as making puppets, drawing, painting, creating with clay or building blocks as a way of responding to a book. After one or two group activities designed to show children *how* to work in these areas, I give the children access to the necessary supplies and the choice to continue such activities on their own during designated parts of the day. Some years I've established response journals for children to write to me or each other after their reading, modeling this procedure after the dialogue journals that Nancie Atwell used so successfully with her eighth graders. Interestingly, most children did not choose this form of written response. Writing about their reading appeared to be a laborious task for these young children compared to the energy intrinsic to their reading and talking about books though the literature time.

Robert Coles (1989), in *The Call of Stories,* writes that the task of those who teach literature is "to engage a student's growing intelligence and any number of tempestuous emotions with the line of a story in such a way that the reader's imagination gets absorbed into the novelist's" (p. 63). At one time I was so wrapped up in teaching reading that I defined "reading" as a repertoire of behaviors rather than considering reading as a process that continues through a lifetime, a continuing process of learning to read that never really ends and that engages intellect and imagination. I want my classroom to be an environment that helps lead children into a lifetime of reading by becoming aware of *all* the purposes for reading, not just the efferent ones of carrying away information. It is the aesthetic purposes that capture minds and hearts and lead individuals back to reading throughout their lives.

CHAPTER 14

Responding to Literature in the Classroom

Author and teacher educator Mem Fox (1990) says, "Writers don't improve their craft unless they have a real purpose, a real audience, and a real investment in their writing" (p. 471). I once used children's books in my classroom as story-starters for writing. Judith Viorst's *Alexander and the Terrible, Horrible, No Good, Very Bad Day* is an example. I'd read the book to the class then ask the children to think of a time when, like Alexander, they had experienced a "terrible, horrible . . . very bad day." The children would write a sentence or two and then I'd edit and type each child's writing and the next day hand these typed pages back to the children to illustrate. Finally, I'd bind all the pages together into a class book. We made lots of these books every year.

Then I began daily writing workshops in my classroom and the children began making decisions for themselves with regard to their writing. From time to time I'd insert one of these class book activities into the workshop, but now I noticed disadvantages to my assigned writing activities.

1. The activity interfered with children's plans for the writing work-shop. "But I was going to write about . . ." was a plea I heard more than once. I was changing the rules on which the workshop was organized and disrupting the children's intentions.
2. Although the security of a writing topic initially seemed helpful, some children had difficulty coming up with a strong response or one they wanted to share.

3. The assignment didn't help the children learn to write. Most children quickly learned the ropes and dashed off a few sentences with little, if any, revision. In contrast, they spent considerable time and energy on self-selected topics.

4. I did most of the work. I planned, presented, motivated, worked (really struggled sometimes) to pull stories out of all the children, typed and bound the books. The amount of my effort seemed to correlate with a lessening degree of involvement on the part of the children.

5. The final clue to the ineffectiveness of these exercises came when I discovered that I could pull such an activity out only a few times before the children lost interest. They sighed or muttered complaints as they went through the motions.

My writing assignments did little for the children's writing development because they provided no real purpose, no real audience, and no real investment for the writers. They were "doing" writing, but they weren't working through the process of writing a piece and, therefore, really were not involved as writers and learners. Writing workshop brought a new approach to teaching and learning, one that responded to children in a manner that was individualized but which, at the same time, worked best within a community.

Children were my teachers. The responsive nature of the workshop approach required highly tuned listening and observation of children. As I developed my skill in "kidwatching" (Goodman, 1985), I noticed a richness of language development and learning connections emerging from children that caused my activities to pale in comparison. Children became more than just fluent writers who wrote longer and longer pieces. These children crafted their work and they learned much about that crafting process from exposure to lots of good books. As writers, the children picked up words, phrases, organization, and structure; they borrowed characters and explored genre. As learners, they explored ideas, discovered meanings, employed imagination, and made connections to their own lives—all though writing and talking, with children's literature as accompaniment.

Children's Literature and Children's Writing

Jody wrote about a firecracker that was a "dud," the word E. B. White used to describe the unhatched goose egg in *Charlotte's Web*. Lori ended her

Christmas story of Santa's visit to her house with lines reminiscent of Clement Moore's famous poem: "Then Santa went up the chimney. He called all of his reindeer. The first one he called is Rudolph, the red-nosed reindeer was the first one that he called. Then Santa went off the roof and he said to all a merry Christmas and to all a good night!" Megan thought of the idea and then wrote a book patterned after Bill Martin, Jr.'s *Brown Bear, Brown Bear, What Do You See?*, reminding me how once I would have had everyone in the class write such a book as a follow-up activity. How often, I mused, we take an idea that works for one child and turn it into an assignment for everyone, establishing more orthodoxies.

Stories such as Eileen's "Babar's First Tooth," where young writers borrowed fictional characters and wrote their own story, occurred often. Children also wrote personal narratives using Arnold Lobel's characters Frog and Toad. Kristen wrote her own Frog and Toad book, for example, with three chapters: Frog and Toad Get a Cat, Frog and Toad Go to the Beach, Frog and Toad Play in the Snow. All three stories are about Kristen and her sister, fictionalized via the characters of Frog and Toad. Jeff used Frog and Toad to write a fantasy adventure entitled "Frog and Toad Meet the Volcano." The story begins, "Bang, swoop! went a volcano. It was erupting. 'Now what should we do? Let's go see where it is,' said Toad." In Jeff's story, Frog and Toad climb a volcano, survive its erupting, only to discover after fleeing that they have ended up in Volcano City. The story concludes with a line reminiscent of the ending of Sendak's *Where the Wild Things Are:* "But just then the world changed and they were back home."

Literature often stimulated topics for writing when a particular book reminded a child of an incident in their own life. When I read Robert McCloskey's *Blueberries for Sal*, children talked of being separated from Mom. Josie wrote "I Was Lost," recounting her experience when she went shopping with her mother and sister for Halloween costumes. When mom went for the car the girls waited for what seemed like such a long time that Josie felt lost and began to cry. Ryan wrote a story about losing mom in the drugstore. "I couldn't find my mom because it was so high in there," he wrote describing the stacks of merchandise. Jeff wrote "I Sneaked Out the Door" after we read Robert Kraus's *Where Are You Going, Little Mouse?* about running away from home. The children became so attuned to finding personal writing topics in books that when stuck for a topic all they had to do was look around at the books in the room to be reminded of something to write about.

The same book often stimulated both nonfiction and fiction writing. Chris wrote about ladybugs after hearing Eric Carle's *The Grouchy Ladybug*. This nonfiction piece explored his own theories about ladybugs.

Some ladybugs are red. Some are yellow and some can be brown. I think ladybugs can fly. I think they have black spots too. I think they live on trees. One time I caught a ladybug and it was yellow and I kept it for a while then in a few days after, it died. Then I caught a red one and it died because I flooded it and it drowned. Then I asked my mom. I said, "Can ladybugs be different colors than brown, yellow, and red?" She said, "There can be gray ones too!" I said, "What color spots do they have?" My mom said, "I don't quite know right now. Go ask Daddy." Then I went to my dad. He said, "Go jump in a lake." So I jumped in the pool instead because I had my bathing suit on. My brother wanted to go in the pool too, but my mom said, "No."

Two months later, Chris wrote a fiction piece patterned after *The Grouchy Ladybug*. However, instead of a ladybug the main character is a honeybee. The class was involved in a social studies unit on China at the time and Chris integrated information from that unit into his story. Here is an excerpt: "He came upon a giant panda bear. 'Wanta fight?' said the bee. 'If you insist,' said the panda bear scooping some honey out of a tree and swallowing a few bees. 'Oh, you're not big enough,' said the bee and kind of scadadelled out of there. He came to the Great Wall . . ."

Several years later, during a year when children brought the term "sequel" to our writing workshop, Adam wrote "The Grouchy Ladybug Goes to the Sky," the story of events after the ladybug's encounter with the whale in Eric Carle's book. It seems the ladybug broke *his* wing when he was hit by the whale's tale at the end of Carle's story. In Adam's story, the ladybug commiserates with the fireflies about not being able to fly. The fireflies search out the whale and have a talk. The whale reports being unaware of having hurt the ladybug. Reporting this back to the ladybug, the fireflies convince him to try to fly one more time. The ladybug's wing has healed and he flies. Adam's story concludes, "He was flying. He soared higher and higher. The wind was in his face. He was the happiest ladybug in the world."

Greg entered school with an interest in the *Titanic*. According to Greg's parents, this fascination began at age three when Greg watched a National Geographic special. Greg's parents bought him books on the *Titanic*, which he shared with classmates. He and his dad read an old book on the *Titanic* that had belonged to my grandfather. Then in the spring, Greg wrote "The Death of the *Titanic*," which he dedicated "To all who went down on the Titanic." (See Figure 14–1.) He spent nearly two weeks drafting his piece in writing workshop and another week revising and editing. He organized the writing into chapters that alternated technical information with the human interest story. He included a glossary at the end because "there's some words in here that some people might not know. So I explained them in

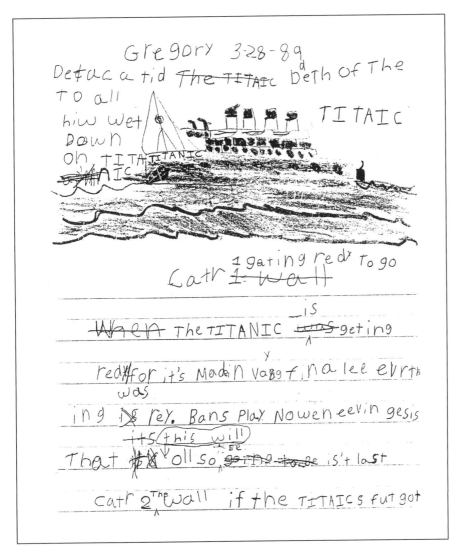

Figure 14–1

"The Death of the Titanic"

the glossary." He also alphabetized his glossary (see Figure 14–2) according-ing to his invented spelling. Here is the story as it was published in the classroom.

The Death of the *Titanic*

Chapter 1 Getting Ready to Go

The *Titanic* is getting ready for its maiden voyage. Finally, everything is ready. Bands play. No one even guesses that this also will be its last trip.

Chapter 2 The Wall

If the *Titanic*'s front got torn off the bow section, one part, the back, called the stern, would still float because there was a wall in the middle.

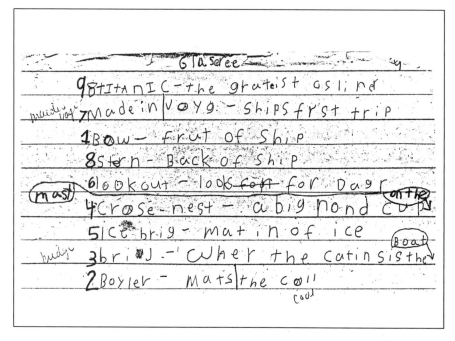

Figure 14–2

Greg's glossary.

But the bow would sink because there wasn't one in the front. But the stern could still go.

Chapter 3   Iceberg

When the *Titanic* had gone a little over half way to New York, the *Titanic Titanic* got into icy water off the coast of Canada. The sea is smooth as glass. The air is bitter, bitter, bitter, bitter cold. It is a good night to be inside but the lookout stays high in the crow's nest. Suddenly he sees a dark shape! It's a mountain of ice! And the *Titanic* is heading right for it! The lookout rings the alarm and calls, "Iceberg straight ahead!" The Captain tries to turn the ship but it is too late. The ice scrapes across the ship's side. Then the Captain runs down below to see if his ship is hurt. Soon he learns the terrible truth. The ice has hurt the ship badly. Over five water-tight compartments are filled! That is too many. The *Titanic* is going to sink! Nothing can be done. Now the Captain gives his order. "Ready the lifeboats! Wake the passengers!" The Captain is worried. There are only enough lifeboats for half and there are 2,227 people on board.

Chapter 4   Water-Tight Compartments

The bottom of the ship was divided into sixteen water-tight compartments made with a switch on the bridge where the Captain steers the ship. A water-tight compartment is a place with two sides but no top so when it gets filled, it overflows into the next one. Two, three, or even four can be filled. Still the *Titanic* will float.

Chapter 5   Explosion in the Boiler Room

When the *Titanic* was sinking, the Captain wanted to keep the lights burning as long as they could. But when you leave the boiler door open you run the risk of water getting in and it changes to steam which makes a big BOOOMM!!!! Sparks flew up the smoke stacks. Outside the *Titanic*, sparks filled the air. Then the stern stood up toward the stars and sank.

Chapter 6   Rescue Ship

Soon the sky grew lighter. Thirteen small lifeboats remained of the greatest ocean liner in the world. It seems as if the help will never come. Suddenly, a light flashes and another and another. It is a ship! The Carpathia! It has come from fifty-eight miles away and its top speed is 8 m.p.h. Everyone is saved but the sea is rough and it takes many hours. Finally, it is done. Everyone is safely on board the Carpathia.

Glossary

Boiler - melts the coal
Bow - front of ship
Bridge - where the Captain steers the boat
Crow's Nest - a big round cup on the mast
Iceberg - mountain of ice
Maiden Voyage - ship's first trip
Stern - back of ship
Titanic - the greatest ocean liner

Ellen captured an essence of good picture books when she wrote "The Very Hungry Princess." In addition to the title echoing *The Very Hungry Caterpillar*, this modern fairy tale reminded readers of Robert Munsch's *The Paper Bag Princess*. Ellen acknowledged that Munsch's book influenced her. The text reads: "Once upon a time there lived a very, very hungry princess. Her name was Chickie. She loved dog food. She would eat it right up. Crunch, crunch, crunch. She always picked the right prince, but she had terrible table manners. Then as you see? She'd (at this point Ellen goes to a new page) . . . disappear in the night. And she has never been seen again."

When I came to publish Ellen's piece, I questioned her because the piece did not make sense to me. Ellen told me, "You have to look at the pictures when you read this book because the pictures go with the writing. Without the pictures it wouldn't make sense." I was still confused. Her sketchy drawings didn't seem to help and I pressed Ellen further. "Well, I think you're having trouble because the pictures are still in my head," she said. "When I publish this, I'll draw the pictures that go with the words and then it will make sense." Sure enough, Ellen's drawings completed the story. In the bedroom of the princess she drew all the things the princess "likes" and on the page where the prince comes into the story she included his interests of playing the piano and reading. I remembered that James Marshall did the same in the illustrations of the bears' rooms in *Goldilocks*; our class discussed those illustrations in literature time. The last two pages of Ellen's book were designed to lead the reader to first believe that the princess disappeared into smoke, but turning the page we see that in fact she took off in a spaceship! Ellen confided to me later that she didn't tell *why* the princess disappeared because she thought readers could figure that out for themselves. "Was it because she was tired of always picking the wrong prince?" I asked.

"That could be one reason," Ellen answered.

When we read Marc Brown's *Dinosaur's Divorce,* Susan candidly wrote the story of the breakup of her family. In her story she recalled a specific incident of violence that she had witnessed. With the permission of Susan's parents, we published the piece and both parents celebrated their daughter's writing. The writing also evoked much discussion in the classroom and several other children wrote stories of the divorces in their families.

In all this child writing I recognize elements of autobiography—connections to the personal stories of the children's own lives, their interests, concerns, experiences. Countless examples of children gleaning meaning from good literature and connecting it to their own lives through writing occurred in the classroom. At the same time, these young writers and readers developed knowledge of the way written language worked and skill in using it for themselves. Nancie Atwell (1982) defines a literate environment as occurring "wherever written language is the natural domain of the children and adults who work and play there" (p. 35). I watched these first graders reading and writing and I understood what she meant. In addition to written language, oral language filled this classroom, weaving in and out of reading and writing. Lots of talk and lots of listening surrounded all of this writing and reading. Even with all of the writing in response to literature—and there was a great deal—talk remained a basic way of responding.

Our Folktale "Unit"

On Monday morning of the third week of school, I put photocopied finger puppets of the characters from *The Little Red Hen* on the children's desks and I write the following note on the chalkboard:

Dear Girls and Boys,
    Good morning! Please color the puppets on your desk.
Love,
Mrs. Avery

The children begin arriving and I greet them at the door. "There's a note on the board to read," I say. These first arrivals look at me slightly puzzled, but put away their lunch boxes and sweaters and then go stare at the board. I move beside them. They look at me, then the board, then back at me.

"Can you figure any part of it out?" I ask.

"I know this says 'Love,' " says one child as he points to the word.

"And this says 'Mrs. Avery,' " says another with a big grin directed my way.

"You got it," I answer. "How'd you know that?"

" 'Cause I already knowed the word 'love' before I came to school. I can even write it."

"Ah, I see," I nod.

"And I just figured 'Mrs. Avery' because you probably wrote it," says another child.

"I knew 'Mrs. Avery' because it's up there," comments another child pointing to our names on the bulletin board above the chalkboard. "I just looked up and saw it was the same."

"Good thinking. Let's read the rest. It starts like notes or letters begin," I say as I point to the first word and start to pronounce "dear" by making only the D sound. The children are puzzled. "Dear," I read and continue across the line slightly enunciating the first letter of each word as a clue. When I get to "boys" a child calls out, "Boys! It's gotta be boys."

"Right! How did you know?" I ask the question that by now is familiar, and the children giggle at the obviousness of the answer. I read the rest of my letter aloud, pointing to the words as I read. Before they go to their desks I tell them that they can help the children who sit near them read the note when they come in.

As other children come in the room, the first arrivals and I help them through the written message. Soon the entire group is coloring the puppets and chatting about the weekend. I move among them and hear Josie telling about sleeping over at her grandma's, Ian awing everyone around him with the story of his trip to Baltimore and the submarine he saw with "real teeth and mouth painted on it," Jeff talking about the ballgame he played with his dad. Their talk is natural, relaxed, and loud. It seems they all need to talk, and I find myself wondering if they're listening to each other's stories.

I didn't plan the blackboard note as a reading lesson nor the finger puppets as an activity for a folktale unit, even though my morning letters on the chalkboard will become part of the class routine and we will be reading lots of folktales. My primary goal this morning, which grew out of a strongly felt need on Friday, was to start our week off calmly and orderly. The way children enter the classroom in the morning sets the tone for the day, and this group had burst in boisterously each morning. A third of them ride the same bus and by the time they arrive at school they've become involved in an assortment of frays—mostly among older children—but that spill over to first graders. Unlike classes from other years that read, or wrote, or created their own puppets and art projects in the morning, this group had difficulty managing this morning time independently. For a while I used directed activities to assist the children in building a structure for working independently.

Some children don't enjoy coloring. Watching this group, I know some of them would rather play with blocks, but they go along with the coloring. Cutting out the little puppets and taping them together gradually brings a bit more involvement. (I suspect using tape has something to do with this.) The children admire Ellen's beautiful coloring job and the compliments prompt several youngsters to go back and add more coloring to their own puppets.

At literature time later that morning, we open Paul Galdone's version of *The Little Red Hen*. The repetitious language brings the children into the story and they chant along as I read. We come to the end and Elizabeth dramatically says, "My mom would just *die* if she had to do all that work! She comes home from work and flops on the sofa and says, 'I have such a headache!' "

"My mom wouldn't do all that work either," says Monica. "But my dad would help her, we'd all help her, and then we'd get done."

Elizabeth and Monica's comments stimulate the ideas of the other children and they talk about distribution of work, Dads cooking dinner, their own jobs at home. "Fairness" comes up, a concept highly valued by justice-minded first graders, and after some discussion the children unanimously agree that "it's fair that the little red hen didn't share at the end because those other guys didn't help."

"But," adds Ian, "if she had chicks, she would share with them because they are her children." The group supplies instant consensus with Ian's statement.

I found the children's discussion fascinating. They began by relating this familiar folktale to their own experiences, expressed strong attitudes about right and wrong, talked among themselves, arrived at a value statement, and concluded by acknowledging a commitment to that value. What's more, they did it without my input. I maintained an observer role and refrained from interjecting my opinion. In fact, the only comments I made were occasional questions such as "What do you think about that?" or "Oh, yeah?"—comments coming out of my own pondering that also served to encourage reflection within the children's minds. I am convinced that this frank and searching discussion would not have occurred if I had taken on the traditional teacher role: censoring, directing, and imparting didactic opinions.

The candid responses continue when we move on to the next book, Paul Zelinsky's *Rumpelstiltskin*. Stacy cries out, "Oh, I just *love* that story. Know why? Because I like when he says, 'The devil told you that!' That parts's *so good.*" The last two words loll out of Stacy's mouth as she emphasizes her relish of the story.

"Yeah, chimes in Aaron, "and I like when he guesses his name and he says 'Stringbones.' "

A chorus erupts as the children repeat, "Stringbones, Stringbones." They savor speaking the unusual name over and over.

At the end of the day I arrange the children in small groups, demonstrate how to use the finger puppets to tell *The Little Red Hen*, then ask them to retell the story themselves in their groups. I move from group to group and discover several complications.

The first problem arises as the children decide who will take what character. Some pretty heated discussions take place while each group works this out. In one group, a single child takes the lead and assigns roles to the others. The mandate falls flat as mandates frequently do. "No!" comes the direct response from one child, "we get to decide too." Others agree. The first child tries to rationally present his reasons, but the group overrides him. After a few moments the dictator relinquishes control. He looks at me and sighs as though to communicate, "Can you believe them?" I shrug my shoulders to say, "Don't look at me," and move to another group.

This second group has selected character roles but is now stuck, unable to get the story started. I help the narrator to get them going. All but one group has this same difficulty even though we've read the story several times; the children solve the problem by using the puppets not to retell *The Little Red Hen* but to tell their own stories, which are blends of fantasy and reality with the cat, the dog, the mouse, and the little red hen (who, by the way, isn't red on most of the children's puppets).

"Once upon a time a hen was going to have a birthday party. 'We have to get ready for the party,' she says. 'Everyone's got to help.' Now you say, 'Not I,' " Jackie cues the next child.

"No," comes the reply, "I got a better idea," and then, slipping into role, he says, "I'm going to watch TV. Do it yourself."

And so it went. The children produced imaginative stories and negotiated the plot as each story developed. Only one group stuck with *The Little Red Hen* and they struggled to recall, sequence, and retell the precise story. It was also the least involved group and I saw the children glance around the room, puzzling over the energy the other groups displayed.

We included a folktale almost every day in our literature time and the children requested many for rereading. In their discussions the children made connections and noticed characteristics of folktales. When we reread *Henny Penny*, Brian noted that these characters "didn't use their heads— they didn't think."

"Like in the *Gingerbread Boy*, those guys didn't use their heads either," said Matt.

"In the *Billy Goats*, the troll didn't use his head with the big billy goat. That was pretty stupid to get in a fight with *him*," commented Max.

"But the big billy goat used *his* head. He *really* used his head," Jeff said, and his eyes twinkled with the awareness of the double meaning in his words. He looked around at his peers.

"I get it. I get it," they said and giggled and repeated Jeff's words.

By the time we read a second version of *The Gunniwolf* in mid-October, the children had developed a rather sophisticated awareness of folktales. They immediately compared the second version to the first, noting differences such as the jungle becomes a woods, the mother character a father. When we came to the end of the second story I asked, "What will happen?"

Ryan, so good at humorous one-liners, immediately recalled a line of poetry we all knew and piped up with, "Gobble, gobble, gulp, gulp, munch, munch, munch."

At the end of literature time that day I pulled out a sheet of chart paper and suggested to the children that we list the characteristics of folktales—what helped us recognize a story as a folktale. In a few minutes the children contributed the following ideas:

- There's usually a bad guy (villain) like a wolf, witch, troll, ghost.
- The characters don't use their heads.
- It usually ends with a happy ending.
- They often begin "Once upon a time . . ."
- They have patterns—like at the beginning they're all right (the characters), in the middle they get into mischief, at the end they get out of mischief.
- They have special numbers—like things happen in three's or there are three characters.
- They sometimes have animals for characters.
- They're "retold." We don't know the author.
- They repeat words a lot.
- Some people use their heads good like the little girl in *The Gunniwolf*.
- They usually run away a lot—like the Gingerbread Boy or Goldilocks.
- People forget or don't follow directions or break a promise and then they get in trouble.

We read through our list when we finish it and again the next day. Then we put it up on the wall. From time to time throughout the year, I saw the children stop, look it over, and perhaps point out their own contribution. Folktales were a regular component of literature time all year.

The discussion of folktales is as close to a literature unit as I get in my classroom. Once, I gathered books on a theme and we spent a week or two reading them. The limitations of this unit approach stifled our thinking and our involvement with books and reading. I felt compelled to read those books on friendship or farm animals every day to the exclusion of a title I longed to read. More importantly, the children displayed a diminishing interest in the themed books. "Read this one," I'd hear from a child as she handed me another title when I picked up my theme selection. Along with a selection of books for a unit, I believed the children needed follow-up activities, and these activities became time-consuming in both planning and implementation with results that did not justify that time. The children sometimes "loved" the activity but, I had to ask myself, does that mean it's educationally sound? For many years I justified my classroom practice with statements such as, "The children loved it" or "We really had a good time." While child engagement brings child enjoyment, it does not necessarily follow that enjoyment brings lasting engagement. I strive now for depth of engagement from children along with enjoyment. Units or themes now focus on introducing a particular genre of literature, such as we did with folktales or on the broader themes that compose our social studies or science curricula.

"Just Read"

Soon after I moved away from the basal to children's literature for reading instruction, I came across an activity book on Arnold Lobel's Frog and Toad books. I was ecstatic. This neat little package provided many creative things to do with Lobel's books. Of course I purchased it. Well, it sat on my desk for weeks, months. Occasionally I flipped through it but nothing appealed at any moment. At the end of the year I put it away with a sigh, thinking I'd get to it next year. A year later I sat down to figure out why I had never used this wonderful resource book. The activities were blackline masters with fancy story starters, or fill in the blanks. Many of the same ideas that emerged in conversations surrounding our reading of these books had been formatted into worksheets. The puppet patterns paled next to the puppets the children and I had created together. What had struck me as so creative now appeared as busywork. Why had I initially been so enchanted with this book? It presented a bridge between the workbook culture of a reading program and the dynamic responses of children reading real books. At that time I needed that bridge—or thought I did—to make the shift. I never used the book because the classroom talk as we read and reread Lobel's books provided richer, more in-depth study.

For a while the activity mentality tempted me to select books with an eye for how I might "use" a particular title in the classroom. I came dangerously close to abusing children's literature. When I first saw Mem Fox's *Koala Lu* I thought of using this book in conjunction with our annual spring field day. I would read the book and then we'd have a discussion about winning and coming in second and that everybody can't win a blue ribbon, etc. Fortunately, the children saved me from such didacticism. When I read *Koala Lu* the children talked about climbing trees! What's more, as they talked they reminded me of a time years ago when I looked out a second-floor window to see my three-year-old son Nathan swaying back and forth in the top of a young sapling—at my eye level! The children and I talked on and on about tree climbing from both a parent's and a child's perspective, a conversation filled with connections far more meaningful than my notion to connect winning or losing to field day. If the *children* had made the field day connection, then of course the book could have facilitated a discussion on this topic. I might have even brought it up at some point, as long as I guarded against the impulse to use the book to "teach" a lesson.

Still, the notion of soliciting children's responses to literature through teacher-planned activities crept in. A student teacher, required by the university to create learning centers during her time in my classroom, crafted a gorgeous and clever center with activities on a particular author and his books. Three weeks later this perceptive young woman commented, "You know this center stuff is really dumb! This didn't help these kiddies learn about this author. It didn't even get them into his books. The only reason they do any of this center is for *me*—because I want them too. It's all a waste of time, mine and theirs!" She was right.

I led the children through an art activity left over from my days as an elementary librarian after reading Burton's *The Little House*. Like the student teacher's learning center, the children completed the activity *for me,* and I could not detect that they had made the connections to ecological issues and urban/suburban environments that I had envisioned. The final products looked uncannily similar. On the other hand, Aaron's sequel to *The Grouchy Ladybug* became a play the children presented for their mothers at our Mother's Day program. In the course of a class discussion on entertainment for the program, the *children* suggested dramatizing Carle's story *and* Aaron's. The idea, planning, and implementation all came from the children. One child went through both books, for instance, listed all the characters, and went around to all the children and negotiated who would take what parts. Another drew the program cover. Still others helped classmates learn their parts. Of course the children needed my guidance with this production and specific resources from me at times, such as help in drawing the costume they made from sheets of butcher paper, but the production developed from the children's needs and purposes.

Under the guise of making connections or curriculum integration, I came close to falling into the trap of creating rigorous follow-up activities that shifted the focus away from actual reading, with all the meaning making and connections inherent in that process, to the activity as an end in itself. This was part of *my* process in weaning myself from heavily programmed reading instruction. Reader response theory does not mean that after reading a reader must respond by doing something, or that my job as teacher is to plan and implement such activities. For children to make the connections that are the basis of learning, those connections must take place within the children themselves. Teacher-planned connections belong to the teacher. In a learner-centered environment where children become risk takers, make decisions, and take responsibility for their learning, children become involved in books and reading and learning without all the embellishments of activities. And so I don't take one book, or a group of books, and plan numerous extension activities to go with them. My role is to set up the environment where connections can begin and then to nurture those connections as they naturally develop. The best way I know to do this is through lots of reading and natural talk in a classroom community.

There is also a push to teach skills with literature. Of course I am responsible for teaching my students the skills necessary for them to learn how to read, make sense of what they read, and appreciate literature. But there's a place for caution. Exposing children to a literature-rich environment may help them understand the structure of written language, literary conventions, characteristics of specific genre—all the demonstrations that books can provide—so long as the focus stays on the *readers*. There is a fine line when it comes to teaching with literature. I want to take care not to cross that line. I taught for many years without big books. When I finally had a couple of them, I thought I ought to try skill instruction as the accompanying guide suggested. I stopped reading and started talking about some traditional skill—I think it may have been rhyming words—when Natalie, seated at my feet, tapped my knees to get my attention and then quietly said, "Just read, Mrs. Avery." I looked to the other children and they nodded in agreement with Natalie. The skill lesson had nothing to do with helping readers understand or enjoy the book.

Professional writers have begun to voice their concerns about the manner in which children's books are being used in the classroom.

- Natalie Babbitt (1990) speaks out on her concern that "real stories are being used in the same way that the old texts were used. . . . A good story is sufficient unto the day. It is complete as it stands. If it has something to teach, let it teach in its own sufficiency. Let it keep its magic and fulfill its purpose. In other words, let it be" (p. 697, 703).

- Nancy Larrick (1991) laments the "teacher's guides for these exciting trade books for children—guides modeled directly on those for the basal readers—with diagrams for recording new vocabulary words, questions with space for writing answers, lists of words for filling in the blanks, and so on. . . . We are heeding the first cry of children: 'Give us books!' But we are moving dangerously close to disaster, when we introduce those books in such a way as to destroy their beauty, their significance, and thus deny the children's plea: 'Give us wings!' " (p. 82)

- Lee Bennett Hopkins (1991) answered the question of a major publisher who asked what they might do to get kids to study a book thoroughly by replying, "Leave it alone. Let teachers read it aloud, have children read it on their own, and leave it alone" (p. xiii).

- Louise Rosenblatt (1991) writes: "It is teachers who need to be clear theoretically about efferent and aesthetic reading. As they commendably seek to present more 'literature' in their language arts curricula, they need to be careful not to 'use' the appeal of such texts simply or mainly for their efferent purposes of teaching grammar or 'skills.' Also as teachers plan to include aesthetic elements in the work in social studies or natural science or to utilize the interest of story in the teaching of mathematics, they need to realize that they have a responsibility not to create confusion about primary stances appropriate to different purposes" (p. 447).

When I think of responses to literature I think of Chris closing the book he's finished reading, hugging it to his chest, and staring into space with a quiet smile on his face. I think of overhearing Josie, holding Aliki's *The Two of Them* and whispering to Monica, "This is a really good book. The cover looks sad, but it's not sad inside. You liked *One Foot, Now the Other* (dePaola) and *Marianne's Grandmother* (Eggar), you'll *really* like this one." I think of Ryan coming to me in a somewhat demanding manner and saying, "Do you have any other books like this one, because this is a really good book. I like this book and I want another." There was no need for me to require these children to do something to demonstrate their involvement or to prove to me that they read, or even to extend their reading.

Children's literature authority Charlotte Huck (1986) wrote "If you want to develop readers, you have to read to children, give them time to read real books, and opportunity to discuss them, respond to them, value them" (p. 69). These authors and experts on literature know what's important in regard to children's literature in the classroom. Natalie was only six, but she and her classmates knew also: "Just read, Mrs. Avery."

and which
you were probably
saving
Forgive me
they were delicious
so sweet
and so cold.
Poetry
Illustrated Poems

CHAPTER 15

Books for the Children

Children's author Katherine Paterson (1990) lists three properties the scientist ascribes to beauty: simplicity, harmony, and brilliance. Paterson applies these same attributes to the art of children's books and describes Patricia MacLachlan's book *Sarah, Plain and Tall* as a "beautiful book."

> Simplicity? . . . the book is complete in itself—direct, and without superfluous words. Harmony? You'd have to look far to find a book in which the parts—character, setting, and plot—so gracefully conform to one another and to the language of the whole. Brilliance? . . . we aren't talking about cleverness but about clarity—about the light that the book sheds not only on itself but beyond itself, to other stories and other lives. Don't you keep thinking of it? Don't you compare other books to it? Don't you know the prairie better now? And what it means to care about another person? (pp. 158–159)

Paterson believes this test of beauty applies to the art of children's books, "for the stories that have endured, the stories to which we turn as we seek to shape our lives, are all beautiful in this sense" (p. 159).

Children are very good at recognizing beautiful books. They remember words and phrases. Jeff says, "I been saying those words at home at lot," and he goes on, in his best witch's voice, to quote a line from a Lillian Moore poem. They remember characters. Jenny hugs herself and says, "I just *love* Templeton [the rat in E. B. White's *Charlotte's Web*]. He's so *nasty*!" A husky laugh ripples from her before she quotes the rat, "What do you think I am, a rat of all work?" and then another deep laugh. Children remember books that touch their lives. Josie loves stories about grandparents and older people; her favorite is Barbara Cooney's *Miss Rumphius*, and she regularly works on learning to read it for herself. Darren requests rereadings of Carol and Don Carrick's *The Accident* again and again and he keeps the book in his desk for months. We all have books that have endured for us because they helped us to understand ourselves, others, and our worlds a little better. They are the books we turn to as we seek to shape our lives, and undoubtedly they are different for each of us. In my classroom I introduce children to many, many books. Some will qualify as "good literature" and some will never make any list of great books. But by hearing lots of books from a range of genre, styles, and even literary quality, young children will find ones that endure for them because of their simplicity, harmony, and brilliance. Children return to these books again and again because they touch their lives in mysterious and magical ways.

The books children find to shape their lives may not be appreciated by adults. Robert Munsch's *Mortimer*, the story of a child avoiding bedtime, is a book youngsters request again and again. Yet *Mortimer* doesn't make any list of great literature. When Maurice Sendak's *Where the Wild Things Are* was published, much of the adult world rejected it for children with arguments that it was too frightening, but children loved it. I've seen many preschoolers listen to this book and identify with Max, who temporarily escapes the troubles of his real life to an imaginary world where he controls all the frightening wild things. The children's embracing of Sendak's book made it a classic. Children often know good books because they quickly sense powerful meanings. Sendak (1990) himself observed how his own niece saw immediately that *Higglety Pigglety Pop!* was a book about death when reviewers missed that basic point. "It's the way children dive into symbology or metaphor," says Sendak, "they get it. They may not like what they get, but they know how to go right to the heart of the matter" (p. 56). Children have taught me that I must read lots of books to them and let them decide what is best and what they want to hear again and again. If I determine which are the best books, using adult standards, I may well miss some books that will touch their lives.

Of course, the books I choose for the classroom and those I select for reading aloud influence what children read. Though children eventually discover books on their own, young readers first move toward the ones I read aloud. Even later in the year, the books read aloud remain the focal books in the room. So I choose books carefully but not cautiously. I apply no readability formula other than seeking out a few books in September and October that will be manageable for beginning readers because of the shorter length, perhaps predictable language patterns, and the physical format (avoiding small print or too many words on a page). The first year of reading workshops I searched for easy to read books because I was tied to the notion of controlled vocabulary. One day I handed Chris a folktale retold in a controlled vocabulary that I thought would be easy for him to read. Later I checked with Chris, asking him what the book was about. "I don't really know," he said, "I think it's 'Jack and the Beanstalk.' The pictures look like it is, but there's not enough words to tell." At that same time Chris fluently read books with words such as "astronaut," "forest," "happened," "wizard." So much for controlled vocabulary. Children have continually astounded me with what they are able to tackle as reading material.

I choose books that I enjoy and that I anticipate the children will like. I make some poor choices, books that bomb when I read them to the class or receive a lukewarm response (though they may have been a great hit with another class). There's room for some junk reading. As Atwell says, we all have our "beach books," the ones we read for no other reason than relaxation or escape. I'm grateful to my elementary school teachers for introducing me to the Bobbsey Twins and encouraging me to read series books. I not only got lots of practice and subsequently became a more fluent reader, but by reading the Bobbsey Twins and Nancy Drew and Ginny Gordon, I honed my awareness of the structure of books: plots, settings, characters, etc. These books captured me as a reader and kept me reading so that I was ready to savor *Little Women* when it came my way. The series books rarely worked as rereads (that's why readers need another in the series), but I reread *Little Women* several times, each time identifying with a new character or seeing things I'd missed earlier. My close association with Nan and Bert, Flossie and Freddie Bobbsey provided a prelude to meeting the far more complex Meg, Beth, Amy, and Jo. I couldn't read *Tom Sawyer* myself when Mrs. Howard read it but I knew it was there waiting for me someday. By introducing me to a range of quality and variety of books, my teachers helped me develop reading tastes and skill in making choices, and they validated reading for a range of purposes. I strive to do the same for my students.

Considerations in Selecting Books

Choosing books for the classroom is an important task for teachers. As the professional in the classroom I need to know good books and how to seek out new ones. The following are some of the characteristics I consider when selecting books for my classroom.

1. Tried-and-true favorites: books I love and that other classes have loved and books that have become classics.

2. Books representing a variety of cultures and peoples and that avoid stereotyped roles for individuals. I strive to achieve a balance of male and female protagonists.

3. Books that connect with specific curricular areas that I teach. For example, I'm always on the lookout for new books on China, ecology, dinosaurs.

4. Books that provide good reading that matches the interest and reading development of my students. For beginning readers, for example, I look for books with predictable or repetitious phrases, books with a strong story line in a few words (but that also avoid a controlled vocabulary), books with print that is easy to read.

5. Books representing a range of topics, child interests, and genre.

6. Books that are well written: the language flows, the book has rhythm, rich vocabulary, well-turned phrases, wonderful images. The book is a pleasure to read aloud!

7. Books by favorite authors. Children await the next book by a favorite author just as adults do.

8. New books: not only newly published books or books unfamiliar to the class, but also books with different or unusual formats, illustrations, or presentations. Someone has taken a risk and tried something new.

9. Books with attractive format:

   - print is easily read, not embedded in the illustrations or compressed tightly together
   - text correlates with the illustrations on the page
   - illustrations are high quality, with a diversity of artistic styles
   - cover is appealing (though we've all heard you can't judge a book by its cover, one of our first invitations comes from the cover)
   - paper quality is sturdy
   - size of book is easy to hold and read (not too small or too big)

10. Book jackets that give information about the author or the process of writing this particular book is a nice addition, though certainly not necessary.

I began my own professional development in this area during an undergraduate children's literature course. Our text, *Children and Books*, by May Hill Arbuthnot (1964), like a similar one by Charlotte Huck that I like, provided a rich introduction to the depth and breadth of children's literature. However, the most valuable part of the course was reading several hundred children's books. I maintain my knowledge of children's books by reading and talking with others (especially children) about my reading. Resources such as Jim Trelease's (1982) *The Read-Aloud Handbook* and *The New York Times Parents' Guide to the Best Books for Children* provide handy references. I maintain a file of bibliographies clipped from journals or picked up at conferences and workshops. I watch for the "notable lists" printed each year in *Language Arts* or *Reading Teacher*. Skimming new bibliographies such as these helps to keep me current, and the file becomes a resource when I want books on a particular topic, genre, or by a specific author. I also read reviews of new books in journals such as *The New Advocate,* or *Hornbook* as a way to browse through new books without leaving home.

Of course, nothing substitutes for holding a new book in your hands, opening the cover, relishing the pictures, tasting the words. One of the best ways I know to keep in touch with new publications is to visit a good bookstore. One teacher I know plans a bookstore visit once a week. She's established a rapport with the proprietor, who pulls out the new arrivals when she comes in the door. Visiting a bookstore will lead to buying books of course, but one advantage in owning children's books is that they go with you rather than staying in the classroom during the inevitable transfers that teachers make. Once I spent money on activity books and resource books to help me create lesson plans; no longer. Now I buy children's books. They are the tools of my trade.

Building a Classroom Library

My classroom library started as a collection left over from my sons' childhoods plus the books left in the classroom by other teachers. Actually, those old classroom books were dregs; the teachers leaving didn't want them and, eventually, neither did I. On a shoestring budget, my classroom library grew through the following tactics:

- I scoured garage sales, used bookstores, and an annual used book sale in our community.
- By using bonus points and some of my own funds I purchased books through mail order book clubs.
- Donations from parents and friends were requested, with a clearly stated "no strings attached" policy: I wanted to be able to discard at my discretion.
- I requested that monies previously allocated for workbooks be channeled to books for the classroom library. (When I first made this request, it was denied; the decision was later reversed.)

- Parents were presented with the option at back-to-school night of giving a book instead of gooey cupcakes for birthday treats (one paperback is less expensive than two and a half dozen cupcakes). Many families chose this option and we'd receive books inscribed, "To Elizabeth's first-grade class in honor of her seventh birthday." We celebrated the birthday by reading the book and remembered the day throughout the year during rereads.
- I purchased books myself.
- I checked out several dozen books from the school library on a long-term basis. The professional librarian, a key person in today's school, knows good books; keeps up on the reviews of new books; and knows the needs of curriculum, faculty, and students.

It didn't take long to build a classroom library. I didn't need lots of books nor did I need multiple copies for first graders. Young children "read around" in lots of different books, noticing words here and there, reading the pictures—generally acquainting themselves with books as meaning-conveying objects. When they begin reading entire books, the books are short and so one child doesn't tie up one book for long stretches of time. Eventually I collected extra copies of some of the most popular books (such as Arnold Lobel's *Frog and Toad*), but my limited resources initially prevented this luxury. Had I been teaching older children, who read longer books that take more time, I likely would have acquired multiple copies to simply facilitate access to popular books. I also didn't need big books. When I eventually acquired a few I found them a pleasant addition and I appreciated the enlarged illustrations. However, like all the books in the classroom, children chose the *best* ones for browsing or reading and the size had little relevance. The important thing was to have a selection of *quality* books to accommodate the diversity of children within any classroom.

A Year's Read Alouds

During one school year as a personal research project I listed all the books I read aloud to the children. I recorded each title the first time I read that book, making no attempt to note the numerous times I reread. This record keeping was an eye opener. Almost immediately I realized that I shared with children only a small fraction of the books I knew and loved. October came to an end and there remained many wonderful Halloween and autumn books that I hadn't read to this class. How important my teacher choices were! As I recorded books, I realized that even though I gave a daily chunk of time to reading aloud I could easily get into ruts. The list helped me see the total picture and strive to incorporate new authors and genre and broaden the range of books I read to the children. The listing definitely prodded me to read more (the final list included over 300 titles) and forced me to confront the fact that in previous years, I really didn't read as much as I thought I did. Lest anyone think I'm recommending creating a list of books to read (to cover) each year, let me say that this was not my purpose. In fact, such a list is an anathema to good a literature program. Much of the joy of our literature read-aloud time derived from the spontaneity and responsiveness of our selections. One book naturally led to another and another. The children requested favorite titles and authors again and again. I read books that connected to interests that surfaced in the class. All of this process of selection and choice provided children with a model of the way real readers select reading materials and how choices lead to further choices. A predetermined list definitely would have restricted the children's developing awareness of books and authors and reading for a range of purposes.

But keeping a list for one year was instructive for me and caused me to make more thoughtful choices. In addition to adding more variety of authors and genres, I noticed my list was lean on books reflecting a range of cultures; there were few books about Native Americans, for example. I would address this lack in the future. What also struck me as I perused this list was that most of these books were stories. Stories have gotten a bad rap in the past with lines such as, "Oh, it's only a story," or "You're just reading a storybook." At the English Coalition Conference in the summer of 1987, we sixty educators discussing critical issues for education in the twenty-first century realized that each of us told stories from our teaching experiences to communicate to the others. Gordon Wells (1986) observed the significance of stories: "Making sense of an experience is to a very great extent being able to construct a plausible story about it. . . . Storying becomes the means whereby we enter into a shared world, which is continually broadened and enriched by the exchange of stories with others. . . . Storying is . . . the way in which the mind itself works" (pp. 196–197). The great teachers throughout history understood the significance of stories. Stories are the path to learning. I chose stories for most of the classroom read alouds because the children craved them.

Another class will never hear the same books read aloud. Why? Because they will be a different group and I will be a different teacher. There was a day when, as an elementary librarian, I believed good teaching developed from repeating and refining great lessons from year to year. (It would become easier each year too!) I saved certain books for reading to particular grade levels. Each year I read *The Christmas Cookie Sprinkle Snitcher* by Vip to first graders and then led them through a dramatization of baking cookies;

Cranberry Thanksgiving by Devlin to second graders and then baked cranberry bread as a follow-up activity; saved *The Funny Little Woman* by Mosel to start my third-grade folktale unit. I managed and controlled those books because I wanted to be the first to read them to children, and I had my activities to reinforce my claim. I realized that my teacher-librarian activities rose from *my* needs and were not necessarily in the best interests of the children. There was no other reason other than my agenda why the children needed to wait to read *Cranberry Thanksgiving* until they were in second grade. Plus, I have to acknowledge that baking cranberry bread had no real purpose that I could articulate. "The children loved it" or "It was fun" were the justifications I professed. In truth, although it was fun, the activity was designed to make me appear to be an exciting librarian and convince myself that I was a creative teacher.

Sometimes I still feel twinges of disappointment when I pull out a book of which I'm particularly fond and the children say, "Oh, we read that in kindergarten." Then I remember I want children to know good books and I say, "Wonderful! I love to read good books again and again. Let's read this one again. Just remember for some folks here this might be the first time they've heard it."

"Yes! Read it. I really like it," comes the response. And when we close the book there are usually comments such as: "I forgot some parts of that" or "I really like when . . ." or "That's a really good book. Can we read it again?"

While good books bear reading and rereading, and while I certainly want children in my classroom to value rereading favorite books, at the same time I want to respect my colleagues and their choices. A unit on Japan is part of the third-grade curriculum and so I generally stay away from Japanese folktales or other books related to the third-grade unit; our first-grade unit on China will provide a taste of Eastern culture. On the other hand, I read *Charlotte's Web*, as does a second-grade teacher in my building. The children come to school knowing the story because it's been on television several times. They love this story and reading the book exposes them to good writing.

How sad to establish a list of grade levels for books or to "save" books until later. It's impossible to do anyway; children will discover these books on their own or through the library, bookstores, friends, and siblings. The world of English studies has a canon, a list of the books that everyone "should" read. We all experienced this canon in our journeys through school—everyone in tenth grade reads *Silas Marner* or *Julius Caesar*, for instance. Usually our reading lacked any connection with reading in our real worlds, in part because the teacher's polished reading was the "correct" reading—the right interpretation. A canon, or a list of books to read, immediately becomes inclusive and exclusive. To make such a list we include particular titles, genre, cultures. But the very nature of choice also excludes possibilities. Not only may we close the door to riches beyond our own current experiences, but we may unwittingly restrict reading to the "tried and true" thus eliminating new choices yet to be published.

I find that an important goal of reading instruction is to help children diversify, to find what they like and then move on from there with one reading experience leading to another and another. My classroom observations teach me that this happens best through the interactions among a community of readers rather than by imposing a list that presumes the directions or sequence in which readers will grow. I can't imagine having to read the same books year after year with children. My enthusiasm would wane quickly and my weariness would spill over to the children, for I know that *my* enthusiasm for particular books is necessary for the children to develop the interest to plunge into a book. I'd also soon fall into routines with the books and impose my responses or those of other classes onto the new group. I'd bridge on "basalizing" the books, which is just what I worked to get away from! Some books will surface from year to year, but even those choices will depend on the context of teacher and culture. Inherent in any reading list lies the danger of orthodoxy, and so the list of books that emerges for each class must be ever fresh and new so that the stories of children learning may likewise remain fresh and new.

CHAPTER 16

Suggestions for Reading Aloud to Children

"When you read a book aloud," my first graders tell me, "you have to read it with expression—so people will want to listen. Otherwise, it gets boring."

"And you have to take your time. You can't hurry 'cause people can't listen as fast as you might read."

"You gotta stop and let people think, let them talk some, in between."

As usual, the children had it down. They knew what made reading aloud enjoyable. Teachers who read to children develop their own techniques, but here are some of mine:

1. Introduce the book with a few brief comments—tell something about the author or why you selected it to read even if it's just "I've never read this book before and I'd like to know what you think of it."

2. Talk about the end pages, title page, dedication page of some books, but definitely not every book.

3. Use an expressive voice that picks up the tone of the story and the voices of the characters.

4. Use timing for emphasis. Pause for listeners to digest, contemplate, consider ideas.

5. Watch expressions on listeners' faces and adjust the reading in response to the audience.

6. Vary your approach with different readings. For example, sometimes read straight through without comment from either yourself or the

listeners. Another time, pause and elicit a few responses through open-ended questions such as, "What do you think about that?" Sometimes share your personal responses taking care not to thwart the responses of listeners who may look to you as the authority.

7. *Invite* talk about the reading:

   - to predict then confirm or disprove the prediction as the book unfolds
   - to make connections to other books
   - to make connections to personal experiences
   - to consider characters and what makes them tick
   - to express likes and dislikes about the book
   - to consider the author's language, style, and strategies

   However, avoid addressing all these areas with every book.

8. Accept all ideas expressed and demonstrate the value of everyone's contribution.

9. Strive to understand the thinking behind the ideas expressed.

10. Ask questions to which you do not know the answer.

11. Repeat well-turned phrases that appeal to you and tell the listeners why you like them.

12. Point out techniques with language or construction that the author uses. Generally, this is best done after the first reading of a book.

13. Take your time. Enjoy the reading and the talk!

Many different individuals read to my children throughout the year: mothers, grandmothers, peers, older students, student teachers, the principal, the reading teacher, other classroom teachers. I've noticed that each brings a unique style to the presentation of a book to the class. One reader evoked criticism from the children because he read too fast. On another occasion, children expressed delight in the voice tone of a particular reader. When a child reader stopped suddenly in a story she was reading aloud and asked, "Why do you think he did that?" I saw the listeners perk up, catch the twinkle in the child's eye, and begin thinking of unexpected events for the story. Exposure to different readers contributes to the children's understanding of the reading process.

Children's Choice

As the year moved along, I found myself barraged with daily requests to reread particular books. To solve this minor issue I established a procedure we called Children's Choice. I listed the children's names alphabetically on a small chart and taped it to the wall. Each day, following the sequence on the list, one child selected a book previously read for rereading. The procedure took on a vigor beyond expectation. Anticipating their turn, children spent days making a decision and great secrecy surrounded their choices. Sometimes a child whispered a decision to me only to come back a day or two later to retract that choice in favor of another. The children chose books they personally liked but also considered what would be a hit with classmates.

In February it was my turn to do the hall bulletin board. I asked the children for ideas. They suggested we "do our good books." We blocked off the bulletin board into a large calendar, made a title "Books We Love," and then each day of the month a child illustrated a scene from a book and added it to the large calendar display. A small heart with the title, author, and child's name completed the child's contribution. When children selected books for rereading they took into account books favored by the community, but when they chose their book for the bulletin board they operated independently. When I look at those choices, I see no surprises. The choices reflect the children's individual personality, interests, and values. Each chosen book had been a hit with the selector on the first reading. A child just beginning to read in February chose a wordless picture book. The choice of *Mortimer* by two boys matched their own senses of humor. The child who chose *Mufaro's Beautiful Daughters*, an African tale, had been intrigued with the lush jungle illustrations and the African characters and early in September had spoken out for causes of minority people. Matt, who chose *Make Way for Ducklings*, had been the child who wanted to talk to the ducklings when I first read the book in September.

Between the first week of January and the end of the school year the following books made the Children's Choice list. The starred books are the ones that children chose for the bulletin board. Numbers after a title indicate the number of times that particular book was chosen as a Children's Choice.

Arnold, Tedd, *No Jumping on the Bed*

*Asbjornsen, Peter C. and Jorgen Moe, *Three Billy Goats Gruff*

*Bang, Molly, *The Grey Lady and the Strawberry Snatcher*

*Brett, Jan, *Goldilocks and the Three Bears*

*Browne, Anthony, *The Piggybook*

*Bunting, Eve, *Ghost's Hour, Spook's Hour*

Burton, Virginia, *The Little House*

*Carle, Eric, *The Grouchy Ladybug* (2)

Carle, Eric, *A House for Hermit Crab* (2)

*Carle, Eric, *Papa, Please Get the Moon for Me*

Carle, Eric, *The Very Busy Spider*

Carrick, Carol, *The Accident* (2)

Carrick, Donald, *Harold and the Great Stag* (2)

Cauley, Lorinda Bryan, *The Trouble with Tyrannosauras Rex* (2)

*Cooney, Barbara, *Miss Rumphius*

Cooney, Barbara, *Island Boy*

dePaola, Tomie, *Big Anthony and the Magic Ring*

*Emberley, Barbara, *Drummer Hoff* (2)

Gantos, Jack, *Rotten Ralph's Trick or Treat*

Haley, Gail, *Jack and the Bean Tree*

Hoff, Syd, *Danny and the Dinosaur*

*Hoff, Syd, *Merry Christmas, Henrietta*

Hoff, Syd, *Stanley*

*Lester, Hester, *Tacky the Penguin* (2)

Lionni, Leo, *Swimmy*

Locker, Thomas, *The Boy Who Held Back the Sea*

Marshall, James, *George and Martha*

*Marshall, James, *Goldilocks* (4)

Marshall, James, *Red Riding Hood* (3)

McCloskey, Robert, *Blueberries for Sal*

**McCloskey, Robert, *Make Way for Ducklings* (2)

McCloskey, Robert, *Time of Wonder*

Munsch, Robert, *Love You Forever*

**Munsch, Robert, *Mortimer* (3)

*Munsch, Robert, *Thomas' Snowsuit* (2)

O'Conner, Jane, *Lulu Goes to Witch School*

Polacco, Patricia, *Rechenka's Eggs*

Rylant, Cynthia, *The Relatives Came*

*Seuss, Dr, *The Lorax* (2)

*Steptoe, John, *Mufaro's Beautiful Daughters* (3)

Van Allsburg, Chris, *Two Bad Ants* (3)

Williams, Vera, *Cherry Stones and Cherry Pits*

*Wood, Audrey, *King Bidgood's in the Bathtub*

Yolen, Jane, *Owl Moon*

*Zelinsky, Paul O., *Rumpelstiltskin* (2)

Zemach-Berson, Kaethe, *The Funny Dream*

Poetry

During literature time and at moments throughout the day I read poetry aloud. Shel Silverstein has become the modern counterpart of Mother Goose in that his poems are the first heard by many of today's children. His catchy rhymes and rhythms in *Where the Sidewalk Ends* and *The Light in the Attic* have led many children into poetry. I begin the year with Mother Goose and the light verse of Silverstein and Jack Prelusky. Then I add poems from my collection of children's poetry books which includes several anthologies such as *The Random House Book of Poetry for Children* and *Sing a Song of Popcorn*. Smaller collections such as the ones compiled by Lee Bennett Hopkins focus on a particular theme (e.g., dinosaurs, Halloween, or the sea). Slim volumes in picture book format such as *Eats*, by Arnold Adolff, or *Balloons and Other Poems*, by Debra Chandra, invite us to indulge in one poet and become familiar with that poet's style. Georgia Heard's book on teaching poetry, *For the Good of the Earth and the Sun*, was not only a wonderful reading experience for me, it also inspired me to read more and more poetry with children and to encourage child poets in the classroom.

I hope to make children poetry readers and so we just read and read and enjoy. "Listen to the sound. What sounds do you like?" "What pictures come to you?" "What do you feel?" are some of the questions I ask to invite responses. Sometimes we get up and move (dance or mime) to a familiar poem as we recite it together. I display posters with favorite poems and copy poems on chart paper for reading together and for children to reread on their own. The children have construction paper folders in their desks and I provide copies of favorite poems for them to keep in their folders. The children regularly select these folders to read during reading workshop; the familiar lines and rhythms support their reading.

When I read lots of poetry and invite children to respond to the rhythm, sound, and images that poetry evokes, children begin writing poetry. I've never been comfortable with the formulas for writing poetry that the old language arts texts suggested. The children who write poetry in my classroom follow the model of the poems they have heard and only a small portion of their finished poems rhyme. Courtney published an entire volume entitled "Poems." On the final page, with the heading "Author Speaks," she wrote: "When I read poems, they make me feel something inside because they are so graceful."

Wordless Picture Books

For years I tried to incorporate wordless or nearly wordless picture books into my classroom. I urged children to tell stories, but they rendered bland versions with "and thens . . ." as they turned each page. When I broadened my view of literacy beyond word-by-word identification and saw reading as constructing meaning from the page, wordless picture books took on new significance. I explained to the children that in this kind of book the author/illustrator invited readers to use their imaginations and tell the story in their own words by reading the pictures. Then I opened Tomie dePaola's *Pancakes for Breakfast* and demonstrated (with a not particularly exciting rendition) how to look at pictures and tell a story. "Your stories will be different from mine and I'm sure a lot more interesting," I said before I handed the book over to the children.

During the early part of the school year the children told original but simple stories. As they became conscious of story construction through their own written compositions and through listening to lots of stories, the stories they told took on more vitality. Children crafted each telling, expanding on each version, yet taking care to make it different from those told by peers, by reading illustrations carefully and looking for undiscovered details. They practiced their stories in order to present them to the group. Frankly, I was amazed at their intricate and imaginative storytelling.

In late February, Jeff presented his version of Molly Bang's *The Grey Lady and the Strawberry Snatcher*. He held up the book, opened to the first page, and began telling his tale. With the ear of a true storyteller, he adjusted the pace, volume, and tone of his voice throughout the telling. "Once upon a time there was an old lady who bought some strawberries. 'Umm, what delicious strawberries! I'll take them home to my family.' " He turned the page and continued.

"She just walked by the flower shop saying, 'La-la-la-la-laa.' " Jeff sang a casual melody. Then suspense grew in his voice as he continued. ". . . not knowing the strawberry snatcher was getting closer and closer."

"She just passed the bakery. He came closer and closer."

"Getting closer and closer and closer and closer."

"Finally, he started running after her! She screamed, 'Ahhh!' " Jeff screamed a delicate scream fitting of the grey lady, then continued, escalating the pace of the telling as he spoke. "She started running. Dun-da-dun-da-dun-da-dunt!"

"She saw a lady on a skateboard with a bucket of snakes. She ran right by. The strawberry snatcher was still after her."

"The strawberry snatcher—she got on the bus. The strawberry snatcher hit the bus and hit the lady and the snakes fell down on him. He smashed them." The grave tone in Jeff's voice suppressed a few giggles among the children responding to the idea of snakes falling on the strawberry snatcher.

"Then the bus went. The grey lady got off on the other side, walked over to the other side. The strawberry snatcher was on a skateboard." By this time it was obvious that Jeff's voice took on a light-hearted tone when he spoke of the grey lady and became ominous when he spoke of the strawberry snatcher.

"The strawberry snatcher began running after the grey lady again."

"He jumped!!"

"He landed in the water. The grey lady started running. She started running—'cuz . . ." at this point Jeff paused in the storytelling to explain this point to his audience. " 'Cuz, see I figured out, see that's her and she's running again. The strawberry snatcher's after her."

"She hid behind a tree. The strawberry snatcher's still looking for her."

The drama picked up as Jeff built to the climax of his story with the pace and tone of his voice. " 'Ah, I *found* you,' he said. She started climbing up a tree. He started climbing up after her."

"She jumped onto a vine and swang down." Jeff emphasized this sentence then dropped his voice for the next one. "The strawberry snatcher was at the top of the tree after her still, but she jumped down."

"She landed!"

"She started running again. The strawberry snatcher started running after her. He stopped!" Jeff inserted a dramatic pause before he continued.

"He started looking around, not knowing she was hiding." The last five words rolled off Jeff's tongue with all the intrigue of a detective story writer.

"The strawberry snatcher started looking a little more—went into the bushes."

"He started eating some berries. 'Umm, what delicious berries. Yummy!' "

"He fell down. His hat fell off and his hair popped out! And the grey lady blocked him."

"They had a big—wait." Jeff stopped and corrected his telling when he saw the next picture. "She brought home the strawberries to her family and they started eating a bunch of strawberries. Bum-da-bum-da-bum-daa!" Jeff's sound effects polished off the story before his final line: "They ate them all up."

When he finished, a delighted audience asked questions. "What's your favorite picture?" said Nicole.

"Oh," said Jeff as he flipped through the book to the page where the strawberry snatcher's hat pops off to reveal a head of curly red hair. He shows the group and someone asks why this picture is his favorite. "Well, because, he had a hat on and his hair went BOINNGG! I think it was because he ate those berries and it made his hair go BOINNGG! And Greg told me that and I thought that could have happened, when I was reading it."

Matt asked, "Why did you want to read this story?"

"Well, it's because I like it and it's kinda funny and I thought it was neat. Stacy."

Stacy asks, "How'd you think up that story, to make up with the book?"

"Well, I was thinking of a different story that was kinda boring and then I thought of this one. How I thought it up was, the minute I heard it, the minute she started reading it (referring to my introducing the book to the class earlier), I started making up my own story for it."

Like all reading in our classroom, the reading of wordless picture books is as diverse as the readers who bring meaning to those books.

Some of the other wordless books we enjoy include:

Anno, Mitsumasa, *Anno's Journey*

Briggs, Raymond, *The Snowman*

Day, Alexandra, *Good Dog, Carl*

Hutchins, Pat, *Changes, Changes*

Martin, Rafe, *Will's Mammoth*

Mayer, Mercer, *A Boy, a Dog and a Frog*

Spier, Peter, *Peter Spier's Rain*

Turkle, Brinton, *Deep in the Forest*

Willard, Nancy, *Simple Pictures Are Best*

Informational Texts

Many of the informational texts that I read in my classroom connect with the social studies and science units of the first-grade curriculum. But I also look for informational books that primary-age children can learn to read. Byron Barton's bold pictures and brief texts in books such as *I Want to Be an Astronaut* and *Machines at Work* appeal to beginning readers, as does Gail Gibbons's book *Tool Book*. When I choose information books for the classroom, the most important criteria is accuracy of information; close behind is that the information be presented in an interesting and appealing format.

Certain authors have gained a reputation for merging accuracy with an appealing presentation for young readers. Two examples that come immediately to mind are Patricia Lauber and Aliki. One year I read Lauber's *Volcano* to the class over several days as part of our literature time. The children talked about volcanos the rest of the year. In our dinosaur study we frequently found conflicting information in books, which led us to check the copyright dates. Aliki's several books about dinosaurs became popular with the children, and they noticed that she had revised her books to keep up with current knowledge. Byron Barton's *Dinosaurs, Dinosaurs* and *Bones, Bones, Dinosaur Bones* also provided good reading about dinosaurs for beginning readers.

Books that invite playing with language and words, focussing on the sounds of language and language construction, also come into literature time. *The King Who Rained,* by Fred Gwynne, *One Sun: a Book of Terse Verse,* by Bruce McMillan, and *Quick as a Cricket,* by Audrey Wood, all lend themselves to playing with language. I will read *One Sun*, for example, and respond to the natural talk that I know will come from children as they try out terse verse for themselves. Depending on the degree of group response, I might write some of their terse verse on chart paper and then continue to collect terse verse on that chart in the days and weeks that follow. With *Quick as a Cricket* I explain similes and ask the children which similes they liked best and why. For myself, "sad as basset" appeals where "happy as a lark" is a cliche. I point out that good writers use new similes—ones that we haven't heard—and avoid cliches. Then I invite children to consider this for their own writing. Sometimes we collect unusual similes on a chart. Always, though, I keep my teaching in response to the children. I might have to read a book to a class more than once before the children's responses indicate that such follow-through is appropriate.

One year I read Ruth Heller's *Kites Sail High: A Book About Verbs* with the children, and we talked about verbs and that every sentence needed one. In writing workshop I read two pages: "A VIGOROUS VERB is super superb. It tells you fireworks EXPLODE or horses THUNDER down the road." Then I pointed out that good writers use strong verbs to help their readers get good pictures in their head as they read. One young writer came to me at the end of writing workshop and said, "I was writing about my horse and I wrote that word 'thunder' that you read. When I was writing, it just popped into my head!"

"It was a strong verb, better than another one you were going to use?"

"Yeah," came the reply, and his tone and expression told me that this young writer made a connection. The next day I pointed out the word choice to the entire class for a mini-lesson.

In a similar manner, Heller's book *Many Luscious Lollipops: A Book About Adjectives* lends itself to talk about language that connects to writing. The opening sentence defining an adjective is a mini-lesson in itself. After reading the opening line I add, "Writers put adjectives into their writing to help their readers understand but good writers don't use *lots* of adjectives—only ones that help them be specific." Then I write a sentence with five "verys" in it, in imitation of what I've seen children do, and point out that one "very" will do and perhaps we don't even need one or we could find a more specific adjective. Rereading these books on language extends again the gentle invitation to children to explore written language.

Novels

My family got a television set when I was ten—in time for the World Series that year. My students are shocked to hear this; they can't imagine a world without television. "But," I add, "we had the radio, and every day when I came home from school there was one half-hour program that I listened to—a different one every day." I tell them about "The Lone Ranger," "Sargent Preston of the Yukon," "Sky King," "Superman," and how I sat beside the radio and made the pictures in my head as I listened to each story. Each of these radio series eventually evolved into television programs, and I still remember how disappointed I was when I saw Sky King. The image in my head was much better than the character on the television screen.

"As I read this book without pictures on every page, this is what I want you to do—make the pictures in your head just as I did when I listened to stories on the radio," I explain to the children as a way of introducing them to the reading of longer children's books, the ones the children call "chapter books." As part of the opening of each school day I read aloud a section (usually about a chapter) from a longer children's book. Can first graders sit for this kind of reading? Yes! This read-aloud time becomes an important part of the beginning of our school day. We talk for a moment about where we left the story the previous day, and the talk and ensuing reading play a part in bringing our community back together to move into another day.

In contrast to literature time when the children sit on the storyrug, during this read-aloud time the class is seated at their desks and I sit at the conference table. In the beginning we talk about comfortable ways to sit for long stretches without having to move restlessly: keeping hands still, and if they tend to get into trouble to have these hands hang on to each other; feet flat on the floor; sitting straight; desks cleared and leaving things inside the desks alone. This may seem rigid but I've found it works in getting wiggly first graders to focus on listening. In a matter of days the procedures are established. "Listening positions," I announce as I pick up the book, and the children straighten in their seat and look at me beaming, ready to listen. Each morning, before we start the next chapter, we recall the events in the plot as it unfolded the day before, and sometimes we speculate about what will happen next. During the reading we stop and talk about our responses to the story and perhaps discuss the meaning of some unfamiliar words that confuse us or hinder our understanding of the story. For example, when I read *Mr. Popper's Penguins* none of the children knew the term "icebox." I explained. When I explained "tripod" we made connections to triangle and tricycle. If I set up this procedure early by stopping and talking about a specific vocabulary word or two, the children feel comfortable to ask about words they don't understand as we encounter them. "I don't get that. What does . . . mean?" We stop and work out meaning.

What novels do we read? The list, which we put up on chart paper, changes every year. Here is a list of books from a recent year in the order in which they were read.

Charlotte's Web, by E. B. White

J.T., by Jane Wagner

A Toad for Tuesday, by Russell Erickson

Molly's Pilgrim, by Barbara Cohen

The Magic Sled, by Nathaniel Benchley

Ramona the Pest, by Beverly Cleary

The Great Christmas Kidnapping Caper, by Jean Van Leeuwen

A Certain Small Shepherd, by Rebecca Caudill

Mr. Popper's Penguins, by Richard and Florence Atwater

Jump! The Adventures of Brer Rabbit, by Van Dyke Parks and Malcolm Jones

The Hundred Penny Box, by Sharon Bell Mathis

The Mouse and the Motorcycle, by Beverly Cleary

I'll Meet You at the Cucumbers, by Lillian Moore

The Enormous Egg, by Oliver Butterworth

James and the Giant Peach, by Roald Dahl

The Boxcar Children, by Gertrude Chandler Warner

Sarah, Plain and Tall, by Patricia MacLachlan

Seven Kisses in a Row, by Patricia MacLachlan

Charlotte's Web, by E. B. White

I begin every year with *Charlotte's Web.* At the end of the year the class votes from the list we've compiled throughout the course of the year and chooses one book to read again. I've done this every year to demonstrate the importance of rereading books that most touch our lives. Every class has chosen *Charlotte's Web* (though *James and the Giant Peach* has been a close second in some years). In the September reading, first graders identify with Wilbur, the helpless little piglet who depends on Fern to care for him. By the time we read the book again at year's end, the children identify with Charlotte, the good friend and good writer. There are always mixed feelings about "poor old Templeton," E. B. White's "rat of all work." Every teacher who has taught first grade knows that this is the development of first graders: from egocentric, dependent "babies" to children who thrive on peer relationships and strive to work independently.

Some books, like *Charlotte's Web,* have become standard for me; I've read them to every class for the last ten years. Others drop off the list one year and then reappear the next. Some other successful read alouds that don't appear on the previous list include:

The Trumpet of the Swan, by E. B. White

Stuart Little, by E. B. White

Winnie-the-Pooh, by A. A. Milne (a child asked me to read this one)

Henry Huggins, by Beverly Cleary (I read only one Cleary book a year.
    That's enough to lead the children into reading these themselves.)
Ribsy, by Beverly Cleary
The Best Christmas Pageant Ever, by Barbara Robinson
Warton and the Castaways, by Russell Erickson

I'm always on the lookout for new books to read aloud. A good review
or two is enough for me to try a book with the class; I don't have to read
it through first. Occasionally I start a book that I abandon. For example,
several years ago I began to read a highly recommended book with a
wonderful story that just didn't read aloud well. One day I simply started
another book. Not one child seemed to notice. Today I'd do that differently,
though; I'd talk to the children and get their opinion before making the
decision.

Like all the books shared in the classroom, we stop and talk about
passages and lines that are worth savoring. Take *Charlotte's Web* for example. When I read the chapter that describes the children swinging on the
rope in the barn I urge the children to imagine themselves on this swing as
I read the paragraphs. "Read it again!" Matthew cried at the end. "I could
feel my stomach jump to my neck." The children giggle at the geese and
goslings repeating everything three times each time they speak, and they
delight in the complaining Templeton rescuing Charlotte's egg sac. When
we read the chapters describing twilight and dawn we recall our visits to
the planetarium where we learned about the rotation of the earth as the
cause of day and night; we also remember Barbara Berger's beautiful book
Grandfather Twilight. Charlotte called the meeting of the barnyard animals
together by announcing, "Attention, please. Attention, please." When I
use the same phrase to get the attention of the class a child says, "I know
who said that. Charlotte." The line becomes a familiar one that I use again
and again throughout the year. "Yes, Charlotte?—I mean, yes Mrs. Avery?"
replied a child one day with a twinkle in his eye.

Occasionally, after completing one of these books, I suggest that the
children think of a part of the book that they especially liked and that they
paint or draw an illustration and write a short passage telling why they like
that particular part. I put these pictures together into a class book, type the
written words, and paste them on the page opposite their picture (which is
the back of the preceding picture). The book then circulates to the children's
homes on an overnight basis. Parents write responses on a page labeled,
"Reader's Comments." A book of watercolor illustrations and responses
after reading *James and the Giant Peach* were laminated and turned out
especially lovely. One parent wrote, "This is one of the most beautiful
books I've ever read—I loved these pictures!" When I read the comment to

the class the next morning a child piped up, "Probably they're good because we made those pictures in our heads when you read the book."

Author Study

A dozen years ago, when I asked a group of first graders for their ideas about an author, the children said, "He made the book." Then they speculated that the author literally "made" all of their books by painting, writing, and sewing together each and every copy. Today, due to writing workshop, children understand authorship and are familiar with authors and illustrators and their styles. First graders notice an illustrator's style before they notice the writing style of authors. Tending to the work of illustrators establishes a natural bridge for examining the individual styles of authors.

During the first week of school I pull out a picture of Eric Carle when I read his name on the title page of one of his books. "He grew up in Germany and he didn't like school much," I tell the children, relating tidbits of information about Carle that I've picked up from publishers' brochures, book jackets, and a magazine article. I add that he makes the pictures for his books by painting brightly colored tissue paper and then cutting and pasting the paper. "I read that he has drawers full of colored tissue that he's painted for his illustrations." The children suck in their breath, imagining such a sight. We put Carle's picture on the bulletin board beside us and read. We've read several of his books by now, and the children notice on this day that he often has the sun or the moon somewhere in his books. One year I bravely led one group of children through painting tissue and making collage pictures, Eric Carle style. The project was a major undertaking and one I didn't repeat in other classes. Such an activity is the rare exception in connection with author study. I've found it's enough to add authors' pictures to our bulletin board and to share some bit of information about each person.

Through the years I've built a file on authors by collecting journal articles and publishers' brochures. Book jackets provide information and several reference books are available on authors, which any librarian can quickly locate. Student book clubs now provide letters and tapes by and about authors. The author bulletin board continues to grow throughout the year with pictures of our favorite authors, many of them photocopied from book jackets or brochures. On the day of our authors' party, when the children first publish, I add each of their pictures to the bulletin board of authors. Author study is a rather simple, yet ongoing, activity that acquaints children with authors' and illustrators' styles and with some of the decisions authors make as they write.

Books provide models of strategies writers use, and in our talk I share information that I've learned about authors and their processes from conferences I've attended and my own reading. For example:

- Don and Carol Carrick wrote *The Accident* about the death of their dog and *The Foundling* about their new puppy. This might have been one story, but they recognized that this was really two stories in one and wrote two separate books.

- Tomie dePaola's *The Art Lesson* is autobiographical but he didn't write a biography that tells *everything* about his life. Instead, he focussed on one incident and told everything about that event. We learn much about his life throughout the book but the focus is on one incident. He also changed the teacher from a second-grade teacher to a first-grade teacher because it worked out better in the construction of the book and didn't change the meaning.

- Steven Kellogg's books about Pinkerton are based on escapades with his own dog. Kellogg wrote about a topic he knew well.

- Patricia MacLachlan's idea for the title of *Seven Kisses in a Row* came from her husband's ritual of giving their daughter seven kisses in a row at bedtime.

- Ann Turner first got the idea for *Dakota Dugout* as she pulled waxed paper off the roll and thought of oiled paper for windows. Then she asked herself who was looking through this window, where was this person, and why was she there. She answered the questions from her own imagination, then researched life on the prairie to write her book. When she wrote *Nettie's Trip South* she felt the writing wasn't working, and from her writing group came the suggestion to try the piece in the form of a letter.

- Maurice Sendak's wild things in *Where the Wild Things Are* started out as horses. The wild things remind him of visiting relatives when he was a child.

All this talk about authors and their processes connects to writing and reading. Frequently, mini-lessons for writing workshop are quick reminders of an author's strategy that we discussed in literature time.

We celebrate child authors in the classroom too. I started an Author of the Week activity focussing on one child. I read that child's books and the child and I made a poster for the room about the child as an author. I'd interview the child about writing and reading, typing the words as they spoke, then put these comments on the poster along with a photo. The child would write other information, such as favorite book, family, etc., and perhaps add a drawing. I ran into trouble, however, trying to get all the children in before year's end, what with short holiday weeks and so on. So I cut the rigid weekly schedule and changed the title to Celebrating Author . . . The celebration of child authors boosted children's concept of themselves as authors and helped them recognize the similarities and differences in their processes.

Sometimes children write to authors. Chad wrote to Maurice Sendak in late fall. He loved *Where the Wild Things Are* but was puzzled over a line in the book. "That part about out of a week and over a year, I don't get it," Chad said. "I been thinking about it and thinking about it and that just doesn't make sense to me. What does the author mean?"

"How could you find out?" I asked.

"Well, I could ask him only I don't know where he lives."

"You could write him a letter," I suggested. Chad looked interested. "If you write and revise it like you do when you publish, I'll send it." So Chad wrote to Sendak. Besides his question, he told Sendak that he was an author too and that he had just published his first book. Chad wanted to send a copy of his published book. I typed his letter, Chad signed it, and we sent it off with the original draft, one of Chad's school pictures, and the published book. Several weeks later Chad received a postcard reply from Sendak explaining that the line in question meant that Max used his imagination. On the postcard, Sendak lined out a word and used a caret to insert, a new word, as Chad had done in his draft.

The children write to authors on their own initiative when they have a question or because they have become so involved with the author's books that they want to connect with the author. Jody wrote to Aliki because he loved her dinosaur books so much that he had asked for nothing else for Christmas. She wrote her reply to him in England but explained in the letter that she would mail it when she got back to the United States so he would get it sooner. After he read the letter, Jody ran to the globe to find England!

I've never given a class assignment of writing letters to authors. Only a few children choose to write to an author over the course of a year, but almost everyone who chose to do so received a personal reply, and all of the class participated in the experience of opening and reading those letters. In *Workshop 1*, edited by Nancie Atwell, author Ann Martin (1989), writing about letters she receives from children, makes an observation about the class assignment letters. "For the most part, these letters are short, follow some prescribed form, and lack spontaneity or imagination. Many actually end with, 'P.S. If you write back I'll get an A' " (p. 31). To be meaningful to both the receiver and the sender, the letters children write to authors need to spring from real purposes that the *children* feel.

Reflections

The task of choosing children's books for the classroom and engaging young minds through those books can seem overwhelming. There are so many wonderful books to choose from. Like the little old man in Wanda Gag's *Millions of Cats* we might wish we could choose them all and do all the wonderful activities that we read about. But we can't. We must make choices. In the beginning I thought I needed lots of follow-up activities. The outward rationale was to connect children with good books; the inward need was to assuage the fear that I really might not be teaching. I found myself falling into the trap of an activity-oriented curriculum rather than a learner-centered classroom. Activities shifted the focus away from the richness of the literature to the activity itself. I learned that children did not necessarily make the connections I presumed they'd make. Learners completed activities for me or for the final product rather than truly turning to the literature for the sake of the meaning and the light it shed on their own lives. I had to make a choice. I chose to read and share books with children and to listen to their ideas rather than imposing mine.

When I let go of the notion that *I* knew and therefore could teach children what they needed to know, I discovered the rich world of children's thinking, which taught me how to really teach. I discovered that the responsive teaching style that Don Graves found essential to the teaching of writing was also essential to the sharing of children's literature and to the development of readers.

> The aim is to develop the habit of aesthetic evocation from a text. If the young readers are allowed in the early years to retain and deepen that ability, we can cheerfully leave for later years the more formal methods of literary analysis and criticism. . . . For, after all, the experienced work is what should be analyzed or criticized. The great problem, as I see it, in many school and college literature classrooms today is that the picture—the aesthetic experience, the work—is missing, yet students are being called upon to build an analytic or critical frame for it. No wonder they so often fall back on published 'study aids,' which give them all the (efferent) answers required. (Rosenblatt, 1980, pp. 393–394)

Reading

CHAPTER 17

Reading Workshop

"Can you read?" I asked my first graders during individual interviews the first week of school. The children shrugged, shifted uneasily, or looked surprised before they answered "no" or "not yet" or a hopeful "I'm almost learning to." One child answered, "I can read a little. I learned some words," and another said, "Yes, I can read." Then I asked, "How does somebody learn to read?" With the exception of three children who had moved into our community over the summer, and two who said they could read, every child replied, "By sounding out."

"How does a reader sound out?" I asked.

Matt answered, "I don't know, but that's how people learn to read. I know *that!*" Matt's reply was typical of the children's answers.

Of the three newcomers, two children told me they didn't know how one learned to read and the third said, "You learn from school." The two children who said they could read gave different replies.

One paused a moment, then answered, "I looked at signs—you know like 'Stop'—and I asked my mom 'What did that say?' and she told me and so I could read."

The second child said, "Well, I don't know how other people do it, but I can tell you how *I* did. My grandma and my mom read to me and I started asking, 'What's that word?' and they'd tell me and then I started remembering and then I just learned to read! I started with little words and then I got into bigger and bigger words."

I knew phonics was considered important in our area, but even I was surprised at the consistency of the replies in these interviews. The method of sounding out appeared embedded in the culture of our community as the dominant, if not the only, way one learns to read. The children's notion of one pathway to reading bothered me, but I felt an even deeper concern with what seemed the underlying attitude: Learning to read is difficult. I heard it in the grave tone of their comments, saw it in their eyes, noticed it in their restless squirms.

Over twenty years ago my oldest son went off to first grade. At the dinner table after his first day his dad and I asked the question asked all over the United States that night, "How was school today?"

"Fine," Tim replied, "except she didn't teach us to read yet." Whereupon, as responsible parents, we informed Tim that learning to read took a long time and required a lot of hard work. Sure enough, reading was difficult for Tim. At parent conferences, teachers quelled our worries about Tim's reading progress with adequate test scores (which we truly did not understand), then raved of his strength in math. Tim was great at taking tests; I realize now his mathematical and mechanical abilities enabled him to tackle tests as another puzzle to be solved. However, Tim did not choose to read on his own, and when we asked him to read to us he stumbled through the passage. In September of his sixth-grade year we expressed our concern to his new teacher.

"I'll get back to you," the teacher said. A few days later we received a phone call. "You're right. He can't read," he said. He outlined a plan for reading instruction focussing around Tim's major interest, sports. A former pro football player, this teacher brought in old football plays and sports magazines. He started Tim reading—and writing and designing—football plays. He suggested we order *Sports Illustrated*. The pieces came together. One night as winter turned to spring Tim announced at dinner, "I just read a really good book." Well! We nearly fell off our chairs. The book? *The Mouse and the Motorcycle*. Tim was eleven years old. He's been a reader ever since.

We, Tim's parents, had colluded with the school in making reading difficult. Tim learned the parts of reading—he demonstrated that on tests—but he had not put those parts together in a way that was either useful or meaningful. I think we were typical parents: willing to question and become involved in our child's learning, yet believing that children learn to read in school and shying away from intruding for fear of confusing this complex process. Yet, sadly, we tacitly taught our son that learning to read is difficult.

When I moved inside an elementary classroom as a teacher rather than a parent, I found elaborate procedures surrounding reading instruction laid out for me in the thick manuals, word cards, workbook skill sheets, charts, etc. Most of the morning was devoted to reading instruction, much of it to the development of skills, especially phonics skills. I'd introduce a particular skill, the children practiced that skill on worksheets or workbook pages, then I'd correct their work. Periodically, maybe one day in five, the sequenced lessons in the manual allowed for the reading of a story in the reading book. Periodically I administered tests in forms similar to the practice skill sheets provided by the reading program to determine children's success as readers. If children did well on the tests, every one, myself included, considered them to be progressing satisfactorily. In *Broken Promises: Reading Instruction in Twentieth-Century America*, Patrick Shannon (1988) writes of the tragedy of reading programs:

> The biggest losers are the students who are processed through these recognized programs. . . . Virtually no one, including the teacher, is offered a literacy which asks readers to go beyond the word and literal translation of text to tackle the sense, feeling, truth, and intention of an author through the words he or she used in a text. . . . [N]o one is asked to develop his or her ability to express understanding of a text—what it does and might mean in one's life. In short, no one is asked to be truly literate by any criterion beyond a standardized text. (p. 111)

When I taught reading with a "program," most of the class time was spent on skill instruction and a small proportion of time went to actual reading. Now, without a program, the distribution of time has flip-flopped and the largest chunk of time is devoted to *reading* real books. Certainly I still teach skills, but skill instruction now consumes a small slice of time and serves the process of meaning making, and the practice of those skills takes place during actual reading. The groundwork for this approach to reading instruction began for me in the late 1970s when my school district asked me to create an "individualized reading program" based on the work of Jean-nette Veatch (1959) for five children who were entering first grade as fluent readers. The success of those five youngsters in reading and discussing trade books (Veatch 1964, 1966), coupled with the research on a workshop approach to teaching writing, naturally evolved into teaching reading as a process in a workshop environment.

A reading workshop, modeled after writing workshop, provides the structure for reading instruction in my classroom. However, adjusting to a workshop approach for reading instruction, and becoming comfort-able teaching reading without the trappings of workbooks and sequenced skill lessons, came slowly for me. In the beginning I felt anxious. What if these children didn't learn to read? But as that first year unfolded my anxiety gave way to amazement. The progress of children in former first grades paled in comparison to the strength and solid achievement of these young readers. I recognized that teaching with a program often misdirected children's natural learning processes and asked them to deal with nonsense or trivia. Children learned to read in a literate environment as naturally as they learned to talk. They learned without a scope and sequenced plan of instruction and without all the drills and practice of skills. I learned to teach by observing and responding rather than proclaim-ing and asserting.

Structuring the Reading Workshop

The Beginning

During that first year, reading workshop began with five-minute time slots inserted throughout the school day. As children read their books I moved among them suggesting strategies for figuring out words. Because I was not far removed from the skills orientation of a reading program, my responses in those first workshops addressed decoding and emphasized the correction of errors rather than focussing on meaning and suggesting strategies to get at that meaning. I felt a strong need to be in control of the classroom, to know what each child read and to direct individual progress. I imposed on the children my decisions as to what would be "best" because I believed this was my job. To do anything less felt irresponsible, or as though I wasn't really teaching. But the more I watched children learning to read, I couldn't help notice their energy, their resourcefulness, and their capacity to construct their own learning processes. I began responding to readers by *sharing expertise* and *making suggestions*—sometimes very *strong* suggestions—but always keeping meaning making at the forefront and allowing the child to determine what strategies helped him get at that meaning. I believe I became responsible *to* learners rather than *for* them, and this in turn prompted the children to take responsibility and invest in their own learning.

The same principles of time, choice, and response that worked so well for writing workshop proved to be the cornerstones of reading instruction as Veatch and others advocated in the 1950s and 1960s and Atwell would articulate in the 1980s.

TIME: Just as writers needed time each day to write, so these young readers also needed time each day to read. In the days when I had a reading program I had established SSR, Sustained Silent Reading, in my classrooms during the spring of each year. In SSR everyone in the room read materials of their own choosing. During those fifteen minutes the children all sat at their seats, book in hand, head in book, and read—no moving about, no talking allowed. SSR was a beginning, but reading workshop required more.

Young readers need chunks of time from the beginning of the school year to browse through books, become comfortable with the process of growing as a reader, and to sink into the luxury of real reading. At first, I honestly believed that first graders couldn't sustain long periods in a reading workshop, especially in the fall months. The children showed me differently.

After that first year, I started reading workshop on the first day of school. The first few workshops last approximately ten minutes, but in a matter of days we work up to twenty, and within a few weeks, thirty minutes. By mid-winter there are days when the group sustains forty or fifty minutes and protests when I announce that it's time to stop reading. Some days, when reading is going well, I extend the time, borrowing from science or social studies, knowing that on other days these content areas will require more time and I can borrow from reading. My first graders no longer sit silently, as they did in SSR. Reading in reading workshop includes the telling of stories from illustrations, retelling a story based on memory of hearing the book read aloud, exploring books through browsing, sharing particular books or parts of books with others, reading alone or with a partner. I learned that children needed *lots* of time and that a broader structure accommodated the diversity of experience levels among child readers.

CHOICE: Like SSR, readers in reading workshops choose their reading material. They make other choices too. They choose *how* they will read, whether it be by telling a story through the illustrations, as a child named Sarah did with *The Very Hungry Caterpillar;* or reading the captions under illustrations and ignoring the remainder of the text, as Greg, Brian, and Michael did with a book on the *Titanic;* or singing the text, as Laura did with *Oh, a Hunting We Will Go;* or practicing until able to read every word accurately. They choose to reread books, to move among several books, or to abandon reading they have begun in favor of something else. They choose the kind of books they will read, including the level of difficulty, the genre, and topic. They set their own intentions and purposes, such as reading to learn about dinosaurs with *Bones, Bones, Dinosaur Bones,* or to laugh at the plight of Big Anthony in *Strega Nona,* or to indulge in the imaginative world of *Rumpelstiltskin,* or to identify with the sibling rivalry in *Mufaro's Beautiful Daughters.* They also choose the reading strategies they will use to figure out words in order to get at meaning. They choose how to respond to what they read and they know that they are not required to "do something" after completing everything they read.

Learning to make all these choices helps children become good readers who choose to read outside of school as well as within the reading work-shop. Parents are the first to testify to this. In November conferences I hear frequent comments such as, "He's trying to read everything in sight." At the end of the year parents write comments such as this one by Jenny's mother: "Jenny carried from school to home her desire to learn. She reads everything she can get her hands on." And Stacy's dad wrote, "A conservative estimate of the number of school books and those purchased by me through a book club which Stacy has read *and enjoyed* would be about 250. A celebration in itself."

RESPONSE: A major way in which reading workshop differs from SSR is that in a reading workshop the reading is surrounded by interaction with others. First-grade readers need responses *as they read*. In the beginning of the school year, teacher responses provide encouragement and briefly demonstrate ways to crack the print code while maintaining a focus on meaning. As young readers acquire decoding strategies and develop a vocabulary of words they recognize, responses enable them to articulate their ideas, thoughts, and feelings about what they read. This responding requires me to first listen, thus providing an audience for a child's ideas and wonderings, then offer suggestions or ask questions. Not all responses come from me, the teacher, however. Soon the children learn from my model how to respond to each other. They figure out words together and talk about the books they read. Responding involves the entire reading community—teacher and children.

Every reading workshop is different. A single, precise description threatens to become a formula that robs the workshop of its essential characteristic: responding to children within the context of a particular classroom at a particular moment in time. Only by telling stories can I illustrate the dynamic workings of reading workshop.

Starting a Reading Workshop

Reading workshop begins on the first day of school. The children have come in from lunch recess and settled in their seats. On their desks lay books they selected before they went to lunch. "I know you can all read," I begin. Immediately the children look away. Some begin searching in their desks for something, anything; others look around the room or stare at the floor. I can almost read their thoughts, "Oh-oh, I'm in trouble. She doesn't know." Or "What do I do now?" Or "I didn't think you had to read until after you've been in first grade." Then I point to the narrow strip of bulletin board above the chalkboard where I've mounted all of our names. "What does this say, Beth?"

"Beth," she answers.

"How about this, Jason," I say as I point to his name.

"Jason."

"See, I knew you could read." I continue pointing to names. After five or six successes, I point to the name of a shy child or one likely to be unsure. Hesitantly she answers—correctly. Soon the children recognize names of friends or siblings. "There are other things I bet you can read too," I add. I write "I ♡ you" on the board, then run my hand under it and ask, "Who has an idea what this says?"

"I love New York!" cries out one little boy.

"Good try! But, it's tricky. Let's look closely," I reply as I point to the first letter and say, "This letter is an 'I' and it says . . . ?"

"I!" a child says.

"Right. 'I,' and the heart means?"

"Love?"

"Right again. 'I love . . .'" I run my hand under the words again to focus the children's attention to specific letters and then say, "This looks like New York." (I write "New York" on the board as I speak.) "It has some of the letters—Y and O—but New York has an N. Hear it?" I emphasize the N in "New." Then a child says, "I know! It's 'you!' I love you! That's what it says."

"How did you know that last word 'you'?" I ask in mock disbelief.

"I don't know. I just did. The other part said 'I love' so that part had to be 'you.'"

"Good thinking! 'You' is what makes sense, isn't it? New York would make sense too, but it needs an N and there's no N here. There are other words you can probably read too." I show the class a stop sign and they respond by crying out, "Stop." "For the next few minutes everyone will read the book they chose. One way you can read it is to look at the pictures and think about the story that the pictures tell. You may even find some words you know. While you read, I'd like you to stay in your seat and not exchange your book for another. If you finish it, go back to the beginning and go through it again. You'll probably notice something you didn't see before. I'll come around and you can tell me what your book is about when I come to you. I may not get to everyone today, but if not, we'll do the same thing tomorrow and I'll try to see you then."

This was the beginning of one reading workshop. Through the years I've started our workshop in similar ways, yet each one different and each one in response to the children's comments and to what they communicate through their attitudes about reading. One of my initial goals is to help children view themselves as readers and to see reading as easy rather than difficult. In the days that follow, I will strive to develop the concept of a reader as someone who makes sense of what they read, whether that be written language, pictures, or environmental print. Some years we collect words from environmental print and make a scrapbook. The children de-light in turning the pages and reading Wendy's, Burger King, McDonald's (and pointing out the difference in the names of these fast-food places), Tastee Cakes, Crest, K-mart, Kellogg's, Captain Crunch. They begin to see that reading is easy and that sounding out is not the only way to learn to read. Within a few days the children have learned the routine of coming in from lunch recess, choosing a book, and settling into reading. I ask them to choose only one book or possibly two. Some children want to select a stack of books and then hurry through them, believing that going through a quantity of books means success. Helping them slow down and reread instead of going on to another and still another book encourages more thoughtful choices and, eventually, leads the child to probing beyond a superficial perusal.

Mini-Lessons for Reading Workshop

Writing workshop begins with a brief mini-lesson each day, followed by a time for writing, and concluding with sharing time. I initially designed reading workshop to follow this same format. However, I soon discovered that many of the topics for mini-lessons had been covered during the rich discussions we had about books, genre, and authors in our literature ime. Other mini-lesson topics were embedded in writing workshop or in language lessons during other parts of the school day (see Chapter 19). In the Giacobbe/Atwell (1985) workshop I learned more tips on reading mini-lessons. Most reading mini-lessons became brief reminders, suggestions, or tips to assist readers. These might be a particular strategy for getting at unknown words or suggesting a particular author or genre. Like writing workshop, the first mini-lessons in a school year address procedures and basic ways to begin reading. Some of those first topics include:

- procedures for selecting books
- how to "read" books (reading illustrations, retelling, etc.)
- the importance of thoughtful reading and *rereading* rather than moving through several titles
- how to hold books, open them, and turn pages
- the concept of *word* and how words are put together to make sense
- the directionality of print on the page and connecting one picture to another
- using soft voices when sharing with a person nearby
- the underlying premise that reading must make sense

Once children understand how the workshop operates and have a clear notion of beginning reading strategies such as these, I find that the need for daily mini-lessons diminishes. Mini-lessons for reading workshop are short—two or three minutes in length—and these lessons occurr once or twice a week.

One kind of mini-lesson is a book talk in which I present a genre of literature, or the books of one particular author, or a specific title. For example, I gather several poetry books or biographies or wordless picture books, share them quickly, then offer them to children. Or, when I read a book by an author such as Pat Hutchins during literature time, I suggest other titles by Hutchins at the beginning of the reading workshop. In a book talk to introduce a particular title, such as Arnold Lobel's *Owl at Home,* I might begin by saying, "Some of you liked reading *Frog and Toad* and Pat Hutchins's *Good Night Owl.* You might like this book about an owl by Mr. Lobel. It's called *Owl at Home."* I read the table of contents or perhaps a few lines from parts of the book to entice readers. Then I offer the book to the class. Frequently, invitations to read particular books are embedded in literature time, and as a mini-lesson I only remind the children of those titles.

Some mini-lessons present strategies for reading. For example, on the chalkboard I write, "We went to the . . ." Then I cover the next word and write, "to get a book." We read the sentence together and I ask the children to suggest words that could make sense in this sentence. They list "shelf," "store," "library," "desk," "school," "house," "bookstore," "table." I uncover the first letter of the hidden word to reveal the letter S. We eliminate some possibilities. I show the last letter, or perhaps the second, and we quickly arrive at the covered word. I recap the process of using context and letter/sound clues to figure out unknown words. With other mini-lessons I might present a reminder of a particular skill addressed earlier in the day, during writing workshop, for example. Sometimes, I suggest to the children that if they notice words with a particular phonetic element (a blend, a vowel pattern, a punctuation mark) that they point them out to me when I stop to confer.

At first I planned for reading workshop to end with a formal sharing time, just as writing workshop does. Then I noticed that children shared their ideas and recommendations for books in very natural ways both during the workshop, in literature time, and throughout the school day. Incorporating a sharing time in the workshop seemed redundant, a stilted repetition of what was occurring naturally. Eliminating a daily formal sharing also provided a bit more reading time. Occasionally we close with a *brief* sharing. Like writing workshop, the reading workshop is based on a predictable structure, one that works for *us,* but is always open to revision because the structure flows with the needs of the community.

Unlike the SSR times in my former classrooms, the low hum of children's voices reading to themselves or with a partner pervades the room. Children want to hear the words they read; silent reading is an advanced skill for far more experienced readers than most six-year-olds. Later in the year, many of the children will read silently, shaping the meaning in their minds from the words they see on the page, but at the year's end the majority of children read by whispering softly to themselves. Moving away from the silence of SSR was only one of the many traditions surrounding reading instruction that I left behind.

Choice in Reading Workshop

Children select books for reading workshop from the dozens displayed around the room. On the first day of school the selection processes are as varied as the readers' personalities. Jared picks a book about a cat and returns to his seat. He flops his arms over the book and watches the other children. A few seconds later he opens the book, quickly shuffles through the pages, then closes the cover and heads to exchange this book for another. Lucas and Brian sprint for *The Very Hungry Caterpillar*. Brian wins and shouts, "Look, I got the one you read." Amy walks around the room, picks up a couple of books, then returns them before she finally settles on *The Napping House*. She slowly moves back to her seat, opening the book and smiling at the contents as she walks. Danny walks directly to a dinosaur book, grins, and says, "I know which one *I* want." Melinda sits shyly at her seat until I take her hand and lead her to the counter and make suggestions. Ryan picks up a poetry anthology and says, "I got a *big* book. See how thick it is?" Jason asks, "Where's that book about the billy goats—the one you read us?" Jenny stacks six books in her arms, until I remind her that one is enough. "Ohhh," she protests, "I want to read them all." Jessica stands with a finger pressed against her chin as she ponders her choice between two books. Finally she says, "This one," and picks up a richly illustrated fairy tale.

Children select books with varying degrees of thoughtfulness and for a range of reasons. Watching first graders select books provides clues about the children's experiences with books and also with making decisions. Some parents naturally incorporate decision making into children's early experiences. One mother I know turned to her eighteen-month-old daughter and asked, "Jamie, do you want the yellow or the red cup for your milk?" She waited the few seconds while her daughter decided, then went on with meal preparations. The process took a bit longer than if the mother had made the decision for her daughter, but the extra moments help Jamie learn to make choices for herself. Learning to make decisions is an important part of this classroom. Children will be selecting their own reading material all year, and from the beginning of school I work with them as they learn to make these choices.

Jackie can choose a book with ease. Her mother read to her before she left the hospital at birth and Jackie is familiar with lots of titles. She selects books for her family's read-aloud sessions each evening. She already knows how to read the pictures for a sense of story, understands the role of print in conveying the story, and grasps details of format such as the left-to-right, top-to-bottom flow of print on the page. She needs little assistance from me in selecting books other than to guide her to choices she has not yet found. Jenny also has experiences with books but she wants to quickly read them all. Part of this is her personality, for I've noticed that she wants to be first, to hurry through any task, and to claim success if she has done "a lot." I'll respond to Jenny by asking her to choose one and set the others aside for later. "Good readers take their time," I'll say. "I want you to look through this book very carefully and, if you finish before our time's done, go back through it again and look for things you missed the first time."

Jared has few experiences with books and he opens the book he picks from the back cover. Within thirty seconds he announces, "I'm done," and gets up for another book. To help Jared with his random selection process, I direct his choices by selecting two or three titles and then saying, "Choose one of these." When he has difficulty deciding, I hand him one title saying, "Try this one. It's a favorite of mine. I think you might like it too." In the next few days I'll do some brief mini-lessons on how to choose books suggesting that the children select books that appeal to their individual interests, look interesting and possible to read, either through pictures or text. In addition, I'll observe the children and help them individually.

As children begin learning to read entire books, they sometimes have difficulty choosing books they can manage. I address this minor hurdle by recommending specific books to children. "Try this one. Let me know how it goes," I say. Sometimes a child comes back a few minutes later and says, "This book's too hard," and then we look for another together. Other times the youngster plunges in and later reports, as Stacy did, "You know that book you gave me? Well, it's a really good book. I can read it!"

A few children believe that they must always read challenging books, as one little boy announces while searching the room for such a book for himself. "It's all right to read some hard books and some easy ones too," I say. "Every good reader does that. Good readers choose different books at different times. At night in bed I like to read easier books." I suggest that the way to make this decision is to read a little of the book to get an idea of how hard it is. I make a comparison to the three bears: "Some books are easy. Some books are hard. And some books are just right. You have to decide which one you want and remember to mix them up. It probably wouldn't be a good idea to read all hard books or all easy books." The children catch on quickly. One day Julie says, "I can read this book, even though it's a pretty hard book, because you read it to us. When I finish I'll choose something easier to give my mind a rest."

Experienced readers develop a repertoire of strategies for choosing books, and individual readers employ these strategies with varying degrees of emphasis. In an activity similar to one from my Giacobbe/Atwell workshop, I've asked teachers in workshops to brainstorm the ways they select books to read. Remarkable similarity emerges in the lists from a dozen or more groups of teachers. Here's a composite of those lists:

- recommendations by others, especially someone whose tastes are similar to yours or who you respect as a reader
- personal knowledge: subject matter that connects with your life or interests in some way
- subject matter that appeals to personal tastes
- need for particular information
- time: time available for reading influences length and kind of book chosen
- author: one you like or have heard of
- easy reading: there are times when a reader wants "escape" with a book
- book talk or hearing a book read aloud on radio, etc.
- newspaper and magazine reviews
- television interviews and reviews
- books that have been movies or television shows
- best-seller lists or "everyone's reading this book"
- appealing cover
- something different: subject matter or genre that breaks an individual's reading pattern
- size: thick or thin
- inside appearance: size of type, amount of white space, illustrations, texture of paper, layout of text and illustrations, etc.
- the first paragraph or the last—many readers report nearly always reading either or both before they make a final selection
- blurbs, summaries, and recommendations on the book jacket
- well-worn cover (indicates lots of readers)
- pictures or illustrations (how many, attractiveness, etc.)
- books from a series or a collection
- catchy title
- cost: maybe wait for the paperback if hardcover is too expensive
- amount of time available for reading: more reading time in the summer allows for longer books

This list demonstrates ways real readers choose books. The real readers in my first-grade classroom compiled a similar list in a group brainstorming session in the spring.

How to Choose a Book

1. Ask another person "What book have you read?"
2. Look in the book to see if it's a book I like—the pictures, the title—or to see if it's too hard or sometimes too easy.

3. I read the first page and if I get stuck on too many words it's too hard. It's like a test. If it's too many easy words, like *Arthur's Nose*, put it back and get *Ghost's House*, *Spook's Hour* and it's in between.

4. I ask the librarian for really good books that I know or sometimes I ask for good books.

5. I like books by certain authors—like Jane Yolen.

6. Read a little and see if it's interesting.

7. Look for books I've listened to.

8. Ask somebody what a book is like—what they think of it.

9. I look for books with big words (big print), like *Mortimer*.

10. Look around the room for books that look really interesting to me.

11. I look at the cover, the title, and the pages to see if it looks good.

12. Sometimes you change your mind later after you put it back and get it.

13. If the cover and title sound neat I try it and if I don't like it I put it back.

14. Pick books by authors I like or books I think are funny.

15. Everyone likes different books to read. They have to be interested in it.

Not every child used all these selection strategies; a strategy that was significant to one child was less important to another. But the same was true for adults. Readers choose books through a range of strategies, and validating individual strategies is important.

Choosing to abandon a book is just as important as choosing to read it. With so many good books available, I want children spending their reading time with a book they find satisfying. From the beginning, I teach them to set aside books that they don't like or that are too difficult or that they just can't get into; they can always come back to a book later.

I make basal readers from the district's adopted reading program available as choices for the children's reading. The children quickly dismiss the preprimers. One little boy summed up the reason one day: "Who would read this book? I mean, I don't get it. It just keeps saying the same words over and over. It doesn't make any *sense*." However, the "first readers" intrigue the children for a time because they are "thick books." Children choose these books because when reading them they perceive themselves as truly accomplished readers. After a time, as one by one the children discover that these books contain only a few stories that match their individual interests, the enthusiasm for these "thick books" wanes. One day two children decided to read a particular story together. One picked up the paperback version and, not finding a second copy, the other located the same title in the basal reader. It wasn't long before they realized that they read different texts! The children were outraged. "How could someone do that to an author's story!" they demanded. "You can't change what an author writes. It's his *writing!* Only the author can change it."

"How did you choose this book?" is a question I ask over and over again of young readers. In the beginning, they often respond with "I don't know. I just picked it." I nod without comment or sometimes say, "Umm. That's something you might want to notice next time—how you choose your book." When children have heard the question over and over they begin answering.

"It looked kinda good when I saw the pictures so then I tried it and I thought I'd like to read it."

"Melanie told me it was a good book and so I thinked I'd like it too."

"I really like James Marshall books so I figured I'd like this one."

"I tried out the words, I read a little bit, and I thought I could learn to read it."

" 'Cause it's funny. I like funny books.

"I have a cat so I just wanted to read a book about a cat."

The school librarian reported that the children use their knowledge of books to choose their library books. "They ask for specific titles or authors. These kids know what they want," she said. Readers who have learned to make choices take responsibility for those choices and actively seek out the books they want to read.

Children make other choices surrounding their reading. Selecting their own reading material helps them develop a range of purposes for reading, and they move among these purposes as they read, making choices appropriate to the material and their interests. And this heightened self-awareness is evident in the comments they make when I ask how or why they chose particular reading materials.

Melinda and Elizabeth read a book over and over. "We're practicing this book so that we can read it to the class with lots of expression—so people will want to listen," they say.

"I been reading this book of riddles and I'm just skipping around 'cuz that way I find the funniest ones. I don't read it one right after the other. That got boring to me," Jeff comments.

Michael, Matt, and Greg pour over a thick volume on the *Titanic,* seeking out the most interesting pictures. "Look, it's a clock. Oh, it the same one as here, in this picture, before it sunk." They read the caption under both pictures and confirm their observation. It takes all three of them to figure out the words in this one-sentence caption. When I ask what this book is about, they flip to the cover and read the title. Title, pictures, and captions serve their meaning-making needs. The text is far too difficult for them at this time and they pay it no heed.

"I'm trying to read *Charlotte's Web* because I love this book and I been wanting to read it for a long time. There's some words I don't know, but I can still read most of it," says Lori.

Jody browses through a book about trains, a passion of his. He chooses a section about old locomotives and begins to read. He painstakingly reads the first sentence, then shifts to the labels on the drawing of an old train. "I'm reading the parts of old trains. It's like when I been on the Strasburg Railroad and I remember some of them parts and some I don't."

Kelly spends the entire workshop engrossed in her book. "This book's so good I was just reading and reading to find out what was going to happen to the girl. I didn't even hear you say reading time was over," says an amazed Kelly.

Jason and Edward read poems from their poetry folders. Jason comments, "Me and him are reading poems in our poetry folders because we both like poems. We know how to read all of these," Jason points to one stack, "and these are a little hard, and these we don't know [about] yet. We didn't try them."

Reading strategies are connected to purposes. Readers read difficult books because these are books they are longing to read for themselves. They read rapidly and they read slowly according their interest, experience/ skill level, and the pace of a particular story. They reread favorite books, read parts of books, or practice reading texts because these strategies connect with the needs they feel or the meaning they desire.

Underlying all of the purposes for reading is meaning that connects to the reader's experiences, interests, and needs. The meaning-making purposes of reading influence the strategies readers use as they tackle unknown words.

Elizabeth says, "I skipped that word because it was too hard and I just keep reading and then I figured out what it was."

Stacy and Emily come upon the name Mr. Vinegar in a story they read together. "What's his name?" they ask me when I stop to confer with them. After I tell them, Stacy says, "Oh, because we didn't know so we just said 'Mr. Whatever.' "

Greg carries his book up to the chalkboard and gazes up at the list of vowel digraphs we've compiled over the course of several short whole group presentations. "Hmm," he says, "a-i says A." He looks back to his book, hunts for a word with his finger, and then puts the digraph sound between an M and an N, reads the surrounding words, and then suddenly says, "main! That's it, main." He heads back to his seat, reading as he walks.

Amy covers up the first four letters of "whenever" and then says to herself, "Ev . . . ever. Whenever."

Max comes to me, leading a small group of youngsters. "Mrs. Avery, we need to ask you this word. We can't figure it out and we asked lots of people, even Monica." I tell them the word and Max says, "Ohhh. We thought of a couple words it could be but those didn't make sense." The small group and I chat a moment about why the familiar strategies didn't work in this particular case and I comment, "That's the way it is. This language of ours just doesn't always work the way it seems it ought to. You learn one rule and then right away there's an exception to that rule. You just have to remember that the rules don't always work and keep trying out different ways."

"Yup," grins Max. "Thanks," he says, and the group goes back to their reading. I muse over his words ". . . and we even asked Monica." No one ever proclaimed Monica to be the best reader in the room, as the consensus of this band of children seemed to imply. But the children knew each other's strengths and where to turn for the help. From the beginning I had urged them to try to solve their difficulties and answer their questions on their own and to use me as the last resource. These children knew how to make decisions to help themselves because they worked in an environment where they continually made choices and learned from both error and success without penalty or extrinsic reward.

Initially, children look to me to provide the answers for the dilemmas they encounter, whether it be choosing books or knowing how to begin reading those books or learning individual words. I supply solutions to those problems, for this is certainly not a guessing-game environment. However, I provide those solutions in the form of tips, suggestions, or invitations by demonstrating possible methods to solve particular dilemmas. As I work with individuals, I show children how to apply those methods as they read. I want to avoid presuming that a particular solution is appropriate for any individual. Children become skillful readers when presented with many strategies and then with opportunities to choose those that are most effective for them at a given moment.

Children's author Katherine Paterson (1990) wrote, "I believe in freedom of choice as much as anyone. But the young don't know the rich variety of choices that are available. Someone they trust must be wise and bold enough to hand them something they would never have known to choose" (p. 150).

During the early days of reading workshop, I felt uncomfortable letting children make their own choices; I was accustomed to seeing the needs of one as being the needs of all. Programmed instruction had lulled me into believing that success depended on every student reading every story and learning every skill in specified sequence. Really letting go of that was one of the hardest things I had to do! At first I required that in addition to their own choice of reading materials the children read the stories from the basal program. I was caught by my own conceptions of how learning to read had to be: quiet, orderly, with everyone on task as I defined that task and as I could witness that behavior. When I let go of that notion and let children make choices about what they read and how they read, the world of real reading opened up in my classroom.

Responding to Readers

Responses to Get Readers Started

The heart of the reading workshop is reading. As the children read I move among them, stooping beside individual children and responding to their reading. "Tell me what this book is about," I say. Most children can make some opening statement, and the rest of our conference develops from there. Like writing conferences, my role in these brief reading conferences is to listen and respond by asking questions that lead the child into expressing her ideas and also to share my own knowledge, as appropriate, to suggest new ideas for a child to consider. If a child seems confused with my opening comment, I guide that child into examining the illustrations with me and we chat together about what we see. "Read to me," I might say to a more experienced child, and the child reads a few words. If she stumbles on a word, I suggest an appropriate strategy or simply supply the word, depending on my knowledge of the child's reading development and the context of that particular moment. There are no hard and fast rules; I listen and respond to nurture the reader. I "read" the child and the situation, using my intuition and my professional knowledge gleaned from prior experiences with children and reading and learning.

These conversations took place in a September reading workshop.

"What's this book about?" I ask of a child with Bill Martin, Jr.'s *Polar Bear, Polar Bear, What Do You Hear?*

"A bear."

"Ah, do you know which one of these words might be 'bear'?" I ask running my finger under the first line of the title. The child pauses to look closely at the words, then points to "bear."

"You're right. That says 'bear.' How did you know that?"

"It has a B."

"Sure does. 'Bear' begins with B. This bear is white. What do we call those white bears, the ones that live at the North Pole?" The child looks puzzled, but the question is addressed to anyone within earshot.

"Polar bears," comes the answer from somewhere in the room.

"That's it. Polar bears," and I turn back to the book and the child I still crouch beside and ask her if she might find that word 'polar' on the cover. She looks and then points to the word. "How'd you know that?" I tease.

She giggles as she says, "I just knew it. It begins with P."

"Yes it does. Read with me." We point to the words as we read together, " 'Polar bear, polar bear.' Look at that! You read it all! Go on and look at the pictures and read some more." My goal has been to suggest to the child a strategy and urge her to apply the same strategy to the next pages on her own. The repetitious language of this particular book will help a beginning reader. Many books will not provide this support, but the strategy of using the pictures and then connecting with words and initial sounds can work for most texts.

Word-by-word accuracy does not concern me at this time. Nor am I concerned with presenting reading strategies in a specific sequence. The central focus now and throughout the year is deriving meaning from the illustrations and print on the page. In these brief conferences I demonstrate many strategies, which are interwoven in the process of shaping meaning. I urge the child to try these strategies independently of me, trusting the child's capacity to select those strategies that are most helpful for him at a particular time. I must encourage the child to risk, to plunge in and try, and so I try to maintain a playful tone and communicate my confidence in the child's ability to figure things out himself. Of course, to maintain credibility with learners, I've got to accept—indeed delight—in the results whatever they may be. Initial efforts won't produce perfection. I believe that children develop language usage, whether it be spoken or written language, by approximating the correct form of language in the beginning and then refining that language through usage. *Responding*, part of the craft of teaching, means: "reading" the child in a particular context, enriching the context in a playful way, and gently inviting the child to explore new possibilities.

When I stop at another desk a child reads hesitantly. "Read with me," I say. Then I point and the child points and we read together. At times my voice drops out and the child takes over. When the child pauses I pause. The child looks at me when he's stuck. "How could we figure this out?" I ask. He shrugs his shoulders and looks to me for an answer. "Let's read the rest of the sentence." So together we go on. "Now go back to the beginning and let's think what will make sense." We read from the beginning to the problem word, I pause for the blank, then read the rest of the sentence. "What makes sense there?" I say as I point to the word again and begin forming the initial sound.

"Ball!" His eyes brighten.

"Right! Let's read the sentence again." We start from the beginning and read the entire sentence with the newly discovered word.

I stop beside another child, who reads an entire sentence to me. "I'm impressed!" I say, "You read that all yourself. How did you do that?"

"I don't know," comes the answer with a shrug and a grin.

"*That's* something to think about. How *did* you do that?" Children will give me the "I don't know" answer at first, but I keep asking the question. By leaving it unanswered, leaving it with the child and knowing that the child will internalize the question, one day when I ask they'll say, "I don't know" and then proceed to supply an answer. Soon they'll have a ready answer when I ask such a question, and eventually they'll say, "And you want to know how I did it?" and continue to explain to me. Becoming aware of the process and then putting it into words serves to further enhance learning.

At Jared's desk I help him read the pictures. "What's happening in this story?"

"I don't know."

"Well, what's happening in this picture?" I ask in mock amazement, implying that he knows. Jared tells me about the illustration. Then I move to the next picture. "And this one?" More explanation from Jared. "Ah, so here the bear was . . . and here he . . . You can read these pictures. And you told me you didn't know how to read," I tease. Jared beams. "You can do this yourself, I bet. You don't need me to read this book and figure out what happens." Jared smiles.

And so I move around through the room, stopping and lending expertise, sharing a strategy, encouraging, helping children discover the power they have to think for themselves by working *with* them and then leaving them to explore on their own. It works. To support and encourage young learners takes time and patience and a playful tone. I keep reminding myself: Let's not take ourselves too seriously here. Everyone will learn to read in good time. I'm here to help, but I trust these children to do this without becoming dependent on me or waiting for me to show them the next step.

I spend only a half to a full minute with each child and move on, thus keeping responses focussed and short. Overloading the reader could quickly occur because I can see so many things I could teach at any particular moment. If I stay only a short time I'm not tempted to address all these things, and I also prevent the child from depending on me for all the answers. Actually, I'm rarely giving children answers but rather helping them find answers for themselves; the children quickly pick up this model and use it with each other. Later, when Sara asks if she can teach Ericka to read a particular book, I'll remind them that good teachers don't tell people the answers, they help them figure out the answers for themselves. I overhear Sara say, "Okay, now skip that word and read the rest. Now come back and read it all and figure it out." Or Justin, "Here, just cover up the end. Now what word is it?"

"Smile?"

"Okay. Now put the 'ed' on it. What's it say?"

"Oh, 'smiled.' I get it."

I frequently use a hand-held tape recorder during these conferences (and play the tapes back as I drive home in the afternoon) to capture the patterns of our reading conferences. The conferences start with the child reading or talking about what he's read. Then I ask questions such as:

What do you think about that?

What's that remind you of?

How does this make you feel?

What do you suppose will happen?

Why do you think that happened?

Why do you think [this character] did that?

Did you ever know anybody like that?

Sometimes I make comments to demonstrate responses, such as:

Listen to those words again!

I like the sound of . . .

I like the way the author says . . .

You won't believe this next page . . .

Uh-oh! Guess what?

I don't know about this . . . What do you think?

These questions and comments are similar to those I make when I'm reading aloud to children, and they always come after *listening* to the child. I want the child to be keenly aware of the meaning she understands as she reads, and I hope that my responses help the child work independently, take risks, and develop her own strategies to get at that meaning. Sometimes in a reading conference I demonstrate one possible strategy to keep the child in touch with meaning. Many other demonstrations will follow. I keep these demonstrations short and move on. It's like a parent showing a child how to stack blocks, asking the child, "What will *you* build?" and then leaving the child to experiment on his own for a while.

Responses to Nurture Readers

Roving among readers during the workshop becomes standard procedure. The pace and tone is similar to that of writing workshop, and the children soon know that I will be there to help them if they are stuck or to listen to their ideas about what they read. These interactions between the children and me from one February day are typical.

Jeff is reading *Ben's Trumpet.*

J: I was stuck with this word "stoop" but then I thought of "soon" and it has the double O in the middle like you showed us, so then I thought it's "stoop"!

MRS. A: Ah, so you got this word on your own by thinking of "soon."

J: Yeah, I could've looked up there—you know, at those double O's on the wall, but I just thought of "soon" first.

MRS. A: Good thinking. What do you think of this book?

J: It's got a good beginning. I gotta read more before I can really say.

MRS. A: Okay. Thank you.

Aaron is reading *Building a House.*

A: [reads smoothly then stops when he comes to "cement."] I like this book because it's about building a house and I think it would be neat to do that—build a house.

MRS. A: You'd like to build a house?

A: Yeah.

MRS. A: Read to me a bit. [He backs up and rereads what he has just read, stopping before he comes to "cement."] Go on. I'll read with you. [We reread the last sentence together. Then comes "cement."] Tough word. But look at the picture. And let me give you a clue. The C in this word makes the S sound, not the C like in "cat."

A: [He looks at the illustration. I begin uttering the S sound. He looks at the word, at my face, at the picture, at the word, and I hear him barely utter the "ent" from the end of the word.] Cement! Right? [I nod.] Cement. I just figured it out because that makes sense.

MRS. A: Good going.

Darren is reading *The Very Hungry Caterpillar.*

D: . . . comed a teeny and very hungry caterpillar. [He stops reading to look at me.] I'm reading *The Hungry Caterpillar.*

MRS. A: Good for you. What do you like about this book? [I ignore the fact that his reading is not perfect.]

D: Um, um, I like he eated all them things. [He reads on and is stumped by "though." I supply the word. He continues reading but reads "pears" for "plums." Before he turns the page, I step in.]

MRS. A: Look at that word, Darren. It begins with P like "pear," but is this a picture of pears?

D: Um, I don't know. I mean yes, I mean no. I mean they're not pears. I don't think they're pears.

MRS. A: Right, these are not pears. These are plums.

D: Oh. I didn't know that.

MRS. A: That's okay. Let's read again. [We return to the sentence and, pointing to the words, reread and make the correction.] Good for you. The pictures will help you sometimes, so remember to look at them.

D: Yeah, 'cuz anyway I like the pictures.

MRS. A: Unhuh! Have fun.

Jody is reading "The Karate Test," authored by a classmate. He reads "wait" for "watch" but corrects himself after reading a couple of words further. He reads "knew" for "know," but the text still makes sense and sounds correct to the ear, so Jody takes no heed of the slight error. He reads "but" for "because" but quickly goes back to successfully correct the word.

MRS. A: How did you do that?

J: Well, "but" didn't make sense, so I looked and I thought "be-make" but that's not a word [he laughs] so I knew what the C was so I said "because."

MRS. A: Oh yeah? Interesting.

J: Yeah, because I put the two letters at the beginning together and usually I can figure them out.

MRS. A: What if it doesn't make sense?

J: Then I try again.

MRS. A: Sounds good. Tell me about this book.

J: Well, Jeff wrote it and I thinked I wanted to read his book. He does karate and it'd be neat to do karate. I might ask my dad if I can do karate but he might not because I don't think he ever done it, done karate.

MRS. A: So you chose this because Jeff wrote it and because you'd like to do karate too.

J: Yeah. When I read it to Jeff, I'll take it home and read it to my dad.

MRS. A: Okay. Thanks, Jody.

Josie is reading Susan Jeffers's illustrated version of the Robert Frost poem, *Stopping by a Woods on a Snowy Evening*.

MRS. A: Oh, you're reading *Stopping by a Woods*.

J: Umhum. It's very quiet. It's a quiet book. Just sounds like you should read it softly. I like the pictures in the book—like snow's falling down everywhere. [She shows me the last illustration in the book.]

MRS. A: Ahh, yes. Nice. Quiet.

J: One thing about this book. He's the only thing that's colorful.

MRS. A: Ah. I hadn't noticed. Why do you suppose the artist did that?

J: Maybe because it was snowing so much and if she made the man colorful you would see the man because he's the one who's talking.

MRS. A: Oh, so the artist wanted you to look at the man because he's the one whose telling this story.

J: Yes.

MRS. A: Thank you, Josie. When I read this book again myself, I'll think about what you said.

J: Mrs. Avery?

MRS. A: Yes?

J: You know that chapter book I was reading, the one you gave me?

MRS. A: Yes?

J: Well, I put it on your desk. It was okay, but it was kind of boring and a little bit hard, so I decided to put it back.

MRS. A: I'm glad you did. I think you're enjoying this book much more.

J: Unhuh.

Like we did during reading conferences in the first week of school, the children are placing their focus on making meaning from the illustrations and from those mysterious marks on the page known as words. I respond to each child to help them with that process and keep them focussed on meaning as it pertains to that child personally. In order to respond to children as learners and to teach with a responsive teaching style I must *wait* and *listen,* then think and reply. Learning this teaching style took time, self-discipline, and some self-reprimanding. Every time I came to the conference with preconceived notions of what I ought to teach, I missed the learner. When I listened to the tape of Josie's comments about the Jeffers/Frost book, I heard a metaphor for listening—and subsequently responding. To respond I must be quiet and "read softly." I think of Josie's words: ". . . it was snowing so much and if she made the man colorful you would see the man because he's the one who's talking." He's the one whose talking—the one who's talking. Josie's words echo in my mind and I know that to connect with learners, to be a good teacher, I must listen to the one who's talking—the child.

Peer Responses

Children become natural teachers for their classmates and they often choose to read books together during free-play time in the morning.

Sometimes they read in partners during the reading workshop. Once again, there's no prescription for this reading together. Some groups of children naturally pair off or work by themselves, managing these decisions with ease and constructively carrying out the format they choose. Other classes have difficulty. In these circumstances I step in and build the structure for them by assigning partners or deciding which days they may read with partners. Once the pairing is accomplished, every group of children has easily developed procedures for reading with a peer without my direction. Sometimes a pair of children alternate pages as they read, with one reading aloud while the other follows along; then they reverse roles. Sometimes they read softly together. Still other times the stronger reader reads a book while another follows along, or one child reads a sentence or two and then the partner repeats, echo fashion. And sometimes one reader works on learning to read a book with instruction from a child who has already learned to read this particular book. Though the reading is central, a significant bonus of partner reading is the talk that develops between the pair as they discuss the meaning of what they read. The children become responders to each other's reading process.

During reading workshop one day in early March, children read with partners and I move among them, stopping to listen a moment and to be generally available to lend assistance.

Greg and Matt sit at Matt's desk with Marc Brown's *Arthur's Valentine*. Greg reads and Matt supplies words occasionally. I quickly realize that Matt knows how to read this book and is teaching Greg. When they stumble on a word, their eyes go to the pictures where they find a clue, figure out the word, and continue. They turn the page and look through the illustration before reading the words. Greg reads "2B or not 2B" carved on a door. "Hmm," he says, "That makes no sense."

"Yeah, that's what I thought when I read it too—makes no sense. So I just skipped it, 'cuz I didn't really need it—for the story you know." Greg nods and they continue reading. I move on. I've heard them read, noting strategies they were using. They acknowledge my presence with smiles and keep reading.

Amy and Max read Robert Munsch's *Mortimer* by alternating pages. "We're practicing. Tomorrow can we read it to the class?" Amy asks.

"Maybe," I reply. "Any problems?"

"No," says Max. I notice that Max mouths the words silently as Amy reads. When Max reads, Amy's eyes follow the words.

Laura and Kelly read *The Three Billy Goats Gruff* curled up under the art table. The repetitious language helps Laura and she reads these lines fluently, pointing to each word. The remainder of the text is more challenging and Kelly suggests she skip one word and read the next one. Laura does this but is still stuck, so Kelly supplies the word. "I just got this book today," Laura says, "and I'm just starting to learn it. I know some parts already!"

Monica and Natalie sit leaning against a wall. A stack of books—all with short texts—rests on the floor beside them. "We read *five* books!" says Natalie. "I read the pictures and Monica taught me some words too. It's easy when you're with someone you like."

Partner reading occurs in two or three reading workshops a week. Most groups of children would love to read with partners every day, but I found that the atmosphere in the classroom on some days is not conducive to partner reading. Also, readers benefit from workshops when they read alone and rely on their own resources.

Responses to Oral Reading

Another way I respond to readers is through listening to individual children read books to me that they have practiced to a smooth, expressive fluency. This reading parallels publishing in writing workshop; the reader polishes a piece for an audience. When a child satisfactorily reads a book to me or another adult, the child takes the book home overnight to share with her family. A few days into September I notice that Jackie reads *The Napping House* with no errors. "Can you read all of this book?" I ask in amazement. Jackie nods and beams. "Well, practice by reading it over a few times so that you can read it smoothly like I did when I read it to the class. Then I'd like to listen to you read it to me," I say. A couple days later Jackie tells me that she can read this book "really good" now. "Okay," I say. She sits beside me and reads and I take notes of any miscues and comments she makes (see Chapter 20). When she finishes the reading I ask, "How did you learn to read this?" (I ask this question of all readers when they share a book they've learned to read.)

"I don't know. The cat part was hard. By sounding out," she answers.

"Oh, the cat part was hard and you sounded out. Did you doing anything else?" Jackie shakes her head.

"Umm, that's something for you to think about next time—how you figured out the hard parts." I ask her another question: "What ideas came to you when you read this book?"

"Sleeping. At nighttime I don't want to go to bed and morning I don't want to get up."

"Oh, so you thought about how it is when you go to bed and when you get up," I acknowledge. Jackie nods and we both smile. I tuck a letter to Jackie's parents in the book and hand the book to Jackie to put in her bookbag. The photocopied letter reads:

Dear Parents,

Today your child is bringing a book home to share with you. I hope you will enjoy listening to your child read and that you will talk about the book together. Before you return this book to school please take a moment to write any comments or questions you have. I welcome your perceptions of your child's learning process.

Have fun!!

Sincerely,

I'll send a copy of this letter home with every book throughout the year. Some parents answer, some never do. Whatever parents choose is acceptable. In Jackie's case a reply comes back with the book the next day. Jackie's mom has written:

Carol,

I enjoyed listening to Jackie read *The Napping House*. Jackie liked when the bed breaks while I enjoyed the cat being scared. We talked about the last illustration and agreed the rainbow and playhouse were interesting.

Jackie is excited about first grade and likes (loves?) Mrs. Avery.

Fondly,

Pam

Before the day is out, I answer Pam's letter and send the reply home with Jackie. I photocopy the reply, staple it to Pam's note, and file the stapled letters in the folder where I document Jackie's reading process. Parents are responders to their children's reading and the letters help bridge the chasm that can so easily exist between home and school.

Taking books home provides the children with an extra incentive, though the intrinsic rewards of learning to read provide sufficient motivation. Some children want to take a book home as soon as they've read it once or even without reading it to me. Carrie comes to me as soon as she sees Jackie taking a book home and asks if she can read her book and take it home too. She begins to read, but the reading is halting and full of miscues and errors. I suggest that she practice a day or two as Jackie did. She scowls her disappointment but then brightens and says, "Okay." Two days later Carrie reads her book without errors and with great animation. I can't listen to every book every child learns to read, but I try to get to everyone at least once every ten days or so.

Through our school volunteer program, two adults come in each week for thirty to forty-five minutes and help out by listening to children read before books go home. One is a retired grandmother of one of my students. In her professional life she was both a high school English teacher and a first-grade teacher. The other, the mother of one of my former students and a former preschool teacher, understands the process of our classroom. I had shown each of these women how to keep records as the children read and both proved to be natural responders who nurtured the children's reading processes. Their contribution gave me time to do more conferring during the reading workshop and permitted the children more one-on-one time to read an entire book with an adult.

Small-Group Sharing

As children become more accomplished readers, they no longer need to read aloud to me as they do in the beginning of the year. For more fluent readers I set up small literature discussion groups, where three or four children come together to discuss a book they have all read or to share different books. I remind students not to retell the plot. If someone has read the book, a retelling is boring; if someone doesn't know the story, hearing the entire plot will spoil the reading. The children understand these procedures from literature time and apply them when talking about books in small groups. The following conversations come from two groups of children, three girls and then three boys, as they discuss Jane Yolen's *Owl Moon*. (Normally, groups are mixed. These single-sex groupings were simply coincidental, but interesting.) The first discussion involves Monica, Elizabeth, and Amy.

MRS. A: Tell me what you thought about *Owl Moon*.

M: *Owl Moon* is a good book. It makes me think if I lived on a farm and my father took me owling.

MRS. A: I've never been owling. [All the girls: "No, me neither."] In fact, I've never heard of going owling before I read this book.

E: Yeah, we never go out in the forest.

MRS. A: Is the child in this book a boy or a girl?

M: Girl.

A: Girl.

MRS. A: Why do you think it's a girl?

M: It sounds like a girl in the beginning of the book. It just looks like a girl.

E: Yeah, she wears red.

A: Yeah, 'cause boys don't usually wear red when they're little.

MRS. A: What was your favorite part of the book?

A: The owl. [They flip to the page of the owl.]

MRS. A: You all like this page? Why do you like this?

E: It looks so real. It looks like the owl's just sitting there.

A: For a minute?

M: Minutes. Because it's like a hundred minutes. [At this point the girls go to the book and discover it's three minutes.]

M: I like the part when they go owling. They go "whoo ooo." [The girls start making owl sounds quietly.] It almost sounds exactly like an owl is doing that and it sounds good. It feels good to me . . .

MRS. A: I was wondering about the ending. [I read the last page aloud.] What does that mean to you. Amy?

A: Well, it tells you a little more about the story.

E: Yeah, just needing hope.

M: You need hope—I needed hope in math. And all of us need hope.

MRS. A: You needed hope in math and all of us need hope in something.

M: Because you have to have hope. When I read it, it's like I'm an owl gliding a path in silver owl moon and I feel good.

E: This book made me feel sorta relaxing.

MRS. A: Sorta relaxing.

E: Yeah.

M: It kinda tells you about how to go owling. Like, kinda like the volcano story that you're reading. The story gives information. The story tells you how to *call* an owl, like you don't need words and all you need is warmth.

This second discussion involves Brian, Cory, and Greg. Jeff joins the discussion toward the end.

MRS. A: Tell me what you think about *Owl Moon*.

B: I think it'd be neat to go owling because then you might be able to capture one. You couldn't really keep it for a pet. I wouldn't want to have him for a pet 'cause it just would wreck up the whole house. You don't know what it could do.

C: The owl could bite!

MRS. A: The owl could bite?

B: Yes! It could hurt you.

MRS. A: What did you think about this book, Cory?

C: I like the part with the boy and the man and they're standing there looking and they hear an owl. [Cory begins making whoo-whoo sounds. The other boys join in.]

MRS. A: What do you think, Greg?

G: Well, my favorite part is when they get to see the owl flapping its wings.

MRS. A: Tell me about that.

G: Well, I'd like to see an owl flap its wings, but I wouldn't like to take it as a pet because it could fly around the house and break glass and stuff like that. But I would like to see it in the woods. [More owl sounds from Cory and Brian.]

B: I like that part too.

MRS. A: Why do you like that part, Brian?

B: Because it's real neat.

C: It's real neat because I like how the owl's claws and its wings are colored. I'd like to see his face. [Cory has opened the book to the page that illustrates the back of the owl and the father and child shining a flashlight on it. The boys all talk at the same time as they examine the illustration.]

MRS. A: Is this a boy or a girl?

C: A boy.

B: It's a boy.

G: A boy.

MRS. A: What makes you think it's a boy?

C: Because it looks like a girl. It *looks* like a girl, but it's *not* a girl. It has a girl hat, and a girl's skirt, and girl's boots but it's a boy!

MRS. A: It has girl things but you still think it's a boy?

B: Yes! That silver wings part is like it's talking about giving you a clue about an owl.

G: What do you think, Greg?

G: Well, I think when they say silver wings they mean the moonlight reflecting on the owl's wings.

MRS. A: I see. So you think the ending is talking about what it looks like.

B: Yes. It's sort of a fairy tale ending—a happy ending.

G: I think the ending has to do with that they *saw* an owl.

MRS. A: Oh. What do you think it means that you don't need words or warmth or anything but hope?

B: You don't need warm or stuff like that. All you need is hope that you'll see an owl! Like it says. [He points to the words in the text.]

MRS. A: Okay. Is there any other part of this book that you really like?

B: Yes. You have to go to the forest to find an owl. You just won't see an owl at night flying around the school.

MRS. A: [Jeff, who has been listening to the conversation, sits down at the table.] Jeff, what do you think about *Owl Moon?*

J: Well, it's a good book and through the book it goes whoo . . . whooo.

MRS. A: You all like that part. Why do you like that?

J: Well, it's pretty neat how they say it. I read this book to my dad a lot and he liked it a lot too.

MRS. A: Jeff, is this a boy or a girl?

J: You can't tell, but it kind of looks like a boy. I think it's probably a boy.

MRS. A: Is there anything else important about this book?

J: Yes. It's got a lot of information in a story about how you do owling. It's in a *story*.

B: You have to go owling at night because owls are nocturnal. They won't go out at day because they're asleep.

J: What are these things up here. [Jeff points to the man's cap.]

G: Well, see there's this special kind of hat—I forget what country they used it in—and there's these flaps you can put down over your ears when it's winter and you go out.

J: And you can fold them up. They're Russian.

C: Ohhh, I know what it is—just like this hat—it has bumps you can pull the whole thing down so it can cover your ears so your ears are not cold.

MRS. A: Okay boys. Thank you.

The children have learned to talk about books in conversation, focussing on ideas about characters, about incidents or information in the book, and about how the book connects to their own experiences. They address the total book—both pictures and text. In fact, they pour over the pictures, frequently noticing details that I miss. As they talk together, they stimulate further ideas and extend their thinking about books and the ideas expressed in books.

Reflections

The structure of our reading workshop develops during the first weeks of school. The basics of time, choice, and response provide the foundation but the particulars of the workshop are worked out with each group of children. Complementing the reading workshop are writing workshop and literature time. In each of these component parts of the school day, I try to make written language enjoyable, useful, important, and easy to learn. I want to demonstrate, both directly and indirectly, specific strategies to help language learners. The tone throughout the day must be one that accepts all ideas, indeed *encourages* a diversity of responses. In reading workshop the children know they will choose books and read by themselves or with a partner. They know I will confer with them as they read, provide assistance when needed, and listen to them read the books they have learned to read.

They know they will take books home. Reading workshop accommodates the diversity of interests, experiences, and learning styles of the children.

The structure I've described defines reading workshop in my classroom. In the first years I did not have the luxury of multiple copies and I found it unnecessary since literature time provided opportunity for the entire class to experience the same books. In late spring, as children became proficient readers, they began selecting the same titles and talking among themselves about these books as they read them. The children helped me envision ways to extend the workshop for other grade levels, when children begin reading longer books.

- Three to six copies of a given book could be made available and given out to children. Specific times each week could be set for the group to meet and discuss their reading—with or without the teacher. (I'd probably not restrict a reader from reading beyond any particular point in a book, but I would negotiate with the group if we wanted to discuss up to a certain point by a given time.)
- Occasionally, the whole class might read the same book with discussions along the way. The teacher would have to take care not to "basalize" the book through vocabulary lists, worksheets, follow-up activities, etc.—or with a test when they've finished!
- Perhaps, a few days could be set aside for everyone to read books related to a social studies or science theme. These themes should be kept broad and have many titles for the children to select from. It would be necessary to take some time to establish the context for these books and then look to class discussions to help children make connections between the ideas expressed in various books.

One of the main reasons for incorporating these options in later years is to ensure there are some books that everyone in the class experiences. The power generated by discussions of books that all have read enriches readers' understanding of a book, strengthens reading development, and builds classroom community. I'd still read to older students and keep individual choice reading as the mainstay of the reading workshop. The children and I together would decide on other variations to the workshop design.

The most significant learning for me from reading workshop was that no two children learn to read with the same timing and with identical strategies. No two readers appreciate the same reading material or read at the same pace. I had to confront the hard fact that the methods I formerly used to teach reading actually may have hindered readers. Like writing development, reading development required a "waiting, responsive teaching style."

CHAPTER 18

The Children Reading

I believe that all children, except those with severe brain damage or dysfunction, can learn to read. I also believe that for each child the timing of when he or she begins to read, the pace of reading development, and the strategies the child finds helpful will be unique to that child. There are no reading groups in my classroom. Without groups, I really witnessed children learning to read for the first time. Differences of age and school experiences fell away. Children—all of them—expended tremendous energy to learn to read. They worked together, learned from each other, and applied a range of strategies to get at the mysterious world of print. *The significance and timing of any particular strategy was unique for each child and no two children learned to read with identical processes.* It became obvious to me that methodologies arbitrating the sequence and timing of reading strategies hindered rather than helped children's learning. The heavy body of research and documentation on reading lends considerable insight into reading development and strategies that readers use, but in the end the process is unique for each individual.

Unlike writing, which leaves a paper trail, reading development is more difficult to document because so much of the process remains hidden within the reader. I wanted to understand not only the children's development in decoding and literal comprehension but also their development as aesthetic readers (Rosenblatt, 1978). To understand reading development I listened and observed as children worked at learning to read passages in books and in their own writing. (Reading words, lines, or passages they had composed in writing workshop contributed to reading development in a major way.) I regularly listened to children read entire books they had mastered, recording how they read: the miscues, expression, fluency, use of finger for pointing, and strategies used to figure out words. I asked questions such as: How did you figure that out? How did you learn to read this? What struggles did you work through? What did this book remind you of or make you think about as you were reading it? I recorded the children's replies. Of course, I couldn't record everything that occurred with each child, but note taking during reading workshop served two functions. First, it helped me to see the progress of individual children clearly and thus greatly aided planning for instruction as well as determining responses to help readers. Second, over time it provided documentation of the children's individual processes for learning to read.

What follows are glimpses of individual children learning to read in reading workshop in my first-grade classroom. The first three vignettes are of three rather typical first graders who began reading with ease, though not at the same time or in the same way.

Jackie

A week after school began Jackie read *The Napping House*. Her only error as she read was substituting "sleeping" for "slumbering." Before she took it home to share with her family I pointed out the difference in the structure of the two words and explained that "slumbering" was another word for "sleeping." "Oh, I never heard that word before," Jackie commented. (Children told me that it was hard to read a word if "you don't know that word." When I asked the class what they meant, they explained it was easy to read words you had *heard* before and you could usually figure out the meaning when you read "the whole thing." Children added that they usually knew words because they'd "heard the book before," referring to the reading aloud of books in the classroom.) Jackie liked the part of the story when the bed breaks "because it's funny" and she liked the rainbow on the last page. "It's neat. I like rainbows." Jackie was on her way as a reader.

She continued to learn to read entire books with little difficulty. She figured out unknown words through picture clues, the sound and rhythm of the language, letter clues, familiarity with the text (i.e., she'd heard the book read aloud), and the anticipated meaning—what made sense. She integrated this range of strategies in an efficient, mutually reinforcing manner. In a September interview she said she could "read a little" and that she learned because "every night we have story time and my mom reads to Emily and Maggie and Andy and me." In an interview at the end of the year I asked Jackie how she learned to read. She replied, "I started reading these little books my friend has, like one about a bus ride. Then I started reading harder ones and then I read them for a while and then we started having reading time every night and when I got to first grade I could read hard books." She added, "When I came to first grade I didn't really know how to write but I got the hang of it through writing because we write every day."

Over the course of the year Jackie took home more than thirty books that she had read to me or a reading workshop aide. In addition, she read nearly all the books published by her classmates and numerous trade books, which she did not read to me. Her comments during her reading of *Marianne's Grandmother* in April helped me understand the integrated nature of her reading, writing, and learning processes and the thinking process she undertook when she read. Jackie said,

> Marianne's grandmother is making the dress to see if it fits her. . . . It's kinda like the story that I published about my grandfather only she tells what she used to do with her grandmother. . . . What I wonder is how old Marianne was. Sounds like she's five or six. It doesn't sound like she's eight because she asks lots of questions. . . . This reminds me of a book Elizabeth wrote and it's like *Nana Upstairs Nana Downstairs* because in *Marianne's Grandmother* the grandmother dies and in *Nana Upstairs Nana Downstairs* the grandmother died. They're alike because Tommy visited his grandmother every Sunday and she visited her grandmother. They do things together and my grandma and I do things together too.

Jody

Jody brought *Cookie's Week* to me during the third week of school and asked to read. He read the first four pages from memory without looking at the words. Then he began to stumble. I pointed to the words and said ever so gently, "Here, let's look at the words." But the attention Jody gave each word as he tried to figure it out caused him to lose touch with the ideas those words were meant to convey. I suggested we read together. We read through the book, pointing to the words, with Jody's voice trailing mine. "We read it," I said when we came to the end; Jody smiled. I urged Jody to "practice" reading it and reminded him to look at the words as he did so, then read it to me in a few days. "Okay," he replied good-naturedly, "because I still needed some help." Ten days later Jody read *Cookie's Week*. He made several miscues but all of the words he read maintained the meaning: "upset" for "knocked," "was" for "were," "shut" for "closed," and "trash" for "trash can." Three days later he read *This Old Man* without errors, pointing accurately to the words as he read, and said at the end, "This book's *easy!*"

Two weeks later he read *Building a House*. Pointing to the words as he read was a big help and if he got off track he paused to find his place. The two miscues, "long" for "large" and "done" for "built," maintained meaning. He quickly corrected "done" to "built" when I asked him if this was what he meant to say. When I asked how he learned to read this book he said, "By sounding out and listening off of you and I asked Monica and also Stacy helped me a little." This book had been a challenging leap for Jody but he had wanted to read it from the first week of school. His interest stemmed from his father's occupation as a carpenter and Jody said, "My favorite part's where they're up on the roof 'cause that's what my dad usually does—put the shingles on." Jody continued as an avid reader and writer from that point on. Like Jackie, he read many books in the classroom throughout the year. He read twenty-five of those books to me or the reading workshop volunteer and took them home to share with his family.

When I talked to Jody about reading and writing in September he said, "I can read—sorta. Well, not really yet." He spoke at length about his mother as a reader and writer. "The last time we went to the library, she read every book in the whole library!" he said, and then added, "And she's always writing a letter to our Aunt Judy." In May Jody talked extensively about his reading and writing. Here's one excerpt from those remarks:

> In the beginning I picked up books like *Cookie's Week* and I just started practicing it and I got it. Before I went to school I could read just one book of mine—a little book. I sound out some of the words, but some I don't sound out. I ask somebody. I know how to pick books. It's like yesterday—it was not too warm and not too cold. *Arthur's Teacher Trouble* was like that. It's right in the middle—not too hard and not too easy. I pick a book and stay with it. If I don't know some of the words, I skip to the next word and see if it gives it to me or I use the pictures to give it to me. It's important that you read something every day. If you don't read and write every day you get out of the habit of it. Reading is fun, funner than writing, but writing is fun too—especially when you finish a piece because you worked hard.

Lauren

Lauren read *The Bus Ride* the first week of school and took it home to read. The next morning she reported, "My mom hugged me, she was so happy." *The Bus Ride* is an early reading book for many of the children because its highly predictable structure enables children to recite each page by glancing at the picture. Lauren's reading followed this procedure. During the next month Lauren dipped into many books, read her own writing, and read with classmates and her mom. She proudly brought in her new library card from the Lancaster County Library. Her mother was taking night classes to finish a college degree and Lauren said, "I watch my mom read and write and I just copy her."

One day in late September I suggested in a writing conference that she try to put spaces between the words she wrote, that this might help her read them more easily. "Between?" she asked, bewildered. I demonstrated by rewriting the words she'd written but she was still puzzled. We chatted a minute more, then suddenly her face lit up. "Oh, you mean *after* every word. Does every word have a space after it?" I nodded. "Oh, I didn't know that," she grinned. I heard the amazement and delight in her voice as she grasped this concept. Despite the many large-group lessons, discussions, and demonstrations about spaces between words, Lauren had not made sense of my lessons on this concept. The individual conference provided a forum to tell her when she was ready. The understanding was a break-through. That day Lauren began reading *Cookie's Week*. After a week of practicing this book (interspersed with other reading), she read the book to me. Like Jody, she read incorrect words that maintained the meaning: "garbage" for "trash," "in" for "into," "was" for "were." She learned to read this book by "practicing," she said. Until February, the books Lauren chose for reading to me and for taking home all had a predictable pattern to the language, such as repeating lines or books that were songs. I suspected that integrating decoding strategies with thinking about the ideas pre-sented through the text was taxing to her and the predictable texts offered support to work at both processes. When I suggested books (other than books written by classmates) that veered from predictable language pat-terns, Lauren declined. She was the only child in this particular class who relied on pattern books to this extent. I allowed her to set her own pace.

The first book that differed was *The Funny Dream*, which was a title Lauren had loved when I read it to the class. "This book's so *funny*," she said. "I just love it because it's so funny," and then she'd go on to tell all the parts she thought hilarious. When she read this book in February, she had difficulty with the word "cereal" and read "the orange juice" as "their juice." She stopped throughout the reading to comment on the text. "I like the part when the kitchen's a wreck," she said, "but I wouldn't do this because look at the kitchen." At the end she said, "I learned to read this book because I practiced it a lot."

"Practice," was the consistent answer Lauren gave when asked to describe how she learned to read and write. At the year's end, however, she spoke more fluently about her learning: "If I pick up a book that's too hard for me, I put it down and find an easy book. When I write I just sound out the words and when I read too. Sometimes I ask somebody if I don't know a word and they just tell me and then I remember the word in my head and then I know how to read the book. You have to practice."

Jackie, Jody, and Lauren are rather typical first graders. Their prior experiences with written language, primarily home experiences and attitudes cultivated in their homes, influenced the pace and timing with which they moved into reading. Although these children, and many others, learned to read with this approach, what about those children who have difficulty?

Our school district provides support through the reading teacher to first graders identified by the classroom teacher as being likely to be "at risk." By providing this support at the beginning of a child's school career and continuing for as long as needed, we've found that a child is more likely to become a successful reader. In Jackie, Jody, and Lauren's class, I identified seven children in September for extra support. This number was larger than in any of my previous first-grade classes. Luci Steele, our reading teacher, arranged a half-hour time slot three days a week to see these children. We wanted this time to be in the classroom, but when Luci came to reading workshop to focus on these seven children, what sounded great in theory turned into mass confusion in practice. The children lacked the inner structure to attend to tasks within a large group without continual teacher direction. We revised our plan and had Mrs. Steele work with the group in her own room, following similar workshop procedures, for three days a week. The other two days the children worked in reading workshop, and I usually paired them up with other children. The procedure worked. The children were able to adapt to the workshop structure and Mrs. Steele was able to address individual needs with regard to developing reading strategies.

Three of the seven children left the classroom before the school year ended and new children (often with similar problems) took their place. The following fall, only two of the seven returned to our school. The transient nature of their family lives is a problem many children face. Each of these seven children brought complex personal histories that affected their learning. Without delving into the details of those private histories, here are the stories of four of those seven children.

Natalie

Natalie attended kindergarten in a rural community in another section of the state. "They didn't teach you nuttin' there," she declared in a September interview, then added, "I can only write my name. It's hard to learn, especially when you're my age." The comments seemed to indicate Natalie's perceptions of herself as a learner. However, Natalie wrote eagerly every day and her writing became her first reading material. "My kitten was the best kitten in the world before we moved," she read, taking on an official reader's tone as she read her intended meaning from the randomly selected letters she'd written. She looked me straight in the eye and said, "Do you like it?"

"Yes," and before I could say more, Natalie continued talking, telling me about the kitten they left behind when they moved just before school started.

Natalie could *sing* the alphabet, but she was lost when it came to identifying letters beyond those in her name. I encouraged her to think about what she wanted to say and to put down letters that might make those words. "They don't have to be perfect. Your *ideas*—what you want to tell other people—are the most important part." She readily accepted my suggestion. With concern for correctness easily set aside, Natalie wrote fluently by writing strings of letters across the page. Most of her pieces were fantasies about butterflies and flowers, unicorns and puppies. She continued to read these pieces using the pictures for clues and running her finger under the letters she had written. On several occasions I suggested she listen for letter sounds but her face clouded before she'd reply, "That's too hard for me to do." I backed off. Give her time, I reminded myself.

Natalie loved books and stories. In reading workshop during the first days of school she flipped through the pages of books over and over and sometimes told the story softly to herself. At the end of September she brought me *The Very Hungry Caterpillar* and announced, "I can read this book all by myself." She sat beside me and told the story from beginning to end by reading the pictures. Her version only vaguely matched the actual words in the text. When she finished she beamed at me and said, "I did it, didn't I?"

If the discrepancy between her achievement and that of her classmates occurred to her, it did not seem to bother Natalie. She worked diligently and conscientiously. That her handwriting was haphazard across the page or that her drawings were at times masses of scribble lines in comparison to her peers didn't matter to her or to me. She happily went about her work in the classroom and made friends with everyone. Her only distress came from being teased at the bus stop by older children who called her "fatty." Natalie's parents supported the school program and their daughter's learning. "We don't expect her to be at the top of her class or anything like that. We only want her to learn and to be happy and to enjoy school," they told me.

When Natalie brought back the books Mrs. Steele sent home with her twice a week, she read each of them to me before she returned them to her. "I need to read to you," she'd remind me on busy mornings. In mid-October she commented during reading workshop, "I know how to recognize 'snail' and 'sun' from each other. 'Snail' has all those letters and 'sun' has three."

Natalie began learning the individual letters of the alphabet with instruction from Mrs. Steele, from involvement with language in the classroom, and from strategies she devised herself. She wrote the alphabet with her friend Stacy during play time: "Me and Stacy are practicing handwriting," she said. I noticed her locating particular letters by softly singing the alphabet song and pointing her finger to each letter of the alphabet posted on the wall. "I'm just finding M," she said. I suggested we put an alphabet strip on her desk but she scowled and shook her head. Natalie didn't want to be different from the other children. I thought of putting an alphabet strip on every desk as I had done other years. One previous class had been especially delighted with these alphabets. I made the suggestion to the children. "NO WAY!" came the unanimous reply. "That's *baby* stuff. We did that in kindergarten!" Thank goodness I asked, I thought.

In early December Natalie told me, "Writing's fun! Reading's fun! I'm learning so much stuff." One day she told me she was writing about a trip to McDonald's. "Me and my family," she read, and then added "now I'm going to write 'went'." I looked at the writing. "Me" was there and MI was clearly intended to be "my." WaLe for "family"—the W could be an M reversed and I could hear Natalie pronouncing "family" as fam-a-lee, thus the aLe. She was beginning to listen to the sounds of letters! I sat beside her for a moment.

Natalie said "went" and looked at me, puzzled. I repeated the word and exaggerated the W sound. Natalie watched my mouth, a look of concentration on her face.

"What letter do you hear at the beginning of 'went'?" Natalie shook her head but kept looking at me intently. "It's a W," I said, "but it's a tricky one because W sounds like Y."

"Should I write a W?" Natalie asked. I nodded. Natalie wrote.

"What else do you hear in 'went'?" I asked.

Natalie repeated the word several times, then suddenly said, "A!"

"Write it! Anything else?"

"T!"

"That's the last letter in 'went,' " I said as Natalie wrote. "What comes next?"

Natalie reread her sentence, "Me and my family went . . . to. Is t-o 'to'?" she asked.

"Sure is," I replied. Natalie wrote.

"McDonald's comes next," she said. "That's a long word. I don't think I can do that."

"Well, let's give it a try," I suggested. "I'll help you. You know when you've seen the McDonald's sign?" Natalie nodded. "Well, picture it in your head. What letter do you see at the beginning of McDonald's?"

Natalie squeezed her eyes shut in concentration then suddenly said, "M! I see M!"

"You got it!" I replied with an enthusiasm to match Natalie's. "Anything else?"

Natalie closed her eyes again but this time she said, "I don't know. It's all jumbled together."

"Well, then let's listen to see if we hear any letters. McDonald's," I repeated slowly.

Natalie repeated the name slowly. "Is A next?"

"Write it," I replied.

Together Natalie and I worked through the spelling of "McDonald's" with Natalie writing MaktallS.

"Did I spell 'McDonald's'?" she asked when we finished.

"You sure did. How did you do that?"

"I listened and then I just wrote the letters!" she replied in total delight.

At this point Stacy walked by Natalie's desk. "I could help Natalie, Mrs. Avery. I could be her teacher and show her how like you did."

"Okay, Stacy. Just remember what we said about good teachers."

"Yeah, I know. Good teachers don't just *tell* people the answers, they help them figure it out for themselves. Don't worry, I can do that. So then Natalie will be able to do it herself," Stacy stated in her most grown-up tone.

Natalie beamed. "Yup," she said. Stacy took my place beside Natalie.

Later, when I looked at Natalie's writing I noticed she underlined the word "McDonald's" in her piece and put a star above every letter— a strategy I often used with the children at the end of handwriting lessons when I asked them to assess their own handwriting by marking with a star the letters they felt were best. I had spent slightly over five minutes with Natalie, though I had waited and watched for three months for this "teachable moment." This piece of writing became Natalie's first published book.

A week later three literacy events occurred for Natalie. She brought in a newspaper clipping and read the headline to me, "Santa is a Christmas state of mind." Then she zestfully explained her process: "I looked through the whole paper to see if I could find anything I could read. Then my dad helped me find this picture of Santa and I knew 'Santa' and I knew 'is' and 'a' and 'Christmas' and then he helped me to read it all!" The next day Natalie read *The Bus Ride* to me. She read the book smoothly and her finger moved under each word as she read. When she came to "rhinoceros" she stumbled, then said, "rhino?" and looked to me for help.

"Rhinoceros," I said.

"Oh, I don't know that one. Is this a rhino or a rhinoceros?" she asked, pointing to the picture. I explained the words.

Natalie nodded and said, "Cuz I didn't know they mean the same."

A couple days later Natalie read the typed version of her story about McDonald's at our author's party. She'd had no trouble learning to read it and explained why: " 'cuz I wrote it so I *knew* what it says!"

In the winter months Natalie read other books with predictable language patterns, such as *Cookie's Week* and *All the Pretty Horses*, a book that had been her favorite since September. She began experimenting with punctuation and quotation marks when she wrote by inserting them where she thought they might go. In mid-January I read aloud "The Snowball Fight," a piece she planned to publish. "You can read what I wrote? How'd you do that?" Natalie startled me with her questions, questions I had asked *her* all year. She sat looking at me, waiting for an answer—just as I'd done with her for weeks. She really wanted to know!

"Hmm, let's see." I paused before I answered to ponder just how I *had read* her writing. "Well, I looked at the pictures, and I used the letters you wrote, and I remember how kids spell some words because I've seen them before—so that helped me figure some words out—but mostly, I think mostly, I kept thinking about what you were saying and what made sense."

Natalie looked at me, pondering this answer with a serious countenance, and then replied, "Yup, that's kinda how I do it too."

At the end of the school year Natalie worked on reading Lois Ehlert's *Planting a Rainbow*. This book was a challenge and the first time she read it to me her reading was halting and she missed many words, such as "seedless," "watch," "again," "select," and others. I suggested she choose another book and come back to this later or practice this one some more. Five days later Natalie came back and read *Planting a Rainbow* smoothly and with no errors! When I asked how she'd done this she replied, "I *really* wanted to read this because I just *love* this book with all the colors. So after you told me some of the words I went back to my seat and read it over and over until I just remembered them!"

During the last week of school I asked the class what they remembered from the year that had helped them learn. Natalie said, "I remember the day I spelled 'McDonald's' and you told me I did it right so then I could spell. That *really* helped me. I'll tell you one thing," she added, "I just love to read and write." In an interview during the last week of school, Natalie commented on her reading and writing.

How I learned to read is I learned 'the' because you wrote it a lot and I saw it. The books that you read to us I learned all the words because I heard them over and over again. They [the words] were just up there in my head. My favorite books are Tomie dePaola books. I like his pictures and the way he says things. When I write I know some of the words and I sound out some. In the mini-lesson I do what you said, then I get my story real well. My best piece is "When I Got My Duck." I just like the way it sounds and feels to me. In writing, I like to get the feeling inside before I write. Then I say what I want to write and see if it makes any sense.

Darren

One morning in mid-September Darren handed me a flat box as he walked into the classroom. "What's this?" I asked.

Darren looked puzzled and said, "I don't know." We opened the box, found cupcakes, and Darren said, "Oh yeah, it's my birthday." A moment later Darren joined the other children, who were putting candles with their names and dates of birth on cardboard birthday cakes, one for each month, that were spread out on the floor. When I joined them, Darren looked at me and said, "I don't know what to do. When's my birthday?"

"When *is* your birthday?" I asked.

"I don't know. I don't remember, I mean, I don't know when my birthday is," then he shook his head as though trying to clear his thinking in some way. "I get confused . . ." He smiled as his voice trailed off.

"Didn't you just tell me today was your birthday?" I asked softly.

"Today?" Darren looked startled.

I led him to my desk and looked on my class role. "Yes, today. It says right here. Today's your birthday."

Darren looked at the cupcakes and at me and then said in a puzzled voice, "Yeah, today's my birthday. I'm seven years old today."

If Darren seemed puzzled, so did I. During the first days of school I attributed his frequent confusion to the many recent changes in his life. His mother had remarried and the new family unit had moved into the school district over the summer. But now, in late September, the confusion continued and the range and complexity of his behaviors fell into no discernable patterns. His comments in class brought impatient protests from the other children. DARE-NNN, they'd chorus until I'd remind them that we needed to listen and try to understand Darren's ideas. When we discussed ways animals prepare for winter, Darren suggested that a bear would go to a store to buy a winter jacket. "But bears don't wear jackets," said Matt, "They have their own fur."

"Oh, I never thought of that," Darren replied and the look on his face told me that he truly hadn't considered this idea.

When the class sat at their seats, Darren constantly fidgeted, cutting paper into slivers inside his desk, falling off his chair, or writing on his desk, chair, or his own arms with pencil or pen. He frequently left his seat just to walk around the classroom. "Darren is in a state of constant movement," I wrote in my observational notes at the end of September. When I gave directions to the class, Darren began the particular task only after he noticed the other children beginning. "What are we supposed to do?" he'd ask in a startled voice. Eventually, he came to rely on imitating other children or requesting assistance from me in order to accomplish basic tasks such as finding a page in the math book. When the children took turns telling math stories to illustrate addition facts Darren volunteered, but when I called on him he suddenly became bewildered and said, "I can't. I mean I don't know." A few minutes later he raised his hand again and then repeated the story Emily had just told.

In a September interview, Darren told me that a good reader was one who could "read fast" and that his favorite book was *The Mouse and the Motorcycle*, which his mom had read to him. He hoarded books in his desk as though they were precious possessions that he might never see again if he put them back on the shelf.

One day a child cried, "Darren has about twenty million books in his desk!"

"I just wanted to read them," Darren answered as he pulled them out.

In reading workshop Darren spent most of his time reading with or watching other children. I began to surmise that he *wanted* to read and hoarded the books he wanted to read, but that he truly didn't know how to go about reading. My individual conferences seemed less helpful to him than what he learned from the other children. He imitated them by choosing their favorite books and turning the pages as he'd seen them do. He stayed with reading most when he read with a partner, a collaboration in which the partner child read and Darren closely followed that child's moving finger. Throughout this reading the pair stopped to talk about the book. The process resembled a parent/child storybook reading at bedtime.

In October Darren read one of the books from Mrs. Steele's room to me. This book, about a mother bird teaching her baby to fly, had few words (mostly "up" and "down"). Darren pointed to each word and read accurately, but when I asked him what he thought of the story, he looked baffled. "Who are these birds?" I asked. Darren shrugged his shoulders. "Are they related?" Darren looked puzzled so I rephrased my question. "Do they know each other?" More puzzlement. "Could they be brother and sister or . . ." before I could finish Darren interrupted. "Yes!" he said, obviously glad to have an answer.

"Are they brother and sister? Or could they be a mother and her baby?"

"Yes, I mean no. I mean, I don't know," he said. I asked if the birds in the first picture were the same ones in the second illustration. He told me no. After I went through the book and told the story from the pictures to Darren he replied, "I didn't get that." I wasn't sure he understood even then.

When Darren wrote in writing workshop, he spent most of the time drawing—his favorite activity—and he told me he could write but he couldn't spell. I suspected that when Darren said he couldn't spell, he meant that he didn't understand the connection of letters to sounds or that letters on a page represented words. During a couple of writing workshops I spent a few minutes with Darren, working him through the process of listening for sounds in words then writing letters to represent those sounds. After this, letters began to replace some of the wavy lines in his writing. However, I never heard him attempting to reproduce the sounds of letters when he wrote. All the words he wrote seemed to come from visual memory. I noticed that he frequently wrote words that I had recently written on the chalkboard, even if they had been erased, and he wrote entire words randomly to convey his meaning, even though these words were not the ones he intended them to be. When he had no visual recall he either wrote letters randomly or reverted to the wavy lines. In no time, and sooner than many of his peers, Darren developed a vocabulary of words he could spell correctly. He couldn't always read these words, but when I read them for him he'd say, "Oh yeah, that's right." However, even when he could remember how to write a word, he could not consistently read that same word and he rarely read words together in any way that communicated meaning.

One of Darren's favorite activities in school was handwriting instruction and, even though he often substituted uppercase for lowercase letters or became confused about which line on the paper to write, he produced beautiful papers with precisely executed letters. He recopied handwriting lessons and even the texts of the short books he read for Mrs. Steele, both in free-play time at school and at home, and frequently presented these papers to me. "I'm playing office," he told me during free-play time, and added that this was like his dad's office. He sat with a toy telephone held to an ear and wrote numbers and letters on his clipboard. "I'm filling out claims," he said. He became deeply involved in his play and engaged other children in elaborate scenarios portraying office scenes. If others chose not to play, Darren created imaginary people to visit his office.

Darren especially loved to draw houses, barns, and buggies. His drawings had a distinct artistic style, different from that of any child I'd ever seen. The other children marveled at his talent and his sensitive use of color. They enjoyed Darren not only for his artistry but for his pleasant attitude and sense of humor. "Darren's really weird," commented one child privately to me, "but I like him a lot even though he's weird!" The comment spoke for all of us in this classroom. We didn't understand Darren and his behaviors at times were trying, but we all found him delightful and *so* interesting. Even so, Darren's unique behaviors and thinking patterns led me to discuss this child with the principal and the school guidance counselor. We considered the possibility of a learning disability. The district psychologist talked with Darren and administered some screening tests, but these tools provided no insights.

Darren continued to work in the classroom. In writing workshop, despite the outstanding artistry and correct spellings, the content of Darren's writing confused readers. In his pieces he wrote words and phrases, repeated them, drifted from one topic to another, and rarely could read more than a word or two of what he'd written. When we were working on publishing his first book in mid-November, I eliminated the small-group conference because I believed the procedures would only confuse Darren. He read a sentence; I typed. When I asked him for a title, Darren said, "What do you mean?" Ignoring the fact that we had emphasized titles during literature time and that I had presented several mini-lessons on titles, I explained titles to Darren by showing him several books. "Oh, okay," he said and immediately proposed the title, "When I Went to My Mom's Work." In the days before our author's party, Darren practiced reading his book over and over. Some days he forgot what the words said and asked for help. His peers and I focussed on context clues to help him remember what the pages said. Darren successfully read his book at the author's party.

Learning to read his published writing seemed to inspire Darren to read a book from the classroom library. During the first two months of school, Darren spent reading workshop browsing through books, noticing words here and there that he recognized, sitting with peers as he listened and followed what they read, and generally gaining experiences with books, readers, and reading. Now he settled with one book, *The Bus Ride*. He had been reading books with a few lines of highly predictable written language for Mrs. Steele, but this was the first time he volunteered to read a book to me from the classroom collection. He became stumped on the word "then" and said "en" and he substituted "bunny" for "rabbit." He moved his hand under words as he read, as I had encouraged all the children to do to help them focus on individual words, but I noticed that he pointed to different words than those he spoke. At first glance it seemed he had memorized the text. However, closer observation revealed a complex integration of strategies. To read the book he relied on the book's illustrations, the predictable pattern of the writing, and memory from his many experiences with this book. Those experiences began early in September and included hearing peers read the book, looking through the book on his own, and working to read it both with peer assistance and independently. Darren had made tremendous progress from the beginning of September.

When he read *It Didn't Frighten Me* two and a half weeks later, his finger trailed behind the words he read during the repetitious refrain in the text, but he pointed accurately to the words in all other lines of the book. He had memorized the refrain and didn't need his finger; his finger helped him focus on words that did not repeat, and the focussing helped him attend to each word and read it accurately. A month later Darren read *Catch that Frog*, from the old Scott Foresman Unlimited Series. He substituted "in back of" for "between" and "over" for "under," and when I directed him to the illustrations he was clearly confused by these concepts. However, when he read "went" for "jumped" he immediately corrected the error and turned to me and confided, "I knowed that word 'jumped.' "

Sequencing information and connecting one part of a story to another continued to be a major difficulty for Darren, both in his writing and his reading. In December he wrote about going to visit his grandpa's farm. The story jumped from one incident to another, leaving readers to fill in the gaps. When peers questioned the text because of the lack of clarity, Darren seemed puzzled. The story made sense to him. I spent short snatches of time chatting with Darren about the piece during a writing workshop, getting him to tell me the information that was in his head but not on the paper. When he told me a missing part, I urged him to write it and showed him where it would fit in the text. I moved on to other students while Darren wrote, then came back and read the inserted information in context, trying to help Darren grasp the meaning for himself. We continued through the story the same way. About the same time he read *Building a House*, by Byron Barton. He read "Then put up walls" for "They put up walls." When I asked if this made sense, Darren replied no. We corrected the error together, but Darren made a similar error in the next sentence. I wrote in my notes during that reading, "Not listening to himself for *meaning!*" It appeared that if the words flowed he perceived himself as reading, but that he gave little consideration to the words making sense. However, he had begun to think of the story as a whole, and at the end told me that he would like to grow up and be "one of them guys who make houses like this." Then he went through the book and told me about the pictures and how he would like to do these jobs.

When Darren came back from Christmas vacation he wrote a coherent and (from all I could determine) sequenced story of visiting Longwood Gardens over the holidays. He read "Beyond the Hill" and said, "It's talking about mountains and stars and that kinda stuff," but his puzzled countenance told me the story was baffling to him. His mother wrote that when he read this book to her, he talked about the stars in the book and the stars he saw during the planetarium visit.

In March, when he first began reading *The Happy Day*, a book about approaching spring, he said, "The bears are dancing and they start crying when the flowers are coming up because they're gonna die. That's what I think." Later, when he polished his oral reading of the book, he read it to me before he took it home. On this reading he talked about spring. It seemed that Darren required many experiences with a text, not only to learn to read but to *understand* what that text was about.

About this time Darren began having sudden outbursts, which were untypical of his pleasant, somewhat carefree behavior of the fall months. One day Jody found a piece of Darren's writing in his folder. "Why'd you stick your writing in *my* folder?" Jody demanded.

"Well, I'm *so* sorry," said Darren in a voice that mocked Jody's.

"Don't stick your writing in *my* folder," Jody replied.

"I didn't do it, Jody!" Darren yelled. He grabbed his writing from Jody and began pacing around the room, muttering to himself. The outburst startled all of us. It took several minutes before Darren's rage subsided. He began talking about being mad when he couldn't find his book or pencil or during minor interactions with other children. He began writing about anger and his stories were coherent for the first time!

One day he and Josie began to coauthor a story entitled "Ben's Dog Got Run Over." Josie wrote with Darren for one day and then Darren continued on his own, checking in with Josie from time to time to read the developing piece aloud. In this story, the dog of a boy named Benny is run over. Benny cries "all day and all night and all day in school." When the other children learn why, they too cry. At one point in the story Benny says, "I am mad my dog died." When Benny tells his mom that he will kill the man who ran over his dog, "she sended him to his room and with no supper and he was grounded and he had no supper that night." The next day Darren revised the piece to read "he had a great supper that night." When I read Darren's writing I saw many allusions to his favorite books. Two of those books had been *Ghost's Hour, Spook's Hour*, by Eve Bunting, and *The Accident*, by Carol and Don Carrick. The characters in the former are a boy and his dog, and the latter (a book Darren always reported as his favorite) is about a dog being killed by a truck.

In another story Darren wrote about a character who is mad and "slammed the door in his face." Then one day Darren produced the following story without pausing to line out or even reread as he wrote, a procedure he had not done *all year*. "There was a boy. His name was dummy because he was a dummy. The next day he went to school and everybody made fun of him. He laughed at himself. The people in school laughed harder and harder. 'What's wrong?' he asked. 'You are dumb.' The next day he got very angry. He said, 'Goodby' to his mother and left in a hurry and wrote a note to his teacher. It said, 'Bye, Mrs. Bounds.' I am mad because everybody makes fun of me and it was so very (sic) that the teacher wasn't even there." Darren read the piece to me. I listened, retold the story to Darren, and then gently inquired, since Mrs. Bounds was our art teacher, if this story was about her or anyone we knew. "No. See this is the other school, my other school, not this school, just another school. I just used Mrs. Bounds's name because I like art." Darren's displays of anger subsided after this writing, but none of us ever discovered what had been upsetting him.

Soon after this incident Stacy chose to write about her parent's divorce after hearing Marc Brown's *Dinosaur's Divorce*. Stacy and Darren were good friends and soon Darren chose to write about the divorce of his parents. He graphically described events that occurred and, although the piece seemed disconnected and Darren himself acknowledged he didn't understand all that had occurred at home, I could understand most of his story. Darren spent days on this writing and seemed particularly satisfied with the ending, where he related that his mother and stepfather did not fight. He now read all of his writing without assistance from me, not only immediately after writing it but also on subsequent days. He had a strong grasp of the meaning embedded in his words and used that meaning as well as all the other reading strategies he had developed to read what he had written. When he read incorrectly, he caught the error within a few words and went back to reread and self-correct.

Darren now saw himself as a writer and a reader and identified with professional authors. He wrote letters to authors Eve Bunting and Carol Carrick to tell them how much he enjoyed their books and how many books he himself had published. Carol Carrick wrote a personal letter to Darren and told him how many books she and her husband Don had published and then commented that Darren would soon be ahead of them.

One day in May Darren picked up Thomas Locker's *The Boy Who Held Back the Sea*. When I stopped at his desk during reading workshop he read the page perfectly. "What's happening in this story?" I asked. The old patterns of confusion with meaning appeared as Darren first looked at the pages, then replied, "I don't know," then pointed to an illustration and said, "a boy who lived in the town, he acted like that boy."

"Tell me more about the boy," I said. Darren shook his head as though trying to clear his thinking. "My head doesn't work sometimes," he said. During the last days of school Darren read *A Kiss for Little Bear*. His reading was a close retelling of the story but not an accurate reading. "It gets all mixed up for me," he said.

With books that he read several times and had heard read aloud, Darren began to understand the stories. It was difficult to tell if his comprehension developed from reading or from hearing class discussions. On a word identification test administered by Mrs. Steele, Darren scored a 1.9, placing him on grade level. I knew that a test of his reading comprehension could likely produce a lag behind word recognition. I also knew that Darren would never be a typical student, that his future teachers would be as baffled by him as I was. I also knew that Darren brought a particularly unique view of life to a classroom community and a special talent as an artist. He would always provide an unusual perspective to situations and offer contributions that would not occur to others.

Michael

During free-play time one morning three weeks into the school year, the principal brought Michael, with his mother, to the classroom. Michael, a tall blond boy of seven, smiled shyly. Large spots of tooth decay blackened that smile. He clutched a small pencil case that held colored markers and two pencils. He mumbled a few words when I said hello. I called one of the boys over and asked him to show Michael around the classroom. "Sure," he replied, and the two boys went off together.

Michael had moved to our community from a distant state where he had lived with his grandparents and mother, who was separated from his father. A reconciliation between the parents had brought Michael, his mother, and younger sibling to Lancaster. He had not begun first grade before he moved, though he had attended kindergarten. Later he would bring in paperback books his teacher had given him and a small photo album from his kindergarten year that she had made and brought to his home before he moved. At Christmas this teacher sent Michael another book.

With his former teacher, Michael had obviously established a love for stories and books. Literature time was his favorite time of day; he loved listening to stories. "R-EE-D!" he'd say and then sit in rapt attention as I read. During reading workshop he hugged books to his chest, turned the pages and looked at pictures, and watched other children reading. He also watched and then imitated during writing workshop. At first he drew and wrote only his name and the date. Then he added a few letters, and slowly those letters began to match the sounds he intended. His oral language handicapped him, for Michael mumbled or spoke in baby talk, and he spoke only in one word utterances or sentence fragments. His writing and reading developed slowly. The support of Mrs. Steele, his working in daily writing and reading workshops, and the continuous inter-actions with other children served to nurture that language development. When possible I spent extra moments beside Michael as he read or wrote, helping him develop specific strategies. Michael could compose stories orally and, with my help, he put a story he told me into writing. It became his first published piece (see Figures 10–7, 10–8, and 10–9. At the November parent-teacher conferences I urged Michael's father (his mother was working) to read to his son and to talk with him about books or any experiences they had together. Michael's father told me his work schedule allowed only one night a week when the entire family was together. Michael's mother was at home with the children in the evenings he said, but acknowledged, "I've never seen my wife read." In a later meeting Michael's mother said, "I don't do so good at reading myself. I can't read, really." Once she had told me this, Michael's mother began writing notes (using invented spelling) to me when he brought books home. When she was hospitalized during the winter, an unknown hand wrote a note and Michael's father added his signature at the end.

In early January Michael read *Brown Bear, Brown Bear, What Do You See?* It was the first book he had read from the classroom library. He said that his friend Kevin had suggested it. He read "beautiful children" as "boys and girls"; when I pointed out the correct words he shook his head, grinned, and said, "Boy, I hate that word because it's too hard for me." I was delighted that he had spoken an entire sentence! He spoke as if he had marbles in his mouth, but it was an entire sentence. I asked him to repeat his words more clearly so I could understand and he did, then smiled. The garbled language seemed to indicate a degree of uncertainty about his performance. With encouragement of that performance, he abandoned the undecipherable talk. Michael moved on to other books with predictable language patterns, such as *It Didn't Frighten Me*, and books written by classmates, such as Darren's "I Went to My Mom's Work." He rapidly began developing a vocabulary of words he knew upon sight and specific strategies to figure out unknown words. He used letter/sound clues as well as context. Meaning always led the way for him. He viewed written language as having meaning and used strategies that he first used in writing to decipher words written by other authors.

Near the end of the year Michael read a book about dinosaurs. When he read to me, his only error was "points" for "plates." Referring to a small and rather helpless looking dinosaur, he commented after the reading, "Tyrannosaurus *cannot* eat him!" Then he added, "I like that I can read now."

"How did you learn to read?" I asked.

Michael shrugged and said, "I don't know. I just kept trying and my friends helped me and I look at the words now."

Michael's family moved before he began second grade, and he did not return to our school the following September.

Ellen

Ellen flipped through the book on her desk during our first reading workshop and within three minutes had wandered to the art table where she sat down to draw. When I handed her a new book a moment later and reminded her that this was reading workshop she looked surprised. "I already read my book," she said.

"Well, in this classroom this year, we're all going to read together for a certain time. If a reader finishes one book that reader could reread it or read another," I replied.

"Oh," replied a startled Ellen. Then she took the book, smiled, and returned to her seat.

Many times during the first days of school Ellen drifted away from a group activity to do her own thing. She left the group during literature time and once asked to go outside. She often appeared to be lost in thought, and her comments usually referred to matters we had moved away from minutes before. Directions baffled her. "What do I do?" she'd ask repeatedly when she saw the others begin a new activity. One day when we worked with counters in math class, she looked up and calmly said, "I think I'd rather make Mickey Mouse faces," and sure enough, on her desk was a face made with counters. When she worked on a math paper one day, she looked up and said, "I was counting but when I did, the numbers just went out of my head." In handwriting she asked me to help her find the line on which to write and had great difficulty managing the lines and spaces. One day out of the blue she said, "I know my phone number but I don't know how to dial it."

In writing workshop during the first week of school she wrote "cat," "rat," and her name beside the drawing of a treehouse. "Those are the only words I can write," she told me in our conference. When I interviewed her she said, "I can write. I really learned to write the first word that's not my name in kindergarten. 'Cat.' My teacher told me it." About reading she said, "I learned to read yesterday. I thought and I remembered and read in my mind." Then she sang the song in Robert Munsch's *Love You Forever*, which was also from her kindergarten experience. She added, "I think I can read *Mrs. Wishy Washy*." Later she retold the story emphasizing the "wishy-washy, wishy-washy" lines.

Ellen spent reading workshop reading the pictures in books. The words had little significance for her, but she noticed every detail in the illustrations. She loved reading with her friends, a partnership that usually involved the other child reading words and Ellen pointing out nuances in the illustrations. She faithfully read (by memorizing) the short books Mrs.

Steele sent home with her and, when she read them to me, she paused to talk about the pictures. For Ellen, meaning came more from illustrations in a book than the words.

After a week of writing "cat" to accompany anything she drew, Ellen wrote S I B for sailboat after I helped her listen for the names of letters when she said the word "sailboat." From that point on, she abandoned "cat" in favor of letters to represent the words that told about her pictures. However, she had difficulty reading her writing. Unless I sat beside her when she wrote, I was unable to help her read because Ellen wrote from left to right or from right to left or combined both, zig-zag fashion. Occasionally she placed strings of letters top to bottom or even bottom to top. Frequently, the right-to-left lines were a complete mirror reversal of the correct form. She loved to write just as she loved to read with her friends, and it was in her writing where I first saw evidence that she was looking to the words for meaning rather than just using illustrations. By the end of October, Ellen filled an entire page with ten to eleven lines of her writing. Her invented spelling produced words such as "has" for "house," "cozn" for "cousin," "apltre" for "apple tree." Because she strung her words together without spaces between them, her writing remained difficult for either of us to read. She appeared to listen for the sounds of letters inherent in the letter names, but when we addressed specific phonic sounds she had difficulty discriminating and recalling even the sound of a consonant letter. The visual recall of written language, both in her reading and in the written language that surrounded her in the classroom, appeared to be of more help to her.

The first week in November Ellen read *The Bus Ride* to me. Her reading was entirely a memorization. "I can read this book with my eyes closed!" she said in amazement.

"Yes, but I want you to look at the words," I said. "Use your finger to point to each word as you read. That will help you see the words so you don't get mixed up."

"Okay," Ellen replied. As she read she moved her fingers under the words but the finger did not match the word she read, indicating memorization. I said nothing more about this aspect of her reading, but rather cheered her success. Ellen took the book home to share with her family that evening.

The next book Ellen read was her first published book. When she received the typed version she had difficulty reading every word, but because she was familiar with her topic, she easily recalled entire sections when prompted with an initial word or two; after practicing it a day or two she could read it smoothly and with an expressive tone. After our author's party she read several books authored by her friends. The day we returned from Christmas vacation she read *Cookie's Week*, which she had been working on with her friend Elizabeth before the holiday break. She had wanted to read this particular book for some time—almost since September—but earlier it had been too much of a struggle. Time and consistent effort on her part had paid off and now she said after the reading, "I had trouble with three parts but Elizabeth taught me. I used to say 'water' here but now I say, 'Nope, it's toilet.' " Less than a week later she read *Catch that Frog*. She pointed accurately to each word as she read and stopped if she was not pointing to the word she uttered. After she took it home her mother wrote, "Ellen read this without hesitation and with lots of expression. We all laughed with her as she read about this jumping frog. She *loves* stories that *make her laugh!*"

When I interviewed Ellen again about her reading and writing, she commented about her writing development: "Now in writing I draw short pictures and before I couldn't read it back because I forgot what the words were, but now I can read it. I learned how to read lots of stuff now." I inquired how she'd learned to read and she replied, "My mom and dad read me tons of stories and now I just started reading them."

After reading two books with predictable texts in February, *Brown Bear, Brown Bear, What Do You See?* and *Over in the Meadow*, Ellen took off with reading. She read confidently and enthusiastically, reading nearly fifteen individual titles to me or our reading workshop aide before the end of the school year. Her mother provided continuing support and wrote her observations of Ellen's reading. When Ellen read *The Carrot Seed* and *Where in the World Is Henry?* her mother wrote, "Ellen read both books confidently. She said she liked the books because they both had surprise endings. She said that she did not expect the carrot seed to grow to be a *huge* carrot and that she expected Henry to be a boy—a little brother—not a lion. She also referred to the book *Where in the World Is Henry?* when we talked about the Milky Way and the universe. Ellen said, 'The universe is all of everything everywhere.' "

Ellen's reading influenced her writing just as her writing had influenced her reading development. When she wrote she planned illustrations to accompany the stories, and she put many details into her final drawings. Her book "Down's Syndrome" reads: "Down's Syndrome is when a child gets an extra chromosome in their body. The child learns slower. But you shouldn't make fun of them. They're not so different. My cousin has Down's Syndrome but he loves to read. Down's Syndrome people want to be friends but they are loving. So please do what I said." She included carefully executed illustrations of her cousin, such as the one in Figure 18–1, which also includes a sign on the wall that reads, "No making fun." When she composed "The Very Hungry Princess," she planned text and illustrations to give meaning to each other and

But you shouldn't make fun of them. They're not so different. My cousin has Down's Syndrome but he loves to read.

Figure 18–1

Picture on the wall says, "No making Fun," in this page from Ellen's book, "Down's Syndrome."

commented after the publication, "These pictures are a clue for the story. I don't want to give it away. Pictures give you clues like Steven Kellogg's pictures do."

Reading and books filled her life. After hearing *The Bed Book*, by Sylvia Plath, she told me, "At night if I can't go to sleep, I just imagine my bed's a sailboat flying in the air and it feels like it's *true!*" Ellen's mother wrote a note telling about taking her daughter to a bookstore. "She struck up a conversation with the clerk in the children's section about books and authors and illustrators. Twenty minutes later, Ellen and the clerk were still talking about books—like adults at a cocktail party."

Reflections

At the end of one year a parent wrote, "These children believe they can read anything! My daughter sits down every night with the newspaper and she actually reads it. I've seen her confidence grow [through] her effort and desire to learn and even more important to understand." This parent's child was one I would have assigned to the "low group" had she been in my class a year earlier. This is not to say that the typical "low group" children suddenly make miraculous strides and match all their peers in school learning, but they do achieve solid success as learners. It's impossible to compare their growth to "low group" children in my former classes and *prove* that this group achieved more because all children are different individuals with unique backgrounds and learning styles. However, I *know* that these children were far better off in this community of learners than other children I taught through a reading program, not only in their achievement but also in their investment in learning. The workshop approach permits children to work *with* their peers and to learn from each other. Nancie Atwell (1987) wrote of her eighth graders:

> Less able students need more able models; they need to be surrounded by other learners whose ideas will spark and charge the environment. . . . I'm hard put to be a model sufficient to inspire the whole group or to provide the individual response each student needs . . . a handful of low ability students can catch fire with enthusiasm generated by other kids. (pp. 45–46)

In my first-grade classroom, the models of more experienced language learners helps less experienced ones. The children do not view themselves as superior or inferior to one another. Rather, they value the talents of their peers. The children regarded Monica as an excellent reader, marvelled at Darren's artistic talent, loved Michael's tales of playing in the woods and his knowledge of small animals, and appreciated Ellen's responses to their writing, which was enhanced by her insight and sensitivity to others. At the end of one year, a parent noted one of the most positive aspects of her son's first-grade experience: "Respect and appreciation for his classmates' talents and interests." Alone I could not meet all demands within the classroom. Gradually children learned to look to peers as a resource. We became a community learning together.

Glenda Bissex (1980) writes, "It has become increasingly clear that language acquisition is not merely imitative but systematic and creative, in the sense of the child constructing the rules for himself." As to how much the child depends on instruction in learning to read, Bissex suggests that "the 'truth' perhaps will be found to vary widely among beginning readers, some virtually teaching themselves while others depend more on instruction" (p. 134). In my experience with first graders, some children, such as Jackie, arrive at school already reading or on the brink of beginning. With a conducive environment and a few guidelines they read, relying on their experiences with written language and learning processes they've developed long before they came to school. Other children, for whatever reason, do not seem to have processes for learning written language in smooth running order (according to the expectations of school) when they begin school. Programmed reading instruction did not serve these children well. Rather than allowing the children to build on the systematic and creative processes they had begun, the program required the children to adapt to its procedures. The structure of reading workshop and the tone of the process-approach classroom allowed *all* children to continue their natural learning processes.

Teachers recognize that "low group" children need more time, more demonstrations, more explanations, more direct instruction. Schools often deal with this need by separating these children from their peers and giving them more worksheets, more skill-and-drill—the very activities that had not been working for them all along. Because the remediation often focusses on skills as ends in themselves rather than as strategies for learning to use language, the children aren't able to connect the exercises to actual reading and writing. These children need more language experiences where they can develop strategies in the context of making meaning. These experiences are best acquired in a community of their peers. These children also need more frequent responses than do children with more experience and those responses must come while the children are engaged in reading and writing.

Reading workshop accommodated an individualized pace and provided opportunity for more teacher time for responding on a one-to-one basis. I'd place a small chair beside a child's desk and ask, "Okay if I sit here and watch how you write [or read]?" The children soon accepted my presence as part of the classroom procedure. In those few minutes beside a child I observed *closely* and interjected occasional requests. My role was coach, supporter, and teacher, sometimes providing *very specific, direct instruction* and then expecting the child to continue independently of me.

Jerome Bruner refers to the natural manner in which parents nurture children as "scaffolding." Scaffolding supports the child as learner, helps that child extend learning, and is gradually removed as learners work independently. These seven children worked well with the same procedures as their more experienced classmates, and in the same environment, but they required more support as they acclimated to school learning and moved into reading and writing. The scaffold of the workshop approach gave them this support.

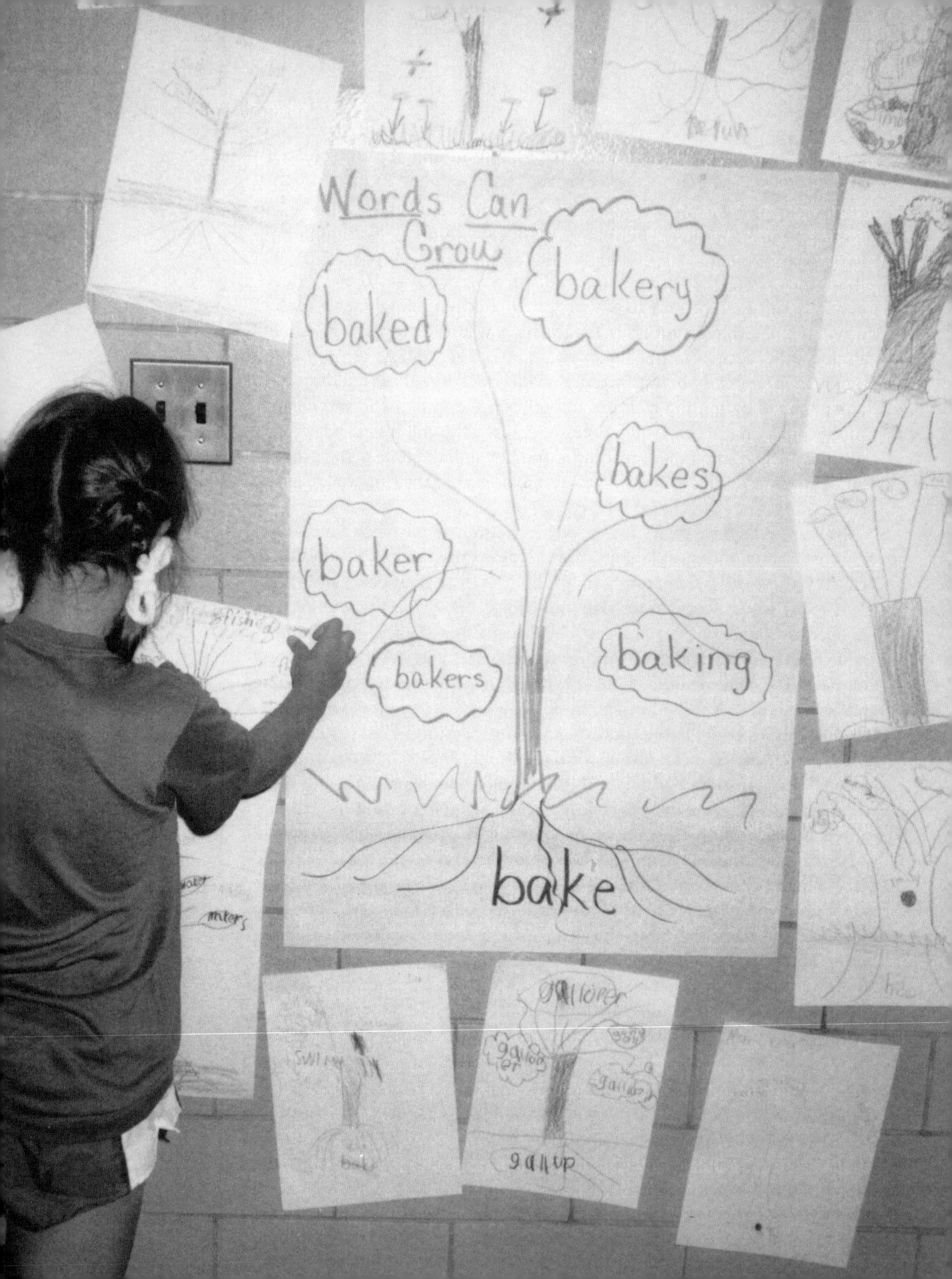
Words Can Grow
bakery
baked
bakes
baker
bakers
baking
bake

CHAPTER 19

But What About Skills?

How does one become a skilled reader and writer? Obviously, by reading and writing. As a classroom teacher I believe this, but I also believe that learners need instruction to learn the nitty-gritty procedures that undergird any refined activity. I considered another area in which I have some competence: needlework. How did I become skillful at needlework?

My first lessons with needle and thread came when I was five. Mom threaded the needle, knotted it, and then showed me how to pull the needle through fabric and continue with a simple running stitch. She handed me the needle and fabric and I continued poking the needle up and down. She applauded my efforts: no criticism, no correction, just delight. When the thread worked out of the needle she came back to rethread it, but a day or two later, I announced that I would do this for myself. She got a needle with a large eye and showed me how first to clip the end of the thread, dampen it slightly to stiffen it, and then feed it through the needle's eye. From then on I was my own needle threader, though Mom was available if I got stuck. Soon I wanted to know how to knot the thread. She showed me how to hold needle in one hand and thread in the other and, maintaining just the proper tension in the thread, to loop the end around my finger, roll it off, and tug ever so slightly to form the knot. Though my first knots were far from perfect, she assured me that this was quite all right. I would get better with practice she said, and with her nurturing and tutelage I did.

Looking back I can see why I successfully learned to sew. First, my mother sewed and embroidered and she placed threaded needle and fabric in my hands as soon as I could possibly manage them because I wanted to do as she did. She trusted my ability to master her craft.

Second, my mother demonstrated a basic stitch, watched for a moment as I tried, then left me to play with this new activity on my own. She came back occasionally to check how things were going and to provide opportunity for me to ask questions. She trusted my ability to work independently and learn through success as well as error and helped when I was stuck. She set high standards at the same time that she tolerated errors. She delighted in my efforts no matter how imperfect and shared my best work with her friends.

Third, she provided quality materials for me to work with, showed me possible stitches and projects, then permitted me to make selections about what I'd like to do next. She provided opportunity to practice with real projects. She took my work seriously but maintained a playful tone. Working to improve my skill was not an end in itself, but an integral part of the process of creating something lovely.

I believe my needlework skills developed to a high level because I experienced success and felt accomplishment from the very beginning. Learning to read and write can be much the same. Give children reading and writing materials, place them in a literate environment with a responsive and supportive community of readers and writers, and they'll plunge in!

But what does instruction look like in this kind of environment? With the mask of a reading program removed I could see—really *see*—classroom learning for the first time. Because the children were not all completing the same workbook pages or reading the same story, I discovered individual learning processes. I began to observe and listen closely. From the children I've learned that every child's learning is continually evolving and that learning is an intricate composite of each child's personality, heritage, previous learning, environment, and group collaborations. Children may share common interests and attributes, but these characteristics combine and operate differently within each child.

How *do* children learn to read? I am still unable to pin down this mysterious, complex process any more than I can state exactly how children learn to talk. Defining the process of learning to read with precision is like trying to capture a moonbeam in your hand, and it strikes me that a major handicap to reading instruction may be that we have attempted to articulate learning to read with such precision that we create inflexible orthodoxies. Every classroom teacher who has taught with a reading program is well acquainted with these orthodoxies, which are impossible to apply to *every* student with any degree of effectiveness. I have come to tolerate ambiguity in the classroom and in the learning process. The children have helped me understand that learning is messy, jumbled, nonlinear, and often unpredictable. If we immerse children in a literate environment where language is not dissected but used in a meaningful whole, reading will occur as a natural process. Learning to read is complex but need not be complicated if we trust children's natural capacities to learn.

Wanting to Read— A Prerequisite to Learning

Many first graders today come to school eager to read and most have experience writing and reading their names, letters of the alphabet, or even a few words. Yet some children have few experiences with books and are baffled when it comes to the paper and pencil and book-reading activities of school. Kurt was a child eager to learn but with little experience with written language in his home. He spoke little and always in one or two syllables. In reading and writing workshops he watched other children and, somewhat hesitantly, imitated them. Then one day in February he said, "I wanna *reeead!*" Though he had been reading a few books prior to this, he had not really been involved with them. Then came a change. His reading skills did not suddenly take off, but he began to approach books with vigor, as though a light had suddenly been turned on. I learned from Kurt that to learn to read and write—and probably to really learn anything—you have to *want to learn.* Kurt had been going through the motions, imitating peers because he wanted to be included among them. His initial motivation was social and he became part of the community, doing what this community did, reading and writing. That experience led him to discover that reading was something he really wanted to do. All of my lessons would not have made Kurt a reader had he not decided to learn to read for himself. Instruction must be grounded in purposes felt by the learner. Inevitably, for most children comes the day when they "crack the code" and discover how written language works. But that moment always comes after the child's decision to want to learn to read.

Demonstrating Strategies for Reading

During the first year without a reading program, I referred to my list of traditional first-grade skills frequently to make sure I hadn't missed anything. In subsequent years I rarely referred to it. I found that I was able to determine what to show readers and writers by observing children. The skill checklist was a helpful beginning, but too much emphasis on skill acquisition turned my attention away from the dynamic processes of learning to read and write. Instead, I continually assessed what readers and writers needed and then provided information in the form of strategies at the time when individuals needed specific help.

Connie Weaver (1988) writes that the difference between *skills* and *strategies* is a crucial distinction as these terms pertain to reading instruction:

> In the word-centered skills approaches, children are taught to use their stock of sight words, their phonics and structural analysis skills, and their understanding of context in order to identify words. Concern with comprehension typically comes later, after the selection has been read. But in a meaning-centered strategies approach, children are actually taught to use their developing comprehension of a text in order to help them identify the words. They are taught to use context of all sorts to *predict* what will come next, to *sample* the visual display, using a minimum of graphic/ phonemic cues to confirm or modify their prediction and to tentatively interpret a word, and to use following context to *confirm* or *correct* this tentative interpretation. Creating meaning from the text is more important than identifying all the words. Meaning is the beginning and the end of reading, and the means as well. (p. 145)

A way to help children develop meaning-centered strategies is through what Smith (1982) calls "demonstrations," the opportunity to see how something is done (p. 108). Many of these demonstrations are the ongoing daily reading and writing activities of the children and myself. Other demonstrations are focussed presentations which, like my mother's needlework instruction, are responsive in nature, take children's work seriously, and maintain a playful tone and a light touch.

Demonstrations in Read Alouds

When reading a book to children I focus on meaning but I also am demonstrating *how* to read. Such demonstrations naturally surround the reading. Occasionally I comment or interject questions to point out the clues the book provides to get at the meaning. When I read Molly Bang's *Yellow Ball* to first graders in September, I began by holding up the book and reading the title while I pointed to the words. A large yellow circle suspended in the sky over the ocean dominates the cover illustration. "Sun" a couple of children said quietly when they saw the cover. Their comment caused me to respond, "This does look like the sun, but this word is "ball" and it begins with B. If it had an S it could be 'sun.' "

Then one little guy commented, "Or bus. At the end."

"Oh yes, if there was an S at the end of this word it might be the word 'bus.' " I acknowledged his contribution by repeating his idea and putting it into a complete sentence. Some children talk in phrases or one-word responses; helping them develop oral language goes on throughout the day, especially when we talk about books in the large group setting.

I read the author's name and noted that "Bang" begins with the same letter and sound as "ball." On the dedication page I asked the children where this story will take place and they quickly identify the setting as the beach. "The pictures tell us that, don't they?" I acknowledged. *Yellow Ball* has twenty pages with a twenty-eight word text. On the opening two pages a little boy holds a large yellow ball and two other children hold out their arms ready to catch the ball. I read the two words on the pagespread: "catch, throw." "Who can tell how the story begins from these pictures and these two words?"

"Throw the ball," commented one child.

"Who will throw the ball?" I asked.

"That little boy."

"Oh, the boy will throw the ball and then what will happen?"

"He's gonna catch it," replied another child.

"Ahhh. So the story begins when the little boy is throwing the ball and the other boy—and the girl perhaps too—are going to catch the ball."

"Yeah," said still another child, "they're gonna play hot potato."

"Hot potato?" I said "Tell me about hot potato." For a moment or two the children explained how to play hot potato.

On the next two pages, four pictures show the ball drifting into the water while the children play on the sand. I asked who could tell what's happening in these pictures, and as I spoke I pointed to each picture in sequence, left to right, top to bottom. I said nothing about the order, just went through the sequence by pointing a couple of times. A child told a story to accompany the pictures as, again, I pointed to each illustration. When she finished, I read "Uh-oh" from the bottom of the second page. The class responded with a series of Uh-ohs and I ran my finger under the word and read it again with them. "You can read this, can't you?" I said. We continued through the book this way, with the children telling the story from the pictures and me validating their ideas by repeating their words, sometimes forming their fragments of meaning into entire sentences. I ran my finger under the words when I read and invited the children to reread with me.

"The fish is looking up at the ball and the ball is *above* him," I noted on one page, emphasizing "above" written under the picture. Then I did the same for the other three pictures and accompanying words on this pagespread. We speculated as to why the water is green in one picture and blue in the other three. A child suggested that "Maybe because it's *under* the water, and the sun above makes it a different color." "Good thinking. That's certainly possible," I commented. We continued through the story, reading the pictures and the few words then telling the story. The ball goes out to sea, is caught in a storm, the ocean becomes quiet, and then the ball comes ashore on a page where a rosy sky meets the water. I asked what time of day this might be to have this kind of sky. A child suggested sunset. We looked at the previous page with the ball floating on a moonlit ocean.

"It's dusk—when the sun comes up," suggested another child.

"Oh, you think it's dawn, when the sun comes up," I say, restating the comment but substituting "dawn" for "dusk" without making an issue of this minor error.

"Yup, dawn," replied the child.

Some children were confused about sunrise and sunset and we talked about the difference. The children speculated as to whether the book illustration showed sunrise or sunset and concluded sunrise because the previous page had shown the moon at night. "Or it could be sunset or sunrise on another day if the ball stayed out in the ocean a long time," another child contributed.

"Yes. Good thinking," I responded.

One child told the end of the story to accompany three illustrations: a woman and a child walking along the beach, the pair finding the yellow ball, and the child picking up the ball. "Hug" I read under the third illustration.

"He hugged it and they went home," concluded the child. We turned the page to see the child sleeping with the yellow ball under an arm and the final word, "Home."

"You're right!" I responded. "They went home. And that's the last word in this book, 'Home.' "

I had spent fifteen minutes on a first reading of this book and, through demonstration, incorporated many traditional beginning reading skills.

- "reading" the illustrations
- left-to-right directionality of written language
- top-to-bottom and left-to-right movement through pages of a book
- word decoding strategies of beginning and ending sounds
- letter/sound relationship
- sequencing
- cause and effect
- vocabulary development
- sentence structure
- setting and characters
- predicting

Yet throughout the reading the focus remained on making meaning from Molly Bang's illustrations and brief text. I did not plan these demonstrations and I'd certainly not choose a book and read it aloud with the primary purpose of demonstrating reading strategies. When I first held up the book that day, my only purpose was to present a new book I liked to the children. Skills came up as strategies to get at meaning, and we never allowed them to dominate, to take over or take away from the central purpose of reading. Children will employ these strategies in the same way when they read books on their own because children naturally imitate from the demonstrations around them. Later, after children begin playing with these strategies, I nudge their development as readers further by helping children identify a specific strategy they might use or be using. *The skills never take on a life of their own independent of the meaning-making process.* When we teach them as strategies in the context of reading and writing, we keep skills in perspective.

Word of the Day

As part of our morning opening every day we play Word of the Day, an activity that demonstrates a number of language skills. I select two children from the class and they come to the front of the room where they each select a word card from the dozen or so cards spread fanlike in my hands. I've preselected the cards somewhat. Since we're in September I include words such as these: me, my, I, a, the, go, in, on.

Each child reads the word on the selected card, figures it out using phonetic clues (usually initial and final consonants), or asks another person—the child next to him, me, or a nearby child. The idea is to identify the word quickly, using the most efficient strategies. (This is not a test to determine children's sight word repertoire or their phonetic decoding skills.)

On a day in September, the words are "get" and "the."

"Who has a sentence that uses 'get' and 'the'?" I ask.

Emily raises her hand and suggests, "Get the teddy bear."

I place the word cards on the chalkboard edge and Emily begins to dictate the writing of her sentence. I carry out her directions.

"G," she begins, "no, I mean *capital* g, e, t, space, t, h, e, space." At this point Emily stops to reread. "Get the . . . teddy bear . . . t, period, b, period. I put periods after the T and the B," she adds, "because I know there's more letters, but I don't know how to write them yet."

"Good enough, Emily. Let's read the whole thing and see if there's anything we'd revise." I point to the words as Emily reads her sentence aloud and when she's finished I say, "If we were going to publish this for lots of other people to read, we'd have to finish the spelling of teddy bear. Would you like me to show you how we'd do that?"

"Yes," says Emily.

I draw a line through "t.b." and write "teddy bear" above it adding, "This is the way a writer makes changes; they line out, then write the new words or ideas."

"Only I don't think I could spell 'teddy bear' yet," says Emily.

"Of course not. Someday you will, but until then there are other ways—like writing t.b. And later, you could revise by getting help from someone else or by looking it up in a book." Emily nods and smiles.

I underline "get" and "the," the two words of the day. " 'The' begins with a th. Say it with me. Notice where your tongue goes when you say th at the beginning of 'the.' " The children repeat "the" over and over, and we note how our tongue goes between our front teeth. "When you're writing, you might want to remember how your tongue goes between your teeth when you say the t-h sound in 'the.' Can you think of any other words with that sound?"

The children think a moment, then hands go up.

"That."

"Think."

"Theron, anyways, that's my name," says Theron.

"Right! We've got a great way to remember the sound for *th*—just remember the beginning of Theron's name."

The two words remain on the chalkboard ledge throughout the school day and the sentence stays until we need the chalkboard again. Tomorrow I will put the words in a box that holds all the words from previous days. I *never* drill the children on these words, the phonetic sounds, mechanics of composition, or revision strategies that we've just addressed. The lesson is short and spontaneous. Each day we address whatever issue arises through the draw of the words and the sentence a child contributes: punctuation, patterns and irregularities of phonetic elements, capitalization, etc. There's always something to talk about, and over the course of the year we address many conventions of written language. Of course, the sentence we write always must make sense. During the first days of school, the children often suggest sentence fragments when I ask for a sentence. When children selected the words "my" and "red," another student volunteered, "My red car."

"Ah," I said, "but what about your red car? For this to be a sentence, you must tell me something about your red car."

The child thought a moment. "My red car . . ." I said, restating the child's line with the words hanging, waiting for completion.

". . . is fast," he replied. We went on to talk briefly about sentences. The children quickly develop an intuitive "sentence sense." Sometimes, a child comes forth with a sentence that goes on and on and on. "Whoa!" I say. "Let's shorten that a bit. We'll be here all morning writing that long snake of a sentence." They laugh and help the child revise before we write.

Later in the school year the children begin examining what they have dictated. "How would you revise that?" I ask, and the child looks at the sentence and corrects spelling, punctuation, words that were left out, spacing between words (for if a child does not tell me to put a space in, I leave it out). Other children begin raising their hands with suggestions, and when the composer of the sentence has taken it as far as he can, he calls on classmates for their suggested revisions. Sometimes revisions create an error. The ensuing discussion enables us to examine the reasoning behind specific ways of writing or spelling or correcting written language. We always end with a correct version. Word of the Day shows children conventions of written language in a nonthreatening, enjoyable way.

Charts and Lists

Carrie writes "two" for "to" as she composes. I explain the difference between the words to Carrie and then suggest we tell the entire group. A short while later Carrie helps me explain homonyms to the class. On a large sheet of chart paper I write the three forms: two, to, too. I comment that there are other words that have two meanings and many of them are spelled differently. Jason suggests "for" and "four." With a different colored marker we add to the chart. We collect homonyms from that point in the school year. Sometimes a child comes upon one in reading and, checking with me, adds it to the chart. Some children bring in lists they've brainstormed with family members at home and we tape these papers to the chart. One day John says, "I've got one: 'fish' like you 'go fish' and the fish that you catch." We take a moment to discuss the different meanings and I point out that "fish" has two meanings but one spelling and so doesn't quite qualify for this list.

We add other charts too, such as ones for compound words and contractions and ones related to a particular topic, holiday, or season. We draw a chart and title it "Words Can Grow." I write "bake" on the roots of a plant that extends to the top of the chart, with branches bearing "baker," "bakery," "baking," etc. Sometimes, the children made similar charts.

We also create charts over the course of several mini-lessons, such as this one on punctuation:

Punctuation
- *Period* . To end a sentence. (says "stop")
- *Exclamation mark* ! To show a lot of emotion (anger, excitement), a lot of expression.
- *Question Mark* ? To ask a question.
- *Comma* , To separate words in a series; in the greeting or closing of a letter; to signal the reader to pause.
- *Quotation Marks* " " To show someone talking.

At the end of the mini-lesson on periods, I started the chart by writing the brief statement about a period. The chart grew on subsequent days as I addressed other forms of punctuation. The chart served as a reminder for students as they wrote and I referred to it during later mini-lessons.

Some charts, such as ones on good writers and good readers, list ideas from group brainstorming sessions. All of the charts hang in the room until the last day of school. Because we create the charts together the children experience the purpose of each, and thus find them useful. On the last day of school, as we clean out the room together, I distribute the charts, the lists of blends, picture reminders for vowel sounds—all the language reminders we have used all year—to the children. "Who wants the compound word list?" I ask. I take it down, roll it up, and it goes home with Suzanne. Next year I'll make new charts with the next group of children—charts that will be meaningful for *those children*.

Word Games

We play word games at the large chalkboard and sometimes with individual chalkboards the children can hold at their desks. These games are ones that teachers and children have played for decades, such as starting with a root word and then adding letters to form a new word. Or I might dictate four words that rhyme for the children to write on their individual chalkboards and ask the children to notice the structural similarities. I find it rather easy to come up with playful activities such as these, but I also know that a little goes a long way. If I pull the individual chalkboards out too frequently the novelty fades, the children moan, and the play diminishes to drudgery; once a month is enough to maintain children's interest. I try also to diffuse any tone smacking of testlike competitiveness. "He's copying mine," a child protested one day. "That's okay. In fact, it's great. One way to learn is by watching others," I responded, and I suggested that we move desks together in pairs so that the work could be more collaborative. So much of what we do in schools is set up as a testing situation. The purpose of using the chalkboard is to experiment with written language together and to learn through the experience. Errors and working together need to be part of that process.

Handwriting Lessons

I teach handwriting to first graders through teacher-directed lessons where I write on the chalkboard while the children write at their seats. At the beginning of the year I demonstrate the way to form uppercase and lower-case letters on lined paper. From then on, handwriting is a matter of practice. I've learned that I can take children through a daily handwriting lesson of fifteen minutes duration or spend fifteen minutes two or three times a week and obtain the same results when it comes to producing legible handwriting. I want children to be aware of situations that call for one's best handwriting. A writer can't attend to producing lovely handwriting while drafting a piece of writing because the focus is on the ideas the writer wishes to communicate. However, a final draft, one meant to be read by the public, requires an attractive presentation. The purpose of good handwriting is to enhance our final written products. Therefore, we learn to form letters and then practice for legibility. I emphasize the purpose of handwriting through the invitations or notes we write and send home.

Rather than a repetitious drill of letters or copying items such as poems, I involve the children by incorporating activities such as these.

- Word play: We write "cat." I ask children to change one letter to make a new word. We write "can" at a child's suggestion and go from there. Another day we may write rhyming words, or contractions, or any one of numerous possibilities.
- Language usage: We write a definition of quotation marks or the rule for forming a plural or possessive. To prepare for addressing valentines, we write the names of the class members, alphabetizing them as we write.
- Phonics: I write "flower," point out the fl blend and then ask children to volunteer other words that begin in the same way. Or we write words with a particular vowel sound or a word ending.

Instead of collecting and correcting handwriting practice papers I ask the children to look over their work and circle letters or words they feel are done well. Often I walk around the room and place a sticker or a stamp on *all* the papers while the children are attending to this self-assessment. Practicing handwriting has less drudgery now that the children are involved in more than copying letters from the chalkboard.

Spontaneous Demonstrations

Opportunities to point out how language works come up throughout the day in the classroom. These simple unplanned demonstrations of language usage occur when I point out *how* something is being done or examine a particular aspect of written language. For example, as I write a sentence on the board I say aloud, almost as if I was talking to myself, "Of course, I'll use a capital letter because this is the first word in a sentence." Or I might talk aloud about my end punctuation or some other aspect of the sentence to help children "see" my thinking. The talk is incidental to the task of composing the sentence, but gives children one more opportunity to find a useful strategy for themselves.

When we read the directions in the math book we come across a one-word sentence: "Subtract." I might ask a question such as: "How do we know that word is 'subtract' and not 'add?' " "What does the writer do to show us this is a sentence?" "How can this sentence have only one word?" "Did you notice the tr blend is in the *middle* of that word?" We take a moment to discuss a particular point and go on with the math lesson. I believe every teacher is provided countless opportunities during the day to point out strategies to make sense of written language.

As I talk with a child during a reading or writing conference, I may remind them of one of the conventions of written language or a strategy to figure out a word by simply showing them how it will apply to what they are doing at the moment. "This is something that might help you," I'll say as a form of introduction, and then present whatever I have to say. Sometimes while working with a child, I'll point out a particular strategy—a phonetic element, for example—and comment, "You may run across this as you read today. If you do, you'll know how to use this." Sometimes class discussion will turn for a few minutes to a specific phonetic structure or perhaps to a punctuation mark in the books the children are currently reading. "Do you find any questions marks in your book?" or "Can you find a word that begins with a *kn?*" I'll ask. As children spot examples, I write them on the chalkboard and we talk about using these strategies as we read. Often, days after such discussions, children tell me about a particular strategy that they've used: "See, I found the oo like you showed us and so I knew this word."

Opportunities for spontaneous instruction on language come up throughout the school day. I keep such instruction short, focussed, and playful. The idea is to continually help children become aware of how language works by pointing out or reflecting on some of the demonstrations that come up.

The Children's Strategies

Each child acquires a complex, unique, and integrated set of reading strategies as they read in an environment rich with demonstrations centering on making sense of written language. The *timing and the ordering of those strategies is different for each child*. Though I continually introduce, suggest or remind children of ways to approach reading, I leave the decision concerning the use of specific techniques up to the individual child. Often no child uses a particular strategy immediately and certainly not every child in the room will find every strategy helpful. Children pull from the repertoire of strategies in the environment as they experience the need to do so. Children are naturally efficient learners, dealing with what makes sense to them at a given moment and ignoring that which, from their perspective, is non-sense. Allowing children to choose their own strategies in an environment where they are surrounded by demonstrations permits children to maintain and expand their efficient and natural learning capacities.

While there is no one sequence to the development of reading strategies, I have observed some particular techniques that children exercise as they learn to read.

Retelling Stories and Using Memory

Some children "read" books to me during the first days of school by talking about single illustrations, by retelling the stories in sequence using the illustrations, by reading words here and there that they recognize on the pages, or through a selection and combination of these strategies. Children who talk through a book, even if they omit most of the actual text, are participating in a natural process of beginning reading. The books they choose to read in this fashion usually are ones I have read aloud to the class.

Familiarity with a text and memory of phrases helps readers. It is easier to read or retell any book for which one has a context rather than a book filled with unfamiliar names, places, or story line. Children use memory of a particular book to recognize words. For example, when I asked Adam how he learned to read *Cookie's Week* he said, "I remembered you reading it and when I came to words I didn't know I could just hear you saying them, so then I knew the word." Children made similar comments even after becoming fluent readers. Of course, as they begin reading, children use other strategies besides memory of a text to figure out unknown words, but memory plays an important part in the initial process. Children read and reread books, and those repeated experiences with words *within a meaningful context* contribute to the development of a sight word vocabulary. Children may not recognize words they have been reading in a book when presented with these same words in isolation, but recognizing words in context is part of the developmental process of meaning making. Requiring children to know all the words before reading is like requiring children to know how to spell before they are permitted to write.

Even after children become fluent readers they continue to rely on familiarity with books—usually ones read to them at home or at school—to select reading material. Familiarity with a text helps make a book or part of a book predictable, a characteristic that helps beginning readers. Also, patterned language of books, such as *Cookie's Week* or *Ten Little Bears*, support beginning readers. However, some books are too predictable, using so many repeating lines that children rely on memory exclusively. The book does little to support growth in the reader because it fails to provide opportunities for the child to explore other strategies or even to look closely at the words. Often these books are written for the specific purpose of creating predictable texts and many are quickly rejected by children because they are not fun to read.

Pointing to Words

When children read books, I suggest they point to the words. I find that pointing directs a child's attention to the words and actually helps children learn individual words by focussing on those words as they read and reread particular texts. Most children naturally point when they begin browsing through books whether they discuss illustrations, pick out a few words, or read entire books. Pointing is similar to the pointing parents and preschoolers do as they first explore books together; it is a way of focussing on particular aspects of the book. I've noticed that the few children who do not point are those who have had scant experiences with parent/child storytimes. For these children, I point toward myself as we talk about a book and they soon pick up on this strategy.

As children begin reading entire books, I encourage them to follow along in the text by pointing. Observing the way a child points provides glimpses into that child's awareness of individual words. At times children move their fingers under each word, accurately pointing to the word they read aloud. Carrie read *Cookie's Week* with this kind of pointing. When she read "garbage can" for "trash can" she noticed the miscue and made a correction without prompting. Pointing helped her focus on the individual word, thus enabling her to notice the mismatch with the initial letter (T) and the initial sound (G) she read. Other children make general sweeps across the printed line, often indicating memorization of the text.

Cory moved his fingers under the lines of *This Old Man* when he read it. His errors did not interfere with the meaning, but he obviously was not attending to individual words. Most children go through a period when they rely on pointing in a word-by-word fashion but, as they become fluent with a particular text, their fingers begin to glide under the words. Eventually, on their own, most children abandon pointing to words except when they come upon a difficult word. When Jody came upon the word "decided" his finger suddenly pointed to the word while he focussed momentarily on it. On numerous occasions with fluent readers, I observe a child's finger dart to a position below a challenging word, hear the child read that word, and then see the finger retract. I've even noticed adults (including myself) do the same thing occasionally, especially when reading aloud. Sometimes I ask a child, "Can you read this now without pointing?" as a nudge toward moving away from pointing if I sense that the pointing is no longer needed. The strategy of pointing enhances the initial meaning-making process by helping children focus.

Learning to Read New Words

As children read new texts and reread others, they begin developing, *in an integrated fashion*, strategies to figure out individual words. The following strategies help many children learn to read unfamiliar words.

PICTURE CLUES: From the beginning children look at the illustrations in books with intense interest, an activity that takes on almost a ritual quality and that continues throughout the year. Newkirk and McLure (1992) noticed the same thing in other first-grade readers and described them as "milking" the illustrations. As children begin tending to the words on a page, they connect the ideas in pictures to the meaning conveyed by those words. Even after they abandon memorization as a way to read, they glance at illustrations when they are unsure of a word. As children become accomplished readers, they naturally ease out of relying on this strategy for word identification but still spend considerable time reading the pictures and discussing illustrations with their peers. Reading the pictures, noticing details in the illustrations and making inferences and predictions from those illustrations, seems to be a significant activity, one that leads to reading written text with the same attitudes toward comprehension.

CONTEXT CLUES: Sentence structure and word order, expected word meaning, words surrounding an unknown word, and illustrations all help readers. The children's entire experiences with language—written and oral as well as with books—enhance the development of reading. They expect a text to make sense and they use their knowledge of how language works to make sense of written passages as they read. Since the structure of written language is not identical to spoken language, reading aloud to children is critical in helping them develop an ear for written language so then they can use context clues.

VISUAL CLUES: The appearance of a word—the shape, length, specific letters, and patterns of letters—helps when reading. Children often make comments such as David's, "I learned 'something' because it's so long and it has *ing* at the end." We share such comments in the classroom, making one child's experience available to all the children. A variety of experiences with written language, from both outside and inside the classroom, contribute to a child's using visual clues.

PHONETIC CLUES: Children say they sound out, meaning they use phonetic clues, especially initial consonants. I observe children developing an awareness of patterns in the structure of words as they write and read and then applying those patterns when they come upon unknown words in their reading. Rarely do I observe children sound out an entire word; the context usually provides supporting strategies so that the child figures out the words by using only some phonetic clues. When I asked Jody how he sounded out he explained, "I looked at the *bl* at the beginning and the *t* at the end and then I got it."

MULTIPLE CLUES: Children employ their own multiple approaches to deciphering words, such as asking another reader, skipping the word, testing and rejecting possibilities for meaning, reading other words around it for clues, and using the strategies listed above. Time and choice are the children's allies in developing their strategies. When Monica first attempted to read *Mufaro's Beautiful Daughters* she had the option to decide to give herself more time. Monica talked about her process. "This book was once too hard. Then I tried it and there were only three words I didn't know. My reading had gotten better by reading so much. When I get stuck I think really hard—like once I forgot 'stop.' I thought really hard what could I use for it. I look at the vowel in it. It's easier for me to use the vowels now but sometimes they don't always work for me. I get nonsense words. So I try other ways. Like 'approaching'—I thought of hundreds of words and then one pops in my head. I read the page and it usually works out. I figured out 'silhouetted' that way." Monica chose when to read this book, when to set it aside, when to return to it, and what strategies to use to decode.

Practicing

When children tell me how they learned to read a book they often talk about "practicing." Adam smiled and told me, "I keeped on practicing and I had a little bit of words from you and on most of the words I tried to get it [to] make sense, so then I knew what the words were."

Jody said, "I was just practicing. When there were words like 'spilling,' I hardly knew what they were. I skipped it and went on."

In a voice brimming with pride Stacy answered my question about her reading approach. "How? When I got [this book] and was practicing on reading it. I tried it a month ago and I couldn't read it and now I know more words and I got the hang of it."

Glenda Bissex (1980) sees "practice being as crucial for reading success as for playing basketball or piano or any other skill." In observing her son Paul's reading development, she noted that one important form of practice was rereading books. She writes, "Perhaps it gave Paul, as a beginning reader, clearer feedback on his own progress; he could tell he was reading the same book more fluently than before. . . . Personal selection of materials was important for this kind of practice" (p. 171).

Children have the freedom to decide if and how long to practice by rereading a book, though occasionally I urge a child to reread when I feel such guidance to be in the child's best interest. Once in a while a child chooses to stay with one text until able to read that book fluently, but most children set books aside, sample other titles, or read with friends and return to the original book from time to time until that book can be read with ease. Practice in learning to read a book means working on a particular title, alone or with other children, with some regularity but interspersing that reading with other reading materials. Only one child ever complained about rereading a book. "I got tired of this book because I read it so many times—over and over." When I asked, "What could you do if this happened again?" she giggled, then replied, "Get another *book!*"

Writing Helps Reading

In *When Writers Read*, Jane Hansen (1987) says "Writing is the foundation of reading; it may be the most basic way to learn about reading. . . . when writers read, they use insights they have acquired when they compose. . . . when our students write, they learn how reading is put together because they do it. They learn the essence of print" (pp. 178–179).

"You can read your writing because you wrote it and you know what it says," Mark said one day. The children concurred. When children read words they have just written they focus on meaning and then use phonetic and context clues to read. They transfer these processes to reading other materials with relative ease, though the pace of this transfer is unique to each child.

Early on, many children's reading of their own writing is an approximation of the exact text. Some children go through a period when they write pages and then are unable to read it all. Both cases parallel the stage when children "read" books by retelling a familiar story using the pictures as a guide. To help children with reading in both reading and writing workshops, I urge children to look at the words and attempt to figure them out. "Remember what this story is about and then let the letters and pictures help you," I say. I applaud the success of reading even a few words and don't require youngsters to figure out entire passages. With time, experience, and nurturing support, children naturally incorporate context, visual, and phonetic clues to decipher their own writing. They transfer these strategies to the reading of books by professional authors.

A child's published books are the easiest reading material in the classroom for that child. The books of classmates follow next. The children are familiar with these books because they hear them read in sharing sessions during the writing process. Seeing their own and their classmates' writing in print—with conventional spelling, punctuation, etc.—helps children develop a vocabulary of words they can both read and write.

That insight from years ago that "it will work," that children could learn to read by writing, turned out to be credible even if somewhat simplistic. When children compose in daily writing workshops, read their writing, share, receive responses, revise and edit for the purpose of meaning making—when they are involved in the writing *process*—they naturally integrate multiple strategies for working with written language which carry into their reading processes. Reading and writing mingle, complement, and augment each other as children learn written language.

Teaching Phonics and Spelling

One of my biggest concerns about moving away from programmed reading instruction was the fear that, without the help of phonics worksheets and spelling lists, children would fail as readers and spellers. Leaving these tools behind felt risky. Looking back now, having witnessed children's success without these instructional trappings, I wonder at my reluctance.

Using Phonics Every Day

After the first speech I heard Don Graves give I asked, "What about phonics? How do children learn phonics with this approach?" Graves answered the question with a statement that children use phonics every day as they write. I agreed with him; I had seen this in my own classroom. Yet I found his answer somewhat frustrating for he gave no precise *method* for addressing phonics that connected to phonics instruction as I knew it.

Then I watched children write. I heard my students repeat a particular word over and over to themselves, listening for letters and perhaps searching for a visual recall of that word in order to write it for themselves. They didn't really sound out but they did seem to connect the names of letters to the sounds they heard when they repeated words over and over to themselves. "Ball, ball, ball—b! Yes, it's B. I know it's B" I heard Dylan say to himself while writing. I'd always had a gnawing sense that our approach to phonics was not necessarily helpful for children in learning to read. Countless examples of children writing confirmed this.

The first year without all the programs, workbooks, and worksheets that revolved around phonics, I felt more anxiety about phonics than any other issue. Throughout the year I presented phonics to children through short focussed lessons that addressed the rules of phonics and identified specific letter/sound correspondences. During our brief conferences in reading workshop I helped children draw upon these rules and apply them as strategies that might be helpful. The formal phonics instruction was minimal compared to previous years, and most of it came in the latter part of the year after children had begun reading. The children became the most energetic, voracious, and skilled readers I'd taught to date. However, the following year when the children went on to second grade, I learned that other teachers expected children to be able to identify and auditorially discriminate between the various vowel sounds, and to attack unknown words by sounding out.

I revised my instruction for the following year to balance the demands of the school culture with the needs of children by presenting phonics as I had done the previous year, but also by incorporating some phonic worksheets and playing word games to develop more awareness of specific phonetic components. Quickly I recognized that the children were learning two forms of phonics: one was a strategy for reading, the second was a foreign language of sorts, phonics as an end in itself. Children who could complete the drill exercises could not necessarily apply the phonetic skill to reading, and children who used phonetic strategies as they read could complete drill exercises but certainly not with 100 percent accuracy. Children used a *range* of strategies as they learned to read; phonics was only one of those strategies, one with varying degrees of usefulness for individual readers.

I soon eliminated the phonic worksheets and relied on focussed teacher-directed lessons to show children a particular phonic form that might be helpful in learning to read. I attempted to expose my students to the *concept* of consonant blends, rather that learning all the individual sounds of *fl, gr, st,* etc. I showed children the difference between long and short vowels but did not require them to practice auditory discrimination of these sounds with worksheet exercises. I presented phonic rules and we wrote these rules for handwriting exercises and played word games to develop awareness of the patterns in spelling that resulted from phonic rules. I emphasized that rules have exceptions and abandoned all talk of sounding out. Even so, the children still told me they sounded out when they came to unknown words. "Show me what you mean?" I'd ask, and most often children demonstrated the use of beginning or ending consonant sounds as clues to decoding, a process they labeled sounding out. Though I felt my teaching ran counter to the culture of reading instruction, I focussed on responding to children's learning needs and to anticipating—not deciding—what might be helpful for them. Frank Smith (1988) says, "The most that can be expected from a knowledge of phonics rules is that they may provide a *clue* to the sound (or name) of a configuration being examined" (p. 139).

I've come to view the helpfulness of phonics for beginning readers as stretching along a continuum. At one end of the continuum is a child such as Clarence. Clarence searched my face for any hint to confirm that he'd found the correct answer as he attempted to replicate a specific letter sound. He did not hear the precise discriminations between short vowel sounds at all and barely those of consonant letters. (He also had difficulty carrying a tune when the class sang together.) Clarence did use letters as clues when he read. One day I watched him come to a word beginning with the letter B. He tried out several words that began with B—words that he *knew* started with that letter. He happened to hit upon the correct word, "balloon," by looking at the picture. A *visual* memory of words beginning with B rather than an auditory one helped Clarence. I had to admire his resourcefulness. Clarence learned to read.

At the other end of the continuum is Shelly, who relied on letter/sound relationships and sounding out as the dominant strategy for tackling unknown words in her reading. She quickly mastered the sounds represented by letters or combinations of letters and loved the precision and patterns the rules of phonics provided. She became frustrated by words that failed to follow the rules and dealt with these by learning them and giving them her own category. "I know 'because' now. It's *different* from the others," she said. Shelly enjoyed math computations and begged for extra math worksheets, which she completed with neatly formed numerals. Her desk was always organized. She appeared to view the world of phonics with the same precision.

Phonics was never very helpful for Clarence, but Shelly began using phonics soon after she acquired a small vocabulary of words that she readily recognized (and she did this through her writing). For many children phonics makes sense only after they can read. I present phonics to children as one of *many* strategies good readers use. Opportunities for phonics instruction pop up continually throughout the school day. Mills, O'Keefe, and Stephens (1991) provide a detailed description of an approach to teaching phonics throughout the school day in their book *Looking Closely*, a book I recommend for teachers. The approach I use in my classroom is much the same as Tim O'Keefe's with his students. From the children I learned that too much emphasis on phonics detracts from reading for meaning, especially as children first learn to read. As children learn more about written language, they attend to phonetic aspects. It may be that the degree of reading achievement is *one* factor in an individual child's receptivity to and the effectiveness of phonics instruction, but to determine that phonics is a "must" puts some children at a disadvantage in their development as readers.

Developing Spellers

The movement to allow inventive spelling with young writers carries a concern that children will always be poor spellers. I discovered that conventional spelling develops when children write every day in a classroom filled with language. The writing of Jan, Danny, and Trevor over the course of the school year is typical of this spelling development.

On the first day of school Jan wrote A for apple, O for orange, P for pear in her self-selected writing topic about Eric Carle's book *The Very Hungry Caterpillar*. Under a picture of his family's boat, Danny wrote LF.JKT (reversing the J) and read "lifejacket," adding, "When you're on the boat it's real important that you wear your lifejacket." Trevor drew dinosaurs and wrote ONE TIME LOG LOG AGO BCEOSU. WEAID AS HIVE AS TEN ELAFN. (One time long, long ago brachiosaurus weighed as heavy as ten elephants.)

All three children expressed reluctance to write because they couldn't spell. "That's okay," I reassured them, "no one expects you to spell correctly right now. We'll work on spelling later. What's important now is your *ideas*. You can write saying the words you want to write slowly to yourself and writing the letters you hear." I wanted to start children taking risks through invented spelling. Giacobbe taught me this way of responding to children's spelling.

When children respond as these three children did that September morning, I must respond with *delight*—no matter what they've written. This is no time to correct errors. An enthusiastic and accepting response encourages writers and paves the way for them to continue. When Jan read "apple," "orange," and "pear" to me, I replied by saying, "I'm impressed! How did you do that?"

Jan grinned. "I just remember seeing them in my alphabet book. And this is me," she continued, pointing to her drawing.

"Can you write 'me'?" I asked.

Jan paused, then nodded and said, "Yup, because I seen 'me' before."

When Danny wrote "lifejacket," he stopped after every letter to ask, "Is that right?"

"Looks fine to me," I commented. When I asked if he wanted to write anything else he declined and I accepted his decision.

Of the three children, Trevor was most concerned about correct spelling. "I can read, you know," he said in response to my urging to set aside concern for correct spelling and it seemed as though he was telling me that he *knew* that words were spelled one way and only one way. He became very frustrated with me when I would not spell for him. "Is there an N in 'long'?" he asked.

"What do you think?" I turned the question back to him because I knew that if I spelled one word I'd end up spelling the dictionary. Reluctantly, Trevor wrote "log" and continued.

When he read his writing he asked, "Is there an E in 'weighed'?" and before I could respond he answered his own question, "I think there is," and immediately inserted the E. "Is that right?" he asked.

"Yes, there is an E in weighed," I answered.

"Yes, but I want to know if that's the right way to spell 'weighed'?" he demanded.

"That's not the perfect way, but I can read it and I know that you will learn to spell 'weighed' and lots of other words correctly by spelling it the best you can and by going back later and editing it as you just did." Trevor looked at me dubiously a moment, then seemed to accept my answer.

"I put periods after 'brachiosaurus' and 'elephants' " he said. "You want to know why? I'll tell you. See, I don't know how to spell those words so I put periods to make them abbreviations."

Mary Ellen Giacobbe (1991) writes of her students: "I learned that all children can write and that I must value their temporary spellings as clues to their thinking. Their inventions are windows on their minds—a way they reveal their thinking about how our language works" (p. 26). These three children had just given me a glimpse of their thinking and experience with language. I would learn more from each of them as time went on.

Writing samples from late November/early December show how their spelling had evolved since September.

On December 5th, Jan wrote: MY DAD GOT ME CHRISTMAS CARDS THEY HAVE CARE BEARS MY DAD GAVE THAM TOO ME ON SUNDAY THEY WERE 3 97 (read by Jan as "three dollars and ninety-seven cents) I AM GOING TO GIVE THAM OUT ON THE DAY BEFOR. . . . Jan's story about the Care Bear Christmas cards continued for several pages. She spelled most of the words throughout the piece correctly. When I commented on Jan's development as a speller at our parent conference in November, her mother said, "Yes, the other day she wanted to spell 'McDonald's' at home and I just told her to close her eyes and see it in her head. Then she could spell it." My amazed look caused Jan's mother to comment, "That's how I spell."

About the same time Danny wrote:

My Sidr and Hr Frend I wos	My sister and her friend (I was
thar to we wor paing up	there too) we were playing up
frot and wen I kam dan	front and when I came down
to gat my drtgun wit eight	to get my dart gun with eight

drs I wax wrd then I wut	darts, I was worried. Then I went
in sid to tell my Mom to sk to got	inside to tell my Mom to ask to get
my sidr to hulp me find my Drt	my sister to help me find my dart
gun with eight durs my sidr shu	gun with eight darts. My sister showed
me sum plass wer I didt lok fur	me some places where I didn't look for
my dar gun my sidr and I wnt	my dart gun. My sister and I went
in to tull my mom at my sidr . . .	in to tell my Mom that my sister . . .

Danny's story continued for several pages, telling of the dart gun that was never found. He correctly spelled several words consistently: "I, and, then, to, my, Mom, find." He copied "eight" from the classroom wall. His willingness to risk with temporary spelling allowed him to develop close approximations of the correct spelling of other words, which served not only his writing but also his growing awareness of correct spelling.

Trevor wrote about baseball in late November, correctly spelling most of his words. The piece begins:

> Base-ball is a fun Game. You have something called a bat. And there is some one called a picher who throws something called a baseball! And then you try to hit the base-ball and run to little things called bases. 1st 2end 3td And if you get to home plate you're team gets one point. if you miss the ball. . . .

Freedom from the concern for correct spelling enabled each child to write fluently and focus on ideas. Spelling, like all of their language development, continued to develop as these samples from late spring show.

Jan loved unicorns and in May she wrote a fictional piece about a unicorn.

THE UNICORN

> Once a pounatime thre was a unicorn and her name was Joy and she was good because she did what her mom said/says [Jan wrote "says" over "said" when she reread the piece because she was unsure of the correct word. "Says" most nearly represents her spoken language patterns]. One day her Mom told her to clean ["clean" was revised to "wash"] wash the dishes so she washed the dishes and dried the dishes. then her Mom said "thank you."

Jan's story continues for several pages.

Danny wrote a story entitled "My Life," spelled "My lighf."

> When I was three or four weer old. this is war I was. I was in a stor with my mom. When I got lost. this lady came and pit me up and omost tock

me to the lost and fond ofist. When my mom soall that I was not thair. she ran to fin me. then she fond me. The end.

In late April, Trevor wrote a piece about penguins. He began his draft with a dedication page: "Deadacated to Hector and Justin an enimie in football." The body of the work begins:

> Penguins are fasinating creatures. They are birds. The adelies have a misoin in the fall. The Adoult-Adelie's go on the misoin. The Adelies live around the South Pole. The misoin is to go to the South Pole They pick a serten Penguin. They pick the stongest penguin. The Penguin swim from there [changed to "their" during editing as a result of teacher instruction] home land to the South Pole. There they try to find their mates from last year. Their mate is the penguin thet had the baby. The penguin thet swam to the South Pole is. . . .

Trevor misspelled more words in this piece than he did in his baseball writing. However, he had become a writer willing to use the words he wanted rather than only the ones he could spell correctly.

Every year I see first graders develop as spellers. I believe three factors intertwine to influence spelling. The first, and perhaps the most important factor is *writing every day in a writing community on topics of choice*. Children care about their writing topics because they choose them and they want the writing to communicate to readers. Good spelling helps readers. The amount of time we devote to writing permits practice in playing with spelling and refining the spelling of words. The community of writers supports all the writing. This conversation overheard between three children during a workshop is an example:

"How do you spell 'city,' with a C or an S?"

"It's a C."

"No, I think it's an S. Listen s-s-sity."

"No, it sounds like S but it's really a C. I remember seeing it."

"C? S? C. I'm gonna write C. I think it's C." Countless examples of children discussing correct spelling occurred in the classroom.

A second important factor is the proliferation of written language in the classroom. Children see and hear examples of written language in chalkboard writing, in books they hear read aloud and that they read themselves, in the writing done by peers, teachers, and authors from beyond the classroom walls, in the charts and posters the class creates. Children report remembering words they have seen and thus being able to write them. I correct all words when I type children's final drafts for publication, and children notice the corrections.

The third factor is teacher instruction. Even in environments where children are learning to spell naturally, I believe it's important that the teacher address spelling. I've heard too many intermediate grade teachers report that their students say, "This is *my* writing. I can spell any way I want." I suggest that these teachers explain why spelling is really for readers and, therefore, before turning in a piece to be read, it is the writer's responsibility to have as much correct spelling as possible.

From the *beginning* I demonstrate the place of conventional spelling and *gradually* help young writers take responsibility for their spelling. I address spelling by extending children's successes. For example, I point out patterns in words: If you know how to spell "cat," you can easily learn to spell a whole list of words that follow the same pattern. I add that we cannot count on these patterns to spell all words. I affirm children's explorations with spelling. One day Chris said, "I just learned how to spell 'little.' See, I sounded out l-i-t. That's *l* and then *it*. But I didn't know how to write the rest. So I kept saying *l*. Then I thought 'camel.' I said 'camel' and 'little' and they end the same. They have the same sound so then I could write *el*, l-i-t-e-l, little!"

I smiled as I searched for words. "Chris," I began, "I'm really impressed with your thinking. I think it's amazing the way you discovered that. There's just one thing."

"Yeah?"

"Well, even though it seems that's the way to spell 'little,' it's not right. *But that's not your fault*. It's this crazy language of ours. It doesn't always work the way it seems it should," I explained.

"Oh," replied a somewhat subdued Chris.

"Would you like me to show you how to spell 'little'?" I asked.

"Yes," Chris replied with renewing enthusiasm. I wrote the word on a scrap of paper and Chris revised the spelling in his draft.

I addressed the unpredictable nature of spelling with the entire class. One day early in the year I asked the children to spell "because." In the next few minutes I wrote on the chalkboard ten spellings from ten different children:

becos	becoe
becalls	becuke
becase	bekos
becouse	becas
bekoue	bekis

As children spelled, they made comments such as, "I think it has an S in it." "I think there's a U or an O." "I know it begins with *be*." After compiling the list, I wrote "because" correctly and explained that it was one of those words you just have to learn. No pattern will give much help. I wrote "because" on a piece of oaktag, mounted it on a wall, and told the children it would be there when they needed it. I also suggested that if they came across other words that didn't fall into a pattern, we could add them to our list. Periodically a child would suggest a new word, which I would then add to our collection of irregular spellings. Soon our list included: was, said, were, does, been, friend, done, once, come, want, have. We mounted "would," "could," and "should" because the children asked to have them available for ready reference. "Those words are hard to find in your pictionary," commented Matt.

A few weeks after the lesson with "because," Laura said as I conferred with her in a writing conference, "I know how to spell 'because' now. You know how? I just wrote it so many times!" Laura had not written "because" over and over as a study technique to prepare for a test, but rather she had written it when she needed it for her writing, referring to the correct spelling on the classroom wall.

Correct spelling was essential for the children's published books, which went beyond the walls of our classroom, and we addressed spelling as part of the publishing process. I never expected a child to spell every word correctly but they all knew I expected them to assume responsibility for correcting some misspelled words. The children used pictionaries in their desks and there were larger picture dictionaries and children's dictionaries available in the classroom. However, I discouraged children from looking up words until the final editing. Some children wanted to look up every word during the drafting of a piece of writing, which severely inhibited their composing process.

From the children I learned that spelling develops through visual as well as through auditory means. Experience with written language—reading, writing, and *reflecting* on language—aided spelling development. Reflection occurred throughout the school day as the children and I worked with language and noted how words were spelled.

In late spring in one of our class brainstorming sessions I asked the children, "How does a writer spell?" The group compiled the following list, which, like our other charts and lists, I recorded and hung on the wall as a reference for them.

Spelling
1. You could sound out—but that might not always work.
2. Ask other people.
3. Look in your pictionary or dictionary.
4. Look for the word in the room.
5. Look in a book.

6. Ask Mom or Dad or sister or brother.
7. Look on a map or glove (for state or country).
8. Look in the newspaper.
9. Look on a shirt.
10. Look on a crayon.
11. Try to remember words.
12. Remember little words. "I learned 'hit' because 'it' is in it."
13. Use a word a lot. "I learned 'go' that way."

As we finished the list Bradley announced, "I got a humongous mind and I just keep words there."

Becoming Good Readers

On a spring morning, after several years of close observation and documentation of first graders learning to read, I asked my first graders a question similar to what Nancie Atwell (1987) asked her eighth graders: "You are all good readers; what do you do that good readers do?" I wrote their responses on chart paper and soon had to run to the supply closet for extra sheets. The class produced the following list.

Good Readers . . .
1. . . . know how to pick books they can read.
2. . . . know how to pick books they like.
3. . . . know when to abandon a book because it's too hard, boring, too easy, not interesting.
4. . . . tell other people about good books.
5. . . . figure words out by:
   a. sounding out but it doesn't always work
   b. asking another person
   c. skipping and coming back after reading the sentence and then seeing what makes sense
   d. looking at the letters for clues
   e. sometimes sounding out the two beginning letters
   f. using the pictures to help
   g. covering up half the word to figure it out
   h. looking at the shape of the word

6. . . . read to other people.

7. . . . listen to other people read.

8. . . . write because reading and writing match.

9. . . . like certain authors and pick their books.

10. . . . write to authors.

11. . . . talk about authors and poets and illustrators.

12. . . . go to bookstores and buy good books like *Two Bad Ants.*

13. . . . *read* a lot!

14. . . . don't always know all the words because they're still practicing when they get a book.

15. . . . *look* for books. They don't just grab the first thing they see.

16. . . . think about books when they're not reading them.

17. . . . know *how* to tell people about good books.

18. . . . look for new authors.

19. . . . spread out and read *lots* of authors.

20. . . . pick books they've never read before.

21. . . . go to the library and reread favorite books again and again.

22. . . . read to find out things they want to know about.

23. . . . go to the library.

24. . . . *love* to read!

Much discussion and agreement surrounded the compiling of this list. When Matt contributed "looking at the letters for clues" (5d), a discussion ensued in which the children said that you "first you have to *look* at the words. After you look at the words, you notice the letters." Some children had already developed this particular strategy when they entered first grade. Others acquired this strategy through involvement in the classroom. I realized that "looking at the words" was a critical breakthrough for each reader.

When Max contributed item 19, "Good readers spread out," I thought at first he spoke of the way children liked to spread out on the floor throughout the room as they read. "No!" he protested, amused at my ignorance. "Good readers read different things—they read different authors. They don't just stay with the same kinds of books or authors. Add 'pick books they've never read before.' "

After we finished our list we reread it and at the end I asked Monica what she meant when she said, "Good readers write because writing and reading match."

"Well, it's like this," she began. "It's kinda hard to explain, but when you write, you write about your life—you know, things you did or things you know something about—and that makes you think of things you've read.

And, when you read, you think about things in your life and then you want to write about them to get them all down and then you can read about your life too." She paused and then her face lit up. "It's about your *life!*" she continued. "Reading and writing match because they're both about your life. They both make you think about your life."

The children listened and acknowledged that indeed this was true. I was dumbfounded. Monica expressed what many adults may have forgotten or perhaps never experienced: Reading and writing are tools for meaning making and meaning making is a *life* process.

Reflections

At Kendall Demonstration Elementary School, on the campus of Gallaudet University in Washington, D.C., I worked with classes of deaf children. One group of six- and seven-year-olds, comparable in age and interests to my first graders, could knock the socks off of many of their peers throughout the country when it came to reading and writing. It was February. They wrote clear, organized pieces of writing that were for the most part spelled and punctuated correctly. They read voraciously. One child was reading the books of Laura Ingalls Wilder. These children are deaf (most since birth); they do not learn language auditorially and obviously phonics is not part of their instruction. However, they are immersed in language-rich environments in their homes and at school, their first language being American Sign Language. They learn language *by using language for meaning-making purposes.* Their example inspires me to maintain that stance for all language instruction in my classroom.

Direct instruction has never left my classroom; neither has skill instruction. However, direct instruction no longer dominates the day and skill instruction takes the form of informing students of helpful strategies. We also take time to reflect on language usage. I ask children: "How did you do this?" "Why did you decide to do it this way?" "What struggles did you find as you did this?" "What did you learn?" "What might you try to solve this problem?" "Why do we need a capital letter for that word?" "What other words end with 'ing?' " Reflection leads children to formulate their own theories about how language works and how it can better serve their purposes. Jerry Harste, et. al. (1984) writes: "Theory, we argue, is fundamentally a set of beliefs upon which you are willing to act" (p. ix). Theory defined this way is a vital component of learning. I try to incorporate instructional practices that allow children to continually construct and revise their theories about language as they use language for their own purposes.

After several years of close observations and documentation of first graders learning to read, I know only that *every child learns to read differently*. Just as Donald Graves stated that writing demands a "waiting, responsive teaching style," so I believe that reading requires a waiting, responsive teaching style. When I began teaching writing with this responsive approach, I realized that it was not enough to establish an environment and let children write. To help writers develop, I had to be familiar with strategies that writers use and to develop an ongoing awareness of the qualities of good writing. Similarly, to teach reading with a responsive teaching style, I had to bring to the classroom expertise about reading strategies, a knowledge of a wide range of available reading materials to accommodate individual interests, and an awareness of the many purposes for reading. I had to strive to incorporate all of these aspects into the structure. I continue to work at this approach, learning from and with the children.

Looking at
Student Progress

CHAPTER 20

Documenting Student Growth

For the classroom teacher, student evaluation—and teacher accountabil-ity—is the bottom line. That accountability often discourages teachers from taking risks. The programmed instructional packages provide a degree of safety with their built-in methods for documenting progress. The reading programs provide tests, worksheets, and cumulative record sheets, break-ing reading down into minute parts. These tools offer "proof" of children's progress—a safe way to measure achievement and to demonstrate "ac-countability." After all, who can argue with numbers and checklists.

Without the reading program I was faced with how to deal with the sensitive issue of evaluation. I had been using the measuring tools in the reading programs, even though I recognized the shallowness of test results and drill exercises to demonstrate reading achievement. I knew that I could give the same test to the same student on a different day and get different results. I knew that I could give a student two different tests on the same day and come up with different reading levels. I knew that the "grade level" parameters varied from test to test and from program to program even though everyone expressed concern that a child be "on grade level." And I knew that the report card grades I gave were based on more than test re-sults and the accuracy with which children completed worksheets and drills; my subjective knowledge of each child played a part in the grades my first graders received. The problem was that I had no way of documenting this knowledge. As I considered the ramifications of the changes coming in my classroom, how I would document student achievement presented a challenge I needed to address immediately.

In August, before that first September without the reading program, I devised an elaborate system for keeping careful records on each child's progress. I set up a thick notebook with sections for each child containing an assortment of record sheets for noting specific achievements, e.g., when a child began to write in complete sentences or use a specific phonetic element. I planned to log observations on each child daily (or weekly at least). Well, my ambitious plan quickly disintegrated. The notebook was cumbersome, the recording too time-consuming, and the premise faulty, for there was no one day when a child suddenly began writing complete sentences or using any other language conventions. Individual learning was too recursive for such specific documentation. I soon found it more important to note my surprises, wonderings, and concerns as I worked with children. The extensive records I kept that year were mostly in my own journal and in folders I eventually set up for each child. I learned that record keeping, to be effective, had to be efficient. Too much recording becomes burdensome, requiring extensive sifting of data later, but too little provides inadequate documentation and leads to generalizing about children's intricate learning processes.

The second year I thought I'd conquered the record-keeping problem, but at the end of that year I found myself still struggling. I kept looking for neat definitive answers. Eventually, I realized that my difficulty resulted from attempting to use the old ways of documenting (e.g., describing achievement in terms of discrete skills) and from seeking a precise system to use year after year. What is the *purpose* of record keeping, I asked myself. The answer always came back: to help me *understand* the learning process of individual children, thus informing instruction, and to provide data to communicate with parents. To these ends, I needed to know what my students did, how they learned and why they made the decisions they did as they worked. Though still faced with the reality of report cards, which required me to grade thirty items on a 1 to 5 scale, I wanted to document the children's ongoing development with information I could show to parents. Instead of *telling* others *about* a child with my interpretive judgment, I tried to *show* a picture of each child, allowing others to *see* a child's progress. When I placed more emphasis on the child as an individual rather than comparing the child to others, so did the parents. We focussed on individual growth from a perspective of success rather than from a deficiency model. Perhaps most important, I recognized that assessment is deeply embedded in the day-to-day process of teaching and learning and involves everyone—teachers, students, and parents. I was finding ways to document what Yetta Goodman calls "kidwatching." "Kidwatching," Goodman (1985) writes, "is used as a slogan to reinstate and legitimize the significance of professional observation in the classroom. . . . The best way to gain insight into language learning is to observe children using language to explore all kinds of concepts in art, social studies, math, science, or physical education" (pp. 10–11).

I am an advocate and practitioner of kidwatching, of closely observing children in order both to note their progress and struggles and to improve my teaching approaches. As I observe children, I keep notes on their learning efforts, trying to be as specific as possible. These notes provide documentation of student growth and enable me to share detailed accounts of a child's acutal progress rather than numbers or phrases that are open to varied interpretations.

I am far more comfortable with this approach to discussing student growth than one that places me in a position as judge and authority on the learner. Kidwatching advances valuing of the learner and takes into account context, which is essential to understanding the growth of individual learners.

Recording Writing and Reading Development

With my last class of children, I prepared two folders for each child before school opened, one for reading and one for writing. I color-coded the folders (red for reading and blue for writing) and kept them on my center table where I had easy access to them at all times. Inside the writing folder I stapled blank paper for anecdotal records and a form devised for taking notes during publishing conferences. Inside the reading folder was also a paper for anecdotal records and a form for recording notes when children read books to me. These record sheets were the core of the folders, but the folder also provided a place for me to file any additional documents or data that contributed to the picture of a child's reading or writing development. I change these forms slightly each year. If I were working with another grade level or if I needed records for another curricular area, I'd design another form and revise it to meet my needs.

Writing Records

Traditionally, products have been the way to determine student achievement. However, when children began writing in my classroom every day, their "products" caused me to reexamine my thoughts about assigning grades to writing. The final product could be examined in isolation, but the context surrounding any piece of writing enriched my understanding of a child's development. I saw growth as unique, individual. How could I possibly give grades to individual papers? Instead, I began looking at growth over time and considering all that children said and did as they wrote. Product *and* process were essential to documenting student growth.

The writing folder that I maintain for each child does not take the place of the writing folder the children keep. Children's folders hold the majority of their writing. My folders hold primarily the drafts of published pieces of writing (the writing that a child has put the most time and effort into), along with my notes from the publishing conferences related to the published pieces. The record sheet for publishing conference notes, stapled to the inside of the folder, provides places to note the date of the conference, the title of the piece, strategies/skills addressed, observations, writer comments, and plans. This form guides my note taking during publishing conferences. However, adhering to the form too strictly hinders record keeping. Better notes come from simply writing what occurs.

My writing folders also hold notes children write to me, as well as vacation journals. When parents plan a family vacation and request their child's "work" to take along, I send a book parents and child can read together and a stapled booklet of blank paper for the child to write in during the absence from school. Jody requested such a booklet for Christmas vacation. He returned it in January with the title, "Christmas Day and Another Day." Eventually, this vacation journal went into his writing folder as additional documentation of his involvement in writing.

On the anecdotal record sheet in the writing folders, I jot down incidents relating to a child's writing. Usually, I make a quick note during the writing workshop to remind myself and then record it later so that this note taking does not rob time from conferences in the workshop itself. I find I end up with extensive notes on some children and brief notes on others. I go though these anecdotal notes periodically and reflect on *all* the children, especially considering those for whom notes are minimal. I've come to trust that the volume of notes has little correlation to my knowledge about a particular child. It is the *anomalies* that I want to understand, and writing helps me reflect on those anomalies.

I can't hope to record everything that happens with a child's writing, but short notes written at the time when events occur provide specific information and also spark my memories of those moments. Finding ways to make efficient notes challenged me. For a brief time I tried taking notes on peel-off address labels, which I planned to transfer to the individual writing folders. Some teachers tell me this technique works well for them; I found the extra step of peeling labels time-consuming and I ended up with piles of untransferred labels. Instead, I devised a single record sheet where I could record notes for the entire class on any given day by sectioning one sheet of paper into blocks and writing each child's name in the corner of a block. I photocopy the record sheet and use it for both reading and writing

Figure 20–1

*Jenny's writing,
September 14.*

workshops. I file these record sheets chronologically in a separate folder. Since each child's notation appears at the same place on each page, I can quickly peruse the records, get a chronological record and also see a given child's work in relationship to other children in the class on a particular day. I use this form one or two days a week for writing and maybe three days a week for reading.

My notes and samples of children's writing over the course of the school year provide a developmental picture of each child as a writer. For example, from the writing samples and my notes, I can construct a vignette of Jenny as a writer. One week into September Jenny produced the piece of writing shown in Figure 20–1.

I MRABCA AM MOMAJEZ
BCA

JeMYB 4-22

Figure 20–2

*Jenny's writing,
September 22.*

SEPTEMBER 14: Jenny writes T for table, F for food, F for fork, and ME to indicate herself. In conference she tells me about the good chicken her mom fixed the night before. I suggest she write a sentence. She tells me she can't because to do so is too hard and her hand hurts. I leave. When I return she has written "I like chicken" and reads the sentence to me. She throws up her hands and says, "I did it. I didn't know I could. But I did it. I wrote a whole sentence." Going out the door that afternoon Jenny says, "I'm gonna tell my mom I wrote a whole sentence today."

SEPTEMBER 22: Jenny draws a school bus (bus #14) with her mom behind the wheel and herself seated in the front seat (see Figure 20–2). She tells me her mom was the substitute bus driver this day and she got to ride

EM NMMoM
r Go To
kall Fwey
MY Dad NTaraN
Mac K.I
Lie g To
GoTo

Ka ll FlN
er
D you
Lieg
ToGO
? To K alIFINI

Figure 20–3

Jenny's writing, October 21.

the entire route. She reads her sentence, "I am riding a bus-a and my mom is driving z bus-a." (Her spoken language matches the sounds of letters she has written.)

OCTOBER 21: Jenny draws a car loaded with people, suitcases, and pets. She spends most of her time writing the sentences on a separate page (see Figure 20–3). She reads them to me, pausing to reread and use context to figure the words out and inserting "mi" in the first line when she notices the sentence does not make sense without that word. Then she reads through the piece: "Me and my mom are going to California, my dad and Tara and Mack. I like to go to California. Do you like to go to California?" She points to the question mark and says, "I put one of them things like you

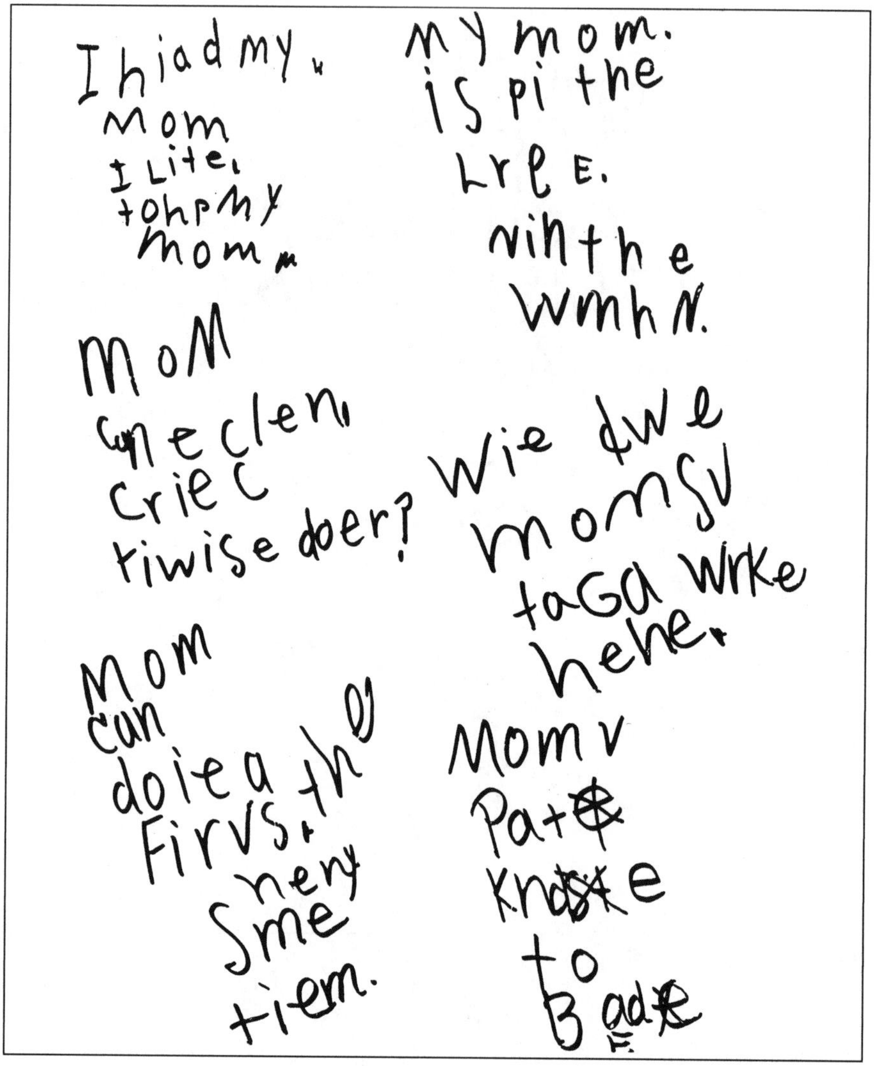

Figure 20–4

Jenny's writing, November 11.

showed us," referring to the mini-lesson that day. She says she crossed out the question mark at the end and moved it to the other end of the line because it was difficult to see in the binding of the writing book.

NOVEMBER 11: Jenny writes a book about her mom (see Figure 20–4). Each segment is on a different page of a small prestapled booklet. She has trouble reading the entire piece to me because her fluency in putting ideas on the page outpaces her spelling development. Together we figure out most of the piece. It reads:

I help my Mom. I like to help my Mom.
Mom can clean [undecipherable].

Figure 20–5

*Jenny's writing,
early December.*

Mom can do a fire in the fireplace sometime. [Jenny uses words more than once when she reads this sentence.]
My mom is putting the laundry in the washing machine.
Why do Moms go to work? Huh?
Moms put kids to bed.

EARLY DECEMBER: Over a week's time Jenny writes a book about herself that is several pages long. The particular page shown in Figure 20–5 has a drawing of her reading in the classroom, the circular conference table, and the other children seated at their desks. The words read, "I like to read. Do you like to read? Ten Little Bears." She inserts the *e* on the end of like when she edits the book for publishing. *Ten Little Bears* refers to a book she has learned to read.

FIRST WEEK IN FEBRUARY: Jenny writes a book about her dog (see Figure 20–6). She draws the scene outside her home and then writes, "My dog likes to dig to hid his bones." She reads her writing without difficulty. She explains a page with five dogs on it (see Figure 20–7): "First I drew this one (number 1) then I thought I could do it better and so then I drew this one . . . I revised." Jenny added the numbers at my request so that we would recall the order in which the dogs developed.

EARLY APRIL: Jenny writes a book about her mom for Mother's Day (see Figure 20–8). This page, one of ten, reads, "My mom cooks chicken.

Figure 20–6

*Jenny's writing,
February.*

Whenever my Mommy fixes chicken she acts like one and she says, 'BOK.'" Using her picture dictionary, Jenny corrected the spelling of "chicken" to edit her piece for publication.

LATE MAY: Jenny again writes about her mother (see Figure 20–9). An excerpt: "My mom loves me. She will not give me away. Maybe for a $100. Would you?"

JUNE 7, THE LAST WEEK OF SCHOOL: Jenny continues her writing about her mother. One page she writes that day (see Figure 20–10) reads, "My mom is so, so, so, so, so, so, so, so great at cooking chicken and meat too."

The teacher-maintained record folders are my first resource for examining a child's development as a writer. If I want to delve deeper, I go to the folders the children keep that hold all of their writing. All writing remains in the classroom until the last day of school, is easily accessible, and provides a history of a writer's development.

Reading Records

Reading development is more challenging to record because reading leaves no tangible product as does writing. A list of titles a child reads over the course of a school year is a beginning, but I wanted more information. I set up reading folders similar to the writing folders. On a record

Figure 20–7

Jenny's revisions of her dog drawings, February.

sheet I called "Reading Record," I note *what* a child reads, *how* the child reads (the struggles, successes, strategies used), *why* the child chose a particular reading material or abandoned it, and the *child's responses* to what he or she reads (thoughts and feelings about characters, actions, author's style and the connections the child makes to personal experience). In the beginning of the year, first graders need to read *to* someone, a process parallel to the publication process in writing. I spend part of my time during reading workshop (and during morning free play, indoor recess, etc.) listening to children read books that they have practiced and polished for fluent oral reading. When children read to me, I jot notes on the

Figure 20–8

Jenny's writing, April.

Figure 20–9

Jenny's writing, May.

My mom is soso
so so so sososo.
grate at cooking
chicken and met
too.

Jenny
June

Figure 20–10

*Jenny's writing,
June.*

Reading Record sheet in their folder. The children quickly came to expect me to write while they read. Later, when the task of listening to young readers grows, I show volunteers how to write observations as they listen.

I am interested in the miscues students make as they read and what they do about those miscues. Describing the significance of miscues, Frank Smith (1988) wrote:

It is not unusual for even highly experienced readers to make misreadings that are radically different visually—like "said" when the word is actually "announced" or "reported" but which make no significant difference to the meaning. Beginning readers often show exactly the same tendency, demonstrating that children will strive for sense even when they learn to read (provided the material they are expected to learn from has some possibility of making sense in the first place). The mistakes that are made are sometimes called *miscues* rather than *errors* to avoid the connotation that they are something bad (Goodman, 1965). Such misreadings show that these beginning readers are attempting to read in the way fluent readers do, with sense taking priority over individual word identification. Of course, reading with minimal attention to individual words will sometimes result in misreadings that do make a difference to meaning, but one of the great advantages of reading for meaning in the first place is that one becomes aware of mistakes that make a difference to meaning. An important difference between children who are doing well in reading and those who are not is not that good readers make fewer mistakes, but that they go back and correct the mistakes that make a difference (pp. 151–152).

I note children's miscues with my own shorthand system. I write the word the child uttered, a slash, then the correct word much the way one might write a mathematical fraction. Then I note in abbreviated form what the child did following such a miscue. My system has evolved to this:

m.m.—maintains meaning

s.c.—self-corrects (after which I note the particulars)

skip—a child skips a word entirely (if child returns to the word, usually because meaning was lost, I note any strategies I observe)

pic.—uses picture clues

s.o.—sound out (often I write the word underlining the part of the word where the child used sound-out procedures; e.g., *bl*anket—the first two letters were sounded)

stop—I interrupt because the oral reading does not make sense. "What did you say?" or "Does that make sense?" or "Hey, I don't get that," I ask in an outrageous and playful tone and then note what the child says and does. I write "IDK" to record the "I don't know" answer I often get from children when I first ask a question.

This coding system emerged as I listened to the children. No doubt had I derived a system ahead of time or followed a system someone else had created, that system would have been difficult to use. The system keeps changing as I work with it. By year's end I have a record of approximately twenty reading experiences with each child in the class. An entry from Jamie's mid-February reading of *Drummer Hoff* is an example of these reading records (see Figure 20–11). The predictable language, the rhyme and rhythm all supported his reading, and when he read Mayor for General, he immediately corrected himself. When I asked him how he knew the word, he replied, "General begins with G and ends with L, so then I could get it."

```
READING   RECORD  Name_____

Date_____Title_____
Observations:



Reader Comments:


Future Plans:
Date   2-13    Title  Drummer Hoff_____
Observations:  Corporal Bammer - s.c.  "I thought it was Corp. Bam."
               Mayor —"No!" s.c. to "General"  How? "General starts with G & it
                                                       also ends with L."
Reader Comments: " I like this book. I like cannons and stuff."
                 "This was in the olden times 'cuz they don't shoot canons today."
Future Plans: IDK
```

Figure 20–11

Teacher's notes on Jamie's reading.

The notes on Jamie's reading do not include all the books that he read over the year. Just as I cannot read everything the children write, so I cannot listen to them read or even talk with them about everything they read. First graders dip into *lots* of books, reading pages here and there, chatting about books with their friends. They reread and practice some books, polishing these titles to read aloud to others. I do not require them to perfect everything they read anymore than I require them to revise, edit, and publish everything they write. To mold them into such a rigid structure would limit the children's reading development. I try to let the children lead. Noting reading behaviors helps me understand children's progress and, in the end, reassures me of growth. In the first year of reading workshop, one little fellow read and reread a page on ships from a book he brought from home. The text was difficult. When I suggested other books he shrugged them off. After three weeks he set his book aside to try something new. I admired his perseverance and I suspect that the idea of finishing this reading had come from his older siblings. Certainly he learned much from working with one page, but I know he lost interest in the meaning of the words he read. I wondered how much he would have achieved if he had moved on to other reading material earlier and then returned to the book he so wanted to read. However, it was important to let him come to this decision for himself. I made suggestions but left the final choice to him. He became an excellent reader. Taking notes through these three weeks helped me see the *child's* perspective and kept me from intruding on his process.

"I want to understand and remember how you read," I explain to the children, "so I'll be taking notes." The children accept the recording as part of the workshop. Occasionally I ask a child to repeat something of particular interest: "Would you say that again?" The children take a keen interest in these notes and sometimes pause to ask, "Did you get that all down?" Of course, I can't capture everything that is said; I'd lose the interaction with the child. We pause, make eye contact, and chat during the reading. Glenda Bissex once told me that if something was important it would appear again and again. Remembering her words gave me permission to relax, listen, and focus first on the child and second on recording. I don't need to record everything. Interestingly, I found that rereading the notes was not critical; the *process of recording* helped me remember the experience, and better understand that child.

Interviews

Even young children can articulate the decisions they make as they read and write. About the midpoint of my first year with workshops I began interviewing children about their progress—a process that naturally evolved from our daily conferences. Those first interviews provided so much information about individual learning that in subsequent years I added interviews to the documenting process. Hearing Carolyn Burke (1984) and Nancie Atwell (1985) speak about interviews helped me refine my interview questions. However, the thrust of all interviews is not the questions but rather the talk by the learner.

I try to interview each child three times a year. Here are three interviews with Greg. The first took place during the first week of school.

MRS. A: Can you read?

G: Ummm, some. [hesitant answer]

MRS. A: How did you learn?

G: From my dad reading to me at night.

MRS. A: What does someone do to learn to read?

G: Saying words and practicing. [pause] I know a lot of opposites I can read.

MRS. A: Can you write?

G: Yeah. [No further comment on writing even in response to questions]

MRS. A: Who do you know who's a good reader?

G: My dad and my mom.

MRS. A: What makes them good?

G: My dad can read a book about Nicolas Knock. It's a two night book! My mom, she reads funny stories and stuff like that.

MRS. A: A two night book?

G: Yeah.

MRS. A: Anything else?

G: No.

MRS. A: Well, who do you know who's a good writer?

G: My dad. He writes most of the checks and stuff.

Greg added that *Nicolas Knock* was his favorite book. As opening interviews go, Greg was pretty talkative in comparison to most of the children, though not especially reflective about reading and writing. In mid-December he had this to say:

MRS. A: Can you read and write?

G: Yeah! I just started a new story today. It's about when Max came over to my house yesterday.

MRS. A: I see. How do you choose your topics for writing?

G: Well, most of the time I write about what I've done. That's stuff like I chose to write about when Max came over yesterday because it was fun and it had some interesting story parts in it, like when we started to put the new roof on my treehouse. It has just one roof that we didn't like so we took some of my wood out and we nailed it on. So the rain won't get in it and rot it.

MRS. A: I see. What can you do now in writing that you couldn't do when school started.

G: Hmmm, that's a hard question. [pause] Well, most of the things I do now that I didn't do when school started is think about like what I did more and I sound out more words than I did when school started. Stuff like that.

MRS. A: If you had to tell somebody what was most important about writing, what would you tell them?

G: Hmmm, that's a good question. [pause] I'd tell them that if you want to be a writer then you have to, most of the time, do a good job on the pictures and stuff—if you can draw pictures. You also have to get your stories to make sense. Like if, say somebody wrote a story and like they said, "I went down to the store" and they put the same thing in again, that wouldn't make sense.

MRS. A: If they said it twice. So what would you do, if you were them?

G: Well, I'd take one of them out. That way it wouldn't say "I went down to the store. I went down to the store." That would be silly.

MRS. A: Anything else that writers do that you're able to do?

G: Well, hmmm. Well, most writers don't make stories that don't have much information. Like when I write. I put information in. That's what I do.

MRS. A: Well, tell me about reading.

G: Well, when school started I couldn't read that much books as I can now.

MRS. A: How'd you learn to read them?

G: Sounding out the words. There's one thing I've learned with most of the books is to keep them for awhile. Like in reading workshop, most of the time I read the same book. If it's too hard for me, I keep practicing it until I get the words right.

MRS. A: So you keep practicing it?

G: Yeah.

MRS. A: What's your favorite book that you've learned to read?

G: Hmmm, favorite book. *Chester.*

MRS. A: What are you wanting to learn to do next in reading?

G: Read some more harder books.

MRS. A: How about in writing?

G: I'd like to try to spell harder words, to get them right.

MRS. A: Okay, thank you very much Greg.

Like his classmates, Greg had begun to articulate his processes of writing and reading. At this point in the year, most of the children spoke more precisely about writing than reading, and almost all expressed a concern about learning to spell correctly. I took notes during both the September and December interviews and ran a tape recorder as backup. Making frequent eye contact and encouraging the children through nonverbal communication was an important part of the interviewing process. For the final interviews at the end of the year, I typed as children spoke, occasionally asking them to pause while I caught up. I only had to ask an opening question for each child to launch into free-flowing talk about reading, writing, and learning, as this interview in the first week of June clearly shows.

MRS. A: Tell me about yourself as a reader.

GREG: I basically learned to read by getting books that I remembered about from other places. I remembered *This Old Man* by remembering the song and if I got stuck on a word, I would remember the song and then I would put the word in place that I would think of and I would use the letters and sounds and probably make out the word. Sometimes I would remember the word from when you read it in the class and then I would memorize it so I would use it in other books. Sometimes I would sound out, but sometimes I come to a word when sound out does not work. Like in *The Boy that Held Back the Sea* [the part where] he was trying to get the guards to believe him that there were pirate ships. I couldn't get the word "arouse." I kept figuring what could it be and then when I read it to you, you told me and then I remembered it when I read to my mom and dad.

MRS. A: How do you choose books?

G: I prefer to pick certain books that *I* like. See, what I do is read two or three pages to see if the book's too hard or too easy. Most of the time now they're too easy.

MRS. A: What's your all-time best book?

G: *Sailing with the Wind*. It makes me think about sailing and their boat almost hit the rocks. It makes me think of when our boat almost tipped over.

MRS. A: What will you do to become an even better reader?

G: Read harder books. I listen to my dad read almost every night and I watch him where he is on the pages and I think of the words he's reading and I try to figure them out myself. When we come to a different chapter, I try to read the chapter title myself.

MRS. A: Tell me about yourself as a writer.

G: I learned to write by writing little stories and I remembered more and did more and I wrote longer and better stories. I wrote about what happens in school and on weekends and some adventures. One thing I want to write about is Mother's Day—how I felt and what it was like, our Mother's Day party. And our Chinese dinner. I also like to write about how to make things and how to do things.

MRS. A: What is your best piece of writing?

G: I think it's "Sailing a Model Boat." It makes me feel like I'm sailing on that little boat and it makes me feel like that boat's real and it might hit another boat or that a propeller might cut up my boat.

MRS. A: What would you tell someone who asked you about becoming a reader and a writer?

G: I would tell them it's important to become a better reader and take books out of the library and buy your own books. If I was to tell them how to become a better writer I'd say, write stories. Don't copy these stories, write about information from books you read. If you learned something, you could put that in your story because that's your information now. Don't write a boring story. Write one that you think readers would like to read. Boring books would say: "Me and my dad went fishing. We had fun. I had fun. My dad had fun. We didn't catch any fish. We went home." If it was a good story it would be: "One day my dad and I went fishing. We didn't catch anything but we had fun trying. At 6 o'clock we went home. My mom was happy to see me again." It wouldn't just go on and on. It would have a good ending and good beginning so it would get the reader hooked and unhooked.

MRS. A: Do you have a favorite author?

G: Yes. Thomas Locker because he writes good books and I like his pictures a lot!

Finding time in a busy school day to interview children isn't easy. During the first week of school I squeeze interviews in during morning free play and at random moments throughout the day—even recess. Often, later in the year, I'm able to interview when a student teacher is in charge of the class. By late spring, the children capably continue their reading or writing while I interview classmates.

Initial interviews in September require much coaxing from me to draw out even one- or two-word answers. Some of the children are eager to sit down with me, some are slightly reluctant, but almost all of them seem baffled by my questions. Had I not experienced the richness of end-of-year interviews, I might become pretty discouraged. I must be content to wait and to trust. I listen and respond to the child during the interview, rather than think ahead about questions I want to ask. It helps me to remember that good interviews get children talking openly about reading and writing rather than answering questions.

The purpose of interviews is to learn from and about children: their perspective on reading and writing. In the beginning I suspect that I was searching for absolute answers about the children's learning to relieve my anxieties and help me conquer, then standardize, these new teaching practices. Instead, I learned from the children that they are as unique as they are alike. No absolutes. No standardization. The children's talk helps me understand each learner a little better, and that understanding improves my total response to that child. These interviews help the children too. A brief, focussed time to talk about their learning with someone with whom they are familiar permits them to give language to experience. I see children pause to think, then talk about their experiences and understanding of those experiences. This same process, in condensed form, occurs during the daily writing and reading conferences. In fact it is these conferences, where children talk about the reading and writing they are doing, that enable children to develop a reflective stance toward learning. Interviews enhance this reflective perspective and extend self-evaluation. Interviews provide opportunity to bring it all together—for both the children and me.

Self-Evaluation

Interviews help children reflect on their own learning and to articulate the process of that learning. So do questions during our workshops that ask how or why the learners make particular decisions as they read or write. Usually, those decisions are below conscious awareness at first, but the questioning—asking children to think and communicate—enables children to develop an awareness of those processes. Self-awareness leads to self-evaluation and, in turn, thoughtful decision making. I knew that our continual classroom inquiries about process helped the children internalize self-evaluation, but I was surprised when Tiffany chose to write a piece about *how* she wrote (see Figure 20–12). Her piece made me more aware of the importance of giving children the opportunity to examine their own processes.

I developed one procedure to help children increase their self-awareness. Occasionally at the end of a writing or reading workshop, I ask the children, "How did writing (or reading) go for you today? I'd like you to think about that a moment and give me a number from one to three. One means it was a great day for writing. Two means an okay day. Three means this was just one of those days when writing didn't go very well. We've all had those days!" I read the class role and the children reply with a number. They know that in this classroom we all have good days and days when we struggle and that there's no penalty for "bad" days, so they report honestly. Because they write *every day*, they are able to self-evaluate and they often explain why a day was a "one," "two," or "three" day. I experienced the power of this brief self-reflection one day when I asked the children to self-evaluate after a writing workshop.

Matt gave himself a three and then added, "You want to know why it was a 'three'? Well, because I just published my new book. I did all the illustrating, and today I wasn't sure what I'd write about. I started a new piece about playing at my friend's, but it wasn't going so good and then I just started talking and I didn't get much done."

"What could you do about that?" piped up Lisa.

"Hmm, well I guess tomorrow I'll start a new piece. I'll think about it tonight," Matt replied.

Jody told the group, "Three. 'Cuz all I could do was draw pictures of micromachines."

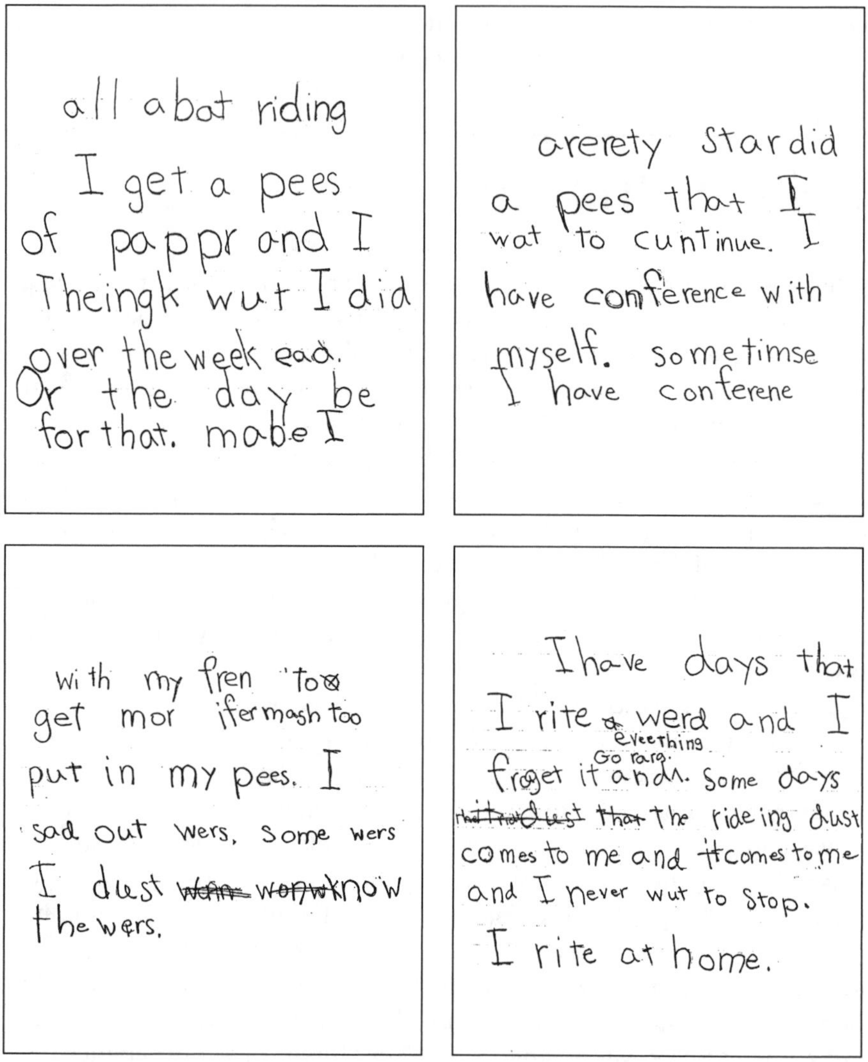

all abot riding
I get a pees
of pappr and I
Theingk wut I did
over the week ead.
Or the day be
for that. mabe I

arerety stardid
a pees that I
wat to cuntinue. I
have conference with
myself. sometimse
I have conferene

with my fren to
get mor ifermash too
put in my pees. I
sad out wers. Some wers
I dust ~~wan~~ ~~wonw~~know
the wers.

I have days that
I rite ~~a~~ werd and I
froget it and everthing Go rarg.
Some days
~~that that dust~~ ~~that~~ The rideing dust
comes to me and it comes to me
and I never wut to stop.
I rite at home.

Figure 20–12

Tiffany's writing about writing.

The children nodded in empathy. "Some days are like that. You can't write the *words,*" someone comments.

Matt and Jody were the only children who gave themselves a "three" and their self-evaluation, as usual, was congruent with my observations. For most of the children, this had been a good writing day. Then Stacy asked, "I'd like to know what it was for you, Mrs. Avery. What was it like for you talking to people about their writing today?"

Her question took me a bit by surprise. "Well, I'll tell you," I answered slowly (I needed to stall a moment to think), "it started out as a three because I was sorta tired, but then it got to be a one because I listened to so many good stories." As I spoke, I became aware that the energy of the community had raised my enthusiasm this day. Giving myself a number required me to be precise in my evaluation, but, like Matt and Jody, I needed to explain my number.

I ask the children to do this self-evaluation only sporadically and I do not record or average these numbers to determine a final evaluation. The purpose is to encourage self-reflection. The children understand that it is okay to have a three, and I think they see that everyone works and learns at varying paces.

At the end of one school year, the district language arts committee decided that a sample of each student's writing would be placed in the language arts folder that went on to the next teacher. Teachers had three options for deciding which piece of writing should be used as a sample:

1. The teacher makes the selection
2. The teacher and student hold a conference and mutually agree on the sample.
3. The student selects the sample and attaches a written summary explaining why he/she selected this piece.

I chose the third option, delighted for the opportunity to involve the children in another self-evaluation strategy. The children plunged into the exercise with vigor. Some children immediately knew what they wanted to select while others browsed through the writing for a day or so before making a decision. All children chose pieces about special times or special interests. The pieces often represented an achievement felt by the child as a writer.

- "This piece is good because I think it has a good lead," wrote one girl. Her lead read, "My sister Erin said, 'Help me with the dishes.' I said, 'NO!' [underlined four times] She said, 'want to fight for it?' I said, 'Yes I do!' " I remembered this young author's delight in writing the conversation between Erin and herself and how much the class had enjoyed that opening to her story.
- "It is a good piece because authors put in funny things and I did that." Kelly's story, "The Lady," was about an incident of seeing a woman's slip fall down in public. The piece had evoked ripples of laughter from the class.
- " 'I Was in the Hospital.' It took me so long. It was probably so long that it took me 11 days to finish it." This child had missed several weeks of school due to an emergency appendectomy and, of all the topics she wrote about over the course of the year, this one had consumed the most effort.

Many of the children explained that their pieces represented a topic that was important.

- "I like this piece because it is a neat piece. It is one of my favorite toys. It is my best piece of writing. It has a good part about putting my micromachine toy together. I didn't even know how to put the stickers on, then my dad put it together. My dad had to switch the stickers around."
- "I think "The Accident" is my best piece of writing because it is about my dad having an accident. That makes the reader feel sad and it has good pictures."

Some children wrote about how the writing affected them.

- " 'Chinese Acrobats.' I like this piece because they were so talented and it really makes me think about China today. It has a lot of information and I like the piece because it is good and well written [and] because it makes me feel stuff."
- " 'When I Got My Duck' because I like the way it sounds to me and the way it feels to me. It is real perfect to me. I love it."

Most children did not choose pieces that I would have selected and it was difficult watching them pass over what I considered to be their best pieces. Yet they all chose solid, well-written pieces. Looking closely, I noticed that the children's criteria for selecting a "best" piece were grounded not only in objective criteria for a quality piece of writing but also in subjective valuing—the writing held special significance for that child. In the process of choosing a particular piece, the children revealed a bit more about themselves as learners and as individuals, and I couldn't help thinking how established standards for "good work" fail to consider the student's perspective. Don Graves (1991) writes, "The child is the most important evaluator in the entire chain of evaluation that leads from child to teacher, principal, system, state, and national exam. If the child plays no major role in the scheme, then the system fails" (p. 175). I saw through this exercise of selecting a piece of writing that children can provide important data about their own learning. Much energy surrounded this self-reflective process. The children chatted for days about their choices and why they chose them. They listened to classmates explain their choices and nodded in understanding and appreciation. The children gained more from this activity than just selecting a piece of writing for the language arts folder.

This concept of self-evaluation and self-reflection developed further for me as an instructor during a summer institute for teachers at the University of New Hampshire. One of the other teachers, Jane Hansen from UNH, had worked on portfolios with teachers and students in the Manchester, New Hampshire schools. In her research project, children and their teachers compiled portfolios by self-selecting items (not just pieces of writing) that showed who they were as literate individuals. They also wrote about the items in the portfolio and why they were included. Jane shared this method of self-evaluation at the institute and inspired me to ask the teachers in the writing group I headed to compile portfolios. "Let your portfolio show who you are as a literate person and what you can contribute to a learning community," I directed, and I compiled my own portfolio with them.

While working on my portfolio, I talked to my son Tim who told me of his recent job search. For the first time in his engineering career, prospective employers asked for a portfolio. Rather than evaluations from current or former employers in the form of letters of reference, prospective employers wanted to see drawings and descriptions of projects Tim had worked on. They wanted his thoughts about what had gone well, what he'd learned, what he'd do differently with these projects. Tim's experience introduced me to new ways of evaluation in the business world, supporting the practicality of developing portfolios in school.

The exercise of compiling a portfolio with teachers in the writing institute also helped me appreciate the personal value of creating a portfolio. I wanted to share my portfolio with others just as my first graders had wanted to talk about their best writing selections. I experienced the same energy surrounding this process that I had witnessed among them. Several months later in a workshop I conducted with teachers, I discussed portfolios and then asked the group to list items they would consider for portfolios of their own. Within a few minutes everyone generated a list. One teacher quickly listed thirty-three items. "I've gotta cut this," he commented. "No one wants to know about all these things." Several teachers shared their lists and commented on the process:

- "Most of my list deals with items related to drama, which is a rather recent interest in my life. It was affirming for me to see this."

- "I've thought of myself as someone responsible for someone else's literacy. Doing this showed me that I'm responsible for my own literacy. That feels good."

- "A few minutes ago when I started this list I thought, 'I don't consider myself a very literate person.' Now, after doing this, I realize I *am* literate."

I asked my first graders what it was like for them to choose their best pieces of writing. They provided answers like, "Great!" "Fun!" "You really had to *think.*" "It was hard to choose." I know I'll want to continue exploring the process of self-evaluation with children. Reflecting on my learning about portfolios, I've compiled the following list of reminders for myself as I help children compile portfolios.

1. *The portfolio has a focus.* Questions to consider: What is the purpose of this portfolio? What is it meant to communicate? Who is the audience?

2. *Every item in the portfolio is included for a reason that the learner can articulate.* Articulating reasons encourages reflection and thoughtful selection.

3. *A portfolio has breadth as well as depth.* For example, in my own portfolio I focussed on teaching and young children, but also included photos of crewel embroidery kits I had designed and an item representing volunteer work in my community. Both items reveal skills I bring to my teaching, but they also show something of me beyond my role as teacher.

4. *Portfolios are ever-changing.* One item in my portfolio is a list of ten books that have had a strong influence on me. (I found it important to set a limit.) Some books have remained constant on that list while I change others; portfolios will change because we change.

5. *Portfolios include thoughtful choices.* I noticed while compiling my own and watching other teachers select items for portfolios that we all had an inclination to include too much. Too many items become overwhelming for the reader. It might be helpful to negotiate a maximum number of items to encourage careful choices.

6. *Portfolios are for self-reflection and communication.* Because this is the basis of the entire process, I would not grade these portfolios nor place any other value judgments on them. I realized with my own portfolio that its significance is in the insight I gained and that sharing the insights became a basis of communication with others. For anyone to impose a grade would negate the process; had I anticipated a grade as I compiled my portfolio, the portfolio would have been quite different, and I would have lost a degree of investment in the entire process.

Since I began playing with portfolios in my classroom, their use as an alternative means of evaluation has spread across the country. Sometimes format and content are prescribed. For me, I want to guard against standardizing portfolios for then I'd lose the premise of honest self-reflection and the evidence of individual diversity that are their strength. Because of the evolving nature of my teaching, I may discontinue using portfolios at some point in favor of something more effective, but I know that student self-evaluation in some form will always be a part of my classroom.

Case Studies

Learning to document student progress in new ways took time and stretched me professionally. One technique that helped was conducting case studies in which I followed one or two children in the classroom very closely, documenting their growth in depth. One teacher doesn't have time for intense documentation on every child in the classroom but when I looked closely at one or two individuals, I discovered that I saw the other children as well. The process of looking closely at one child taught me how to keep efficient, yet detailed records. Most important, the case study approach taught me how to look at learning with goals of understanding rather than judging and valuing rather than evaluating.

Glenda Bissex (1980), my teacher in how to do case studies, writes that "case studies can only disprove the universality of generalizations; we cannot generalize from one case to many. Conversely, we cannot presume to know an individual in terms of generalizations drawn from groups. In our schools, we usually teach to groups, though children (like the rest of us) learn as individuals in the context of groups" (p. 39).

Collecting data for a case study is an extension of kidwatching and provides another way of looking at student growth. Kidwatching helps me put first priority on the learner rather than on the curriculum. When I do that, I find I can accomplish a more effective job of bringing the learner and the curriculum together.

Tests

My initial implementation plan to teach without a basal included testing. In that plan I wrote: "The school district uses the Scott Foresman Systems

Unlimited Reading Program. Levels 1–4 are normally covered in first grade. . . . The end of level tests for Levels 1–4 will be administered to the children at appropriate times for assessment and comparison." After administrators reviewed the plan they also decided that the California Achievement Test (CAT) be administered at the year's end to both first-grade classes in our school. The district maintained a low profile on testing in those days, especially the testing of young children, but administrators told me they needed documentation from an "objective" measurement tool to verify the results of this new program. I couldn't blame them: Testing was the most acceptable means of refuting criticism.

In December of that first year the children took the Level 2 test from the reading program. (We omitted Level 1, a prereading level, since we had never given it to all children in previous classes anyway.) A score of 45 was considered passing; the children's scores ranged from 46 to 50 with nine children scoring a perfect 50. In my years of teaching the reading program, only part of each class had taken the test before January and occasionally scores had dipped to the low 40s. These test results reassured both me and administrators. The major part of that test consisted of stories with comprehension questions. The test also contained a section testing knowledge of consonant blends by requiring children to choose a word that named a picture. Since this group of children had not completed any of the worksheets from the reading program, several days before the test I introduced the children to worksheets. We worked through dittoed worksheets together so that the children understood how to complete similar test exercises.

The children continued to do well on the tests throughout the year. A major hurdle for a few was the section testing vowel sounds in the Level 3 test, and this section pulled the scores of three children below the 45 passing grade. All three of these children correctly answered all of the comprehension questions at the end of the stories on the test; only identifying vowel sounds out of the context gave them difficulty. Testing with CAT at the end of the year raised my anxiety because this type of test was new for us. I knew these children were good readers, but I had no idea how they would deal with a standardized test. My fears subsided when scores in the group ranged from the 76 to 99 percentiles.

During the first year of this new approach to teaching, we *needed* test scores to confirm that the children's progress matched that of previous classes. Every year we continued these testing procedures with solid results. But as each year passed, the importance of those scores diminished. I became increasingly uncomfortable giving the CAT to only two first-grade classes in the entire district and finally found enough courage to suggest we stop the procedure. Administrators agreed.

Prior to eliminating the testing the district adopted a new reading program and a new set of reading tests came on the scene. For one year the children and I laboriously worked through these new tests. The preprimer test alone was nearly twenty-five pages long. In addition to the significant amount of time we devoted to taking tests, I found that these tests gave no real information about student progress. The stories on the tests from the previous reading program had been interesting, written in language that paralleled the language of the books the children read. In the new program tests were written with the controlled vocabulary of the new reading program. The children complained. "I don't understand this." "It doesn't make sense." "There aren't enough words." I agreed with them. I realized that my classes had done well on reading tests from the former reading program because the children were aggressive readers, tackling unknown words efficiently as they read for meaning. A test with a limited vocabulary was more difficult to read for meaning than a test with an uncontrolled vocabulary. The following year my class went back to the tests from the old program. When we decided to eliminate all the test taking, the reading teacher devised a screening tool from the reading program and other assessment measures to determine reading placement in second grade. Near the end of the year, I introduced my class to workbook pages to prepare them for second grade. I ran off dittos with test-like formats and we practiced answering the questions. The children needed specific instruction on the format of tests and in "test thinking."

I believe tests provide limited information about a child's learning. Yetta Goodman (1985) writes: "Formal tests, standardized or criterion referenced, provide statistical measures of the product of learning but only as supplementary evidence for professional judgments about the growth of children. If teachers rely on formalized tests they come to conclusions about children's growth based on data from a single source" (p. 10).

Ironically, at a time when we are moving into learner-centered teaching practices, education requires more and more testing in the name of accountability. Teachers in one school district reported being asked to write a end-of-year test with two questions for every objective in their new language arts curriculum. The first-grade teachers protested, stating that they had already given their first graders thirty-six tests that year! The teachers made their point; additional testing plans were dropped.

Accountability was the reason administrators required me to test. Tests reassured us because they were a familiar tool. But with each year the results of the tests became less important. More significant information came from the documentation I had gleaned in the classroom as children read and wrote and talked. This information informed my instructional practice and helped me make decisions about how to respond to individual children. It provided solid information to share with parents in conferences. The tests only gave me a fleeting glimpse of one moment in time. Test results are subject to influence by many factors (the day before a test we even suggest kids get a good night's sleep and eat a good breakfast), yet we've often treated the results as the ultimate authority on individual achievement. Tests, I've come to believe, may show trends within large groups, but as far as revealing individual achievement, they can only provide us with one slim slice of the pie, which may not be an accurate reflection of a child's proficiency. I don't think we can measure individual learning anymore than we can measure other human capacities such as love or faith.

National educational organizations have begun to call attention to the consequences of testing practices. In 1989, The National Council of Teachers of English passed a resolution on the testing of young children calling for an immediate end to "the use of norm-referenced, multiple-choice, standardized tests for children in preschool and the primary grades." Part of the background statement of this resolution stated that "scores on standardized tests reflect neither the diversity of children's preschool experiences nor the range of their development. Nevertheless, test results may be used to assign young children to curricular tracks. The use of scores by school boards, administrators, and teacher committees, . . . prompts teachers to replace sound educational practices with undesirable efforts to prepare children in preschool and the primary grades." Resolutions such as this may, in time, evoke change. Recently, some teachers report a decrease in tests they are required to give young children.

When I share test results with parents, I show them the child's actual test or a sample. When parents see the questions the test asks and their child's errors, I've found that the amount of significance they attach to the test diminishes. It's important to explain scores to parents. Friends of mine brought me their child's achievement test scores that had been tucked into the envelope with the year-end report card. "Can you help us understand what these mean?" they asked. "We do our own income tax but we can't figure out this little piece of paper." Understanding the scores was only part of their concern. Most of all, these parents wanted to know if there was any aspect of their child's learning they should be concerned about. Schools often claim that parents require scores, but I suspect that we in schools have relied on test scores to demonstrate that things are going well or not so well for individual students. Parents and the public have now come to view student learning as something that can be measured, and we find ourselves tyrannized by test results. To change this situation we teachers will need to abandon our own emphasis on tests and determine progress of individual students through multiple methods of documentation.

CHAPTER 21

Reporting Student Growth

When I taught high school English, I spent a weekend every nine weeks averaging student grades with an adding machine. The machine tape curled across the floor with the all-important number for each student: the final average for the marking period. When I saw Roger's grade I remember thinking, "This can't be right! Roger's not failing English!" Yet, the numbers said he was. When it came time to transfer grades to report cards, I put a passing mark on Roger's report card—a grade that wasn't a gift. As Roger's teacher, I had knowledge about his progress that wasn't reflected by the numbers in my grade book. I knew those numbers provided only part of the information about his achievement. I understood even then that learning cannot be measured by numbers in the same way that we measure physical stature. Still, I was nervous about Roger's report card because I knew that, if questioned, I couldn't prove that passing grade. I had no documentation of any student's school progress other than the numbers and checks in the grade book. Numbers were the basis of grading. Teacher knowledge didn't count.

As a first-grade teacher I didn't keep a grade book full of numbers. However, I did assign worksheets and workbook exercises, administer tests, and, every nine weeks, determine grades based on student success in the programs of instruction. Through the years I watched those grades take on increasing significance. Children counted the number of As and played one-upmanship with peers. Parents rewarded top grades with money or fancy toys. I noticed how grades encouraged children to view themselves in comparison to others. Some students convinced themselves they were better than others, while other students perceived themselves as failures.

I believe grading results in unrealistic perceptions of self, threatened self-esteem, and pressure on children for perfection that actually can hinder their learning. Children come to believe that the goal of school is receiving good grades. "Does this count?" they ask when teachers give assignments. One evening on the television show "Jeopardy" the host asked a contestant, a teacher of eighth-grade gifted students, "What do eighth-grade gifted students think about most?" "Grades," came the *immediate* reply. In my own classroom a little boy announced, "You have to get all ones (1 is equivalent to A) in first grade so that you can go to Princeton college."

Just as I know that we can use a variety of ways to document student growth, I believe that there are options open to us for reporting student progress. Although individual schools and school districts have found innovative ways to break away from the traditional report card grading, most of us still are tied to some type of report card. I believe that the report card is just one mechanism for communicating about students and that by using a variety of reporting methods, no one method carries all the weight and becomes disproportionately important to teachers, students, schools, and parents.

Report Cards

When it came time to complete report cards that first year, I asked our reading coordinator, Rose Stetler, how she might suggest I mark our district's report card. Assigning numbers to children's progress just wasn't congruent with the dynamic learning going on in my classroom. Rose and I agreed that I could eliminate marking the reading level, which was demonstrated on the report card by drawing an arrow up a scale to indicate the book in the reading program in which the child was currently working. Since we weren't using the program, the scale was not applicable. As to the rest of the report card, she advised me, "Mark it just as you always have." Rose's reply helped me examine how I did mark report cards. I had never really thought it through before. The district report card for primary grades at that time listed thirty items to be marked on a 1 to 5 scale, 1 representing outstanding and 5, poor. When I thought about it, I had to acknowledge that my report card grades were very subjective. I also realized that I had worked out procedures and a philosophy of sorts for marking report cards that I need not change. This is what it looks like.

I take the entire batch of report cards home on a day when I feel really good about the class, not the evening of an approaching snowstorm nor one of those days when everything's been crazy. I plan for a chunk of time when I can get through all the reports and determine the grades for all the children in one sitting. If I can't do it in one sitting I break up the report card into sections and do one section for all the children at one time. To determine the actual grade, I read the topic I'm to grade ("comprehends what is read," as an example) and think about the child in relationship to that phrase. I determine a number from my knowledge and understanding of the child. The number must convey my honest and realistic perceptions of the child's progress and also must encourage the child. Some grades are clear-cut while for others I'll look back at my notes in the teacher-maintained reading and writing folders. I try to avoid comparing children to each other although I know that my knowledge of all of the children is part of my frame of reference when I view each individual child.

When I've finished marking numbers on the report cards, I put them away for a few days. Just before the reports go to parents I read through them and attempt to look at each report from the perspective of the individual child and his or her parents. Will the parents and child understand what I intend to communicate? Will they see strengths and areas to develop? Most important, will this report card encourage the child as a learner? Just as I believe an important goal of writing or reading conferences is to encourage the writer or reader to want to write or read again, so I see one goal of a report card is to encourage the child to want to come back to school the next day and the next, and to want to continue learning in this community. While reviewing the grades I've given I write the narrative paragraph that goes at the bottom of the report card.

I know I have made and always will make some mistakes on report cards. A mother called me several days after report cards went home. "We've got a problem," she said, "there are so many tears here over the math grade." I couldn't even recall what math grade I had written on her child's report card. When I went back to look again at the records, I had to admit that a higher grade was in order. I could only acknowledge that I had made a mistake. However, I believe that most of the grades I give are more fair, more supportive of learning, and less prone to error than those I assigned when I attempted to be clinically objective by averaging numbers for student grades. Can we really be objective with report cards? I think not. Our principal called a faculty meeting once to discuss report cards. As we tenuously ventured our philosophies about giving grades and the ways each of us viewed report cards, we discovered that each of us had our individual ideas about determining grades. The great myth was that we all did it the same and that we all placed the same value on the As, Bs, Cs, etc.—or that it was even possible to do so. I came away from that meeting realizing how important it was to explain to parents our individual philosophies about report cards.

Report cards are changing. I hear of the report cards written by teachers in district committees. Many schools are moving away from letter or numerical grades in favor of checklists, especially for young children. Some districts are exploring the idea of substituting narratives for graded report cards. To cope with the time-consuming nature of writing narratives for an entire class they're looking at building a structure for the narrative (topics to address, for example) and cutting back on the number of times a year these kinds of report cards are given. In one district the teachers prepared a checklist report card. An administrator working with them asked if they wanted to consider a narrative. They decided to include a brief narrative, but when it came time to use the report card the teachers came back to ask if they had to use the checklist. They needed to formulate the checklist as a guide for the narrative, but the checklist, like letter and numerical grades, needed explaining. They chose to eliminate the checklist and write a narrative.

Parents

At Back-to-School Night in September, I talk to parents about the structure of our classroom and the approach to writing and reading that their children are experiencing. I explain invented spelling and discuss the concept of meaning making as the basis of reading. All of the children's writings since the first day of school are on their desks for parents to examine. On a bulletin board is the writing each child did on the first day of school. This display allows parents to see their child's work in relation to other members of the class. I explain to parents why all the writing will stay in school and invite them to stop by to see this writing at any time. I also explain why the children will not be bringing home the papers (worksheets), that they are accustomed to seeing as schoolwork. Our "work" is actual reading and writing, I explain, not just exercises on the little parts of reading and writing. I introduce my lending library for parents, which includes books and published articles on topics such as invented spelling, the teaching of writing, and reading as a meaning-making process. I give out a one-page handout with suggestions for parents that encourage them to continue the natural practices they've begun at home. I also distribute two brochures prepared by the National Council of Teachers of English: "Helping Your Child Become a Better Writer" and "Elementary School Practices." Both pamphlets are written in clear jargon-free language and I find they are helpful to parents.

I try to keep in touch with parents through the letters that accompany the reading children take home, with phone calls, and by maintaining an open door policy. Often parents stop in the room for a brief moment before or after school. I've learned that not all parents are comfortable coming to school. One father came for the scheduled fall conference after breaking several appointments. This large, burly man and I sat on small chairs at a low table while I showed him his son's reading and writing. He fidgeted while he listened and but said little; he never looked at me. "School's important," he finally commented, "I want my boy to do good in school." He took the report card and left, obviously anxious to be on his way. I could only wonder at the experiences that made him so very uncomfortable in a classroom. However, there was no doubt in my mind of his strong commitment to his son and to education. The incident pointed out the diversity of the children's backgrounds and the need to build communication that starts by *valuing* that diversity.

Dialogue Letters with Parents

One means of establishing communication with parents is dialogue letters, described in the Chapter 17. Not every parent wrote letters when children took books home to read to them and no parent wrote about every reading, but over the course of the school year we exchanged several hundred letters. I viewed the letter exchange as an invitation for parent involvement and a means of maintaining open communication. The letters from parents enhanced my view of children's reading development. In their letters, I saw parents evolve in their understanding of reading. Here's the first and last letter from the thick pack of letters from one parent.

September 19

We thoroughly enjoy listening to N. read. She has a love for reading that we share and it heartens us to see our daughter share this joy. N's determination to solve words she is unfamiliar with brings pride to us. Her pride in her own reading gives us many rewards. Her attention to detail (sight words) could use work but for the most part we couldn't be more pleased with her progress.
C. and M. G.

May 23
Dear Carol,

Again, it was a great pleasure to hear N. read these two moving stories. The story *When I Was Young in the Mountains* was especially endearing. N. felt very strongly that she would not like a dead snake around her neck or in her swimming area. We discussed okra and diarrhea. Also, outhouses came up. She knew their use. The baptism in the river was compared to the baptisms she is familiar with. She felt happy that the young girl was so confident.

The second story was a step-by-step discussion of the give/take, gain/loss, love and thanks way of life. She felt I looked like the Mom in *A New Coat for Anna*. The combing and dying of the wool were new ideas to her. She noticed that two of the celebrants at the Christmas party had their payments on (garnet necklace and gold watch). N. appreciated the Mother's efforts and the pride of the new coat felt by the protagonist. Anna's gratefulness was appropriate according to N.

These books were *good*.

Warmly, C. L. G.

These dialogue letters with parents provide a means of addressing parent concerns and questions. One child's mother wrote in September: "We enjoyed listening to him read this book but when we asked him the same words outside of the book, he did not know them. I think he has just memorized this book." In my reply, I explained that memory plays a part in learning to read and that I'd rather a child read by memorizing words in a meaningful context rather than learn by memorizing a list of words. These letters provide a vehicle for me to address issues before they escalate. In addition, I learn much that helps me understand and appreciate the children and the individual cultures of their homes.

I make every effort to answer parent letters on the day I receive them. Often I receive one or two notes a day, but sometimes there are five or six. I write my replies quickly—spontaneously—and send them home that afternoon. I photocopy my note, staple the copy to the parent letter, and file both in the child's reading folder. I want a record in case anyone questions what I've written (though no one ever has). If a parent writes a short letter, I keep my reply short. If the parent's letter is a page long, I write a page. At the end of the first year of writing these letters one mother wrote, "I've really appreciated these letters this year. I especially like that your letters, like mine, aren't perfect. You're willing to scratch out and continue writing. I know that you write these during lunch and when the children are in music just as I write mine at the breakfast table or before I shut off the light at night. If you had taken the time to write polished, typewritten letters I probably would never have written back to you." I realized that communication with parents needed to be down-to-earth and unpretentious.

I first started the dialogue letters with parents several years after initiating writing and reading workshops. The parent letters opened up a whole new area of communication with parents and their views of school and learning, and I found myself wishing I had initiated this letter writing sooner. However, I realize that I wasn't ready. In the beginning I had my hands full just learning to manage the new structures in my classroom and to internalize the intricate process of listening and responding to children. Like the children, I needed time to learn too.

Parent Conferences and Responses

Parent conferences are scheduled at our school in November and teachers give the first report cards to parents at those conferences. The report card used to be the center of the conference, a document I went through grade by grade with parents. Now I usually begin the conference by asking the parents to tell me about their child: how they see the child's response to school, their view of their child's interests and learning style, their questions about the child and school. Although parents are far more of an authority on their child than I, our observations about the children's personalities almost always match. "That's the way my boy's been since he was a baby," is a comment I've heard many times when I share my observations. As we chat, I view a fuller picture of the child and I try to give the parent a realistic picture of the child in the classroom by showing accomplishments and by raising any concerns I have. I avoid comparing the child to other children. When I give the parent the report card at the first parent conference, I say, "Take this with a grain of salt. I want you to know that if I did these grades next week, it's likely they'd all be different." I explain my philosophy about report cards, how I mark them, and what I hope this particular report card will communicate to the child. Then, I spend the rest of the conference time sharing the child's writing and my observations of his or her reading. Because children have been taking books home to read, and because of the dialogue letters accompanying that reading, parents already have a good idea about reading progress. Because of these letters, the reading the child has taken home, and because many parents have seen their children writing on their own at home (a frequent occurrence when children work in daily writing workshops in school), there are usually no real surprises by the time report cards come along. As a result parent conferences are rarely stressful for me or the parents. Many teachers today include children in parent conferences. I know of one fifth-grade teacher who spends time before conferences helping his students reflect on their learning. When the parents come to school, the child leads the conference. I'd like to incorporate this concept into future parent conferences.

Just before school ended one year I sent home a form titled "Parent Evaluation of a Child's Progress." On the first page were ten questions related to school progress; parents were to circle a choice of three answers: almost always, some of the time, not yet. I asked the children to complete the same questions in school. As I compiled the results, I saw a remarkable congruence between the child's, the parent's, and my perceptions of learning. On a second page of the parent evaluation I invited parents to write comments on the strengths and weaknesses of this approach to reading and writing, and to express their concerns and any suggestions for improvement. Over three-fourths of the parents wrote responses. The following are a sampling of their comments.

"I must admit at first I thought this approach to reading was questionable, but since November I can see nothing but strengths. I see a great enthusiasm for reading and books. [My child] chooses her books often (at the library) by the author. She can tell me why she likes the book—picking a specific passage that she liked rather than saying generally it was a good book. She has the confidence to pick up any book and begin to read it or try rather than only reading from the 'reading book,' or books she has brought home from school. This was a *great* year for [my child]. She has a lot of confidence in herself and isn't as hesitant to try new things. She is learning to record her ideas, put them on paper, [be] in touch with her thoughts. . . ."

"[My child's] success is a result of *his* effort and the effort of *his* teacher, a very human being. [My child] is very much aware of how the class work *evolved* as a result of the students' efforts. [My child] has an excellent self-image in relation to his reading and writing. Last year in 1st grade [my child] found the prepackaged reading program a standard that was very hard to keep up with."

"Reading big words is so important for [my child] because using just 1st grade vocabulary is so limiting to comprehension. There is a flow to [my child's] reading and writing that is not emphasized in the basal program. This flow may be just as important as the specific skills that seem so inhibitory when taught each skill in isolation."

"My daughter . . . loves to read and does so constantly. She began chapter books by October. Her fascination with illustrations reflects her own interest in Art and her new awareness of the genre itself (illustrations). She discusses certain authors with such aplomb that I must remind myself she is only six. Her desire and determination to tackle and unlock vocabulary in the stories is strong. She has experienced many foreign notions and ideas from the grand assortment of authors as well. The moral aspects of some stories reflect strongly on your choices and have aided in reaffirming or discovering how she correctly perceives her own morals."

"Trying to be extremely objective I can see no weaknesses in learning to read with this approach. Among the strengths I would include diversity of material and instilling a love for reading at an earlier age due to a 'non drill like' learning environment. I wouldn't change a thing."

Three concerns surfaced in the parent responses:

- "The weakness I see is in his spelling. I work with him at home on this and he seems to be getting it, although slowly."
- "Will this approach be carried through into second grade? If not, will it be a difficult transition for the child to switch to another learning approach?"

- "As parents we had no benchmark to compare [our child's] progress. We did not know what was considered normal progress, therefore at times we did not know what [our child's] weaknesses were and how we could or should help her. Was [our child] getting the reading help she needed? Also we had no means to tell how [our child] was progressing [in relation] to her peers . . . in the other first-grade classes." (This comment came from the parents of a strong student—one I had no concerns about—showed me that I must *tell* parents I have no concerns.)

I've heard these concerns before but hearing them again—if only from a few people—communicates that these issues continue to be important for parents. Usually these concerns come from parents who are sending their first child to school, reminding me that education of the community at large is an ongoing task. I hope parents and I can grow in our understanding of each other for the sake of our common interest in the child. For my part, I've found it helpful to attempt to negate the traditional role of teacher as authority by communicating directly and clearly. That's not always easy. Several years ago an articulate mother with more than one college degree wrote a note: "I finally actually saw what you folks call 'word attack.' When he came to a word he didn't know I really saw how he 'attacked' that word to get it." I was appalled at my own insensitivity in falling into educational jargon that blocked communication. How many other terms, acronyms, phrases like "word attack" did I casually rattle off in conversations with parents? I've made a concerted effort to eliminate educational jargon in all parent/teacher interactions.

The Teacher's Role
in Evaluating Progress

A couple of years ago, after wrestling with the terms "evaluation" and "assessment" and "report cards" and "accountability," I brainstormed a list of ideas, writing them down just as they came to me, in order to help me think through what it was I believed about this incongruous mess! Across the top of my paper I wrote: My Attitudes About Evaluation. Then I crossed out "Evaluation" and wrote "Assessment," then I crossed out this word and finally just put a big question mark and continued. What I wanted to do was put on paper some guidelines to myself as I approached all these ticklish issues. Here's my list (unedited) from that time.

1. Look at development and growth—avoid a deficiency model.
2. Recognize that learning/growth patterns are uneven, recursive, and individual.
3. Examine the growth of the individual—avoid comparison with others.
4. Set goals—with students—but be flexible. Remember: growth may go in unpredictable directions; avoid measuring against predetermined standards.
5. Recognize the limitations of tests.
6. Include student self-evaluation.
7. Recognize that *all* assessment procedures and tools have an element of subjectivity and bias—including my own methods.

As a classroom teacher, I must give feedback (for want of a better term). Writing out what I believed helped me clarify my underlying philosophy as I developed ways of documenting observations, influenced my communications with both parents and children, and relieved me of the stress I felt from attempting to match the richness of learning in the classroom to the traditional but inadequate practices of examining student achievement. I found it personally important to articulate not only *what* I did, but *why*.

Recently, I've realized that the terms "evaluation" and "assessment," as traditionally used in schools, no longer reflect my attitudes toward sharing what I observe about my students and I try to avoid those terms in the context of giving feedback. Both terms have come to carry heavy connotations of judgment, leading to a process of focussing on weakness rather than strength, deficiency rather than growth, failure rather than success. My role as a teacher and learner with children is not to be standing in judgment of their growth but to provide honest and helpful responses. I can do that through several modes of communicating with both parent and child. The processes I've developed will undoubtedly change in the natural rhythms of evolving growth but, at this point, I look to these four broad areas to provide information about children's learning:

1. documents of the children's work over time, such as writing samples, and reading records
2. student self-evaluation that includes a strong component of self-reflection
3. observations and insights of parents
4. teacher observations of specific behaviors and reflection on the meaning of those behaviors

The underlying purposes of gathering and sharing any information about children's growth in the classroom is to *understand* each child's process as a learner and to *communicate* with both parent and child.

Reflections

During the first years of this new approach to teaching, the issue of evaluation, specifically report cards, troubled me. Traditional modes of evaluation just weren't congruent with new insights into teaching and learning but I felt stuck. A friend told me a story from her personal experience that expresses the difficulty. My friend needed to move to new office space for her growing business. Though she searched and searched, she could find nothing suitable until she realized that she was searching for space similar to what she currently had. Once she realized that the new space could be different, that it did not have to replicate the past, she realized that lots of possibilities existed. "I was limited by my own vision of the way it had to be," she said. In the same way, I recognize that my vision of report cards and evaluation—in fact of many changes in my classroom—was restricted in the beginning by established practices. "Kidwatching" rescued me! When I looked and listened in my classroom I envisioned new ways of teaching and learning. The children were my teachers. Goodman (1985) states that "observation, evaluation, and curriculum planning go hand in hand" (p. 16). Evaluation is not an activity that occurs after a test, a product, or at the end of a marking period. Instead it is an *ongoing and integral part of the teaching/learning process* that guides me—the teacher—in making daily decisions about instruction. When I understood that evaluation/assessment is woven into everything that occurs in the classroom the incongruence fell away. I was ready to carry the theories I had been developing and refining into the rest of the curriculum and to integrate a responsive approach to learners into teaching math, science, and social studies. But that is the topic of the final chapter of this book.

Question Mark ? to ask a que
, to separate words in
in the greeting & closing of a le
to signal the reader to pause.
Quotation Marks " " show so
North
Canada
United St
Ame
Atlantic
Central
Ameri
Venezuela
South
America

CHAPTER 22

Taking Reading and Writing into the Content Areas

Writing across the curriculum. Learning across the curriculum. Integrated instruction. These terms appeared in the professional literature heralding new approaches for teaching and learning. What did they mean? With writing and reading workshops underway in my classroom, I knew that carryover to the content areas of the curriculum ought to follow. Yet I was stumped. Of course I integrated instruction, connecting various disciplines as I planned curricular units. Hadn't I been doing this for years? With dinosaurs, for example, I sought out a range of books from poetry to fiction to informational literature and read those books to the children. I also incorporated math activities by graphing dinosaurs according to size or measuring their lengths on the playground. I planned craft activities, searched out songs about dinosaurs for music, designed creative movement exercises for physical education (walking like dinosaurs, etc.), and on and on. I maintained an entire resource file of activities and bits of information about dinosaurs, as well as for every other content area of the curriculum. True, the children had fun and they were *active* learners (these were *activities* after all). But something wasn't right. I knew it in my bones even as I shared my fossil collection.

This integrated curriculum concept was a beginning; curricular studies ought not to be isolated from one another. For years, we teachers referred to content units as the "fun things." However, the children now talked about writing as the best part of the day, cried out in dismay if reading workshop was shortened, spoke with anticipation of the books we'd read and talked about in literature time. My old curricular lessons—all those "fun" things—became flat in comparison to the energy surrounding reading and writing. The content area activities lacked the children's *involvement* and *thinking*, which had become a part of the rest of the school day.

For the first couple of years I left math, science, and social studies alone. One thing at a time was enough, and I couldn't possibly have made significant changes in every part of the curriculum at once. But as I became more comfortable with reading and writing workshops I began looking for ways to incorporate reading and writing—and the thinking that comes when children have responsibility for their learning—into other parts of the curriculum. Somewhere along the way I'd donned the hat of the reflective practitioner—become a kidwatcher—viewing the classroom not only in terms of what I implemented and what children produced in return, but also from the perspective of what children did along the way and why. I was impressed by the idiosyncratic nature of learning that surrounded me in the classroom. Like winter snows melting to reveal the sprouting of new life in spring, so moving away from my tried-and-true teaching practices revealed the dynamic and organic nature of learning. I began changing the ways I introduced science and social studies units in my classroom, for the old ways were no longer congruent with what I believed.

Reading and writing workshops worked well because they accommodated individual needs through responsive teaching within a community of children with diverse interests, experiences, and achievements. The range of ideas, the questioning, and the nurturing within this community stimulated far more thinking among the children than I could do alone. I decided to take more risks and play with the theories of learner-centered classrooms, responsive teaching, collaborative learning and language as a tool for learning in content areas of the curriculum.

The little writing we had done as a part of math, science, and social studies had been confined to writing math problems and summary learnings at the end of units of study. I wanted the children to experience writing as a tool for raising questions and seeking answers. When I moved writing to content areas I incorporated the principles of writing workshop. Children needed time to write and explore ideas. They needed to share their writing and talk with others about their ideas. They needed the opportunity to rewrite and revise their thinking through writing. Most important, the children needed to have a large part in forming questions, exploring ideas, and drawing conclusions so that they could develop the involvement that surrounded our workshops.

Experimenting with Writing in the Content Areas

What follows is the story of a first-grade class from February through June as we began revamping the approach to curricular units.

Our class was scheduled to visit the high school planetarium four times during February. Immediately upon returning from the first visit and before any discussion, I asked the children to write what they remembered about the trip or what was important to them. Writing *before* discussion is important. Toby Fulwiler (1985) says doing so gives learners opportunity to discover their thoughts before they speak (a particularly enabling factor for reticent children); commits writers to a stand; and allows writers to arrive at their own thoughts without first being directed by others—including the teacher. Fulwiler believes that "more personal writing is a direct route to more autonomous thinking."

Since the children had been writing for several months, they were comfortable with my request. After a few moments of writing the children shared with a partner, and then a few children read their writing to the entire group. I wrote with them and then moved among them as the pairs chatted. Some children wrote about riding the bus. One or two wrote pieces that began with our departure, included one sentence about the planetarium, and ended with our return. The majority of the writing consisted of one or two short statements such as: "We learned that the sun is a star." "There are nine planets." "Comets are sorta like stars but they're not stars." I was struck by the brevity of most of the writing, a contrast to the fluency displayed during writing workshop. But the writing was enough to start discussion. In the large-group discussion we composed questions, which I recorded on chart paper. For example:

> What is the difference between a comet and a star?
>
> Why are some planets hot and some cold?
>
> If the sun is a star, why can't we see it at night?

Before our next trip we reread the questions, and when the children arrived at the planetarium they posed their questions to the planetarium instructor, who started answering, then stopped in puzzled amazement and said, "You kids certainly have a lot of questions today."

After each visit, and also after reading books or viewing filmstrips on astronomy, we followed the procedures of writing, sharing, discussing.

Sometimes we wrote again after the large-group discussion. With each writing fluency increased; the children became comfortable writing to include new information. I wrote with the children. Each of us kept our writing about the planetarium in individual construction paper folders, which we called our "planetarium logs." This writing differed from the pieces done during writing workshop in that we did not revise or craft the writing in any way.

The planetarium logs were one of several learning logs that the children maintained on different topics of study. The logs were tools for inquiry—allowing children to frame questions and to seek answers. They were another way for children to participate actively in their learning. The use of learning logs varies from class to class, but are vehicles that can be used for speculating, predicting, recording, documenting, webbing, charting, listing, sketching, brainstorming, questioning, imagining, hypothesizing, synthesizing, analyzing, and reflecting. Learning logs should not be graded or corrected. They are not classroom products nor are they just pages for note-taking. Learning logs are places to think and discover meaning.

After the last planetarium visit I asked the children to read through their logs and then write a new piece about something of interest to them. These final writings were not just assorted facts strung together, as children had produced in previous years when I asked them to write at the end of a unit of study. Most of the writing revealed the children's search for answers to questions they had raised.

Jared, who had been fascinated with planets, wrote: "There are nine planets. Mercury is the planet closest to the sun. Mercury is hot. Earth is not hot because earth is not close to the sun. Venus is another planet. Mars is another planet too. You could not live on some planets because they are too cold or too hot. Only earth."

Billy, the child who wrote one sentence about comets after the first visit wrote: "When comets get near the sun it makes a tail. The tail turns away from the sun. Comets are as big as Manheim Township. Comet's orbits looks like a cigar!!!! Comets go very fast! I like comets."

The astronomy unit established writing as an expected procedure for science units, and when we began our study of dinosaurs, the children easily wrote after viewing filmstrips or listening to me read about dinosaurs. The sharing time that followed was sometimes done in pairs, sometimes in small groups, or occasionally in the whole group. Children wrote additional ideas in their dinosaur logs during and after the sharing. I began expanding my role by moving among them as they wrote, asking "How do you know this?" "Why is this important?" "What do *you* think?" The children began posing the same questions to each other. They pooled their knowledge and hypotheses.

The group became interested in two particular questions in regard to dinosaurs: Why did the dinosaurs die? What color were dinosaurs? The children suggested many theories during their writing and discussion. They were not content with absolute answers but were excited to discover *many* possibilities. This phenomenon caught me off guard and both alarmed and delighted me. I was accustomed to managing lessons in the name of "covering the curriculum." Now the children had taken control of their learning. I managed to keep up with the children by following their lead; as for covering the curriculum, well, the children had gone well beyond all the objectives.

At the end of the unit (a misnomer, for I eventually realized that this kind of learning never ends; once inquiry begins, it continues), I asked the children to read through their dinosaur logs and write about dinosaurs using all they knew about good writing: strong leads, interesting information, focussed ideas, clarity, making sense to other readers. They plunged into these pieces.

"This is fun!" said Katie.

"Listen to my lead," said Jeff.

"Can we do this tomorrow?" asked Jon.

When we set the writing aside that day, Courtney had written: "Roar! Roar! Roar! This is the sound of the ancient dinosaurs. They roamed the earth many years ago. They were terrible. We still don't know what color they were. They just guess green. But soon the dinosaurs started to die. No one knows for sure how they died. Some scientists say it got too cold. Some scientists say the land coughed and volcanos blew up. Some . . ." (see Figure 22–1).

Amanda wrote: "Boom! A star fell to the ground. The dinosaurs died. Dinosaurs lived millions of years ago. Dinosaurs could be pink or red or yellow or green or white or blue or orange or even polka dotted. . . ." (see Figure 22–2). Most of the children chose to continue writing and revising these pieces during writing workshop on subsequent days.

Writing and the sharing became a norm for thinking and learning throughout the school day. In math the children used manipulatives and worked in teams to come up with various combinations that could be written as addition facts. They talked as they worked and wrote about how they discovered the combinations they found. We shared the written ideas in the large group, noticing patterns, and articulating strategies that children found helpful. Throughout the year I ask children to explain in writing how to add or subtract. Janelle wrote about addition: "Addition is adding means + the plus sign means you join 2 numbers and you get a big number like $8 + 3 = 11$ and here's another one $2 + 8 = 10$. Melissa had 9 cookies and her mother made two more cookies and now Melissa has 11 cookies" (see Figure 22–3).

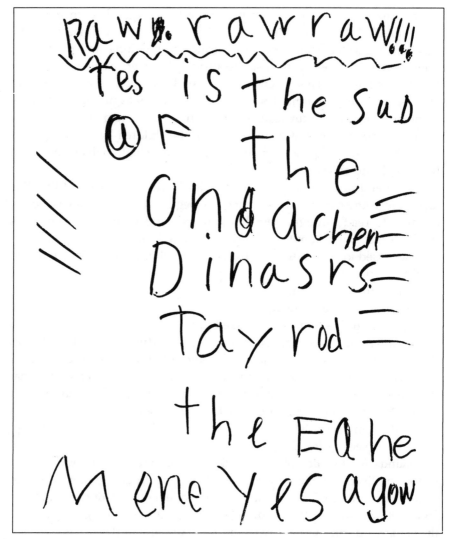

Figure 22–1

Courtney's writing: "Roar Roar Roar. This is the sound of the ancient dinosaurs. They ruled the earth many years ago."

The day before presenting a lesson on the addition of double-digit numbers, I asked the children to try to solve the problem 31 + 42 and then to explain how they did it or to simply state they didn't know how and why. Patrick wrote: "I added 3 and 4 That was 7 and then I added 2 and 1 that was 3—so it was 73."

Billy wrote: "I don't know what this is because there are too much numbers."

A few days later, after instruction, children completed the same problem, wrote about their learning process, and then looked at their first explanations to see their own concept growth.

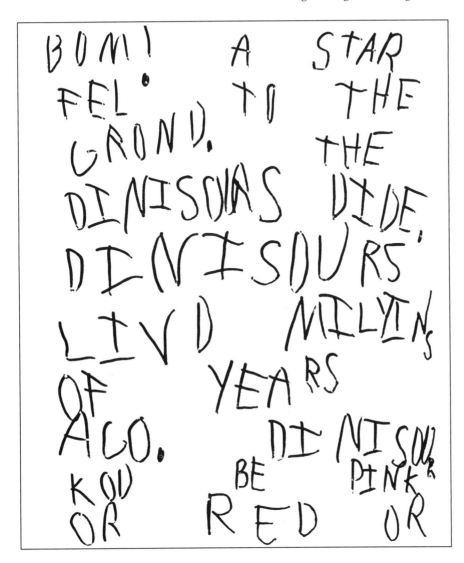

Figure 22–2

Amanda's writing.

In March I brought forsythia branches to school to force blooming and asked the class to observe and write and talk each day on their theories about these sticks and what they might be. Each day the children recorded the changes they saw in logs. Their daily writing reflected the revision in their thinking as the blossoms appeared.

On the first day Chad wrote: "It looks like something that blooms and dies again. It has branches. It has leaves. It looks like any other plant and its branches are skinny and it looks like a plant from a flower shop." And the next day: "Since yesterday it has changed a lot. It use to have leaves on it. But now it has one flower on it My guess about it is its a flower bush!"

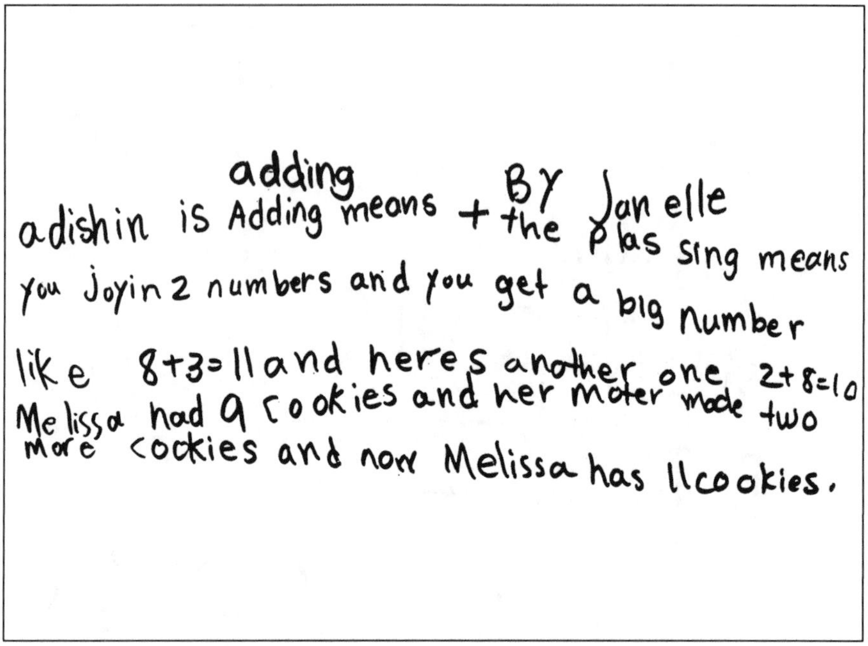

Figure 22–3

Janelle's writing.

And after the weekend: "On Friday it had only a little bit of flowers. Since Saturday and Sunday it has bloomed. Now it has hundreds of flowers on it. It looks like a flower bush that were picked out of a flower garden. I think they are buttercups."

Troy wrote: "I think it is a pussywillow that hasn't bloomed yet—that is a late bloomer." (Troy had just learned to read Robert Kraus's book, *Leo the Late Bloomer*.) And five days later: "It bloomed a lot of flowers. It could have been a pussy willow that bloomed though."

On the sixth day Courtney slipped a note on my desk that said: "Forsythia. My grandmother told me. I asked her what was a plant that had yellow flowers." Later, Courtney explained her process to the class. "Well, I asked my grandma. I told her what it looked like after I'd watched it a few days and she said forsythia. But I wanted to be sure, so then I asked a couple more people. I asked my mom and my Aunt Debbie and they both said forsythia so I figured it probably was." Courtney's observations and questioning led her not only to seek an answer but also to validate her answer with more than one source.

In the late spring, after I read Roald Dahl's *James and the Giant Peach* to the class, we went to the library to learn more about the six creatures from that book: ladybug, spider, earthworm, centipede, grasshopper, and glowworm. The librarian and I helped the children locate poetry books, nonfiction books, junior encyclopedias, and study prints. We asked the children to look and read until they were "filled up," then to close their books and to write what seemed important. In the ensuing noise and bustle (this was NOT a quiet library time!) we overheard comments from the children.

Jon tells one classmate after another, "The ladybug was named after Mary, Jesus's mother."

Jeff says, "I wrote something I think is important. You see this is about the earthworm and how it eats *soil.*"

From Colleen: "I just learned that spiders have *nine eyes!*"

"Centipedes can be poisonous. Did you know that?" asks Jack. He reads the encyclopedia to prove his point.

We took many of these books back to the classroom and set up a shelf for each creature. Among the materials we kept there were writing folders where children placed contributions—poems and illustrations they had collected or information they had written after reading about a particular insect. The children frequently gathered in pairs or small groups to read through the folders and discuss the ideas. Children brought books and artifacts from home to add to the shelves—everything from spiders and caterpillars in jars to a stuffed centipede. A teacher in another room became involved and shared spider webs he had sprayed and captured on black paper.

The children's thinking processes were evident in their writing. Katie wrote a page on spiders (an interest of hers from our reading of *Charlotte's Web*) that began: "Spiders hang from their silk when they want to see a closer view." (See Figure 22–4.) When I stopped to talk with Katie as she worked, she said, "I just wondered *why* a spider would drop down on a strand of silk and then I remembered Charlotte did that when she wanted to see the big pig at the fair and so I think that it might be so they can get a closer view."

Katie continued writing about spiders: "Some spider are poisonous like this. It is black and little of red on its body." [She drew a spider.] "Spiders have two parts. Spiders have jaws to suck blood out of the insect. Some spiders are good and eat grasshoppers because grasshoppers are bad."

Katie had drawn on information from another folder, where Jeff had recorded the devastation grasshoppers can cause to entire fields. Katie concluded her notes on spiders with this line, which referred back to *Charlotte's Web:* "Spiders die before their babies hatch. And I think that is sad."

Their inquiries extended outside of school. One rainy morning Ted came into the classroom and wrote: "On my way to school I saw a puddle. In the puddle I saw a worm this big. [Ted illustrated just how big with a drawing.] I thought a worm needed to live in dirt. But it was water. It looked like its skin was pulling off." (See Figure 22–5.) Ted's writing led to class discussion and speculation as to why we see worms in puddles, why they come out on rainy mornings. A couple of weeks later, David reported reading that

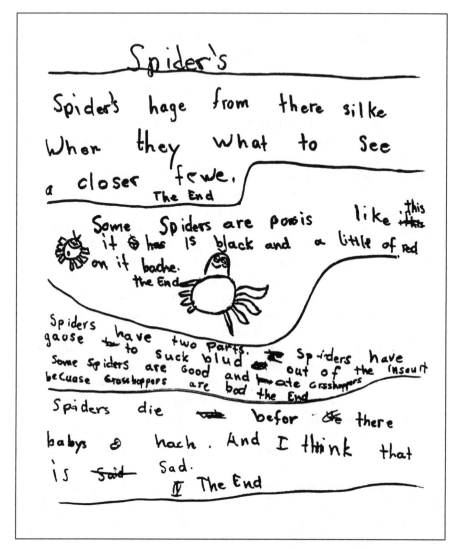

Figure 22–4

Katie's writing.

earthworms drink through their skin. Since earthworms also need air, the speculation went, they probably come up to get a drink and a breath of fresh air since it gets so muddy underground when it rains.

I saw more evidence that the children took their questioning attitude outside of the classroom when we visited the Philadelphia Academy of Natural Sciences. Jon looked at a stuffed rhinoceros, commented that it resembled a dinosaur, and wondered if the rhinoceros evolved from the dinosaur. "Hmmm? How could you find out?" I asked.

Jon smiled, and without further prompting walked over to the attendant and asked. "No," came the answer, followed by an explanation: the

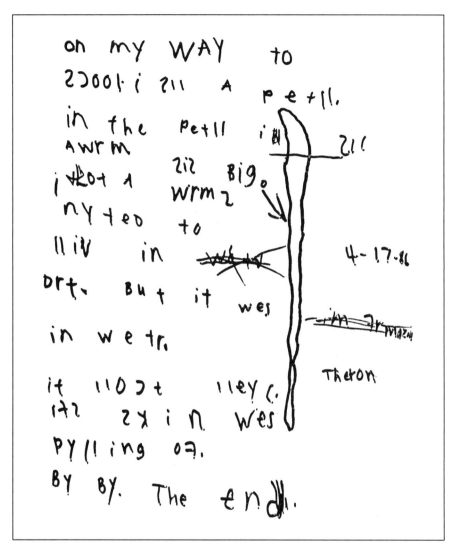

Figure 22–5

Ted's writing.

dinosaur was a reptile and the rhinoceros is a mammal. Jon thanked the attendant and reported the information back to the group. Later he saw a picture of a dinosaur with bright reds and oranges on its head and said, "Look! There's *red* dinosaurs!" The curator explained to Jon a new theory regarding dinosaur colors. As we walked away Jon made a comment that referred to Amanda's final piece about dinosaurs, which had been written nearly two months before. "Amanda was right. They could be any color!"

The importance of talking to peers during this learning became apparent. On the morning after we visited a dentist's office, I asked the children to write what they learned, to share that writing with a classmate, and then to write some more. Later I asked the children if this procedure had been helpful. Laura answered, "Yes! I talked to six people. At first I only knew this much about the dentist [she indicated a page of writing], but now I know this much!" She spread her arms full length.

Writing, talking, questioning, sharing, reading, thinking, and learning together became the expected norm for approaching a topic. When we began our China unit I turned the recording of concepts on chart paper over to the children. Small groups sat on the floor negotiating and composing statements about pandas after viewing filmstrips or hearing books read aloud. Each group shared the chart they produced with the entire class, which prompted more inquiry about pandas. Children also kept individual logs on China. On the last day of school, small groups sat around the room sharing ideas from their China logs. As I walked around the room, I heard Mark reading to his peers: "Pandas like honey. They take honey from bees. Bees can't sting them because they have tough fur."

Jared responded, "No, not tough skin. They have tough inside their mouths! Remember, the film told us."

Mark answered, "Oh yeah, that's right." He stopped to make a change on his page. "I wonder if they have tough skin too. Probably they do or they'd get stung on their fur. I could look it up."

From the tentative beginnings, when I first asked children to write about a planetarium visit, until the year's end, the children demonstrated time and again their ability and eagerness to question, to theorize, to explore, and to learn. A new energy came into the entire school day. The following year I started children writing about science and social studies topics much earlier than February, and another group took up the inquiry process with equal enthusiasm. However, in the spring, I repeated the same activity with the creatures from *James and the Giant Peach* only to discover that neither the children nor I felt the same energy as that of the previous year. We soon abandoned the project, and I confronted the reality that not only every child, but also every group will be different and that carrying identical activities from one year to another is not a good idea.

Learning results, I believe, from an intrinsic need, inherent in each child, to understand the world and make sense of experiences. Children are natural and self-motivated learners who make connections to that which they perceive as relevant and who dismiss nonsense, that which is irrelevant to them at a particular time. As I gained experience, I saw that children's learning was both developmentally and experientially based, that the interplay of physical maturation and life experiences was unique for each child, and that learning resulted from each new encounter with the world. Children are learning all the time, but I cannot assume that they interpret experiences as I anticipated they might. I had come to these beliefs (which I continue to revise and refine) through professional reading, attending conferences, being a reader and writer myself, and most of all, through observing children in the classroom and asking them to tell me how they worked and why they made the decisions they made. Motivation was not something *I* did to them; children motivated themselves. I could only establish the environment and tone for them to take the risks of plunging into new areas of learning. I am reminded of Janet Emig's words: "That teachers teach and children learn, no one will deny, but to believe that children learn because teachers teach and only what teachers explicitly teach is to engage in magical thinking" (1983, p. 135).

Using an Inquiry Approach

I begin content units of study by asking the children what they know and what more they want to explore with a particular topic. At one time I would have dismissed this procedure as inappropriate for first graders. After all, how would these little kids know what to study? How could I possibly manage a couple dozen first graders going in different directions? But children have shown me differently.

About ten days into the new school year we began our study of communities. I taped three sheets of chart paper to the chalkboard and labeled them "rural," "suburban," and "urban." I defined these terms and asked the children for characteristics of these three kinds of communities. In the next thirty to forty-five minutes they produced lists that spilled over to second sheets of chart paper. When we were done, the children had listed all the concepts about urban, suburban, and rural communities outlined in the district curriculum guide intended to cover several class periods. In Lancaster County, Pennsylvania, it is almost impossible to travel even a short distance without encountering all three kinds of communities, and the children had paid attention to the world around them. The talking gave language to that experience. The pooling of knowledge within the group helped everyone. And it helped me know where to begin rather than spending time presenting concepts children already understood.

At the end of discussion on this day I asked the children what they wanted to know more about in regard to these three different communities. For a minute no one responded. Then one brave little guy raised his hand and said, "What I really want to know is how do they fight fires in the country?"

"You mean on farms?" I asked.

"No, what I mean is how do they fight fires *way* out in the country, like in Yellowstone Park, 'cuz I been seeing these fires on TV, on the news, and you can't get a firetruck there. At least I don't *think* you can get a firetruck there very easy."

Wow! I would never have thought of this idea. The rest of the class responded immediately. The television news clips they had seen just didn't match their knowledge of firefighting learned from their experiences both in and out of school. We began searching for information. The library had no resources on this particular question, so we began collecting newspaper and magazine articles and reporting the news we saw on television. I learned too and learning *with* the children was invigorating.

A couple of weeks later I launched our ecology unit. The school district had just added this topic to the first-grade curricular agenda, and a limited number of resource materials on ecology were available through the school. When we began talking about ecology that day I had done no planning, gathered no library books, made no teacher centers, selected no activities. Secretly I was glad for the opportunity to carve out a total unit of study *with* the children. I did have an agenda of my own: I wanted to address farm preservation in Lancaster County, for we have some of the richest farmland in the world, which, to my distress, is being converted into shopping centers and housing developments. I opened this new topic by asking the children, "What does ecology mean to you?"

"Pollution," specifically "litter" came the reply. "How come there's so much litter?" "Where does it come from?" "How come people litter?" The room burst into a frenzy of talk about litter. And this was some time before Earth Day! Now I had "done litter" in the early seventies, the last time this topic came around in curriculum units. With a sinking feeling I realized that studying litter did not hold near the interest for me that firefighting in Yellowstone Park had. Yet the class clearly wanted to explore the issue of litter. "We could pick up litter," someone suggested. However, our custodian maintains litter-free school grounds, and the manicured lawns in our neighborhood were immaculate. Then I had an idea, and before the day's end I'd written a letter to parents asking each family to spend fifteen minutes collecting litter and to send this litter to school the following Friday. "Parent involvement," I told myself, but in truth I hadn't thought this through too carefully.

Not Friday, but Monday morning the bags started arriving. "My mother says you can have this now," said one little boy. All week the bags accumulated. The janitor rolled his eyes but went along with me when I explained that he couldn't throw these bags into the dumpster until Friday. That Friday afternoon we spread butcher paper on the floor, I donned work gloves (the litter was too sordid to allow the children to rummage through it) and began sorting. The children sat around the paper directing the placement of each item into specific piles. Debris from fast-food restaurants constituted a big hunk of this litter, but there also was a car battery pulled from a creek, a multitude of rusted cans and broken bottles, and a large assortment of one-of-a-kind articles. We sorted, categorized, and counted. "How about we make a graph?" I asked the class. We had been making graphs in math class and this seemed a perfect way to demonstrate a purposeful use of graphing. Scowls suddenly appeared on several faces.

"Why should we do *that?*" asked one little girl, "We can see right here which one has more."

"We already got a graph. It's all this stuff."

"But what about showing other people who aren't here?" I prodded.

"Na-aw," came the consensus.

I realized I had work to do to help these children understand that one purpose of a graph is to communicate with others, but now wasn't the moment to address this. They saw no purpose in such an activity.

"Look at all this yucky stuff. Don't you just wish you could *do* something?" came a quiet comment from Marcy.

"Yeah, this is awful."

"Well, what would you like to do?" I asked.

"You could write a letter to everyone in the school," suggested Mark.

"I'm not going to do that for you," I replied with playful outrage.

"Oh. Yeah. Well, *we* could write letters to everyone," came a suggestion.

Then a buzz of discussion broke out, and within a few seconds the children realized the enormity of such a task. Then I told the children about a petition, what it was, how it worked, its purpose. They decided to write a petition and chose two children to draft the document. A few days later, after returning to the class for input and discussing language that would persuade and not demand that others stop littering, the class agreed on their petition. With the children gathered around me on the floor, I recopied the final draft onto a large scroll of paper. The children watched closely. I pointed out the format for a letter of petition, the necessity for correct spelling and punctuation, and the advantage of easily read handwriting. Every child learned to read the petition. Then they signed up for committees and, with a box containing a sampling of their litter, went around to the other classrooms where they read their petition and requested signatures. When they finally posted the petition in the hall, everyone in the school—including every cook, custodian, secretary, even some parent volunteers—had signed it.

The integration of our curriculum had developed from purposes felt by the children. Collecting litter had led to: counting and categorizing, writing with the persuasive language of a petition, learning the form of a letter of petition, handwriting, spelling, punctuation, reading, public speaking, etc. It took place within a community learning together.

We went on to explore other kinds of pollution and the effect on our world, and the children made a connection to the fires of Yellowstone that also had destroyed a part of the environment. I got my bit in about farm preservation, though I had to be content only to raise the children's awareness of this problem. Long after we officially moved on to other curricular issues, the children maintained an interest in ecology, specifically litter, occasionally bringing in newspaper articles, checking out related library books, reporting something they'd heard on television. In the spring, when they noticed candy wrappers on the playground, they determined that they needed to get their petition out to remind others not to litter. They also became keenly aware of the power of the written word through the use of a petition. When I read Tomie dePaola's *The Art Lesson* to them in the spring, part of their response was outrage toward Tommy's teacher for allowing only one sheet of paper to her students. "Yeah, if you did that, we'd write a petition and give it to Mr. Feltman!" they announced. When we studied China at the year's end, the events in Tiananmen Square were taking place. Our China unit took on new significance as the children reported the events they watched on television every evening.

"Those students want democracy," Matt commented in one discussion.

"What's that mean—democracy?" I asked.

"It means you get to choose," said Jeff. "You get to vote." Jeff began exploring his budding awareness of democracy but then had difficulty clarifying further.

"Why don't they just write a petition for what they want?" asked Adam.

And then these six-year-olds sat in amazement as I explained that a petition would probably not be tolerated in a country such as China. Through classroom experience these children had learned something of the meaning of democracy.

Reflections

My risk taking paid off. I watched children invest in subject matter and acquire factual knowledge at levels that far outpaced my previous approach to teaching content units. I came to understand that integration is not something I as a teacher plan and implement, but rather something that occurs *within* learners. When curricular units are broadly framed and begin with the children, building on what they know, connections between all the disciplines occur. Reading and writing and talking and listening really are tools for learning, regardless of the topic.

I still occasionally pull activities from my resource files, but I look for clues from the children to determine when, and even if, to carry them out. When the children speculated about the size of dinosaurs, for instance, we went to the playground and measured dinosaur lengths. We focussed attention on answering the children's questions about dinosaur sizes because this was information they cared about learning, not because this activity is one that's done in dinosaur units.

I want children to learn to question and to understand that answers to those questions—like the world itself—are always changing. I found a model for this approach for content studies in Patricia Lauber's book *The News About Dinosaurs*. Lauber structures the book by presenting facts of what was once believed about dinosaurs followed by sections with the heading "The News Is . . ." where she tells how our theories have changed as we uncover more information. I believe that it is important to help children understand that what we believe today may be disproved tomorrow, that our theories about the world, our understanding, our knowledge is finite. Learning is based on a continuous process of theory making, testing, revising, and new theory making. In this chapter I've only skimmed the surface of the active involvement with learning that goes on now in my classroom in content area studies.

Like teaching reading and writing, I teach content topics with a responsive teaching approach. My process of change was slow and continues to evolve. I know I'll probably never repeat the litter activity with another class, not because of the messiness of bringing litter into the room, but because I understand now that activities must be purposeful to be effective. To discover what is purposeful learning, I must start by listening to the children in each group. As a teacher I have expertise to share with children, but when, what, and how depends on the children. This kind of teaching demands more of me than any of the elaborate activities and intricate planning I once produced. It requires me not only to maintain a cutting edge of knowledge but also to be aware of the learning styles, experience levels, and thought processes of each of my students. Since those individual attributes are continuously in flux, I've got to be attentive so that I can help children take their own learning further. I leave school tired at the end of the day, but it's a good tired, one that comes from the vigorous nature of active learning.

Conclusion

The last morning arrives. The room sparkles through streams of sunlight and refreshing morning air flows through open windows. The children run from the school buses, shouting, singing, some still squabbling. Many bring me gifts: garden flowers, a gift certificate for books, a wooden apple. Monica slips me a copy of *Charlotte's Web* and Ellen presents a book she's authored and published at home about first grade. The children cluster around to help me tear away the wrapping paper; it's like Christmas morning, except they are both Santa and child. And they're just as boisterous as they were on the first day. Cory's gone, and so are Carrie and Eric. Do I miss them? Maybe—individually. But in the group? No. The group dynamics improved as each one left. Our community is shaped by all of us, and even one angry, frustrated child can make life difficult for everyone. It's not been an easy year and I have a jumble of feelings now that it's over.

A visitor asked the children one day what was good about this class and they told her about reading and writing—all the good stuff. When she asked what wasn't so good they told her they were noisy. True. They've been noisy all right—sometimes downright argumentative and nasty with each other. Somehow we've weathered it all.

There have been good moments and several success stories: the class applauding Cory's reading, Ellen's remarkable growth from immature "baby" to the author of "Down's Syndrome" and "The Very Hungry Princess," Michael's and Natalie's becoming readers. But there are also trouble spots. Mark seems to have stood still in the last two months, no longer taking risks. Bradley is still smart-alecky. And Darren? He tells me he hates writing. I think he hates reading too. This way of teaching can't solve all classroom problems. But it's better than it was—better than it was for George who had shared the birth of butterflies over a decade ago.

We start the last day by reading the final chapter of *Charlotte's Web*. When I close the book the children and I exchange smiles; no words are necessary. In writing workshop the children continue to begin new pieces, revise others. That we won't be back tomorrow doesn't seem to enter their heads. I marvel. We clean out our desks and pack up before gathering on the rug for our last literature time. The children choose *Two Bad Ants* to read again. We are reading and talking when the loudspeaker comes on. The principal says his good-byes and a student helper begins calling buses earlier than expected. The children hurry to gather their things. I put down the book unfinished. Our time together has run out. In a few minutes they are out the door and gone. The community that took so long to come together vanishes. Or does it? I never know what vestiges are left.

I remember comments by my son Nathan, who has been visiting my classroom since he was fifteen. "I don't get it Mom. I mean, what's the big deal? What you do's so simple." What a fine compliment. The methodology is simple—much simpler than it was in George's class. Nathan came into this classroom and, even though this was a difficult group, he was able to slip into the routines and work beside me. Yet what's occurred here is far from simplistic; it's intricately complex. We've not been learning *about* reading and writing and math and all the rest, but *been* readers and writers and mathematicians and scientists. We're not getting ready for life; we're living life now. The children shine through. I think on this and I realize that it's not the lessons I teach or the achievement children make or the content we cover. It's the surprises—the unexpected, undefinable moments that define our time together. I saw the first glimmers of such moments in the children's writing. When I first began writing workshop I knew so little about teaching writing: I could do nothing but listen and respond and struggle and rejoice with them. Slowly those first glimmers grew brighter. The children taught me how to teach and how to learn.

When I took that journey years ago to learn about teaching writing through reading, I thought I'd come home with the door wide open—everything clear and revealed. I came home with the door open a crack. Now, after all these years, I realize that I've opened that door only a couple of inches. I've learned that the heart and art of teaching is more than a set of sound practices. The heart and art of teaching is grounded in the theory of each teacher. I know that my own theory of learning and teaching is shaped by *all* of my experiences and the relationships with others that are part of those experiences—my home and family, the work of researchers and educators, my daily observations and reflections in the classroom. Learning to teach is an ongoing process and I know that I'll never really "get there." Every year I begin with the same anxieties, but somehow I get through that first day and each day shows me how to teach the next one. The last day comes and I'm still writing the narrative of my teaching—and my learning—and the story ends only because the school year ends. And then I go back and do it again differently.

APPENDIX A:

Directions for Bookbinding

Materials Needed:
Cardboard or cereal boxes
Wallpaper
Rubber cement
Decoupage roller

Lightweight oaktag
Sewing machine with a large
needle, or a stapler

1. Cut two pieces of cardboard the size you wish the finished book to be.* Score each piece by holding a ruler approximately 3/8″ from the edge that will be the spine and drawing a sharp knife along the edge of the ruler.

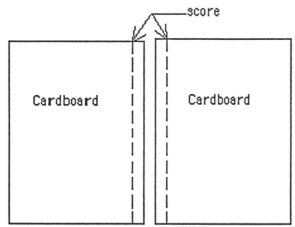

*To make large blank books cut cardboard in 9″ by 12″ pieces. Follow steps 1–4 leaving a slightly wider space between the cardboard sections (step 2). Cut lightweight oaktag approximately 16″ by 11″, or large enough to cover inside of cover when opened. Glue oaktag to inside of cover. Count out 15–20 sheets of 17½″ by 11″ paper (available at office supply stores). Fold paper in half and staple into the spine of the book. (Use a long armed stapler or a saddle-stitch stapler if available.)

2. Cut a piece of wallpaper large enough to leave a 1″ border around all four sides when the two pieces of cardboard are placed side by side with approximately ¼″ space between them.

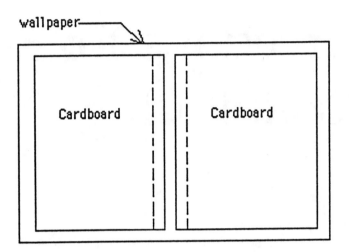

3. Fold the wallpaper in half to form a crease along what will become the spine of the book. Open the wallpaper and, with score lines facing up and placed in the center, glue the two pieces of cardboard to the wallpaper, leaving the ¼″ space between them. Use rubber cement for glueing.

4. Fold the 1″ edges of the wallpaper over the cardboard and glue in place. Do the corners first, then the sides. Going over the glued surfaces with a decoupage roller helps sharpen edges and spread the glue under the wallpaper, thus eliminating air pockets.

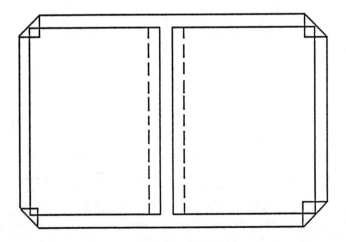

5. Cut paper for the book pages to fit inside the book. Cut a piece of lightweight oaktag twice the width of the book pages and fold it around the pages after typing has been done. Staple or sew through the oaktag and book pages to make an oaktag-covered booklet. (If you use staples, place them close together.) Allow the child to illustrate the book before completing the next step.

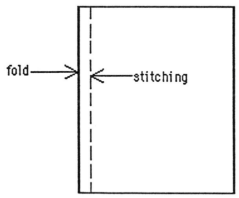

6. Fold cardboard bookcover on score lines to make cover bend at the spine. Open cover. Glue oaktag-covered booklet to cover with rubber cement.

APPENDIX B:

Poetry

Adoff, Arnold. 1982. *All the Colors of the Race*. New York: Lothrop, Lee & Shepard.

Adoff, Arnold. 1979. *Eats*. New York: Lothrop, Lee & Shepard.

dePaola, Tomie. 1988. *Tomie dePaola's Book of Poems*. New York: G. P. Putnam's Sons.

de Regniers, Beatrice Schenk, et al. 1988. *Sing a Song of Popcorn*. New York: Scholastic.

Dog Poems. Selected by Myra Cohn Livingston. 1990. New York: Holiday House.

Eric Carle's Dragons Dragons. Compiled by Laura Whipple. 1991. New York: Philomel.

Good Morning to You, Valentine. Selected by Lee Bennett Hopkins. 1976. New York: Harcourt Brace Jovanovich.

Greenfield, Eloise. 1977. *African Dream*. New York: Harper Collins.

Greenfield, Eloise. 1978. *Honey, I Love*. New York: Harper & Row.

Greenfield, Eloise. 1988. *Under the Sunday Tree*. New York: Harper & Row.

Hey-How for Halloween! Selected by Lee Bennett Hopkins. 1974. New York: Harcourt Brace Jovanovich.

Hopkins, Lee Bennett. 1972. *girls can too!* New York: Franklin Watts.

Hopkins, Lee Bennett. 1974. *Kim's Place*. New York: Holt, Rinehart and Winston.

Kennedy, X. J. 1968. *Brats*. New York: Atheneum.

Kennedy, X. J. 1985. *The Forgetful Wishing Well*. New York: Atheneum.

Kennedy, X. J. 1991. *The Kite that Braved Old Orchard Beach*. New York: Macmillan.

Kuskin, Karla. 1975. *Near the Window Tree*. New York: Harper & Row.

More Poetry for Holidays. Selected by Nancy Larrick. 1973. New York: Scholastic.

More Surprises. Selected by Lee Bennett Hopkins. 1987. New York: Harper & Row.

O'Neil, Mary. 1961. *Hailstones and Halibut Bones.* New York: Doubleday.

Piping Down the Valleys Wild. Selected by Nancy Larrick. 1968. New York: Dell.

Poems of A. Nonny Mouse. Selected by Jack Prelutsky. 1989. New York: Knopf.

Prelutsky, Jack. 1990. *Beneath a Blue Umbrella.* New York: Greenwillow.

Prelutsky, Jack. 1983. *It's Valentine's Day.* New York: Scholastic.

Prelutsky, Jack. 1984. *The New Kid on the Block.* New York: Scholastic.

Random House Book of Poetry for Children. Selected and introduced by Jack Prelutsky. 1983. New York: Random House.

Siebert, Diane. 1989. *Heartland.* New York: Crowell.

Singer, Marilyn. 1989. *Turtle in July.* New York: Macmillan.

Still as a Star. Selected by Lee Bennett Hopkins. 1989. Boston: Little, Brown.

Surprises. Selected by Lee Bennett Hopkins. 1984. New York: Harper & Row.

Thayer, Ernest Lawrence. 1988. *Casey at the Bat.* Boston: David R. Godine.

The Sea Is Calling Me. Selected by Lee Bennett Hopkins. 1986. New York: Harcourt Brace Jovanovich.

Time to Shout. Selected by Lee Bennett Hopkins. 1973. New York: Scholastic.

To Look at Any Thing. Selected by Lee Bennett Hopkins. 1978. New York: Harcourt Brace Jovanovich.

Turner, Ann. 1986. *Tickle a Pickle.* New York: Macmillan.

Viorst, Judith. 1981. *If I Were in Charge of the World.* New York: Atheneum.

When the Dark Comes Dancing. Compiled by Nancy Larrick. 1983. New York: Philomel.

APPENDIX C:

Resources for Keeping Current on Children's Literature

My favorite sources for reviews on children's books or lists of notable books are in the following journals.

Book Links
c/o American Library Association
50 East Huron Street
Chicago, IL 60611

Booklist
c/o American Library Association
50 East Huron Street
Chicago, IL 60611

The Horn Book Magazine
14 Beacon Street
Boston, MA 02108

Language Arts
National Council of Teachers of English
1111 Kenyon Road
Urbana, IL 61801

The New Advocate
Christopher-Gordon Publishers, Inc.
P.O. Box 809
Needham Heights, MA 02194-0006

The Reading Teacher
International Reading Association
800 Barksdale Road, P.O. Box 8139
Newark, DE 19714-8139

The Bulletin
Children's Literature Assembly
c/o National Council of Teachers of English
1111 Kenyon Road
Urbana, IL 61801

The WEB
Martha L. King Center for Language and Literacy
Department of Educational Theory and Practice
29 W. Woodruff Avenue
Columbus, OH 43210-1177

There are many resources that provide lists of recommended children's literature. Most of the following resource books can be located on library reference shelves or by checking with the children's librarian at public or university libraries.

Anderson, Vicki. 1990. *Fiction Sequels for Readers 10 to 16: An Annotated Bibliography of Books in Succession.* Jefferson, NC: McFarland & Co.

Dreyer, Sharon Spredemann. 1989. *The Bookfinder: A Guide to Children's Literature About the Needs and Problems of Youth Aged 2 and Up.* Circle Pine, MN: American Guidance Services, Inc.

Freeman, Judy. 1990. *Books Kids Will Sit Still For,* 2nd ed. New York: R. R. Bowker.

Gillespie, John T., & Corinee J. Nader, eds. 1990. *Best Books for Children Preschool Through Grade 6,* 4th ed. New York: R. R. Bowker.

Jett-Simpson, Mary, ed. 1989. *Adventuring with Books: A Booklist for Pre-K— Grade 6,* 9th ed. Urbana, IL: National Council of Teachers of English.

Kennedy, DayAnn M., Stella S. Spangler, & Mary Ann Vanderweif. 1990. *Science & Technology in Fact and Fiction.* New York: R. R. Bowker.

Lima, Carolyn W., & John A. 1989. *A to Zoo: Subject Access to Children's Picture Books*, 3rd ed. New York: R. R. Bowker.

Kobrin, Beverly. 1988. *Eyeopeners! How to Choose and Use Children's Books About Real People, Places, and Things*. New York: Penguin.

Lipson, Eden Ross, compiler. 1988. *The New York Times Parent's Guide to the Best Books for Children*. New York: Times Books.

McBride, William G., ed. 1990. *High Interest—Easy Reading: A Booklist for Junior & Senior High School Students*. Urbana, IL: National Council of Teachers of English.

Richardson, Selma K. 1991. *Magazines for Children: A Guide for Parents, Teachers & Librarians*. Chicago: American Library Association.

Rosenberg, Judith K. 1992. *Young People's Books in Series: Fiction and Non-Fiction, 1975–1991*. Englewood, CA: Libraries Unlimited, Inc.

Trelease, Jim. 1982. *The Read-Aloud Handbook*. New York: Penguin.

Wilson, George & Joy Moss. 1988. *Books for Children to Read Alone: A Guide for Parents and Librarians*. New York: R. R. Bowker.

There are a number of books that are helpful for learning about children's literature. Some of my favorites are:

Arbuthnot, May Hill. 1986. *Children and Books*, 7th ed. Glenview, IL: Scott Foresman.

Cullinan, B. 1987. *Children's Literature in the Reading Program*. Newark, DE: International Reading Association.

Hearne, Betsy. 1990. *Choosing Books for Children: A Commonsense Guide*. New York: Delacorte.

Hickman, Janet, & Bernice E. Cullinan, eds. *Children's Literature in the Classroom: Weaving Charlotte's Web*. 1989. Needham Heights, MA: Christopher-Gordon.

Hopkins, Lee Bennett. 1987. *Pass the Poetry, Please!* New York: Harper & Row.

Huck, Charlotte S., Susan Hepler, & Janet Hickman. 1993. *Children's Literature in the Elementary School*, 5th ed. New York: Holt, Rinehart and Winston.

Lamme, Linda Leonard, ed. 1981. *Learning to Love Literature*. Urbana, IL: National Council of Teachers of English.

Paterson, Katherine. 1981. *Gates of Excellence: On Reading and Writing Books for Children*. New York: Elsevier/Nelson Books.

Stewig, John Warren, & Sam Leaton Sebesta, eds. 1989. *Using Literature in the Elementary Classroom*. Urbana, IL: National Council of Teachers of English.

Zinsser, William, ed. 1990. *Worlds of Childhood: The Art and Craft of Writing for Children*. Boston: Houghton Mifflin.

Works Cited

Arbuthnot, May Hill. 1964. *Children and Books,* 3rd ed. Glenview, IL: Scott, Foresman.

Atwell, Nancie. 1987. *In the Middle: Writing, Reading and Learning with Adolescents.* Portsmouth, NH: Boynton/Cook.

Atwell, Nancie. 1982. "Class-based Writing Research: Teachers Learn from Students." *English Journal, 74:* 35–39.

Avery, Carol. 1987. "First Grade Thinkers Become Literate." *Language Arts, 64:* 611–618.

Avery, Carol. 1989. "From the First: Teaching to Diversity." In *Stories to Grow On,* ed. Julie Jensen. Portsmouth, NH: Heinemann.

Babbitt, Natalie. 1990. "Protecting Children's Literature." *The Horn Book, 66:* 696–703.

Bissex, Glenda. 1980. *GNYS AT WRK: A Child Learns to Write and Read.* Cambridge, MA: Harvard University Press.

Burke, Carolyn. 1984. Presentation at convention of the National Council of Teachers of English. Detroit, MI.

Calkins, Lucy McCormick. 1986. *The Art of Teaching Writing.* Portsmouth, NH: Heinemann.

Coles, Robert. 1989. *The Call of Stories.* Boston: Houghton Mifflin.

Crews, Harry. 1983. *A Childhood, the Biography of a Place.* New York: Morrow.

Donaldson, Margaret. 1978. *Children's Minds.* New York: W. W. Norton.

Elbow, Peter. 1973. *Writing Without Teachers.* New York: Oxford University Press.

Emig, Janet. 1983. *The Web of Meaning.* Portsmouth NH: Boynton/Cook.

Fox, Mem. 1990. "There's a Coffin in My Office." *Language Arts, 67:* 468–472.

Fulwiler, Toby. 1985. "Writing and Learning, Grade Three." *Language Arts, 62:* 55–59.

Giacobbe, Mary Ellen. 1980. "Teaching Writing in the Elementary School." Presentations at Martha's Vineyard, MA.

Giacobbe, Mary Ellen. 1991. "A Letter to Parents About Invented Spelling." In *Workshop 3: The Politics of Process,* ed. Nancie Atwell. Portsmouth, NH: Heinemann.

Giacobbe, Mary Ellen and Donald Graves. 1983–85. Workshops for Pennsylvania Department of Education. Harrisburg, PA.

Giacobbe, Mary Ellen and Nancie Atwell. 1985. "Reading, Writing, Thinking and Learning." Presentations at Martha's Vineyard, MA.

Giacobbe, Mary Ellen and Nancie Atwell. 1986–88. Workshops for Pennsylvania Department of Education. Harrisburg, PA.

Goodman, Yetta M. 1985. "Kidwatching: Observing Children in the Classroom." In *Observing the Language Learner*, ed. Angela Jaggar and M. Trika Smith-Burke. Newark, DE: The International Reading Association; Urbana, IL: National Council of Teachers of English.

Goodman, Kenneth F. 1969. "Analysing Oral Reading Miscues: Applied Psycholinguistics" in *Reading Research Quarterly*. 5(1):9–30.

Goodman, Kenneth S. A linguistic study of cues and miscues in reading, *Elementary English*, 1965.

Graves, Donald H., for the Committee on Research, National Council of Teachers of English. 1978–81. Articles initiated at the Writing Process Laboratory, University of New Hampshire, Durham, NH, and published in the "Research Update" section of *Language Arts*.

Graves, Donald H. 1983. *Writing: Teachers and Children at Work*. Portsmouth, NH: Heinemann.

Graves, Donald H., 1984. "The Author's Chair." In *A Researcher Learns to Write*. Portsmouth, NH: Heinemann.

Graves, Donald. 1984. "The Enemy Is Orthodoxy." In *A Researcher Learns to Write*. Portsmouth, NH: Heinemann.

Graves, Donald H. 1991. *Build a Literate Classroom*. Portsmouth, NH: Heinemann.

Hansen, Jane. 1987. *When Writers Read*. Portsmouth, NH: Heinemann.

Harste, Jerome C., Virginia A. Woodward, & Carolyn L. Burke. 1984. *Language Stories and Literacy Lessons*. Portsmouth, NH: Heinemann.

Heard, Georgia. 1989. *For the Good of the Earth and the Sun: Teaching Poetry*. Portsmouth, NH: Heinemann.

Heath, Shirley Brice. 1987. Address at the Conference of the Coalition of English Associations, Queenstown, MD, July 13.

———. 1990. Presentation at Conference on College Composition and Communication, Chicago, IL.

Holdaway, Don. 1979. *The Foundations of Literacy*. New York: Scholastic.

Hopkins, Lee Bennett. 1991. " 'Leave Me Alone,' Cries the Poem." *Perspectives*, 7(3): xii–xv.

Huck, Charlotte. 1986. "To Know the Place for the First Time." *The Bulletin*, Spring: 69–71.

Jensen, Julie, ed. 1989. *Stories to Grow On*. Portsmouth, NH: Heinemann.

Larrick, Nancy. 1991. "Give Us Books! . . . But Also . . . Give Us Wings!" *The New Advocate*, 3(2): 77–83.

Lipson, Eden Ross. 1988. *The New York Time Parent's Guide to the Best Books for Children*. New York: Random House.

Lloyd-Jones, Richard, & Andrea A. Lunsford. 1989. *The English Coalition Conference: Democracy through Language*. Urbana, IL: National Council of Teachers of English.

MacLachlan, Patricia. 1990. "Painting the Air." *The New Advocate*, 3(4): 219–225.

Martin, Ann M. 1989. "An Author's Perspective Letters from Readers." In *Workshop 1: Writing and Literature*, ed. Nancie Atwell. Portsmouth, NH: Heinemann.

Mills, Heidi, Timothy O'Keefe, & Diane Stephens. 1991. *Looking Closely: Exploring the World of Phonics in One Whole Language Classroom*. Urbana, IL: National Council of Teachers of English.

Murray, Donald M. 1982. *Learning by Teaching: Selected Articles on Writing and Teaching*. Portsmouth, NH: Boynton/Cook.

Murray, Donald M. 1985. *A Writer Teaches Writing*, 2nd ed. Boston: Houghton Mifflin.

Murray, Donald M. 1990. *Write to Learn*, 3rd ed. Fort Worth: Holt, Rinehart and Winston.

National Council of Teachers of English. 1989. *A Handbook on Public Communication*. Urbana, IL: NCTE.

Newkirk, Thomas. 1989. *More Than Stores: The Range of Children's Writing*. Portsmouth, NH: Heinemann.

Newkirk, Thomas, with Patricia McLure. 1992. *Listening In: Children Talk About Books (and other things)*. Portsmouth, NH: Heinemann.

Paterson, Katherine. 1990. "Heart in Hiding." In *Worlds of Childhood: The Art and Craft of Writing for Children*, ed. William Zinsser. Boston: Houghton Mifflin.

Rogers, Carl R. 1969. *Freedom to Learn*. Columbus, OH: Merrill.

Rosenblatt, Louise. 1938; 1976. *Literature as Exploration*. New York: Noble and Noble.

Rosenblatt, Louise. 1978. *The Reader the Text and the Poem*. Carbondale, IL: Southern Illinois University Press.

Rosenblatt, Louise. 1980. "What Facts Does This Poem Teach You?" *Language Arts*, April: 386–394.

Rosenblatt, Louise. 1991. "Literature—S.O.S.!" *Language Arts*, 68: 444–448.

Sendak, Maurice. 1990. "Visitors from My Boyhood." In *Worlds of Childhood: The Art and Craft of Writing for Children*, ed. William Zinsser. Boston: Houghton Mifflin.

Shannon, Patrick. 1988. *Broken Promises: Reading Instruction in Twentieth-Century America*. Granby, MA: Bergin & Garvey.

Smith, Frank. 1982. *Writing and the Writer*. New York: Holt, Rinehart and Winston.

Smith, Frank. 1986. *Insult to Intelligence*. New York: Arbor House.

Smith, Frank. 1988. *Understanding Reading*, 4th ed. Hillsdale, NJ: Lawrence Erlbaum.

Stafford, William. 1986. *You Must Revise Your Life*. Ann Arbor: University of Michigan Press.

Teale, William H. 1984. "Reading to Young Children: Its Significance for Literacy Development." In *Awakening to Literacy*, eds. Hillel Goelman, Antoinette A. Oberg, and Frank Smith. Portsmouth, NH: Heinemann.

Trelease, Jim. 1982. *The Read-Aloud Handbook*. New York: Penguin.

Tunnell, Michael O., & James S. Jacobs. 1989. "Using 'Real' Books: Research Findings on Literature-Based Reading Instruction." *The Reading Teacher*, 42 (7): 470–477.

Veatch, Jeannette. *Individualizing Your Reading Program: Self-Selection in Action*. New York: Putnam. 1959.

Veatch, Jeannette. *How to Teach Reading with Children's Books*. New York: Teacher's College Bureau of Publication. 1964.

Veatch, Jeannette. *Reading in the Elementary School*. New York: Ronald Press, 1966.

Vygotsky, Lev S. 1978. *Mind in Society: The Development of Higher Psychological Processes*. Cambridge, MA: Harvard University Press.

Weaver, Constance. 1988. *Reading Process and Practice from Socio-linguistics to Whole Language*. Portsmouth, NH: Heinemann.

Wells, Gordon. 1986. *The Meaning Makers: Children Learning Language and Using Language to Learn*. Portsmouth, NH: Heinemann.

Zinsser, William. 1990. *On Writing Well*, 4th ed. New York: Harper & Row.

Children's Books Cited

Adams, Pam, illus. 1975. *This Old Man.* New York: Grosset & Dunlap.

Adolff, Arnold. 1979. *Eats.* New York: Lothrop, Lee & Shepard.

Ahlberg, Janet and Allan. 1978. *Each Peach Pear Plum.* New York: Viking.

Ahlberg, Janet and Allan. 1986. *The Jolly Postman.* Boston: Little, Brown.

Alcott, Louisa May. 1868. *Little Women.* New York: Little, Brown.

Aliki. 1979. *The Two of Them.* New York: Greenwillow.

Anno, Mitsumasa. 1978. *Anno's Journey.* New York: Philomel.

Arnold, Tedd. 1987. *No Jumping on the Bed.* New York: Dial.

Asbjornsen, Peter C., & Jorgen Moe. 1957. *The Three Billy Goats Gruff.* Illus. Marcia Brown. New York: Harcourt.

Atwater, Richard and Florence. 1938. *Mr. Popper's Penguins.* New York: Little, Brown.

Balian, Lorna. 1972. *Where in the World Is Henry?* Scarsdale, NY: Bradbury.

Bang, Molly. 1980. *The Grey Lady and the Strawberry Snatcher.* New York: Four Winds.

Bang, Molly. 1991. *Yellow Ball.* New York: Morrow.

Barton, Byron. 1981. *Building a House.* New York: Greenwillow.

Barton, Byron. 1987. *Machines at Work.* New York: Crowell.

Barton, Byron. 1988. *I Want to Be an Astronaut.* New York: Crowell.

Barton, Byron. 1989. *Dinosaurs, Dinosaurs.* New York: Crowell.

Barton, Byron. 1989. *Bones, Bones, Dinosaur Bones.* New York: Harper Collins.

Benchley, Nathaniel. 1972. *The Magic Sled.* Harper & Row.

Berger, Barbara. 1984. *Grandfather Twilight.* New York: Philomel.

Brett, Jan, retold and illus. 1987. *Goldilocks and the Three Bears.* New York: Dodd, Mead.

Briggs, Raymond. 1978. *The Snowman.* New York: Random House.

Brown, Marc. 1976. *Arthur's Nose.* New York: Atlantic/Little, Brown.

Brown, Marc. 1986. *Arthur's Teacher Trouble.* Boston: Atlantic Monthly Press.

Brown, Marc. 1988. *Arthur's Valentine.* Boston: Little, Brown.

Brown, Marc, & Leurene Krasny. 1986. *Dinosaur's Divorce: A Guide for Changing Families.* New York: Little, Brown.

Brown, Ruth. 1987. *Our Puppy's Vacation.* New York: Dutton.

Browne, Anthony. 1986. *The Piggybook.* New York: Knopf.

Bunting, Eve. 1987. *Ghost's Hour, Spook's Hour.* New York: Clarion.

Burton, Virginia Lee. 1942. *The Little House.* New York: Houghton Mifflin.

Butterworth, Oliver. 1956. *The Enormous Egg.* Boston: Little, Brown.

Carle, Eric. 1969. *The Very Hungry Caterpillar.* New York: Philomel.

Carle, Eric. 1977. *The Grouchy Ladybug.* New York: Philomel.

Carle, Eric. 1984. *The Very Busy Spider*. New York: Philomel.

Carle, Eric. 1986. *Papa, please get the moon for me*. New York: Philomel.

Carle, Eric. 1987. *A House for Hermit Crab*. Natick, MA: Picture Book Studio.

Carrick, Carol. 1976. *The Accident*. New York: Clarion.

Carrick, Carol. 1977. *The Foundling*. New York: Clarion.

Carrick, Donald. 1988. *Harald and the Great Stag*. New York: Clarion.

Caudill, Rebecca. 1965. *A Certain Small Shepherd*. New York: Holt, Rinehart and Winston.

Cauley, Lorinda Bryan. 1988. *The Trouble with Tyrannosaurus Rex*. New York: Harcourt Brace Jovanovich.

Chandra, Debra. 1990. *Balloons and Other Poems*. New York: Farrar, Straus & Giroux.

Cleary, Beverly. 1950. *Henry Huggins*. New York: Morrow.

Cleary, Beverly. 1964. *Ribsy*. New York: Morrow.

Cleary, Beverly. 1965. *The Mouse and the Motorcycle*. New York: Morrow.

Cleary, Beverly. 1968. *Ramona the Pest*. New York: Morrow.

Cohen, Barbara. 1983. *Molly's Pilgrim*. New York: Lothrop.

Cooney, Barbara. 1982. *Miss Rumphius*. New York: Viking.

Cooney, Barbara. 1988. *Island Boy*. New York: Viking Kestrel.

Cowley, Joy. 1980. *Mrs. Wishy Washy*. Aukland, New Zealand: Shortland Publication.

Dahl, Roald. 1961. *James and the Giant Peach*. New York: Knopf.

Day, Alexandra. 1985. *Good Dog, Carl*. San Diego, Green Tiger Press.

Delaney, A., retold and illus. *The Gunnywolf*. New York: Harper & Row.

dePaola, Tomie. 1973. *Nana Upstairs and Nana Downstairs*. New York: Viking.

dePaola, Tomie. 1974. *Charlie Needs a Cloak*. New York: Prentice Hall.

dePaola, Tomie. 1975. *Strega Nona*. New York: Prentice Hall.

dePaola, Tomie. 1978. *Pancakes for Breakfast*. New York: Harcourt Brace Jovanovich.

dePaola, Tomie. 1979. *Big Anthony and the Magic Ring*. New York: Harcourt Brace Jovanovich.

dePaola, Tomie. 1981. *One Foot, Now the Other*. New York: Putnam.

dePaola, Tomie. 1988. *Tomie dePaola's Book of Poems*. New York: G.P. Putnam's.

dePaola, Tomie. 1989. *The Art Lesson*. New York: Putnam.

de Regniers, Beatrice Schenk, et al. 1988. *Sing a Song of Popcorn*. New York: Scholastic.

Devlin, Wende and Harry. 1977. *Cranberry Thanksgiving*. New York: Parents Magazine Press.

Eggar, Bettina. 1986. *Marianne's Grandmother*. New York: Dutton.

Ehlert, Lois. 1988. *Planting a Rainbow*. New York: Harcourt Brace Jovanovich.

Emberley, Barbara. 1967. *Drummer Hoff*. New York: Prentice Hall.

Erickson, Russell. 1974. *A Toad for Tuesday.* New York: Lothrop, Lee & Shepard.

Erickson, Russell. 1982. *Warton and the Castaways.* New York: Lothrop, Lee & Shepard.

Fox, Mem. 1988. *Koala Lu.* New York: Harcourt Brace Jovanovich.

Freeman, Don. 1968. *Corduroy.* New York: Viking.

Frost, Robert. 1978. *Stopping by a Woods on a Snowy Evening.* Illus. Susan Jeffers. New York: Dutton.

Gag, Wanda. 1928. *Millions of Cats.* New York: Coward.

Galdone, Paul. 1968. *Henny Penny.* New York: Seabury.

Galdone, Paul. 1973. *The Little Red Hen.* New York: Seabury.

Galdone, Paul. 1975. *The Gingerbread Boy.* New York: Seabury.

Gantos, Jack. 1986. *Rotten Ralph's Trick or Treat.* Boston: Houghton Mifflin.

Gibbins, Gail. 1982. *Tool Book.* New York: Holiday House.

Golenboch, Peter. 1990. *Teammates.* New York: Harcourt Brace Jovanovich.

Greenfield, Eloise. 1988. *Under the Sunday Tree.* New York: Harper & Row.

Gurney, Nancy. 1965. *The King, the Mice and the Cheese.* New York: Random House.

Gwynne, Fred. 1970. *The King Who Rained.* New York: Simon & Schuster.

Haley, Gail. 1986. *Jack and the Bean Tree.* New York: Crown.

Hall, Donald. 1979. *The Ox-Cart Man.* New York: Viking.

Harper, Wilhelmina, retold. 1967. *The Gunniwolf.* New York: Dutton.

Harste, Jerome C., & Janet L. Goss. 1981. *It Didn't Frighten Me.* School Book Fairs.

Heller, Ruth. 1988. *Kites Sail High: A Book About Verbs.* New York: Grosset & Dunlap.

Heller, Ruth. 1989. *Many Luscious Lollipops: A Book About Adjectives.* New York: Putnam.

Hoff, Syd. 1961. *Chester.* New York: Harper & Row.

Hoff, Syd. 1958. *Danny and the Dinosaur.* New York: Harper & Row.

Hoff, Syd. 1962. *Stanley.* New York: Harper.

Hoff, Syd. 1980. *Merry Christmas, Henrietta.* Champaign, IL: Garrard.

Hutchins, Pat. 1971. *Changes, Changes.* New York: Macmillan.

Hutchins, Pat. 1972. *Good Night, Owl!* New York: Macmillan.

Isadora, Rachel. 1979. *Ben's Trumpet.* New York: Greenwillow.

Jeffers, Susan. 1974. *All the Pretty Horses.* New York: Macmillan.

Johnson, Hannah Lyons. 1974. *From Seed to Jack-o-lantern.* New York: Lothrop, Lee & Shepard.

Knight, Eric. 1940. *Lassie Come Home.* Philadelphia: John C. Winston.

Kraus, Robert. 1971. *Leo the Late Bloomer.* New York: Thomas Crowell.

Kraus, Robert. 1985. *Where Are You Going, Little Mouse?* New York: Lothrop, Lee & Shepard.

Krauss, Ruth. 1949. *The Happy Day*. New York: Scholastic.

Krauss, Ruth. 1971. *The Carrot Seed*. New York: Scholastic.

Langstaff, John. 1974. *Oh, A-Hunting We Will Go*. New York: McElderry.

Larrick, Nancy. 1968. *Piping Down the Valleys Wild*. New York: Delacorte.

Lauber, Patricia. 1986. *Volcano*. New York: Bradbury.

Lauber, Patricia. 1989. *The News About Dinosaurs*. New York: Bradbury.

Lester, Hester. 1988. *Tacky the Penguin*. Boston: Houghton Mifflin.

Lionni, Leo. 1963. *Swimmy*. New York: Pantheon.

Lobel, Arnold. 1964. *Giant John*. New York: Harper & Row.

Lobel, Arnold. 1970. *Frog and Toad Are Friends*. New York: Harper & Row.

Lobel, Arnold. 1971. *Frog and Toad Together*. New York: Harper & Row.

Lobel, Arnold. 1975. *Owl at Home*. New York: Harper & Row.

Locker, Thomas. 1986. *Sailing with the Wind*. New York: Dial.

Locker, Thomas. 1987. *The Boy Who Held Back the Sea*. New York: Dial.

Lord, John Vernon. 1972. *The Giant Jam Sandwich*. Boston: Houghton Mifflin.

MacLachlan, Patricia. 1983. *Seven Kisses in a Row*. New York: Harper & Row.

MacLachlan, Patricia. 1985. *Sarah, Plain and Tall*. New York: Harper & Row.

Marshall, James. 1972. *George and Martha*. Boston: Houghton Mifflin.

Marshall, James. 1985. *Four on the Shore*. New York: Dial.

Marshall, James. 1987. *Little Red Riding Hood*. New York: Dial.

Marshall, James. 1988. *Goldilocks*. New York: Dial.

Martin, Bill, Jr. 1983. *Brown Bear, Brown Bear, What Do You See?* New York: Holt, Rinehart and Winston.

Martin, Bill, Jr. 1991. *Polar Bear, Polar Bear, What Do You Hear?* New York: Henry Holt.

Martin, Rafe. 1989. *Will's Mammoth*. New York: Putnam.

Mathis, Sharon Bell. 1975. *The Hundred Penny Box*. New York: Viking.

Mayer, Mercer. 1967. *A Boy, a Dog and a Frog*. New York: Dial.

McCloskey, Robert. 1941. *Make Way for Ducklings*. New York: Viking.

McCloskey, Robert. 1948. *Blueberries for Sal*. New York: Viking.

McCloskey, Robert. 1957. *Time of Wonder*. New York: Viking.

McMillan, Bruce. 1990. *One Sun: A Book of Terse Verse*. New York: Halliday House.

Milne, A. A. 1926. *Winnie-the-Pooh*. New York: Dutton.

Minarik, Elsie. 1968. *A Kiss for Little Bear*. New York: Harper & Row.

Moore, Lillian. 1988. *I'll Meet You at the Cucumbers*. New York: Atheneum.

Mosel, Arlene. 1972. *The Funny Little Woman*. New York: Dutton.

Munsch, Robert. 1980. *The Paper Bag Princess*. Toronto: Annick.

Munsch, Robert. 1985. *Mortimer*. Toronto: Annick.

Munsch, Robert. 1985. *Thomas' Snowsuit*. Toronto: Annick.

Munsch, Robert. 1986. *Love You Forever*. Scarborough, Ontario: Firefly.

O'Conner, Jane. 1987. *Lulu Goes to Witch School*. New York: Harper & Row.

Parks, Van Dyke, & Malcolm Jones. 1986. *Jump! The Adventures of Brer Rabbit*. New York: Harcourt Brace Jovanovich.

Piper, Walter. 1945. *The Little Engine That Could*. New York: Platt & Munk.

Plath, Sylvia. 1976. *The Bed Book*. New York: Faber.

Polacco, Patricia. 1988. *Rechenka's Eggs*. New York: Philomel.

Prelutsky, Jack, comp. 1983. *The Random House of Poetry for Children*. New York: Random House.

Rey, H. A. 1941. *Curious George*. Boston: Houghton Mifflin.

Robinson, Barbara. 1972. *The Best Christmas Pageant Ever*. New York: Harper Collins.

Rylant, Cynthia. 1982. *When I Was Young in the Mountains*. New York: Dutton.

Rylant, Cynthia. 1985. *The Relatives Came*. New York: Bradbury.

Scarry, Richard. 1964. *Richard Scarry's Best Word Book Ever*. New York: Random House.

Schwartz, Alvin. 1984. *In a Dark, Dark Room and Other Scary Stories*. New York: Harper & Row.

Scott, Foresman & Company. 1976. *The Bus Ride*. Glenview, IL: Scott Foresman.

Scott, Foresman & Company. 1976. *Catch That Frog*. Glenview, IL: Scott Foresman.

Scott, Foresman & Company. 1976. *Ten Little Bears*. Glenview, IL: Scott Foresman.

Sendak, Maurice. 1963. *Where the Wild Things Are*. New York: Harper & Row.

Sendak, Maurice. 1967. *Higglety Pigglety Pop!* New York: Harper & Row.

Seuss, Dr. 1971. *The Lorax*. New York: Random House.

Seuss, Dr. 1985. *How the Grinch Stole Christmas*. New York: Random House.

Silverstein, Shel. 1974. *Where the Sidewalk Ends: Poems and Drawings*. New York: Harper & Row.

Silverstein, Shel. 1981. *The Light in the Attic*. New York: Harper & Row.

Spier, Peter. 1981. *Peter Spier's Rain*. New York: Doubleday.

Spinelli, Jerry. 1990. *Maniac McGee*. Boston: Little, Brown.

Steptoe, John. 1987. *Mufaro's Beautiful Daughters: An African Tale*. New York: Lothrop, Lee & Shepard.

Thorson, Charles, illus. 1946. *The Story of the Three Bears*. Kenosha, WI: John Martin's House.

Turkle, Brinton. 1976. *Deep in the Forest*. New York: Dutton.

Turner, Ann. 1985. *Dakota Dugout*. New York: Macmillan.

Turner, Ann. 1987. *Nettie's Trip South*. New York: Macmillan.

Twain, Mark. 1936. *Tom Sawyer*. New York: Heritage Press.

Van Allsburg, Chris. 1985. *The Polar Express*. Boston: Houghton Mifflin.

Van Allsburg, Chris. 1988. *Two Bad Ants*. Boston: Houghton Mifflin.

Van Leeuwen, Jean. 1975. *The Great Christmas Kidnapping Caper.* New York: Dial.

Viorst, Judith. 1972. *Alexander and the Terrible, Horrible, No Good, Very Bad Day.* New York: Atheneum.

Vip. 1969. *The Christmas Cookie Sprinkle Snitcher.* New York: Windmill Books.

Wagner, Jane. 1969. *J.T.* New York: Van Nostrand Reinhold.

Ward, Cynthia. 1988. *Cookie's Week.* New York: G. P. Putnam's.

Warner, Gertrude Chandler. 1942. *The Boxcar Children.* Chicago: Albert Whitman.

White, E. B. 1945. *Stuart Little.* New York: Harper & Row.

White, E. B. 1952. *Charlotte's Web.* New York: Harper & Row.

White, E. B. 1970. *The Trumpet of the Swan.* New York: Harper & Row.

Willard, Nancy. 1977. *Simple Pictures Are Best.* New York: Harcourt Brace Jovanovich.

Williams, Vera. 1986. *Cherry Stones and Cherry Pits.* New York: Greenwillow.

Wood, Audrey. 1984. *The Napping House.* New York: Harcourt Brace Jovanovich.

Wood, Audrey. 1985. *King Bidgood's in the Bathtub.* New York: Harcourt Brace Jovanovich.

Wood, Audrey. n.d. *Quick as a Cricket.* Child's Play (International) Ltd.

Yolen, Jane. 1987. *Owl Moon.* New York: Philomel.

Zelinsky, Paul O. 1986. *Rumpelstiltskin.* New York: Dutton.

Zemach-Berson, Kaethe. 1988. *The Funny Dream.* New York: Greenwillow.

Ziefert, Harriet. 1986. *A New Coat for Anna.* New York: Knopf.

Index